BUREAUCRACY AND PUBLIC CHOICE

BUREAUCRACY AND PUBLIC CHOICE

edited by
Jan-Erik Lane

SAGE Modern Politics Series Volume 15
Sponsored by the European Consortium for
Political Research/ECPR

SAGE Publications
London · Beverly Hills · Newbury Park · New Delhi

Editorial material, Preface, Chapter 1 © Jan-Erik Lane 1987
Chapter 2 © Gert de Bruin 1987
Chapter 3 © Rune Sørensen 1987
Chapter 4 © D. Chisholm 1987
Chapter 5 © A. Dunsire 1987
Chapter 6 © C. Hood 1987
Chapter 7 © R. Murray 1987
Chapter 8 © K. Ståhlberg 1987
Chapter 9 © R. Rose 1987
Chapter 10 © E. Page 1987
Chapter 11 © G. Peters 1987
Chapter 12 © A. Wildavsky 1987

First published 1987

SAGE Publications Ltd
28 Banner Street
London EC1Y 8QE

SAGE Publications Inc
275 South Beverly Drive
Beverly Hills, California 90212

SAGE Publications India Pvt Ltd
C-236 Defence Colony
New Delhi 110 024

SAGE Publications Inc
2111 West Hillcrest Street
Newbury Park, California 91320

British Library Cataloguing in Publication Data
Bureaucracy and public choice.——(Sage
 modern politics series; v. 15).
 1. Bureaucracy
 I. Lane, Jan-Erik
 350′001   JF1411

 ISBN 0-8039-8067-1
 ISBN 0-8039-8068-X Pbk

Library of Congress Catalog Card Number 87–060207

Printed in Great Britain by J. W. Arrowsmith Ltd., Bristol

Contents

Preface

The chapters assembled in this volume grew out of an ECPR venture. The ECPR Research Group on Bureaucracy and Public Resource Allocation met for the first time in Florence in September 1984. It was oriented towards the interpretation of the place of bureaux and bureaucrats in public choice processes whether public resource allocation or redistribution. The work of the group included theoretical as well as empirical pieces evaluating from various angles current conceptions about bureaucracy. There was a kind of consensus about the need at the present stage of knowledge to try to assess the notion that bureaucratic behaviour is all of one kind: inefficiency, waste, organized chaos and lack of control.

The idea of bureaucracy may be approached as a concept denoting an organizational entity, a *group* of people making up an institution — the basic question then becomes to identify what characterizes these institutional entities. Alternatively it may be approached as a *property* concept connoting some property, or sets of properties of organizations — the crucial question then is which entities these properties are true of or denote. Taking the first approach we enquire into what characteristics the set of people that populate the entities called "bureaux" are testing different assumptions about the basic traits of bureaucracies. Starting from the second approach we try to elucidate the extent to which various concepts of bureaucracies, identifying some typical property, are applicable to the set of people that inhabitat bureaux. The difference between the two approaches is one of focus. Taking the first route it is clear what the concept of bureaucracy is, but not what the meaning of the concept is, whereas the second route is the other way around.

To the participants in this ECPR research group it was obvious that any theory about the place of bureaucracies in public choice processes has to refer to the, nowadays, sizeable staff of administrators, professionals and workers employed at various levels of government in the public sector. However, it was far from obvious what the characteristics of these groups of people are as the group took a critical view of prevailing concepts of bureaucracy. Two distinct modes of modelling bureaucracy were identified as the basis for the deliberations of the group — the organizational framework derived from mainstream public administration theory and organizational sociology on the one hand and the public choice approach on the other. An attempt was made to cover the variety of theories and hypotheses within these two basic frameworks. When the group met for its final session in

Barcelona in 1985 it turned out that all the authors had something to contribute to the theoretical and empirical assessment of prevailing theories of bureaucratic behaviour, with reference to the applicability of that concept to the public sector. It was considered necessary to ask some scholars to submit articles in order to make publication of the work of the group possible.

Jan-Erik Lane
University of Umeå, Sweden
1987

I
THEORETICAL EXPLORATIONS

1
Introduction: the concept of bureaucracy

Jan-Erik Lane

Introduction

Public resource allocation would be impossible without the existence of bureaucracy. Budgetary provision of goods and services implies a structure of bureaux making and implementing decisions as to which goods and services are to be supplied, in what amounts, to various groups of citizens-consumers. In a similar vein it may be established that public resource redistribution depends on the existence of administrative personnel to handle transfer payment tasks in accordance with a publicly enacted system of rules. In the welfare state the role of bureaucracies is extensive as a considerable part of total resources is allocated over the budget (Dunleavy, 1985). Although there is unanimous agreement about the necessity for bureaucracies in the welfare state, there is wide disagreement about the basic characteristics of bureaucratic behaviour. The issue under contention concerns how efficient bureaux tend to be. Actually, the *problem of efficiency* may be regarded as a key issue in understanding the nature of bureaux and the fundamentals of bureaucratic behaviour, as Gert de Bruin argues in Chapter 2.

Organizational theory and public choice theory imply three mutually inconsistent propositions about bureau operations — (1) bureaucracies are capable of the highest level of rationality or efficiency (Weber); (2) bureau behaviour is characterized by social inefficiency and administrative waste (Niskanen and Tullock); (3) the logic of bureau operations is irrationality (March and Olsen). How do we test these propositions in order to find out which one has empirical support, or which of them the data or the evidence supports the most (Goodsell, 1983)? It seems important to insist upon some kind of empirical procedure in order to find out how bureaux operate, because bureaucracies are, in the last resort, a phenomena independent of the theoretical frameworks of the scholarly community. However, it is impossible to bypass some theoretical problems as to how bureaucracies are conceptualized in these opposing theories. Maybe the disagreement is the outcome of different uses of the key terms — 'bureau', 'bureaucracy behaviour' and 'efficiency'. By looking at the concept of bureaucracy implied in general statements about bureau characteristics, we may not only find out how the key terms are defined, but such an examination will also give us clues to the kind of test that is appropriate to such statements. It is by no means to be taken for granted that these terms are employed in similar senses, because semantic investigations have revealed that the concepts of administration, including terms like 'bureau', 'bureaucracy' and 'efficiency', are often used in a variety of meanings. Let us begin with a glance at these semantic findings.

Two distinct approaches to bureaucracy may be identified — the organizational framework and the public choice approach. Theories regarding bureaux and bureaucratic behaviour derived from mainstream public choice theory tend to be individualistic, atomistic and economic in their assumptions, whereas the organizational approach displays a preference for structure, holism and power. How to integrate these two research traditions is the major task facing any study of bureaucracy. Just how far this is at all possible is an open question. One theory proceeds from the assumption of individual utility maximization, whereas the other emphasizes complexity and unintended functions as Donald Chisholm shows in his article in Chapter 4.

The semantic approach to bureaucracy

A look at usage or definition displays ambiguity as well as confusion between the descriptive and normative employment of 'bureaucracy'. This is shown in Martin Albrow's *Bureaucracy* (1970). These various meanings may be structured in a way that enhances the understanding of the variety of phenomena and properties denoted by the term. Fred W. Riggs examines the variety of meanings of 'bureaucracy' in order to find that the concept may denote aggregates or systems, wholes or parts, as well as a variety of properties having various emotive connotations (Riggs, 1979). It is not likely to be possible to reduce such a set of different meanings to a common conceptual core, nor is it probable that the procedure of explication is the correct one. 'Bureaucracy', it appears, is what is referred to as a 'theoretical term', i.e. it derives its meaning from the theoretical context in which it operates and as an abstract concept it needs the elaboration of indicators to be applied to observable phenomena. Though it is well to be reminded of the semantic predicament with regard to the use of 'bureaucracy', it does not solve any problems in itself.

One could draw the conclusion that the term is too ambiguous and that it should be banned from scientifc discourse altogether. This remedy is illusory because the word 'bureaucracy' is too entrenched in various theories and there are no neighbouring terms available that do not suffer from a similar ambiguity. To resort to 'administration' does not constitute a viable option, as Andrew Dunsire shows in *Administration* (1973). To some the concept of bureaucracy enters the broader concept of administration, though it is far from clear what type of administration bureaucracy is. Such a *per genus proximum* and *differentia specifica* approach cannot inform us about the concept of bureaucracy, because the concept of administration has a semantic predicament not very different from that of bureaucracy. Dunsire lists fourteen meanings of 'administration', but which ones are relevant to the specification of the concept of bureaucracy? If the semantic predicament of the word bureaucracy is one of rather extreme ambiguity and terminological controversy, and if broader terms are of little help, then we certainly have a problem when testing different assertions about the nature of bureaucratic behaviour.

The theoretical nature of the concept of bureaucracy means that it is necessary to look at the specific context of each of the propositions concerning bureaucratic behaviour that we wish to test, in order to find the reference of the word. After such an examination it is possible to decide whether the controversy is a real one or the unhappy outcome of different meanings for the same term. Let us begin with the classical bureaucracy analysis, the Weberian rationality hypothesis. At the same time we will look at the concepts of efficiency in order to find out what is implied in assertions to the effect that bureaucracies are efficient or inefficient. It could be the case that there is also a variation in the meaning of the word 'efficiency', thus creating additional confusion to that which derives from the unhappy semantic predicament of 'bureaucracy'.

Bureaucracy as rationality

Max Weber is often considered as the main adherent to the theory about bureaucracy as efficiency. Weber makes a number of claims in his *Wirtschaft und Gesellschaft* that point towards some theory about bureau rationality or efficiency. Let us take one quotation:

> Experience tends universally to show that the purely bureaucratic type of administrative organization — that is, the monocratic variety of bureaucracy — is, from a purely technical point of view, capable of attaining the highest degree of efficiency and is in this sense formally the most rational known means of exercising authority over human beings. (Weber, 1978: 223)

The association of bureaucracy with efficiency is very clear in Weberian administrative theory. However, there are some key problems of interpretation in relation to the quotation that must be resolved (Rudolph and Rudolph, 1979). What is meant by 'bureaucracy', 'experience' and 'capable of'? It is not the case that Weber stated not that bureaucracy *is* efficiency, but that bureaucracy *may* be efficiency? Moreover, the use of the phrase 'experience tends universally to show' indicates that the proposition, or the theory, is intended as an empirical generalization about the comparative contribution of various administrative forms to efficiency. This is not an absolute concept of efficiency, but a relative one, comparing the historical evidence about various types of authority structures in order to rank these types in terms of their *relative efficiency*. The Weberian claim about bureau efficiency rests on his famous model of bureaucracy, an ideal type comprising the following properties (Weber, 1978: 220–21) — impersonal authority structure; hierarchy of offices in a career system of specified spheres of competence; free selection based on achievements in accordance with specified rules; remuneration in terms of money in accordance with clear rules; discipline and control in the conduct of office. It may be pointed out that the formal model of bureaucracy contains nothing about bureaucratic motivation.

Of course, bureaucratic efficiency cannot simply be a function of the formal structure of the bureau, but depends crucially on what goals are expressed in the behaviour of bureaucrats as well as what means are considered. Maybe the lack of any requirements concerning the motivation of bureaucrats in the model explains the phrase 'capable of', since it opens up the possibility that bureaucracies that are close to the Weberian ideal type characteristics nevertheless perform poorly, simply because the bureau officers do not care too much about efficiency or productivity. How bureaux operate will depend on more factors than those specified in the model. We are not told what these other factors are but learn that formal bureaucratic organization in accordance with the model makes bureaux 'capable of' 'the highest degree of efficiency'. The missing link is supposedly supplied in the Weberian theory of bureaucratic behaviour as a vocation:

> Rather, entrance into an office, including one in the private economy, is considered an acceptance of a specific duty of fealty to the purpose of the office (Amtstreue) in return for the grant of a secure existence. It is decisive for the modern loyalty to an office that, in the pure type it does not establish a relationship to a *person*, like the vassal's or disciple's faith under feudal or patrimonial authority, but rather is devoted to *impersonal* and *functional* purposes. (Weber, 1978: 959)

Weber argues from a historical perspective, comparing modern bureaucracy with other types of government or authority. The statement about the efficiency of modern bureaucracy is only a *relative comparison*. Judged in relation to other types of authority and government, modern bureaucracy is more efficient, but it does not follow that modern bureaucracy is efficient according to other criteria. Thus, Weber may be both right and wrong. The relative efficiency judgement may be correct depending on experience, but the strong efficiency judgement that modern bureaucracy is capable of 'the highest degree of efficiency' — an *absolute comparison* as it were — has certainly not been proved and does not follow from experience.

The basic Weberian idea is that the transition from a personal relationship to an impersonal one establishes the concept of an office to which the office holder is more devoted than to any person (the ethic of Beruf). This may be a step towards more efficiency, but it does not make modern bureaucracy efficient in an absolute sense. We have here a sort of fallacy, the fact that a bureaucrat is devoted to his office does not ensure that the motivation problem is solved. It is still possible that the office holder is thus devoted because it maximizes his own personal utility or because they wish to maximize the utility of the bureau — a functional purpose. Both these goal functions may not be conducive to efficiency, as other analysts of bureaucracy claim. The emphasis in the Weberian analysis is focused too much on a formal structure emerging from a historical perspective. What matters very much to efficiency in bureaucratic behaviour is the ends and means of such behaviour. Also, it does not follow that bureaucrats pursue ends and means that are in the public interest simply because they are oriented more towards their office than towards personal loyalty to someone else.

The Weberian *ideal type* of bureaucracy makes no claim with respect to descriptive realism. It is an open question how it relates to reality. The model may be employed for the purpose of *evaluating* actual practices in two distinct senses — it may identify deviations from the rational or efficient requirement or it may hold up an ethnical challenge that may be conducive to changes in existing practices. The model is in no way a realistic one claiming that public administrative bodies typically or on average have the properties specified. The model may also be employed for *comparative* purposes in order to pinpoint the range of variation in the bureacratic phenomenon, by looking at how the basic properties in the model vary. Even if it is true that public administrative bodies are not bureaucracies in the Weberian model sense, the relevance of the model may in no way be affected by the lack of correspondence between model and reality. In Chapter 10, Edward Page shows not only the relevance of the Weberian approach for comparing country variations, but also its moral attractiveness.

Dysfunctions in bureaucracies

Much of the research about bureaux and bureaucratic behaviour has been conducted within the framework of the Weberian model. It has been the starting point for numerous investigations within public administration and organizational sociology. Although the Weberian model was used as a framework for analysis, it did not meet with unanimous agreement because several findings indicated that there was a gap between theory and reality. Not questioning the basic mechanism of the Weberian model — bureaucracy as neutral and rational machinery — several scholars revealed that bureaucracies could display traits other than rationality and efficiency. There was an inherent danger of so-called dysfunctions in bureau operations.

In a couple of well-known articles Robert K. Merton argued that the sharp distinction between means and ends, typical of the Weberian model, tends to be blurred in bureau operations. The older a bureaucracy the stronger the tendency to a displacement of means and ends. From the beginning the bureau was a means to promote external social ends, but as a result of organizational inertia the interests of the bureau itself tend to replace the basic function to promote external goals. The bureau itself becomes the end for which it operates. Merton argued in *Social Theory and Social Structure* (1957) that bureaux cannot be understood if one does not pay attention to the unintended consequences of bureaucratic behaviour, dysfunctions.

Philip Selznick in his *TVA and the Grass Roots* (1949) came to a similar conclusion. Selznick showed that a bureaucratic apparatus tends to develop in a democratic organization. The drive towards autonomy of the bureaucracy derives, according to Selznick, from its possession of specialized knowledge about the operations of the organization. Technical expertise and the specialization of the knowledge base of the organization is typical of bureaux, which can, however, be conducive to a vicious circle, where the bureaucracy within the organization tends to overemphasize the need for expertise. In due time the experts will take over the organization — one of the dysfunctions of bureaucracy. Selznick stated a number of methods to counteract this type of dysfunction, including a broad composition to the board of the organization and an explicit emphasis on its democratic ideology.

It may be generally argued that the Weberian model did not fully realize the implications of expertise for the structuring of bureaucracies. It is necessary to introduce another distinction between two kinds of personnel within bureaux: administrative personnel and professionals (Parsons, 1947). Harold Wilensky showed in the book *Organizational Intelligence* (1967) that bureaux cannot operate without strong elements of specialist and expert knowledge which counteract the tendencies of bureaucracies towards centralization and homogeneity. There is an inherent conflict between the professionals in a bureau, who base their position on the possession of a monopoly of expert knowledge, on the one hand and the administrative staff which conducts the bureau on the basis of their rule authority. Since the employment of knowledge has become increasingly important for bureaux the tension between administrative power and expert knowledge within bureaucracies may lead to dysfunctions.

In his *Patterns of Industrial Bureaucracy* (1954) Alvin Gouldner criticized the emphasis on subordination in the Weberian model. According to Gouldner this element in the model bypasses the negative consequences of controlling the behaviour of subordinates. A strong surveillance of people within a bureaucratic organization may lead to a severe dysfunction, i.e. that the control strengthens tensions already in existence which the surveillance should counteract. Gouldner argued that it is not possible to direct the organization toward goals which all agree upon. Organizations consist of different groups of individuals with varying interests and goals which can only partly be balanced against each other.

The theme of dysfunctions was developed into a general reaction against the Weberian administrative theory in the human relations school. Criticizing various organizational theories — scientific management, the division of labour and the Weberian administrative perspective — various authors developed a number of hypotheses about the individual in the organization which broke away from prevailing notions about rationality and mechanization. Instead of hierarchy they emphasized the informal structure of the organization and the need of the individual for integration into it. Bureaucracy denoted the inhuman, the formal external framework of the organization, whereas what really happened in an organization was what Weber had not noticed — implicit norms; individual motivation and satisfaction; integration and identification (Argyris, 1960; Likert, 1961; Roethlisberger, 1955; Whyte, 1956).

The idea that bureaucracies may be plagued by dysfunctions amounts to a minor criticism of the Weberian perspective. The idea that bureaucracy is a predictable machine that operates in a rational mode under normal circumstances, has to be revised. Bureaux display inherent tendencies to operate suboptimally due to unintended and unrecognized consequences of behaviour in a complex structure. The theme of the human relations school implies a more serious criticism of the Weberian model because it denies the basic mechanism which is implicit in it. Crucial for the capacity of the organization to accomplish its goals is the informal structure, as Chris Argyris showed in *Understanding Organizational Behavior* (1960). According to Argyris, there exists an undeniable conflict and tension between the demands of the formal organization and the legitimate needs of the individual. The characteristics of bureaucracies — division of labour, subordination, hierarchical structure and control — are not in agreement with the needs of the individual in his mode of functioning within an organization. Informal behaviour systems compensate for the inhuman and mechanistic nature of organizations. These informal behaviour patterns are crucial if the organization is to operate successfully, rather than the formal characteristics of the Weberian model (Argyris, 1960: 1).

Bureaucracy as rigidity

It is readily recognized that bureau and bureaucracy are not synonymous. Whereas the meaning of the word bureau tends to be rather unambiguous, the semantic predicament with regard to bureaucracy is quite another thing. The *Oxford English Dictionary* states as one of the meanings of bureau 'an office for the transaction of public business; a department of public administration'. Sometimes bureaucracy has the same denotation. However, often bureaucracy does not stand for some object or entity like an institution or a set of people, but refers to properties of organization. In particular, bureaucracy is often equated with rigidity, though the word bureaucratism is often used in this more pejorative meaning of bureaucracy. As a matter of fact, to some scholars the distinguishing feature not only of bureaucracy but also of bureaux is rigidity. Let us look at a few quotations that entail that bureaucratic behaviour is characterized by inflexibility, whether this may be true of the concept of bureaucracy as a definition of the term or as a matter of fact:

> Bureaucracies tend to reduce administration to the application of a set of rigid rules and formulas and to insist on a slavish devotion to routine, with the effect of exasperating the people and delaying public business. (Smith and Zurcher, 1944)

> Bureaucratism is usually characterized by adherence to routine, more or less inflexible rules, red tape, procrastination, unwillingness to assume responsibility and refusal to experiment. (Fairchild, 1955)

> The third usage corresponds to the vulgar and frequent sense of the word 'bureaucracy'. It evokes the slowness, the ponderousness, the routine, the complication of procedures, and the maladapted responses of 'bureaucratic' organizations to the needs which they should satisfy . . . (Crozier, 1964:3)

In his *Inside Bureaucracy* (1967) Anthony Downs develops a public choice theory of bureaucratic behaviour in which rigidity looms large. Downs identifies two sources of rigidity in bureaux, one is called 'normal', the other 'abnormal'. There will be a normal increase in rigidity as bureaux grow older and augment their size. However, there may also be a rapid, abnormal outgrowth of rigidity when bureaux enter a rigidity cycle exemplifying the ossification syndrome. The inherent tendency of bureaux to expand is, according to Downs, counteracted by an opposite force — the decelerator effect. As new bureaux reach their mature age further expansion becomes increasingly difficult due to a loss of original function, growing hostility from other bureaux, difficulties in maintaining efficient output, internal problems of recruiting talented people and handling conflict. The reaction on the

part of the bureau to the inevitable stagnation of the growth period is to resort to various expressions of rigidity in order to maintain the status quo and protect the organization against bureau death. The move towards rigidity measures takes different forms:
— development of more formalized rule systems;
— shifting the emphasis from carrying out the goals of the bureau to protecting its size and autonomy;
— less capacity for innovation;
— more emphasis on routines and administration.

The combined effect of these rigidity trends is to make bureaux conservative (Downs, 1967: 5–23), which means that large bureaux seldom are abolished and that the older the bureau the less likely is it that it will die. This theory about the normal development of rigidity in bureaucratic behaviour is certainly open to empirical test. Following Downs we may formulate some test implications of the rigidity hypothesis. We may take a longitudinal perspective on the development of a bureau in order to investigate the extent to which there is a goal displacement from external functions towards internal goals, as well as look at the relationship between innovation and administration in the bureau. This requires the construction of empirical indicators, but the test should be possible to carry out. The literature on administration includes empirical studies of innovation, formalization and adminis-trative routines (Blau and Scott, 1963; Blau, 1955, 1974; Blau and Schoenherr, 1971).

It is not clear if such a test of the rigidity hypothesis also covers the hypothesis about abnormal rigidity. Some bureaux tend to run into the so-called rigidity cycle. The hypothesis about a rigidity cycle implies that the rigidification of bureaucratic behaviour may be so severe that the bureau no longer produces any output and that it will face strong demand for reorganization or even abolition. The answer to the rigidity cycle is the reorganization cycle, according to Downs. As there may be other reasons for bureau reorganization than ossification, it is hard to tell when there is a normal process of rigidification and an abnormal one. Case studies in bureau development may be employed to find out what is going on in bureau growth, mere size expansion, rigidification or ossification. The basic problem is to separate the amount of formalization or rigidity that is neutral in relation to bureau operations, or that may even be beneficial in relation to some bureau tasks, from the type of routinization that is dysfunctional for bureau operations. Krister Ståhlberg shows in Chapter 8 that the designation of what is functional or dysfunctional in a bureaucracy may be context dependent and rather complicated.

Bureaucracy as 'Beamtenherrschaft'
At this point it seems relevant to recall what Max Weber regarded as

the inherent danger in bureaucracies — the drive of bureaucrats to become their own masters. As Guy Peters points out in Chapter 11 the conflict between politicians and bureaucrats is endemic to the administration of modern society. According to the orthodox theory of bureaucracy it is a tool for efficient administration, but its goals are to be determined outside of bureaucracy. But how are bureaucrats to be confined to decision making concerning the means of public policy and not its ends? Also, is there really such a neat and clear distinction between ends and means in public policy making? How is a separation between politics and administration possible?

The growing complexity of modern society, as well as the strong expansion of bureaux at all levels of government, seems to have strengthened bureaucratic power. Literature on government overload (Rose, 1980) and organized democracy (Olsen, 1983), as well as on intergovernmental dependency (Hanf and Sharpf, 1978) and on the relation between democracy and bureaucracy (Etzioni-Halevy, 1983; Saltzstein, 1985) all suggest that typical of modern bureaucracy is penetration into the spheres of political power. According to one conception of bureaucracy this is not just an accidental development typical of some historical period, but derives from the essence of bureaucratic behaviour — a thesis which Page challenges in Chapter 10.

One may here refer to modern theories about the policy process as a network of organizations, both private and public, in which bureaux play an important role. Policy making within the structure of major governments includes the interaction between bureaux and private organizations, in relation to both the making of public policy and its implementation. Thus, bureaux tend to be dependent upon, and interact with other organizations in society. At the same time, this pattern of interaction enforces the independence of the bureaux in relation to government. In the so-called mixed economy public programmes are initiated through interaction between bureaux and interested organizations and these programmes are often implemented in the form of collaboration between the public and the private sector (Hernes, 1978). The increasing complexity of society is conducive to interdependence and interaction between public authorities and private organizations, in order to have well-functioning public pro-grammes (Richardson and Jordan, 1979). Strong bureaux enter policy-networks which are responsible for various public programmes. Co-operation between the public and the private sector may not only stengthen 'Beamtenherrschaft' in relation to government, but there is also a clear risk for what Weber called 'Satrapenherrschaft' and what we may refer to as lobbyism or interest politics (Page, 1985). Jim Sharpe emphasizes that bureaux as part of a network of organizations, may have a positive effect on the functioning of public programmes

(Sharpe, 1985). The literature on neocorporatism argues along similar lines (Schmitter and Lehmbruch, 1978; Lehmbruch and Schmitter, 1982). Varying forms of corporatism at various levels of government feed on the interdependence between public and private organizations within a policy area (Cawson, 1985; Streck and Schmitter, 1985). The development of a third sector between the public and the private or 'private interest government' (PIG) is another indication of the fact that bureau independence may be a necessary condition for fruitful co-operation between the public and the private sector. One must, however, remain alert to the danger of the power of distributional coalitions (Olson, 1982) which may operate unrestrained under the auspices of either 'Beamtenherrschaft' or 'Satrapenherrschaft'.

Bureaucracy as chaos

A new set of principles modelling organizational choice has been suggested by critiques of rational choice models (March and Olsen, 1976). Organizational decision-making is to be understood in a way very different from that which a rational model implies:

> Suppose we view a choice opportunity as a garbage can into which various problems and solutions are dumped by participants. The mix of garbage in a single can depends partly on the labels attached to the alternative cans; but it also depends on what garbage is being produced at the moment, on the mix of cans available, and on the speed with which garbage is collected and removed from the scene. (Cohen, March and Olsen, 1976: 26)

The model has been applied in particular to public sector organizations or bureaucracies. It seems appropriate to ask what general contributions to the description and explanation of bureaucratic behaviour could be expected from the garbage can model. Now, it must be stated that the model is just as lucid as it is loose. It identifies four part 'streams' of decision making: (a) problems; (b) solutions; (c) participants and (d) choice opportunities. The model is based on the assumption that decision outcomes are a function of (a)–(d):

> Although we have treated the four streams as exogenous for most of our discussion, it should be clear that we view the understanding of the lawful processes determining the flows of those streams as fundamental to understanding what is happening in organizational choice situations. The more complete social theory into which these ideas would be embedded would include . . . (Cohen, March and Olsen, 1976: 36)

Maybe it is presumptuous to evaluate the model before it is complete. Yet, we argue that the garbage can model is defective as a general theory of bureaucratic systems. The emphasis here is on 'general' as we may wish to identify the garbage can processes within public administration at times. However, far from denying the relevance of this model to special processes of bureaucratic behaviour, the test of the chaos hypothesis concerns whether the garbage can model identifies something typical of bureaucratic behaviour, that is, something which is inherent in the essence of bureaux. How would we go about testing the general chaos hypothesis that bureaucratic behaviour amounts to a garbage can process?

The garbage can model may be derived from a more general model of organizational choice building on the Thompson categories of preferences and technology (Thompson, 1967). Bureaucratic behaviour as an organizational choice is a function of the preferences involved and the technology to be employed. Collective preferences may be more or less ambiguous and technologies may be more or less certain. Thus, as in Table 1.1 we have a 2×2 Table:

TABLE 1.1
Goal function

		Unambiguous	Ambiguous
T E C H N O L O G Y	Certain	1	2
	Uncertain	3	4

Whereas rational decision models would be applicable to decision situations 1 and 3, they would obviously fail in situations 2 and 4. If bureaux always faced decision predicaments 2 and 4 they would perform badly on any efficiency criterion. If the goals are not clear and if the technology is uncertain, then how could there be bureaucratic efficiency? It seems somewhat exaggerated, however, to claim that all types of bureaucratic behaviour are to be found in the decision predicament most typical of the garbage can model, i.e. situation 4. This is an empirical question that has to be decided by investigating different decision processes in bureaux.

The Weberian model of bureaucracy has met with various kinds of response. One criticism was that it had neglected dysfuntions stemming from an idealized model of abstract properties and their interaction. In reality there were bound to occur unintended consequences and unrecognized functions. A more severe kind of criticism was launched within the human relations school which questioned the basic mechanism in the Weberian model. Organizational efficiency or productivity is not a function of the abstract model properties of the Weberian framework. Finally, the introduction of the garbage can model in the study of bureaucracy means a radical rejection of the Weberian administrative approach. Bureaux, like all organizations, cannot in principle attain rationality in collective choice. There is thus a trend towards a post Weberian administrative theory that rejects more and more of the original Weberian model. Turning to the public choice approach to bureaucracy, we find even more criticism of the classical model of bureaucracy.

Bureaucracy as oversupply

Even if it is true, as Weber claims, that in modern bureaucracies the bureaucrats are devoted to their offices and the functional purposes inherent in these, it may be the case that modern bureaucrats are so devoted to their functions that they only care for them at the expense of other considerations. Devotion to office may become so pervasive that the enlargement of the bureau becomes the sole preoccupation of the office holder. Such a vocation may certainly not be conducive to efficiency. On the contrary, such motivation could result in bureaucracy in the pejorative meaning of the word as it is listed in standard dictionaries:

> *Bureaucracy*: 1. government by bureaux. 2. the body of officials administering bureaux. 3. excessive multiplication of and concentration of power in administrative bureaux. 4. excessive governmental red tape and routine. (*The American College Dictionary*)

A coherent theory derived from the public choice approach about bureaucratic behaviour, which implies that the maximization of the bureau itself is a typical feature of bureaucrats, has been put forward by William Niskanen in *Bureaucracy and Representative Government* (1971). Obviously, the hypothesis that bureaucrats maximize their budgets is intended as a fundamental characterization of bureaucratic behaviour. Niskanen pays little attention to the concept of bureaucracy as shown in the first two meanings listed in the quotation above. Also, an organization is a bureau only if it has two public features:

> Bureaux specialize in the supply of those services that some collective organization wishes to augument beyond that supplied by the market and for which it is not prepared to contract with a profit-seeking organization. (Niskanen, 1971: 20)

Thus, typical of a bureau is its public character, receiving some grant or appropriation from a government budget as an essential source of its revenues. The Niskanen bureaucracy model consists of a few equations modelling the interaction between the bureau and its government (sponsor), which allows some painstaking conclusions about the nature of bureaucratic outputs and efficiency. The equations are:

1. The demand curve of sponsor: $B = aQ - bQ^2$.

2. Bureau's cost curve: $TC = cQ + dQ^2$.

3. Bureau's motivation: budget maximization.

4. Sponsor's motivation: operating a programme in toto at a certain level.

5. Information: the bureau has full information whereas the sponsor has partial information.

The first derivation from the model concerns the nature of the equilibrium outcome of the interaction between the sponsor and the bureau in the budgetary process, characterized by bilateral monopoly on the part of the bureau due to its information advantage. How large will the bureau budget be? Given a budget constraint, meaning that the output of the bureau cannot be larger than the appropriation of the sponsor, Niskanen derives the implication that:

> At the equilibrium level of output, there is no 'fat' in this bureau; the total budget just covers the minimum total costs, and no cost-effectiveness analysis would reveal any efficiency.

However, and this is the surprise:

> The output of this bureau, however, is higher than the optimal level. The equilibrium level of output is in a region where the minimum achievable marginal costs *hf* are substantially higher than the marginal value to the sponsor *hg*, offsetting all the potential net benefits of the service that would be generated by efficient operation at lower outputs levels. (Niskanen, 1971: 47–8)

The conclusion is, of course, that bureaucratic behaviour is inefficient:

> Given the demand for service represented by the collective organization, all bureaux are too large, that is, both the budget and output of all bureaux will be larger than that which maximizes the net value to the sponsor. (Niskanen, 1971: 50)

Since the sponsor may be equated with government and in a representative system with the electorate, bureaucratic behaviour results in social waste, i.e. an inefficient allocation of the resources of society, given the preferences of its citizens. *Social inefficiency* does not necessarily imply *bureau inefficiency*, however. Niskanen is careful to point out that his model of bureaucratic behaviour does not imply that bureaux operate with internal waste, i.e. with different production functions a lower cost could be attained for the same level of output. Whether there will also be bureau inefficiency besides social inefficiency depends on other things, and one cannot rule out the combination of social inefficiency and bureau efficiency. If bureaucratic behaviour implies social waste, then what are the remedies?

Niskanen suggests a number of reforms in the structure of bureaux, which are all directed towards abolishing their information advantage. Thus, we have bureau competition for the supply of similar services, the recognition of private incentive mechanisms for efficiency promoting behaviour, more use of private business for public provision, as well as a strengthening of the control and review process. These reform suggestions would improve the social efficiency of bureaucratic behaviour, though they would strip the bureau of the Weberian model properties. The basic question is whether such drastic changes of bureaucracy would bring about an allocation state where marginal benefit would equal marginal cost for the provision of the goods or services handled by bureaux. The validity of the Niskanen model may be tested from two angles.

Theoretically, the model may be contested because it is misspecified, given the present knowledge of budget behaviour in the public sector (Eavery, 1984; Bender and Moe, 1985). Rune Sörensen argues along this line in Chapter 3 showing that there are system constraints on bureaucratic behaviour not recognized by Niskanen. It has been argued against Niskanen that the theory about the budget maximizing bureau is inherently difficult to test. What could be the empirical consequences? It is somewhat astonishing that there has been wide acceptance of the Niskanen analysis though there have not been many empirical tests. The Niskanen bureaucracy model does not simply state that the bureau budget will be a large one, whatever that could mean, nor is the model a longitudinal one predicting that bureau budgets will grow at a certain rate. The Niskanen analysis implies that bureaux are socially inefficient, meaning that their budgets are too large in relation to effective demand. Thus, it is a cross-sectional hypothesis about the relationship between demand and supply for the services and goods that bureaux provide. The criterion of size is the standard efficiency condition in micro-economic theory, i.e. that the marginal revenue equals marginal cost. The only way to find out whether a bureau is too large, too small or about the right size, is to measure demand and supply and compare them. But how can we do this for these kinds of goods? As a matter of fact, the difficulties of testing the Niskanen bureaucracy model are profound. What the marginal evaluation of an extra unit of bureau supply may be is often far from clear. Obviously, there may be different demand curves revealed in the political process, which may make it very difficult to judge whether marginal benefit equals marginal cost (Miller and Moe, 1983).

The Niskanen model does not predict that bureau inefficiency will be done away with if the control and review process is strengthened, because the Niskanen model is not a theory about bureau waste. Instead it refers to the occurrence of bureau oversupply. Thus, the model implies that if the sponsor gets hold of enough accurate information they will cut back the size of bureau operations until social efficiency is reached. However, the only way to test this implication is to conduct real life experiments, changing the political system in rather drastic ways. Since there is little likelihood that the Niskanen reform proposals will be accepted — shifting bureaux among alternative functions; creating independent policy analysis institutes to look into budget requests — it also becomes difficult to find data that supports or negates the theory.

Moreover, the Niskanen model predicts that a shift to less bureaucracy and more market operations will be conducive to social efficiency. Again, as it is hardly likely that the Niskanen reform proposals will be implemented — competition among bureaux without predetermined functions; private incentives of various kinds to bureaucrats who reduce bureau fat; privatization of bureau functions including even some types of military service — we have difficulty finding the necessary data to corroborate or negate the theory. There is a limited amount of evidence concerning how bureaucracy compares with market in relation to some services and goods (Borcherding, 1977; Kristensen, 1982), but the conclusion is far from straightforward. In any case, such comparisons are only possible outside the range of public goods which bureaux provide. Thus, in that considerable range there is no way to test the Niskanen model except by conducting social experiments, which are not likely to be initiated. Richard Rose in Chapter 9 raises a warning against the strong market preference that is an implicit assumption in the work of Niskanen. Rose shows that what matters is accountability and it is not the case that markets always do better than bureaucracies in this crucial respect. Aaron Wildavsky claims in Chapter 12 that the notion of accountability expresses a cultural view of social life and Christopher Hood in Chapter 6 examines the general application of the public choice approach to bureaucracy reform.

Bureaucracy as size maximization

Growth and size are often associated with bureaucracy. It is no accident that the list of definitions in the *Webster's Dictionary* contains, amongst other characteristics, the following:

Bureaucracy: (1a) the whole body of nonelective government officials. (b) the administrative policy-making group in any large organization. (2) systematic administration characterized by specialization of functions, objective qualification for office, action according to fixed rules, and a hierarchy of authority. (3) a system of administration marked by constant striving for functions and power, by lack of initiative and flexibility, by indifference to human needs or public opinion, and by tendency to defer decisions to superiors or to impede action with red tape. (*Webster's Third Unabridged Dictionary*)

The 'constant striving for function and power' as the typical feature of bureaucratic behaviour has been seized upon by several scholars (Breton, 1974; Downs, 1967; Starbuck, 1965; Parkinson, 1957). The size argument, that bureaux strive for growth, is not just a variation on the Niskanen theme. The Niskanen model is a cross-sectional one stating that bureau operations are too large in relation to effective demand for bureau goods and services. The size argument is different from the oversupply hypothesis as it does not involve social efficiency. Instead it predicts not that market type decision mechanisms will reveal the bureaux as too large, but that the bureaux, over time, tend to become larger and larger in various ways. Thus, the size argument is not necessarily about waste or inefficiency, it is about the internal dynamics of bureaucratic behaviour. Why, then, is the maximization of size vital to bureaux?

The hypothesis that bureaucrats maximise their own utility and that their personal utility is a strict function of bureau size, is a simple one. As simple is another version of the size argument, which argues that growth is the essence of organizations, including one species, viz. bureaux.

> In fact, all organizations have inherent tendencies to expand. What sets bureaus apart is that they do not have as many restraints upon expansion, nor do their restraints function as automatically. (Downs, 1967: 16–17)

Not all versions of the size argument state that size is such an uncomplicated property of bureaux. Actually, more complex arguments about the functions of size have been presented. William Starbuck argues that organizational growth is typical of organizations, because size has a number of separate effects — economies of scale; better chances of survival; more resistance to external pressures; more stability and less uncertainty (Starbuck, 1965). The size argument should not be difficult to test. If it is true that bureaux have one dominating goal — organizational growth — then we would expect the following to be true:

— new bureaux would grow rapidly;
— old bureaux would maintain themselves, if not grow still more;
— the older the bureau the larger the bureau;
— new bureaux would grow either by internal diversification or by means of external merger;
— bureaux would tend to grow steadily except when amalgamations take place.

These test implications are amenable to scientific study without awaiting social experiments, as was the case with the oversupply hypothesis (Meyer, 1985). Comparative studies in the long-term development of the bureau structure in various nations would provide data that may corroborate the size argument. The coming of bureaumetrics is an important step towards an empirical evaluation of this theory, as Andrew Dunsire argues in Chapter 5. Dunsire finds that bureaux may have to face considerable cut-backs in periods of retrenchment (Hood and Dunsire, 1981).

Bureaucracy as uncontrol
The ideal type concept of bureaucracy does not only equate bureaucratic behaviour with rationality and impersonality but also with a tendency towards concentration of power. The *Dictionary of the Social Sciences* contains the following definition:

1. Bureaucracy, conceived as an ideal type, refers to principles of organization that find varying degrees of expression in a wide variety of organizations. The characteristics of the ideal type are rationality in decision making, impersonality in social relations, routinization of tasks, and centralization of authority. (Stone, 1969)

This typical feature of bureaux, to centralize power, may be interpreted in two very different ways. Either the centralization tendency may be inherent in the entire hierarchy in which the bureau is placed — *system centralization*; or the centralization drive may refer to the internal division of authority within the bureau. According to the *Oxford English Dictionary* a 'bureaucrat' is an 'official who endeavours to concentrate administrative power in his bureau'. The outcome of such internal bureau processes may be the opposite to system centralization — *bureau autonomy* and bureau irresponsibility. Gordon Tullock in his *Politics of Bureaucracy* (1965) considers bureau autonomy as the typical characteristic of modern bureaucratic behaviour, and the outcome of such 'bureaucratic free enterprise' is inefficiency, irresponsibility and waste. Firstly:

It can only be concluded that, in a very large organization of this type, for the greater part of its specific activities, the bureaucracy will be 'free' from whatever authority it is allegedly subordinate to. 'It', the bureaucracy, will do things, will take actions, not because such actions are desired by the ultimate authority, the center of power, in the organization, but because such things, such actions, develop as an outgrowth of the bureaucracy's own processes. (Tullock, 1965: 168)

The phenomenon of bureaucratic free enterprise has its source in the hierarchical structure of bureaux with its implications for loss of reliable communication and preciseness as well as impossibility of control of the superordinate over the subordinate. Secondly:

We are saddled with a large and basically inefficient bureaucracy. Improved efficiency in this sector could, looking at the matter economically, raise our national income and improve our rate of growth. Politically, it could both increase the degree of control the citizen, *qua* voter, has over many fields of our national life and enlarge his personal freedom. This apparent paradox is the result of the peculiar form taken by the inefficiency of bureaucratic free enterprise. (Tullock, 1965: 221)

As a matter of fact, there is a growing literature about the tendency of bureaucratic behaviour to find its own goals and enlarge its discretion at the expense of its sovereign, the body politic. It is argued that the traditional simple model of public administration, with its distinction between politics or values and administration or facts, as well as its naive conception of public administration as mechanical and impersonal execution, has no relevance to the realities of politics and bureaucracy (Dunsire, 1973, 1978). The literature on policy implementation has further eroded support for the idea that bureaux may be controlled for the purpose of perfectly carrying out administrative functions that are in the public interest (Hood, 1976; Pressman and Wildavsky, 1984). Again, the main line of development in policy analysis tends to confirm the critique of the simple public administration model (Wildavsky, 1979). The adherents of the garbage can model may be regarded as extreme advocates of the hypothesis that bureaucratic behaviour is basically uncontrollable (March and Olsen, 1976).

The uncontrollability hypothesis may be subjected to an empirical test by the derivation of some test implications. We may wish to separate two ideas in the uncontrol hypothesis: the notion that bureaux tend to become autonomous or that bureaucracy processes tend towards garbage can processes on the one hand, and the idea that these bureau trends result in inefficiency on the other hand. Bureaucracy as free enterprise is one state of affairs and inefficiency is another, but there may be other causes of inefficiency than bureau autonomy. In Richard Murray's chapter, he presents an analysis of productivity in bureaux which highlights both theoretical and empirical problems.

The bureaucracy as uncontrol hypothesis has two elements which must not be mixed up. Firstly, we have to find out whether bureau officials really tend to have a large amount of discretion. Then, should this happen to be the case, we must inquire into the consequences of such a large amount of discretion. It certainly does not follow that because there is a control problem, leaving each bureau with more discretion than intended, that this autonomy will be employed for other purposes than carrying out the tasks of the bureau. Actually, some implementation theories argue that autonomy is a precondition for successful implementation (Sabatier and Mazmanian, 1979; Williams, 1980; Elmore, 1982; Sabatier, 1986). Thus, it is an open question as to what the implications of far reaching discretion will be for bureau operations. In order to arrive at the conclusion of Tullock that bureaucratic behaviour is inefficient because bureaucrats cannot be controlled, one assumption is implicitly made, that bureaucrats do not care about their official goals. This is a separate assumption that should be identified for special scrutiny.

Bureaucracy as private choice

Whereas it used to be claimed that there existed a special type of behaviour or motivation — the bureaucratic vocation — it is often stated in modern administration theory and decision-making approaches that the distinction between public and private choice is an invalid one. As Andre Breton states in his *The Economic Theory of Representative Government* (1974):

> The hypothesis implies, even when stated in its simplified form (bureaucrats seek to maximize the relative size of their bureaus), that it is through the maximization of this objective that bureaucrats are able to achieve the highest possible income and prestige consistent with the constraints to which they are subjected . . . (Breton, 1974: 162)

Such an objective function would, perhaps, not be conducive to the propagation of the public interest or the even more mundane public goals of the bureau. However, such a bureaucratic mentality, or unbureaucratic one as it were, does not necessarily imply inefficiency. If the successful operation of the bureau was made a function of the private incentives of bureaucrats, then the maximization of a private objective function in a bureaucratic setting does not have to result in waste or bureaucratic free enterprise. A Swedish economist has suggested that efficiency promoting mechanisms of a kind that ties output to the private incentives of the officials, should be introduced into public administration as a recurrent phenomenon (Jonsson, 1985).

Two versions of the private objective function hypothesis may be identified. According to a weaker version bureaucratic behaviour is not only affected by the public interest, but also by private motives, whereas in the stronger version there is no such thing as the public interest. In his cautious argument, Downs follows the weaker version:

> Specifically, the theory rests upon three central hypotheses:
>
> 1. Bureaucratic officials (and all other social agents) seek to attain their goals rationally . . .
> 2. Bureaucratic officials in general have a complex set of goals including power, income, prestige, security, convenience, loyalty (to an idea, an institution, or the nation), pride in excellent work, and desire to serve the public interest . . . But regardless of the particular goals involved, every official is significantly motivated by his own self-interest even when acting in a purely official capacity . . .
> 3. Every organization's social functions strongly influence its internal structure and behaviour, and vice versa. (Downs, 1967: 2)

Although the number of basic assumptions in the Downs theory are not large they have so much content that almost anything is deducible. If we happen to find bureau inefficiency, then this may be due to the private motives of officials, but if we happen to find efficiency then maybe another motive is at work — the public interest? The Downs assumption about bureaucracy motivation is so complex that hardly anything specific can be deduced about bureaucratic behaviour.

The stronger version of the private choice argument in a bureaucracy setting is more specific. It states that public officials maximize their own interests whatever they may be and that bureau size is conducive to this maximization. How can we test the hypothesis that bureaucratic behaviour is the maximization of private gain? What would be the behaviour implications?

One set of test predictions would simply be the occurrence of a confusion of public and private roles in the traditional understanding of what is public. It is hardly likely that we will find massive private action in bureaucratic behaviour, like the use of the resources of the office for private ends or the manipulation of bureau resources for other purposes than those intended. A more sophisticated set of test implications would insinuate that private goals are enhanced at the same time as public targets are achieved, in particular bureau expansion. Typically, the public choice approach regards bureau growth as the primary manifestation of the private objection function. However, it has been argued that bureau expansion may not be totally accounted for by means of the private choice hypothesis. When officials make priorities among their private goals, then security may loom larger than the other ones, as Herbert Kaufman has argued in *Are Government Organizations Immortal* (1976). Growth is risky, it may bring bureau disaster. The self-evident aura surrounding the private choice hypothesis should be replaced by empirical inquiries into the nature of bureaucratic motivation. In Chapter 11, Guy Peters proceeds to exactly such an examination of the complexity of bureaucratic motivation. In his chapter Andrew Dunsire tests a number of implications derived from this theory of bureaucratic motivation, among others the hypothesis that the salaries of bureaucrats tend to increase over time.

Bureaucracy as waste

Whatever model of bureaucratic behaviour one adopts the question of bureau efficiency is bound to come up. From the various models available has resulted a contention between hypotheses on the performance of bureaux that must be decided by means of empirical research. Some definitions take a prejudged approach to the problem of bureau performance stating from the outset that bureaucracy is rationality or that bureaucracy is rigidity, whereas other definitions imply that the concept of bureaucracy is not in itself related to bureau performance. A bureaucracy is simply a set of people in a bureau — a part of government — that may or may not operate efficiently. Whatever approach one adheres to — the analytical one making performance judgements part of the concept, or the synthetical meaning that the concept is neutral in relation to performance judgements — the problem of bureau performance is still an empirical one. In the analytical interpretation it becomes a problem of the applicability of the concept, but in the synthetic interpretation it concerns the truth of an empirical generalization. However, even if we manage to pinpoint the various characteristics stated as typical of bureaucracy — impersonality, hierarchy, legitimate authority, size maximization, lack of control, rigidity — we still must have evidence of inefficiency before we draw the conclusion that bureaux are rationality or bureaux are waste. How do we conceptualize efficiency in bureaucratic behaviour?

Although there are several definitions of organizational efficiency in the literature, we use the oft quoted Etzioni concepts of organizational efficiency and organizational effectiveness. In his *Modern Organizations* (1964) Amitai Etzioni argues that there is a basic distinction: on the one hand, efficiency is the 'amount of resources used to produce a unit of output', and on the other, effectiveness is the 'degree to which an organizational realizes its goals' (Etzioni, 1964: 8). The distinction between efficiency or productivity and effectiveness or goal attainment allows for the possibility that bureaux may score well on one dimension but poorly on the other. Thus, we have a four–fold table.

TABLE 1.2
Effectiveness

E E F F I C I E N C Y		Goals success	Goals failure
	Cost minimization	I	II
	Waste	III	IV

Categories II and III deserve some further comment. Category II may appear to be a contradiction, how could bureaux be efficient and at the same time produce outputs that have no relation to their ends or that may even be counterproductive to their purposes? Category III appears almost as peculiar. How can bureaux be effective and at the same time be wasteful in terms of the employment of resources? It is doubtful whether the Etzioni distinction helps very much. Would we not regard a bureau that operates meaningless activities in an efficient manner as wasteful? Would we not deny the rationale of a bureau that, though achieving its tasks, does not allocate its resources in an optimal way? The Etzioni distinction, however, brings out clearly that we must not only focus narrowly on cost minimization but pay attention to the desired output or outcome, the standard as it were. Efficiency in bureaucratic behaviour cannot be a function of goal attainment solely or only be interpreted in terms of cost minimization. Both elements must enter the efficiency equation, as Roland McKean states in his *Efficiency in Government Through Systems Analysis* (1958):

> The consequences of an action fall into two types: (1) those positive gains which we like to increase, or the achievement of objectives, and (2) those negative effects which we like to decrease, or the incurrence of costs. Neither type by itself can serve as an adequate criterion: the maximization of gains without regard to cost or resource limitation is hardly a helpful test, and the minimization of cost regardless of other consequences of the alternative actions is nonsense. (McKean, 1958: 34)

If we conclude that efficiency in bureaucratic behaviour must include both Etzioni aspects, then we may suggest that efficiency is to maximize gains minus costs, or effectiveness considering efficiency. However, the criterion which maximizes gain/costs requires that gains and costs can be compared in terms of some common standard, which is doubtful in relation to bureau output. Certainly, some goals are more important than others, meaning that costs may be easier to accept in some activities than in others. Efficiency in bureaucratic behaviour is a function of both the provision of goods and services and the allocation of resources. To compare the way resources are allocated in order to reach a level of provision we must hold quality *constant* in some way. Only if we have the same quality and quantity of the output may we compare the efficiency in the employment of resources.

Given a certain level of service quality we can go about establishing inefficiency in two ways, social efficiency versus bureau efficiency. In order to provide its citizens with a certain amount of goods and services at a certain quality level society may use one of its basic allocation mechanisms, market or bureau. Speaking of efficiency we must separate the question of which of these two forms of allocation mechanism is the most efficient — social efficiency — from the question as to how bureaux are most efficient to organize their activities. It is clearly conceivable that there may be bureau efficiency but social inefficiency. Thus, as in Table 1.3, we have a 2x2 table:

TABLE 1.3

	Social efficiency	Social inefficiency
Bureau efficiency	1	2
Bureau inefficiency	3	4

In order to judge whether there is inefficiency or not with regard to a bureau it is not enough to focus only on the bureau itself. Firstly, we must ask whether the market, or some type of market similar mechanisms, could provide the goods or services more efficiently than the bureau. It may be very difficult to decide whether market or bureaucracy is superior in relation to certain goods and services. This seems to require some theory of the nature of goods and services and their relation to the two basic types of decision mechanisms, market versus bureaucracy or public policy.

To judge whether there is bureau efficiency may also be troublesome. Cost differences between bureaux may be the result of differences in the quality or quantity of goods and services supplied. If we hold bureau output constant we may state how much waste there is. The problem then becomes one of identifying the extent to which the bureau could lower its costs while maintaining the same service level. This is not to deny that the efficiency judgement may focus on the oversupply of bureau output, but it is another problem which is more difficult to solve empirically, as the demand for bureau goods and services is not easily measured. Efficiency and productivity in public resource allocation not only presents difficult theoretical problems. The measurement aspects are as important as they are problematic to handle. Richard Murray in Chapter 7 tackles the basic problems involved in measuring public sector efficiency and productivity.

Relative cost comparisons

The identification of bureau inefficiency is a difficult task as it calls for rather precise empirical measurements. It is necessary to make a number of decisions as to the type of bureaucratic behaviour involved as well as to the nature of the bureau output in question. It seems fruitful to make a *first* distinction between administrative bureaucratic behaviour and service bureaucratic behaviour. This is an analytic distinction, as we may expect to find both types of bureaucratic behaviour in most large public entities. A *second* distinction concerns the separation between a cross-sectional approach and a longitudinal one. Suppose we have a number of public administration units — central agencies, regional or local government entities, local state units — we may enquire into the relative efficiency of these bureaux either by taking a longitudinal approach or by resorting to cross-sectional comparison. The efficiency judgement along one dimension is not the same as that along the other dimension. One bureau may be more efficient than another, yet it may not perform as efficiently as it used to do, or vice versa. There may be two different types of inefficiency — *administrative inefficiency* and *service inefficiency*.

Public administration is typically divided into various sectors of activity on the basis of a more or less hierarchical structure. The lower units in the structure are oriented towards the provision of goods and services, whereas the higher entities or agencies are more involved in administrative work, preparing budgetary requests, policy proposals and deciding on matters of principle relating to the implementation of laws. There is also administrative work within the lower entities dealing with personnel administration and overall fiscal management of the unit. It is possible to separate these administrative functions and analyse them separately from the service functions, in order to study administrative efficiency. The analysis of administrative efficiency may focus on the longitudinal development of the administrative function in relation to the service function, in order to find out whether the administrative function at various levels expands more rapidly than the service function. This process will be called *bureaucratization* (see also Meyer and Brown, 1977). Conversely, the analysis of administrative efficiency may look at the cross-sectional variation in the size of the administrative function in order to find out whether, for example, all local governments employ the same amount of administrative resources for the provision of their services. Alternatively, we may wish to look at differences in the size of the central agencies between various sectors of activity. The cross-sectional analysis of administrative efficiency is highly suitable to test the hypothesis about *administrative economies of scale*. The economies of scale hypothesis means that the administrative component in various local government sectors, as separate from the service functions, will vary as a function of overall size, or that the size of the administrative overhead will fall, relatively speaking, as the size of the organization increases (Blau, 1974).

The well known size hypothesis predicts that the administrative component of an organization declines as a function of the size of the organization (Starbuck, 1965; Blau, 1974). The size hypothesis may be interpreted in two modes. On the one hand the administrative component is reduced in relative size as an organization grows, the *longitudinal hypothesis*. On the other hand, there will be an administrative economy of scale in a set of similar organizations with different sizes, the *cross-sectional hypothesis*.

The status of the size hypothesis is contested. It is part of the structural approach to organizations (Mintzberg, 1979) relating organizational features to contextual variables, including organizational size (Kimberly, 1976). Theoretically, it rests on the assumption of technical rationality and its institutionalization in the normative framework of the organization (Thompson, 1967), which is contested in the public choice approach to bureaucracies. Moreover, it also rests on crucial assumptions about the implications of size for structural diversification and administrative intensity (Astley, 1985; Donaldson, 1982; Grinyer, 1982). Empirically, the support for the size hypothesis is positive but not decisive. The test implication of a negative correlation between size and the relative size of the administrative component, measured by various indicators, has been confirmed in studies of various types of organizations (Melman, 1951; Bendix, 1956; Anderson and Warkow, 1961; Hawley et al., 1965; Indik, 1964; Pondy, 1969). However, the empirical evidence suggests that the relationship between size and administration may be curvilinear, with administrative intensity declining at a decelerating rate (Anderson and Warkov, 1961; Hall, 1974; Knight, 1976; Davis and Lawrence, 1977).

Service inefficiency is of a different kind. It may also be studied by means of cross-sectional or longitudinal analysis, but it is essential to remember the importance of the concept of service level. The public provision of goods and services in terms of bureau operations may display large variations measured by cost index, with the same programme varying in cost quite substantially between different local state units, regional or local governments. However, we cannot simply attribute the cost variation to service inefficiency, as it may be a function of variations in the quality or quantity of the goods or services provided. Only by holding the level of service constant may we explain a cost variation by means of inefficiency. Thus, the service inefficiency hypothesis requires elaborate analysis of the provision of public goods and services in order to separate out what inefficiency accounts for in contrast to costs that derive from the choice of higher service levels, or costs that are incurred as a function of environmental exigencies. The study of service inefficiency links up with the analysis of public policy variations at central, regional and local levels of government (Sharpe and Newton, 1984). To what extent is there X-inefficiency in bureau operations? The concept of X-efficiency emphasizes the importance of taking a wider look at the factors that have an impact on bureau outputs, whether in service production or in administrative functions (Leibenstein, 1966).

To sum up. In order to make hypotheses about inefficiencies in bureaucratic behaviour amenable to scientific test in relation to specified sets of data, we suggest a number of distinctions. Firstly, we must distinguish between social efficiency and bureau efficiency, since some goods and services are more efficiently provided for by the market whereas others better suit public policy and public administration. The best way to increase bureau efficiency may not be to resort to some Weberian ideal type concepts of bureaucracy, but to insert more market similar institutions into public life or to radically alter the decision mechanism involved, substituting the market for the bureau. Secondly, the analysis of bureau efficiency may be conducted in four different modes.

TABLE 1.4

	Cross-sectional	Longitudinal
Administration	I	II
Goods and services	III	IV

Focusing on public administration as sector oriented systems of bureaux tied in some hierarchical structure, the distinction between the administrative function and the service function seems promising. Bureau inefficiency may mean either that the administrative component in the system is too large according to some standards, or that the provision of goods and services is too costly given other such standards. Administrative inefficiency may be interpreted as a process phenomenon — bureaucratization — to be revealed by means of a longitudinal approach. Alternatively administrative efficiency may mean that economies of scale in the administrative function are seized upon — a cross-sectional interpretation. The study of bureau efficiency in the service function is more complicated, as there are more explanations of cost variations in the provision of public programmes than merely a lack of efficiency. Service inefficiency may be regarded as a residual when the amount of cost variation that stems from differences in external conditions, or the choice of service level (quality or quantity), has been recognized. The contributions of Murray, Dunsire and Hood to this volume deal in various ways with the concepts of efficiency and productivity.

Conclusion

There is peculiar tension between the denotation and the connotation of the concept of bureaucracy. If it is taken for granted that 'bureau' refers to the existing organizational entities within the public administration system, then it is far from obvious that there exists any one theory that adequately portrays the distinguishing characteristic of such entities. On the other hand, if we start from a specified concept of bureaucracy, then we must try to specify what its range of application is. It could be the case that the various connotations discussed above are not generally true of bureaucracy, assuming that its denotation is given as the existing bureau structure. Indeed it seems difficult, if not directly impossible, to come up with some valid generalization about what distinguishes bureaux or bureaucracies. We wish to emphasize the multi-dimensional nature of the phenomenon of bureau operations within public resource allocation (Jenkins and Gray, 1983; Warwick, 1975). It may be the case that alternative concepts or theories of bureaucracy have some validity or applicability, but it is certainly the case that bureaucratic behaviour in none of the theories surveyed here can do justice to the bureaucratic behaviour in the huge public administration systems typical of advanced capitalist democracies.

References

Albrow, M. (1970) *Bureaucracy*. London: Macmillan.

The American College Dictionary.

Anderson, T.R. and S. Warkow (1961) 'Organizational Size and Functional Complexity: A Study of Differentiation in Hospitals', *American Sociological Review*, 26, pp. 23–8.

Argyris, C. (1960) *Understanding Organizational Behavior*. Homewood, IL: Dorsey Press.

Astley, W.G. (1985) 'Organizational Size and Bureaucratic Structure', *Organizational Studies*, 6, pp. 201–28.

Bendix, R. (1956) *Work and Authority in Industry*. New York: John Wiley.

Bender, J. and T.M. Moe (1985) 'An Adaptive Model of Bureaucratic Politics', *American Political Science Review*, 79, pp. 755–74.

Blau, P.M. (1955) *The Dynamics of Bureaucracy*. Chicago: University of Chicago Press.

Blau, P.M. (1974) *On the Nature of Organizations*. New York: John Wiley.

Blau, P.M. and R.A. Schoenherr (1971) *The Structure of Organizations*. New York: Basic Books.

Blau, P.M. and W.R. Scott (1963) *Formal Organizations: A Comparative Approach*. London: Routledge and Kegan Paul.

Borcherding, T. (ed.) (1977) *Budgets and Bureaucrats: The Sources for Government Growth*. Durham, NC: Duke University Press.

Breton, A. (1974) *The Economic Theory of Representative Government*. Chicago: Aldine-Atherton.

Cawson, A. (ed.) (1985) *Organized Interests and the State*. London: Sage.

Cohen, M., J.G. March and J.P. Olsen (1976) 'People, Problems and the Ambiguity of Relevance' in March, J.G. and J.P. Olsen (eds) *Ambiguity and Choice*. Oslo: Universitetsforlaget.

Crozier, M. (1964) *The Bureaucratic Phenomenon*. Chicago: University of Chicago Press.

Davis, S.M. and P.R. Lawrence (1977) *Matrix*. Reading, Mass: Addison-Wesley.

Donaldson, L. (1982) 'Divisionalization and Size: A Theoretical and Empirical Critique', *Organization Studies*, 3, pp. 321–37.

Dunleavy, P. (1985) 'Bureaucrats, Budgets and the Growth of the State: Reconstructing an Instrumental Model', *British Journal of Political Science*, 15, pp. 299–328.

Dunsire, A. (1973) *Administration: The Word and the Science*. London: Martin Robertson.

Dunsire, A. (1978) *Implementation in a Bureaucracy*. Oxford: Martin Robertson.

Eavery, C.L. (1984) 'Bureaucratic Agenda Control: Imposition or Bargaining?' *American Political Science Review*, 78, pp. 719–33.

Elmore, R.F. (1982) 'Backward Mapping: Implementation Research and Policy Decision' in Williams, W. (ed.) *Studying Implementation: Methodological and Administrative Issues*. Chatham: Chatham House.

Etzioni, A. (1964) *Modern Organizations*. Englewood Cliffs: Prentice-Hall.

Etzioni-Halevy, E. (1983) *Bureaucracy and Democracy: A Political Dilemma*. London: Routledge and Kegan Paul.

Fairchild, H.P. (ed.) (1955) *Dictionary of Sociology*. Totowa, NJ: Littlefeld, Adams.

Goodsell, C.T. (1983) *The Case for Bureaucracy*. Chatham: Chatham House.

Gouldner, A.W. (1954) *Patterns of Industrial Bureaucracy*. Glencoe, Il: The Free Press.

Grinyer, P.H. (1982) 'Discussion Note: Divisionalization and Size: A Rejoinder', *Organization Studies*, 3, pp. 339–50.

Hall, R.H. (1974) *Organizations: Structure and Process*. Englewood Cliffs: Prentice Hall.

Hanf, K. and F.W. Scharpf (eds) (1978) *Interorganizational Policy Making*. London: Sage.

Hawley, A.W. et al. (1965) 'Population Size and Administration in Institutions of Higher Education', *American Sociological Review*, 30, pp. 252–55.

Hernes, G. (ed.) (1978) *Forhandlingsökonomi og blandingsadministrasjon*. Oslo: Universitetsforlaget.

Hood, C. (1976) *The Limits of Administration*. London: John Wiley.

Hood, C. and A. Dunsire (1981) *Bureaumetrics: The Quantitative Comparison of British Central Government Agencies*. Farnborough: Gower.

Indik, B.P. (1964) 'The Relationship Between Organizational Size and Supervisory Ratio', *Administrative Science Quarterly*, 9, pp. 301–12.

Jenkins, B. and A. Gray (1983) 'Bureaucratic Politics and Power: Developments in the Study of Bureaucracy', *Political Studies*, 31, pp. 177–93.

Jonsson, E. (1985) 'A Model of a Non-Budget-Maximizing Bureau' in J.-E. Lane (ed.) *State and Market*. London: Sage.

Kaufman, H. (1976) *Are Governmental Organizations Immortal?* Washington DC: Brookings.

Kimberly, J.R. (1976) 'Organizational Size and the Structuralist Perspective: A Review, Critique and Proposal', *Administrative Science Quarterly*, 21, pp. 571–97.

Knight, K. (1976) 'Matrix Organization: A Review', *The Journal of Management Studies*, 13, pp. 111–30.

Kristensen, O.P. (1982) 'Privat eller offentlig produktion ay offentlige serviceydelser: Danskt brandvaesen som eksempel', *Nordisk Administrativt Tidsskrift*, 63, pp. 219–47.

Lehmbruch, G. and P.C. Schmitter (eds) (1982) *Patterns of Corporatist Policy-Making*. London: Sage.

Leibenstein, H. (1966) 'Allocative Efficiency vs. "X-Efficiency" ', *American Economic Review*, 56, pp. 392–415.

Likert, R. (1961) *New Patterns of Management*. New York: McGraw-Hill.

March, J.G. and J.P. Olsen (eds) (1976) *Ambiguity and Choice*. Oslo: Universitetsforlaget.

McKean, R.N. (1958) *Efficiency in Government through Systems Analysis*. New York: John Wiley.

Melman, S. (1951) 'The Rise of Administrative Overhead in the Manufacturing Industries of the United States: 1899–1947', *Oxford Economic Papers*, 3, pp. 62–112.

Merton, R.K. (1957) *Social Theory and Social Structure*. Glencoe, IL.: The Free Press.

Meyer, M.W. and M.C. Brown (1977) 'The Process of Bureaucratization', *American Journal of Sociology*, 81, pp. 364–85.

Meyer, M.W. et al. (1985) *Limits to Bureaucratic Growth*. Berlin: de Gruyter.

Miller, G.J. and T.M. Moe (1983) 'Bureaucrats, Legislators, and the Size of Government', *American Political Science Review*, 77, pp. 297–322.

Mintzberg, H. (1979) *The Structuring of Organizations*. Englewood Cliffs, NJ: Prentice-Hall.

Niskanen, W.A. (1971) *Bureaucracy and Representative Government*. Chicago: Aldine-Atherton.

Olsen, J.P. (1983) *Organized Democracy: Political Insitutions in a Welfare State – The Case of Norway*. Oslo: Universitetsforlaget.

Olson, M. (1982) *The Rise and Decline of Nations*. New Haven: Yale University Press.

Page, E. (1985) *Political Authority and Bureaucratic Power: A Comparative Analysis*. Brighton: Harvester Press.

Parkinson, N.C. (1957) *Parkinson's Law or the Pursuit of Progress*. London: John Murray.

Parsons, T. (ed.) (1947) *The Theory of Social and Economic Organization*. New York: Oxford University Press.

Pondy, L.R. (1969) 'Effects of Size, Complexity, and Ownership on Administrative Intensity', *Administrative Science Quarterly*, 14, pp. 47–60.

Pressman, J.L. and A. Wildavsky (1984) *Implementation* (3rd edn.). Berkeley: University of California Press.

Richardson, J.J. and A.G. Jordan (1979) *Governing Under Pressure*. Oxford: Martin Robertson.

Riggs, F.W. (1979) 'Introduction: Shifting Meanings of the Term "Bureaucracy" '. *International Social Science Journal*, 31, pp. 563–84.

Roethlisberger, F.J. and W.J. Dickson (1939) *Management and the Worker*. Cambridge, Mass: Harvard University Press.

Rose, R. (ed.) (1980) *The Challenge to Governance: Studies in Overloaded Polities*. London: Sage.

Rudolph, L.J. and S.H. Rudolph (1979) 'Authority and Power in Bureaucratic and Patrimonial Administration: A Revisionist Interpretation of Weber on Bureaucracy', *World Politics*, 31, pp. 195–227.

Sabatier, P. (1986) 'Top-Down and Bottom-Up Approaches to Implementation Research', *Journal of Public Policy*, 6, pp. 21–48.

Sabatier, P. and D. Mazmanian (1979) 'The Conditions of Effective Implementation: A Guide to Accomplishing Policy Objectives', *Policy Analysis*, 5, pp. 481–504.

Saltzstein, G.H. (1985) 'Conceptualizing Bureaucratic Responsiveness', *Administration and Society*, 17, pp. 283–306.

Schmitter, P.C. and Lehmbruch, G. (eds) (1978) *Trends Toward Corporatist Intermediation*. London: Sage.

Selznick, P. (1949) *TVA and the Grass Roots*, Berkeley: University of California Press.

Sharpe, L.J. and K. Newton (1984) *Does Politics Matter? The Determinants of Public Policy*. Oxford: Clarendon.

Sharpe L.J. (1985) 'Central Coordination and the Policy Network', *Political Studies*, No 33: pp. 361–81.

Smith, D. and O. Zurcher (eds) (1944) *A Dictionary of American Politics*. New York: Barnes and Nobles.

Starbuck, W. (1965) 'Organizational Growth and Development' in J.G. March (ed.) *Handbook of Organizations*. Chicago: Rand McNally.

Stone, R.C. (1969) 'Bureaucracy' in J. Gould and W.L. Kolb (eds) *A Dictionary of the Social Sciences*. New York: Free Press.

Streeck, W. and P.C. Schmitter (eds) (1985) *Private Interest Government*. London: Sage.

Thompson, J.D. (1967) *Organizations in Action*. New York: McGraw-Hill.

Tullock, G. (1965) *The Politics of Bureaucracy*. Washington DC: Public Affairs Press.

Warwick, D.P. (1975) *A Theory of Public Bureaucracy*. Cambridge, Mass., Harvard University Press.

Weber, M. (1978) *Economy and Society*. Berkeley: University of California Press.

Webster's Third Unabridged Dictionary.

Whyte, W.H. (1956) *The Organization of Man*. New York: Simon and Schuster.

Wildavsky, A. (1979) *Speaking Truth to Power*. Boston: Little, Brown and Company.
Wilensky, H. (1967) *Organizational Intelligence*. New York: Basic Books.
Williams, W. (1980) *The Implementation Perspective*. Berkeley: University of California Press.

2
Economic theory of bureaucracy and public good allocation

Gert P. de Bruin

Introduction

Over the past two decades we have witnessed the remarkable phenomenon that an apparently a-political theory of market behaviour has been applied with increasingly wide acclaim to the analysis of political processes. Since it seldom happens that putting the cart before the horse turns out to be the most successful approach, be it in theoretical research or whatever else, one may wonder whether the analytical results of these endeavours are really as substantial as it is claimed.

This essay goes into some recent results of neoclassical modelling with regard to one particular area of non-market behaviour, viz. allocation processes for public resources, to see what relevance these results might have for a better understanding or arrangement of such processes. Following a by now well-established subdivision in the literature, three different sorts of allocation processes will be considered in separate sections. One section will be devoted to the analysis of voting procedures or *political mechanisms*, as they will often be called to distinguish them from another class of mechanisms which are much more similar in device to a market process. These so-called *economic mechanisms* are reviewed in a second section. Finally, the third section will deal with neoclassical approaches to *bureaucracies and bureaucratic behaviour*.

It would be difficult to discuss persuasively the prospects and limits for the successful application of the neoclassical maxims to this area of research without first saying something about the characteristics of these maxims. The following section will, therefore, give a bird's-eye view of the nature and basic features of neoclassical theory in so far as these seem relevant to the topic. On the whole, however, emphasis on the limitations of neoclassical theory will prevail, due to the fact that the very nature of neoclassical economics virtually blocks any effective application to some highly essential questions relating to public resource allocation. This pessimistic mood is shared by one of the main proponents of neoclassical economics, Kenneth Arrow.

A good deal of the theoretical literature of recent years seeks to describe political behavior as analogous to economic, and we may hope for a general theory of socio-economic equilibrium. But it must always be kept in mind that the contexts of choice are radically different, particularly when the hypotheses of perfectly costless action and information are relaxed. It is not accidental that economic analysis has been successful only in certain limited areas. (Arrow, 1970: 3)

In the concluding section this point is reiterated to see whether Arrow's rather negative view needs to be revised after fifteen years.

Neoclassical theory: its scope and limitations

In the introductory section neoclassical economics have been equated with a 'theory of markets'. However, this delineation still appears too broad. A more appropriate characterization of neoclassical economics would be to say that it is first and foremost a theory or markets *with perfect competition*. The immediate question to be answered then is, of course, by what device neoclassical theory was ordained to such a narrow scope. Facing this question becomes even more important because the answer may also give some insight into when and how the neoclassical apparatus can be fruitfully applied to the analysis of non-perfect competitive behaviour.

What was new in neoclassical economics? In the doctrine literature the differences from its predecessor — classical economics — have been described in many ways. The old school was concerned with *aggregates* (social classes), the new one with *individuals*; the first was *dynamic* in character, the second *static*; classical economics was *supply-oriented*, its successor *demand-oriented*; the earlier theory was pre-eminently *essayistic* in style, the new one firmly *mathematically* based. Without doubt, these dichotomies make sense, but, as is argued below, the decisive change has been the rise to power of mathematics. If all these differences had to be subsumed under one heading, they would show that neoclassical economics started in the 1870s with the introduction of *methodological individualism and the concomitant hypothesis of individual maximizing behaviour*.[1]

At about the same time that the hypothesis of maximizing behaviour was introduced into economics, the Newton–Leibniz theory of calculus became more widely known and applied outside the inner circle of pure scientists. From a history-of-economic-doctrines point of view it would be interesting to know which was first, the marginalist/maximization concept or the choice of differential calculus as mathematical technique. Whatever the answer to this 'chicken-and-egg' problem might be, for our purposes it suffices to note that from the early beginnings of the new economic school there has existed an indissoluble relationship between the maximization hypothesis and the technique of differential calculus.[2] Not surprisingly, therefore, the course of development of neoclassical theory has at least in part been steered by the potentialities of this mathematical device.

For calculus to be applicable to solve maximization problems, it is necessary that the arguments of the function to be maximized are exclusive to that function and do not appear simultaneously in any other function which is also to be maximized. Except for the proverbial Robinson Crusoe case, economies are characterized by intricate patterns of interaction between the participants so that, in general, the arguments of the different individual functions must be highly intertwined:

> Thus each participant attempts to maximize a function . . . of which he does not control all variables. This is certainly no maximum problem, but a peculiar and disconcerting mixture of several conflicting maximum problems. Every participant is guided by another principle and neither determines all variables which affect his interest. This kind of problem is nowhere dealt with in classical mathematics. (von Neumann and Morgenstern, 1967: 11)

In a market system, the most important if not the only kind of allocation process economists in the past century could think of, the 'disconcerting mixture of maximum problems' is evidenced by constant price changes due to the demand and supply behaviour of different individuals. How disconcerting the mixture will be depends on the extent to which prices can be upset by the actions of individual participants. Already many classical economists were aware of an inverse relationship between the number of participants in a market and any single individual's potential to influence price. In his *Recherches sur les Principes Mathématiques de la Théorie des Richesses* (1838) Augustin Cournot, who is sometimes called the first mathematical economist, explicitly introduced the limiting case of market competition where no individual producer's supply would have any *appreciable* effect on market price. By extending this large number argument to the demand side of markets, the founders of neoclassical economics established the key feature of what is now generally called the model of *perfect competition*, i.e. the parametric role of prices for all participants. Gradually the large number argument receded into the background and it was *price-taking behaviour* by all individuals which turned into the defining assumption of perfect competition.

Although the puzzle of the mixture of maximum problems has formally been solved if prices can be taken as parameters by each individual, for the hypothesis of individual maximizing behaviour truly to make sense some additional assumptions are necessary. At least, prices should be known to all participants which, in turn, requires a more or less stationary economy in which technology, preferences and other conditions are not prone to change:

. . . by the very logic of the maximization problem, all true neoclassical economics is economics under certainty, the static framework being closely linked to the plausibility of the implied assumption of full information. (Streissler, 1973: 160)

The early neoclassical economists seem not to have been bothered very much by these exacting assumptions about information and certainty. Their first concern, from Walras on, has been to prove that a market system with perfect competition would work. That is, for given preferences, technology and income distribution there would exist some set of prices such that all markets would be cleared. This research into the existence of perfectly competitive equilibria got a new and decisive impulse when the hypothesis was raised that such equilibria would also yield *socially optimal or efficient* outcomes.

Just like the very model of perfect competition had its less articulated classical forerunners, so had the problem of optimality also been taken up before by classical economists. Indeed, the founder of the Old School, Adam Smith, had already suggested that in the case of what he called free competition, the decentralized actions of self-interested individuals would give rise 'as led by an invisible hand' to a socially optimal outcome. The neoclassical approach was different in two respects. To begin with, the concept of optimality, Smith's rather vague idea of a social maximum, was replaced by the analytically unambiguous notion of *Pareto optimality*. In addition, there was again the difference in mathematical rigour whereby the relationships between competitive equilibria and Pareto-optimal allocations were established.

There is no question but that the standing of both the perfect competition and the Pareto optimality concept in neoclassical theory have been strongly reinforced by the formal analytical result that, *under certain conditions*, perfectly competitive equilibria and Pareto-optimal allocations 'coincide'. Indeed, on the one hand this result has vindicated Pareto optimality as a meaningful efficiency criterion, since there always appears to exist at least one allocation process by which this criterion is met, viz. perfect competition, while on the other hand it has once more emphasized the 'perfectness' of perfect competition. However, this enthusiasm seems rather premature since the conditions to be satisfied are very stringent.

Actually, the nature of the conditions in question is such that non-optimality of perfectly competitive equilibria may be expected to be the rule rather than the exception. As soon as the consumption or production of a commodity by one individual enters the utility or profit function of any other person, optimality will be lost. Neoclassical economics has gathered all these deviant cases under one common denominator, the concept of *externalities* or *external effects*. The name refers to the cause of optimality disturbance, for example changes in utility for some person due to the consumption of someone else are not counted in the market price of the commodity in question, i.e. they are *external* to the price mechanism. To put it differently, market price reflects the *individual* marginal utility of a good, while for Pareto optimality it should reflect *social* marginal utility, i.e. the aggregate of the individual marginal utilities.

Unfortunately, at this general level of analysis about the only thing neoclassical theory has to say on the divergent class of externalities is the suggestion that other, non-market channels of resource allocation should be sought for them. Of course, this suggestion would only be useful if there existed one other allocation process besides the perfectly competitive market, which would yield fully Pareto-optimal outcomes for all externalities. The basic problem with neoclassical theory with regard to optimality is that it only allows for 'all-or-nothing' statements, i.e. an allocation can only be judged either fully optimal or non-optimal. There exists no criterion whatsoever to decide whether some commodity, with external effects, would better be allocated by one process or another. For instance, when the consumption of a single good enters the utility functions of many individuals in the economy, there are clearly external effects, but when are these effects large enough to justify state or governmental provision of the commodity thus calling it a public good? Neoclassical theory cannot tell. The very reason for this deficiency would seem to be that such a comparative criterion would inevitably require some sort of interpersonal utility comparison.[3] Consequently, the analytical framework of neoclassical economics is exclusively directed towards 'limiting cases' and 'ideal type' concepts. It is not by accident that the progress which has been made in the past two decades with regard to the analysis of public resource allocation, is fully due to just another set of ideal types — Samuelson's dichotomy between purely private and purely public goods.

The limiting case character of perfect competition is clearly illustrated when attention is shifted from the statics of equilibrium outcomes and their possible optimality, to the dynamics of how such equilibria could be attained. Indeed, the very same assumption which is essential to the equilibrium of perfect competition, that of price-taking behaviour, at the same time effectively blocks any reasonable explanation as to what behaviour would lead to an equilibrium set of prices.

> Each individual participant in the economy is supposed to take prices as given and determine his choices as to purchases and sales accordingly, there is no one left whose job it is to make a decision on price. (Arrow, 1959: 43)

Walras, the first economist to be confronted with this *stability problem*, introduced the device of an *auctioneer*, somebody whose job it would be to call a set of prices, whereupon all individuals in the economy should indicate the quantities they would like to buy or sell at these prices. If for some goods demand would not equal supply, the auctioneer would call a revised set of prices, and so on, until all quantities supplied and demanded would balance. Only then, would all purchases and sales be effected. The problem with such a trial-and-error, or *tâtonnement* process is, of course, first of all that it has no real-world counterpart. In addition, the device of an auctioneer seems detrimental to the image of the market system as a pre-eminently *decentralized* allocation process. Nevertheless, up until now Walras's *tâtonnement* process is presumably the only solution to the stability problem which is compatible with the assumption of price-taking behaviour.[4]

This stability problem relates to a rather specific and limited notion of dynamics for an economic system in which all important features like number and variety of goods and services, individual preferences, production technology etc. are supposed to remain the same. Real dynamics relate to changes in one or more of these features. Since, within the static equilibrium context, neoclassical theory lacks a criterion to decide whether some good should be allocated by one or the other process, it is especially interesting to know if, from a dynamic perspective, anything can be said about how new commodities arise in an economy.

The standard answer to this question by any neoclassical theorist is, without doubt, that the market process will provide everything that is *profitable*. One objection to this profitability argument would be that, at best, it could only be a partial answer. Almost by definition it is unable to explain how new goods are included in other, non-market, channels of allocation like, for instance, governmental provision.

Recapitulating on what has been found so far then, it can be said that the hypothesis of individual maximizing behaviour has led neoclassical theory to the almost exclusive consideration of a limiting case, the model of perfect competition, in the context of which dynamic processes are difficult, if not impossible to explain, while its static equilibrium outcomes are seldom if ever fully Pareto-optimal, given the stringent conditions to be fulfilled. Despite these negative scores the concepts of perfect competition and Pareto optimality still dominate neoclassical analysis.

To present a complete and truthful picture of neoclassical theory, however, two further additions are necessary. Firstly, the maximization hypothesis has led to *almost* exclusive attention being given to perfect competition. Actually, there is one other model of a market process which is compatible with this hypothesis (and the mathematical technique of calculus), that is *monopoly*. In the monopoly model there is one *price-setter*, the producer, while all consumers are supposed to be *price-takers* again. The monopolist will extend his supply up to the point where the marginal revenue and marginal cost of his product are equal, thus yielding him maximum profit. There appear to be two reasons why the monopoly model has never become as popular as the perfectly competitive one in neoclassical economics. The first is purely analytical. With perfect competition it is possible to look at a *general* equilibrium for an economy. With one or more monopolistic markets this becomes rather troublesome, so that the analysis of monopoly is usually restricted to a *partial* equilibrium for the market in question. The second reason is clearly normative. The outcomes under monopoly are *not* Pareto-optimal. On consideration, this statement seems contradictory to the aforementioned point, since the Pareto criterion strictly applies to outcomes for the economy as a whole. Actually, what we have here is an example of how the perfect competition model serves as a measuring rod for Pareto optimality. Under monopoly the price of a good is higher than marginal cost, under perfect competition these two are equal. A perfectly competitive equilibrium is Pareto-optimal, therefore an economy with monopoly is not.[5] Another way to express the suboptimality of monopoly is by saying that the monopolist's output is too small compared with that of the perfectly competitive producer.

The second addition to the picture of neoclassical theory is the *theory of games*. Of this it can be said without too much exaggeration that it was created to fill the wide gap between perfect competition on the one hand and monopoly on the other, i.e. all those market structures where a 'disconcerting mixture of several maximum problems' would be present. Even in 1959 Oskar Morgenstern, one of the founders of game theory, had still high expectations as to its applicability.

> The theory of games provides a model for economic behavior no matter what the market structure. The logico-mathematical properties of the model are well understood, and it is amenable to computation and numerical analysis. (Shubik, 1959: viii)

If today the enthusiasm regarding the potentialities of game theory is somewhat less, this is at least partly due to the fact that for most game-theoretic situations assumptions as to the level of information on the part of participants or *players* are even more severe than in the model of perfect competition. A participant in a game is supposed to know exactly which actions or *strategies* are open to each of the players (including himself), what outcomes correspond to the different combinations of individual strategies and also which utility or *pay-off* each distinct individual attaches to all of these different outcomes. Most disappointing of all, however, have been the problems with the search for reasonable behavioural hypotheses. Obviously, at least some amendment of the straightforward maximizing hypothesis is necessary, so as to take account of the interaction or mixture aspects in game situations.

Actually, only one sort of game has been fully satisfactorily solved by the von Neumann–Morgenstern theory. Just like the models of perfect competition and monopoly the game in question, the *two-person zero-sum game*, is an ideal type, where the interests of both players are diametrically opposed. From a behavioural point of view the analysis of this game is rather easy because the hypothesis about the behaviour of the other player (opponent) is more or less directly implied by the inverse relationship between the preferences. Mathematically the problem had already been solved by von Neumann in the 1920s, resulting in the *maximin solution* for these two-person zero-sum games.

It proved to be much more difficult to outline a general behavioural hypothesis and a concomitant solution concept for mixed interest games, i.e. games in which interests are partly opposed and partly parallel. The problems involved are reflected by the multiplicity of solution concepts for co-operative as well as for non co-operative games. Although even the question whether some interaction process can best be represented by a co-operative or by a non co-operative game has in general no unequivocal answer, attention here will be restricted to non co-operative games because only applications of these games will be discussed in subsequent sections.

For mixed interest games there does exist one subcategory where the problem of a reasonable behavioural hypothesis is virtually absent since all players have an unconditionally best strategy, i.e. a strategy which against each strategy of the other player(s) yields an outcome which is at least as attractive as the outcome resulting from any other strategy. This is, of course, a situation which comes rather close to one with independently maximizing individuals. There is one important difference though, by choosing his unconditionally best or *dominant strategy* a player can be sure that he never could have done better, but which outcome exactly will result, and therefore what pay-off, still depends on the strategy choices of the other players. For instance, in the following simple two-person game, with two strategies for each player,

		B	
		b_1	b_2
	a_1	1,3	2,4
A			
	a_2	3,1	4,2

both players, A and B, have a dominant strategy. For A a_2 is dominant since this strategy yields better payoffs than a_1 against both strategy b_1 and b_2 of player B, viz. 3 versus 1 and 4 versus 2, respectively. Similarly, b_2 is a dominant strategy for player B. Consequently, the *dominant strategy equilibrium* outcome (4,2) seems the natural solution to this game.[6]

Unfortunately, the subcategory of games with a dominant strategy for all players appears rather small. The solution concept which is most commonly used in games where such dominant strategies are lacking, is that of a '*Nash equilibrium*'. While a dominant strategy is best against *all* possible strategies by the other players, a Nash equilibrium strategy is only best against the corresponding equilibrium strategies of the other players. For example, in the following game the combination of strategies a_2 and b_1 is a Nash equilibrium pair. Clearly, strategy a_2 is a better reply for player A against strategy b_1 of player B than strategy a_1 (3 versus 1).

B

		b_1	b_2
A	a_1	1,3	4,1
	a_2	3,4	2,2

Similarly, strategy b_1 is the better reply against strategy a_2 for player B (4 versus 2). Note, however, that strategy a_2 is not the best reply against strategy b_2 for player A.

Although the Nash equilibrium outcome certainly meets the requirements of an equilibrium to the extent that, once arrived at, nobody is inclined to move away from it again, it is more questionable whether it also meets the requirements for a natural solution. Basically, the problem with the Nash equilibrium concept is more or less the same as with that of a perfectly competitive equilibrium. The associated behavioural assumption is difficult to combine with a sensible dynamic process which would lead to such an equilibrium. Under perfect competition the behavioural assumption is, in fact, that every individual *can* act as if the other participants will not react to his behaviour since, supposedly, nobody has any appreciable influence on the course of events in markets. For Nash equilibrium the assumption is that every individual *does* act as if the others will not react to his behaviour although, except in equilibrium, they clearly will.[7] Needless to say, in those analyses where the Nash equilibrium is taken to be the appropriate solution concept, seldom if ever is any attention paid to the dynamic process by which the equilibrium would be attained.

The problem of how equilibrium could be attained has become even more burdensome in those analyses where the assumption that each player is fully informed about the preferences of all other participants, for theoretically very good reasons, has been dropped. Indeed, it is most probably true that the assumption of *no* information about other players' preferences is more realistic than that of *full* information, but at the same time it seems to become impossible because of this change of assumption for any player to know even *what* his equilibrium strategy is in the most simple games. Note, for instance, in the game matrix above that if player *A* had not known the pay-offs for player *B*, he would be unable to trace which of the four outcomes corresponds to Nash equilibrium. So, the more realistic the assumptions as to information become, the less plausible the Nash equilibrium point as solution concept appears to be. There seem to be two obvious reasons why this equilibrium concept is still the most frequently used solution in recent game-theoretic modelling of allocation processes. One reason is that the existence of such an equilibrium for nearly all relevant games is fairly easily established. The other, closely related one, is that behaviourally more suitable equilibrium concepts are wanting in most games. For instance, the dominant strategy equilibrium as a solution concept is in no way jeopardized by alternative assumptions as to information about the preferences of other players, but does as already mentioned only exit in a relatively small category of games.

Political mechanisms for public
resource allocation: voting procedures

Nowadays the usual method of decision making on public[8] goods is by voting. Formally, any voting procedure may be thought of as consisting of two parts. First each individual participant determines and reveals his preference ordering of the possible alternatives. These preferences are then aggregated, according to a weighting scheme indicated by the particular procedure used, into a *social choice* or socially best element from the set of alternatives. Of course, if individual preferences vary, there is a good chance that for one or more participants the final selected social choice is quite different from their own first choice. Under the circumstances one may expect that, due to individual maximizing behaviour, such participants will try to bring about another outcome under the given voting rule by revealing *false* preferences. In the recent past, neoclassical research in this area has been concerned with whether such individual attempts to manipulate the outcome of voting procedures can be successful.

Since it will be no one's purpose to cheat in order to bring about a less beneficial outcome, a voting rule can be called *manipulable* whenever a participant, by reporting an insincere preference ordering, is able to effect a social choice which is more favourable to him than the outcome which would have resulted, under the given rules, from sincere voting. Clearly then, any attempt to manipulate the choice rule only makes sense for those individuals whose personal first choice does not coincide with the social choice revealed by sincere revelation. To give an extreme example, the dictator, under the dictatorial choice rule, will never have any incentive to manipulate. His own first choice and the 'social' choice always coincide. Revealing false preferences would merely lead to the choice of some alternative which he prefers less.

So, a necessary condition for manipulability of a voting rule is that for at least one participant, personal and social choice do not always coincide. As such, this result does not seem very helpful since potential differences between individual preferences do constitute the *raison d'être* for collective choice rules. In other words, the 'undying unanimity' which non-fulfilment of the above condition seems to require, would make any such rule superfluous. Surprisingly enough, however, in the early 1970s this necessary condition had been proven to be much less trivial for research into the manipulability of choice rules than previously thought. Indeed, as will be shown in the next section, this condition has been the 'key' to the construction of a whole class of non-manipulable procedures.

For our present purposes, however, it suffices to point out that the condition is necessary, but not sufficient, for manipulability of voting rules. The previous example of dictatorial choice may serve to make that point clear. Other participants in the procedure will often have a first choice which is quite different from that of the dictator, but they are unable to change the outcome of the procedure by reporting insincere preferences. The dictatorial rule is simply *not* manipulable.

Obviously, the dictatorial rule is not a very interesting case, since there is virtually no question of aggregation of individual preferences. There do exist, however, other more persuasive examples to show that the condition is not sufficient for manipulability. Suppose, for example, that a committee of three persons has to make a choice out of two alternatives, *A* and *B*, via majority rule. If two members prefer *A* above *B*, then alternative *A* is the majority choice irrespective of the third member's ordering. Moreover, if this third member preferred *B* above *A*, his first personal and social choice would differ. He would still have no possibility whatsoever of changing the outcome of the rule by reporting insincerely. Indeed, the only possible insincere preferences would be either indifference between *A* and *B* or strict preference of *A* above *B*. Clearly, reporting one of these two preferences would only further strengthen alternative A as the social choice.

The non-manipulability of majority rule in the above example is due not to the number of participants, but to the number of alternatives. For any size of committee majority rule remains non-manipulable so long as the number of alternatives remains at two. In the case of three or more alternatives, there may arise situations in which some participant, by reporting falsely, is able to effect an outcome under majority rule which is more attractive to him than the sincere social choice. Generally, it is not enough for manipulation under majority rule that individual and social choices diverge, there should also be enough room for the 'manipulator-in-spe' to report an ordering which is fairly different from his sincere preferences. The required room is lacking when there are only two alternatives to choose from, or when the set of admissible preferences is severely limited.[9] It happens to be the case, for instance, that even with three or more alternatives, majority rule is non-manipulable if the participants are only allowed to announce preferences which satisfy the well known condition of single-peakedness (Blin and Satterthwaite, 1979).

What has been said with respect to majority rule, turns out to be true for each voting procedure. In the early 1970s Gibbard and Satterthwaite formally proved that every non-dictatorial voting procedure is manipulable, unless the choice is limited to two alternatives or severe restrictions are imposed upon the domain of admissible individual preferences.

If one is inclined to consider non-manipulability as a valuable property for choice procedures, the content of the *Gibbard–Satterthwaite Theorem* must have a rather negative ring. Actually, the theorem does clearly not imply that all non-dictatorial voting procedures constantly fall victim to manipulation. What it really says is that announcing ones sincere preferences does not under *all* circumstances yield the individually best possible outcome, i.e. irrespective of the preferences reported by the other participants. In other words, there exists no non-dictatorial voting procedure in which truth-telling, or sincere voting, is *always* a dominant strategy for *all* participants. At the same time it also follows from the theorem that under no voting procedure is any insincere voting strategy always best for some individual.[10] Thus, whether under some given voting procedure revealing one's true preferences or some false ordering yields a more attractive outcome, is strongly dependent on the preferences reported by the voters. The following example is intended to show that at least for some more commonly used procedure opportunities for manipulation, though theoretically present, are virtually non-existent.

As choice procedure the well known majority rule is again selected. If three persons have to make a choice between three alternatives x, y, and z, it needs a complex tableau, similar to Table 2.1 in order to describe all possible preference profiles, i.e. combinations of individual preferences, with corresponding outcomes, even though only strict preferences are considered and indifferences excluded.[11] For some

TABLE 2.1
Game matrix for majority rule in case of three voters, three
alternatives and only strict preferences allowed

Preference ordering of individual: 1:	2:	3: xyz	xzy	yxz	yzx	zxy	zyx
xyz	xyz	x	x	x	x	x	x
	xzy	x	x	x	x	x	x
	yxz	x	x	y	y	x	y
	yzx	x	x	y	y	(x)	y
	zxy	x	x	x	(x)	z	z
	zyx	x	x	y	y	z	z
xzy	xyz	x	x	x	x	x	x
	xzy	x	x	x	x	x	x
	yxz	x	x	y	y	x	(x)
	yzx	x	x	y	y	z	z
	zxy	x	x	x	z	z	z
	zyx	x	x	(x)	z	z	z
yxz	xyz	x	x	y	y	x	y
	xzy	x	x	y	y	x	(y)
	yxz	y	y	y	y	y	y
	yzx	y	y	y	y	y	y
	zxy	x	x	y	y	z	z
	zyx	y	(y)	y	y	z	z
yzx	xyz	x	x	y	y	(y)	y
	xzy	x	x	y	y	z	z
	yxz	y	y	y	y	y	y
	yzx	y	y	y	y	y	y
	zxy	(y)	z	y	y	z	z
	zyx	y	z	y	y	z	z
zxy	xyz	x	x	x	(z)	z	z
	xzy	x	x	x	z	z	z
	yxz	x	x	y	y	z	z
	yzx	(z)	z	y	y	z	z
	zxy	z	z	z	z	z	z
	zyx	z	z	z	z	z	z
zyx	xyz	x	x	y	y	z	z
	xzy	x	x	(z)	z	z	z
	yxz	y	(z)	y	y	z	z
	yzx	y	z	y	y	z	z
	zxy	z	z	z	z	z	z
	zyx	z	z	z	z	z	z

preference profiles there are formally no majority outcomes. These are instances of the famous Condorcet Paradox. All cells in Table 2.1 where the outcome is encircled pertain to 'Paradox'-situations. In this example these deadlock cases have been solved by elevating the relevant first choice of person 1 to the rank of social choice.[12] For instance, for the preference profile:

person 1: *yzx*
person 2: *zxy*
person 3: *xyz*

none of the alternatives is preferred by a majority above both the other two. Therefore, the first choice of person 1, *y*, has been made the social choice (compare highest encircled outcome in the first column).

The outcome, *y*, which thus corresponds to the above given preference profile, happens to be least preferred alternative for person 2. Would it be possible for him to improve his situation by manipulation? Yes, it would. By pretending that his ordering is *xyz* instead of *zxy*, he could change the social choice from *y* into *x* *if* persons 1 and 3 stick to their original preferences. The conditional is essential since the manipulative ordering *xyz* does not yield a more attractive majority choice to person 2 for all possible preference orderings of persons 1 and 3. If, for example, individual 1 adhered to his ordering *yzx*, but individual 3 announced *xzy* (instead of *xyz*), then the sincere preference ordering of individual 2 would lead to alternative *z* as social choice, i.e. his most preferred alternative, whereas the false ordering *xyz* would yield alternative *x* as majority choice, i.e. his own second choice.

This example illustrates that for successful manipulation of a voting procedure, an individual participant needs complete information about the preferences which the other voters are going to announce. But if such 'omniscience' were indeed present, manipulation would become virtually impossible since everybody would then know the sincere preferences of everybody else. This is the main argument advanced by Leif Johansen (1977) to support his proposition that manipulation is a negligible phenomenon in most, if not all, representative bodies. In his view dispersion of information about everyone's preferences is a natural consequence of the lobbying processes which precede the actual vote. In other words, it is impossible to persuade one's opponents of the merits of some alternative without giving notice of one's own preferences.

To some extent Johansen appears to be overshooting his mark with this argument, since it is difficult to believe that, in general, votes are as completely prefabricated as he suggests. Moreover, even the slightest uncertainty about the opponent's voting behaviour is much more deadly to any manipulation plan than Johansen's lobbying process. One look at Table 2.1, which is about the simplest example of a voting process one can think of, is sufficient to show that opportunities for manipulation which theoretically exist, can be ruled out for all practical purposes. The Gibbard–Satterthwaite Theorem and, more particularly, the interpretation that it would prove that all democratic voting procedures are manipulable, is just another instance of the phenomenon that neoclassical theory and its extension, the theory of games, are ill-suited for choice situations with other than perfect information. In addition, while Johansen and the present author both believe, though on different grounds, that the really important decisions are not made during the formal voting stage but during the agenda-building and lobbying processes which precede the vote, the static analytical framework of neoclassical theory has little or nothing to offer as to the analysis of these dynamic procedures.

In total, then, the main neoclassical contribution to the analysis of political allocation mechanisms consists of a theorem which is formally a possibility result as to manipulability of voting procedures, but which informally can best be interpreted as an impossibility result.

Economic mechanisms for public resource allocation: pseudo-markets

In the foregoing section it sufficed to assume some intermingling of individual interests in order to justify collective decision making. However, as soon as Pareto optimality of the outcomes under different allocation mechanisms becomes a central issue, it is necessary to start with a clearly defined concept of public resources. In this section our point of reference will be Samuelson's polar concept of a pure public good, with the characteristic property that it is equally available to all individuals in the economy.[13]

Actually, Samuelson's concepts were not as novel as he had first thought. Similar definitions had been presented and applied by, for example, Lindahl and Bowen, be it that their analyses had been restricted to partial equilibrium level. Presumably, Bowen had been the first economist to specify sufficient conditions under which majority rule would yield efficient outcomes for the allocation of pure public goods. These conditions do seem somewhat unrealistic and odd looking, constant unit cost for the public good, 'normally distributed' individual marginal rates for substitution, and equal tax shares for all participants. The requirement for a strictly symmetric distribution around the median for marginal rates of substitution, appears rather extraordinary. However, given the assumption of equal cost or tax shares for all participants, it could well be the only possibility to allow that under majority rule the sum of marginal rates of substitution equals the marginal cost of the public good (in terms of a numéraire) as demanded for Pareto optimality.

One could do without symmetry if the condition of equal tax shares were dropped and replaced by the assumption that each individual's contribution would be accordant to his marginal rate of substitution. Bowen was well aware of this alternative condition, but at the same time also of the problems associated with its implementation (Bowen, 1969:129). In fact, Bowen preferred equal tax shares which theoretically could only seldom be expected to yield Pareto-optimal outcomes under majority rule, above distinct individual cost contributions which, in theory, would lead to optimality but in practice to insincere revelation of preferences and all kinds of administrative problems. Thus, Bowen foresaw the basic weaknesses of those classes of newly designed allocation mechanisms for pure public goods which were to be introduced in the 1970s.

In general, the Pareto-optimal amount of a public good varies with income distribution and cost patterns. However, in the case of constant unit cost and constant marginal utility of money or income for each person this optimal level is unique, i.e. independent of existing income distribution. More particularly, suppose we consider a simple economy with one private and one public good, where the costs of both goods are constant and equal to each other. Suppose furthermore that in this economy all individual preferences are of the following type:

(1) $u_i(x,y_i) = v_i(x) + y_i$ $i = 1,2,...,n$

In other words, the utility for individual i derived from quantity x of the public good and quantity y_i of the private good, may be taken to be the *sum* of some function of quantity x of the collective good, indicated by $v_i(x)$, and quantity y_i of the private good. Note that for this kind of utility function one additional unit of the private good always gives rise to one extra 'unit' of utility. In other words, the private good serves as an unit of measurement or numéraire for utility. Moreover, this unit of measurement is the same for all individuals. Individual preferences of the form given in (1) which do have the property of constant marginal utility of income, are sometimes called *quasi-linear* (i.e. quasi-*linear* with respect to y_i and *quasi*-linear with respect to x).

If all individuals have quasi-linear preferences and the cost of both goods are constant and equal, then the necessary condition, as derived by Samuelson, for Pareto optimality of outcomes of this economy with one private and one public good, becomes rather simple:

(2) $$\sum_{i=1}^{n} v_i(x) = 1$$

in which $v_i(x)$ represents the first derivative of $v_i(x)$. That is, the *sum* of the marginal utilities of all individuals with respect to the collective good should be equal to marginal cost in terms of the numéraire, which in this case, equals 1.

The first class of allocation mechanisms for public goods which was specially designed to foreclose any profitable way of insincere revelation of preferences on the one hand and to yield Pareto-optimal outcomes on the other hand, incorporated the above necessary condition in a rather direct way. Participants were asked to report their evaluation of the public good, $v_i(x)$, to the Central Organization or Government, who would maximize the following function:

$$(3) \qquad \sum_{i=1}^{n} v_i(x) - x$$

The first term of this function, $\sum_{i=1}^{n} v_i(x)$, denotes the *sum* of individual utilities corresponding to amount x of the collective good in terms of the numéraire, the private good. The second term, x, represents the cost (again in terms of the numéraire) of x units of the collective good. So, maximization of (3) means nothing more than maximization of the total *net* benefits of the collective good. The amazing thing is that at first sight it looks as if apples (i.e. individual utilities) and pears (cost of the public good) are summed together. However, due to the assumption of quasi-linearity and the implied one-to-one relationship between units of utility and of private good, these apparently divergent entities can indeed be compared.

It is easy to see that for the function in (3) to be maximized, the necessary condition for Pareto optimality must be satisfied. For a maximum of (3) the amount x should be so chosen that its first derivative equals O, or

$$(4) \qquad \sum_{i=1}^{n} v_i(x) - 1 = 0$$

which is, of course, identical to condition (2).

It may be taken for granted that each individual tries to maximize his utility function $u_i(x, y_i)$ under the constraints imposed by his income I_i and the individual contribution (tax) T_i which he has to pay for the financing of the collective good. If income I_i and tax T_i are also expressed in terms of the private good, the function to be maximized by individual i is given by:

$$(5) \qquad v_i(x) + I_i - T_i \qquad I = 1,2,...,n$$

Furthermore, since income I_i is constant at any given time, maximization of (5) is equivalent to maximization of:

$$(6) \qquad v_i(x) - I_i \qquad i = 1,2,...,n$$

Both Groves (1973) and Clarke (1971) have discovered that by an appropriate choice of the individual tax formula T_i manipulability of the procedure can be precluded. Groves suggested the following individual tax function:

$$(7) \qquad T_i(x) = x - \sum_{j \neq i} v_j(x) \qquad i = 1,2,..., n$$

If T_i in (6) is replaced by formula (7) the individual objective function happens to be identical to the government objective function given by (3). Here, then, we have an example of the case hinted at in the preceding section, where social or collective choice rule and individual objective function are identical, so that the first choices for both functions always coincide and the necessary condition for manipulability *cannot* be fulfilled. Indeed, it turns out that telling the truth, i.e. announcing the correct and sincere $v_i(x)$ to the government, is a dominant strategy for each and every participant under this procedure.

There is only one problem with this peculiar tax device. Usually, individual tax levels or functions are so chosen that the government budget is balanced, i.e. that the sum of individual taxes equals the cost of the selected public good level. In this case the form of the tax function has been prescribed by the requirements for non-manipulability of the procedure and, unfortunately, these requirements and those for budgetary equilibrium are incompatible. By algebraic manipulation it can be shown that for this particular tax function the government will be confronted with a *deficit* (de Bruin, 1986).

It is true that some variation in the tax function formula is still possible without destroying the non-manipulability property. In fact, any term can be added to formula (7) which is not dependent on $v_i(x)$, as long as the added terms are *constants* from the point of view of individual i. It can be proven, however, that by adding such constant terms a balanced budget can never be ensured. Since apart from the above condition, budgetary equilibrium is also a requirement for Pareto optimality of the outcome, the conclusion should be that decision making via the procedures suggested by Groves and Clarke will, in general, not lead to fully Pareto-optimal results.

In view of this suboptimality the only advantage of the Groves–Clarke procedures, compared with majority rule as suggested by Bowen for decision making on public goods, consists in the solution, at least formally, of the problem of manipulation or free-ridership with public goods. For that reason some researchers, in particular Tullock and Tideman (1976), have not only propounded enthusiastically the actual use of some form of Groves–Clarke procedure, but have also made painstaking efforts to show that the more participants there are in such procedures, the closer the outcome would be to full Pareto optimality. Their arguments as to that point are, however, inconclusive (de Bruin, 1986) and what is probably more important, Pareto suboptimality though perhaps the most significant failure from a confirmed neoclassical point of view, is certainly not the only weakness in the Groves–Clarke construction. Some of the other weaknesses have been treated at greater length by the auctor intellectualis himself (Groves and Ledyard, 1977) than by Tullock and Tideman.

From a purely theoretical standpoint the most striking failing of the Groves–Clarke device is, without doubt, the necessary restriction to quasi-linear preferences which, by their nature, come rather close to cardinal and interpersonally comparable utilities. Practically seen, however, the problem of its *implementability* might be much more important. Each participant is supposed to report his complete individual evaluation function for the collective good in question, $v_i(x)$, to the government. Even mathematicians amongst the participants would, obviously, have great trouble in meeting this requirement. Moreover, the costs of collecting and processing the necessary information would often be higher than the cost of the public good itself. In other words, even if the *theoretical* relevance of the Groves–Clarke construction were beyond dispute, the *practical* implementability would still be zero.

At the time Groves began criticizing his own creation, he had, together with Ledyard, just designed a new class of procedures for decision making on public goods, which supposedly met all the objections raised against his first device. Indeed, these Groves–Ledyard procedures would yield fully Pareto-optimal outcomes, ask for no restrictions as to individual preferences, be non-manipulable, and, in addition, allow for very simple messages from participants to government.

Of course, some price has to be paid for all these sunny prospects. Since the results so far seem to indicate that non-dictatorial, non-manipulable choice procedures fail to exist unless the domain of possible preferences is severely restricted, it cannot be other than that the concept of manipulability has changed. Up until now non-manipulability has been defined in terms of truth-telling being a *dominant* strategy, but in the Groves–Ledyard procedures sincere revelation of preferences is just a *Nash equilibrium* strategy. In view of the criticisms levelled against Nash equilibrium as a solution concept, especially in situations with incomplete information, the question may be raised whether the theoretical and practical relevance of the new Groves–Ledyard procedures are really greater than that of the old Groves–Clarke device. Actually, from both a theoretical and a practical point of view the score of the new procedure is worse. Perhaps the easiest way to present this argument is on the basis of some simple examples of a Groves–Ledyard procedure.

To keep as close as possible to the example of the Groves–Clarke procedure, we will stick to our economy with just one private and one public good and with constant and equal production costs for both goods. It is also assumed that there are *n* individuals in society. The collective choice rule which is part of the Groves–Ledyard procedure looks extremely simple:

$$(8) \quad x = \sum_{i=1}^{n} x_i$$

where x denotes the amount of the public good, while x_i indicates the number of units of the public good individual i would like to add *given* the messages of the other participants as to the level they desire. If, for instance, individual k considers $x = 100$ to be the most desirable level for the public good in question, while the messages, $x_i s$ of the other $n-1$ participants sum to 105, then he should send the message $x_k = -5$ to the government. Obviously, a message like this where just one number has to be reported, is much easier than the announcement of a complete evaluation function as required under the Groves–Clarke procedures. On the other hand, the rule is such that if the individuals differ in opinion about the most desired level of the public good, there might arise an endless cycle of messages. One of the objectives of the individual tax functions in Groves–Ledyard procedures is to bring about consensus between the participants about the most desired level of public good. There appears to exist a wide class of tax functions which can accomplish this task. The most transparent form is perhaps the following:[14]

$$(9) \quad T_i(x) = \left[\; \frac{1}{n} + (x_{i+2} - x_{i+1}) \; \right].x$$

The part between brackets may be seen as a sort of individual price per unit of public good for individual i. This part consists of a fixed

proportional part of the unit cost, $\frac{1}{n}$ and a part which is determined by

the messages of the individuals $i+2$ and $i+1$, $(x_{i+2} - x_{i+1})$.[15] It is this second part of the individual price which is to bring about consensus as to the level x of the public good. Furthermore, notice that overall, nT_i's taken together each individual message x_k appears twice, once with a negative and once with a positive sign. Consequently, when all n tax functions are added, the sum of all second parts is identically equal to zero, and:

$$(10) \quad \sum_{i=1}^{n} T_i(x) = n \cdot \frac{1}{n} \cdot x = x$$

Irrespective, therefore, of the exact numerical value of x tax receipts and cost of the public good are always equal, so that at least a balanced budget is ensured under Groves–Ledyard procedures. What about Pareto optimality and non-manipulability?

Groves and Ledyard (1977, 1980) proved the following: if all participants try to maximize their utility, given the constraints imposed by income and individual tax functions, the resulting outcome will be Pareto-optimal. Furthermore, this outcome will also be non-manipulable to the extent that as long as all other $n-1$ participants 'hold' to their messages x_j, it will never be profitable for individual k to change his message x_k.

At first sight this looks like a rather fundamental result, more so because it is valid for arbitrary individual utility functions. Actually, however, the Groves–Ledyard result is more like an empty shell. To see why, one should try to imagine how a procedure with a collective choice rule as in (8) could function at all. Each individual has to indicate the amount by which he would like to increase or decrease the sum of the messages announced by the other participants. Note, *all* participants have to do this at the same time! That is, a participant is expected to send a message to the government indicating by how much the amount of the public good, as implied by the messages of the other participants, should be increased or decreased *without* knowing these messages. Of course, the only feasible solution to this paradox is some sort of dynamic trial-and-error process, via which the equilibrium messages could be attained, but there is no hint whatsoever in the Groves–Ledyard papers as to what such a process should look like. Just as with the model of perfect competition, the formal results for the Groves–Ledyard procedure relate exclusively to *existence* proofs. That is to say, Groves and Ledyard proved that there do exist individual messages $x_1, x_2 \ldots x_n$ such that the resulting amount of public good is the most desirable outcome for all participants given their preferences, income and tax function.

As long as a dynamic process which would lead to an equilibrium outcome is wanting, even the *theoretical* claim of non-manipulability for Groves–Ledyard procedures remains in doubt, since it could well be that if some dynamic process were found, it would offer ample opportunities for manipulation by participants along 'the road to equilibrium'.

To sum up, due to a weaker game-theoretic solution concept the equilibrium outcomes of the Groves–Ledyard procedures can be formally shown to be Pareto-optimal and non-manipulable, but any theoretical result as to the necessary dynamic process is lacking. On the other hand, the Groves–Clarke procedures can, formally at any rate given the dominant strategy equilibrium concept, do without dynamic process, but require, rather, specific individual preferences and do not yield fully Pareto-optimal outcomes. Finally, voting procedures do not need a dynamic process, or alternatively can be said to incorporate one, but are formally not manipulation proof and do not yield Pareto-optimal outcomes. However, if practical implementability rather than theoretical results is at stake, the score is quite different. In that case, presumably only voting procedures can hold the line. What causes this big difference between political mechanisms for the allocation of public goods on the one hand and economic mechanisms on the other hand?

In the opening paragraph of the last section, it is stated that analytically two aspects or functions of any collective choice procedure can be
distinguished. The first one consists of collecting (sufficent) information
about the preferences of the participants. The second function is to
provide a formal aggregation or weighting procedure to turn the set of
individual preferences into a social choice. The real bottleneck is the
information gathering stage. Obviously, the more alternative possibilities there are, the more information has to be gathered before the
aggregation rule can be applied. The simplest case would arise when
the choice is between a very small number of alternative levels for the
public good in question and, in addition, the tax share is *a priori* fixed
for all participants. If there truly were only a few alternatives to choose
from, participants could be asked to report their complete preference
ordering to the central planner or government. In practice this kind of
multiple reporting is never used, existing voting procedures elicit the
required information in a piecemeal manner by separate and pairwise
votes between alternatives. Furthermore, most voting bodies use the
simplifying procedure that once an alternative has lost in a pairwise
vote, it is dropped. By this and other short cuts the number of pairwise
votes, which would skyrocket with the increasing number of alternatives, is kept within limits.[16] This sketch of how a voting procedure
works illustrates once more that the really important decisions are
already made at an earlier stage since someone must have determined
how many alternatives, and of which type, are offered for choice.

Alternatively, given the infinite number of possible values for the
public good level, as well as the built-in variation of individual tax
rates, it seems hard to imagine that any realistic implementation of
Groves–Clarke or Groves–Ledyard procedures can ever be found
which would allow for the piecemeal information gathering already
mentioned. The conclusion appears to be that the political relevance of
the newly devised economic mechanisms for the allocation of public
goods is at best rather low.

Changing focus from demand to supply:
bureaux and bureaucratic behaviour

So far attention with regard to public goods has been exclusively
directed to problems of revelation and aggregation of individual
preferences, that is, to the demand side. For simplicity it was assumed
that production and supply of these goods would always take place
according to standards of productive efficiency. In another body of
recent literature, however, starting with Niskanen's seminal text
Bureaucracy and Representative Government (1971), the emphasis is on
problems with the supply of public goods or services by (governmental)
bureaux. Here the very existence of some sort of collective demand or
evaluation function is taken for granted. Since the main conclusion

derived by Niskanen and others is that bureaux in general do not operate in an optimal way, there seems to be every reason to study the Niskanen results more carefully. The main problem with his approach is its strictly partial equilibrium character, which makes it rather difficult to compare his results with those already analysed. Therefore, his model needs to be reformulated, as much as possible, in general equilibrium terms.

Bureaux are defined by Niskanen as those organizations which have both of the following characteristics, (1) the owners and employees of these organizations do not appropriate any part of the difference between revenues and costs as personal income; (2) some part of the recurring revenues of the organization derive from other than the sale of output at a per-unit rate. One might think that sale at a per-unit rate would be difficult or impossible because of the indivisibility of the output, but apparently this is not what Niskanen had in mind, since in the subsequent analysis the level of output is treated as a continuous variable. What is meant is that a bureau offers a total output in exchange for a budget, while a market organization offers units of output at a price. Accordingly, the preferences of the Government are 'summarized by what will be termed a 'budget-output function'. Any point on this function represents the maximum budget the sponsor is willing to grant to the bureau for a specific expected level of output, the budget-output function represents the relation among these points' (Niskanen, 1971: 25).

Unfortunately, this summary of preferences is rather ambiguous. From the description it seems most likely that the budget-output function is analogous to the Total Revenue function for market organization. In that case, however, the demand function would be given by the analogue of the Average Revenue function while Niskanen claims that demand is given by the derivative of the budget-output function.[17] Especially in a general equilibrium context, when something has to be said about the (non)-optimality of outcomes, it is important to know exactly the function, since for partial equilibrium to be a special case of general equilibrium it is necessary that the marginal utility of money or income is strictly constant for each person (cf. Samuelson, 1966: 111). Again simple individual preferences are used relating to an economy with just one private and one public good:

(1) $u_i(x, y_i) = v_i(x) + y_i$ $i = 1, 2, ..., n$

If the private good y is taken as the numéraire again, collective or social demand for the public good is given by:

(2) $p_x = \sum_{i=1}^{n} v_i(x)$

Suppose, furthermore, to get as close as possible to the functions used by Niskanen, that every individual value function $v_i(x)$ takes the form:

(3) $\quad v_i(x) = a_i x - \frac{1}{2} b_i x^2 \qquad i = 1,2,...,n$

Then we can also write:

(4) $\quad v(x) = \sum_{i=1}^{n} v_i(x) = a.x - \frac{1}{2}b.x^2$ and

(5) $\quad v_i(x) = \sum_i v''_i(x) = a - b.x$

where $a = \sum_i a_i$ and $b = \sum_i b_i$

Formulas (2) and (5) together imply:

(6) $\quad p_x = a - b.x$

which represents the demand function for the public good. Consequently, the Total Revenue of budget-output function is given by:

(7) $\quad B = p_x.x = a.x - b.x^2$

which is identical to Niskanen's formula for the budget-output function. Finally, the Marginal Revenue function is given by:

(8) $\quad MR = a - 2b.x$

In addition to the budget-output function Niskanen introduces a Total Cost function and a corresponding Marginal Cost function:

(9) $\quad TC = c.x + d.x^2$ and

(10) $\quad MC = c + 2d.x$

Niskanen's model of a bureau is completed by an assumption regarding the behavioural rule followed by the head of the bureau or 'senior bureaucrat'. The assumption is that such senior bureaucrats will try to maximize their budget, the argument being that their income, prestige, power, etc. are positive montonic functions of the budget size, so that budget maximization may be considered a good proxy for utility maximization. Moreover, although formally the bureau–government relationship is one of *bilateral monopoly*, given that the bureau is a monopolistic supplier of a service facing a single buyer, the government, for all practical purposes the bureau had dominant monopoly power according to Niskanen, due to information advantages. So, the bureau will get the budget it prefers subject only to the constraint that the total cost of supplying a particular service must not exceed the maximum available budget.

Before going into further details it may be useful to state first Niskanen's most important and, in any case, most stirring conclusion: 'Given the demand for service represented by the collective organization, all bureaus are too large, that is, both the budget and output of all bureaus will be larger than that which maximizes the net value to the sponsor' (Niskanen, 1971: 49–50). Of course, this remarkable result has given rise to a lot of discussion and dispute. Surprisingly enough these disputes have never related to the optimality concept which is at the basis of Niskanen's conclusion:

> A bureau's production behavior is efficient if it produces a given output at the minimum possible cost; economists sometimes use the term 'productive efficiency' to describe this condition. A bureau's output behaviour is optimal if the level of output generates the largest net benefits; economists sometimes use the term 'allocative efficiency' to describe this condition. (Niskanen, 1971: 47 n)

Niskanen's conclusion can best be understood from Figure 2.1.

Here the budget-output function (B) and the cost-output function (TC) are shown. Given the behavioural assumption, output x will be extended to the point where either B is maximized (but smaller than TC) or $B = TC$. Figure 2.1 depicts the second case, i.e. where $B = TC$ corresponding to output x_{MAX}. Given Niskanen's definition of efficiency, x_{MAX} is an efficient output since it is produced at minimum possible cost. However, x_{MAX} is not an optimal level of output since it does not generate the largest possible net benefits. For Niskanen's optimum output the condition $MR = MC$ should be satisfied. In Figure 2.1 this situation occurs at x_{NISK}. Since x_{MAX} is large than x_{NISK} Niskanen's conclusion follows immediately. Algebraically one can even show that if the functions B and TC are given by the formulas (7) and (9) above, respectively, the output corresponding to $B = TC$, i.e. x_{MAX}, is exactly twice as large as the output corresponding to $MR = MC$, i.e. x_{NISK}:

$$(11) \qquad x_{MAX} = \frac{a-c}{b+d} \text{ and } x_{NISK} = \frac{1}{2} \cdot \frac{a-c}{b+d}$$

What Niskanen calls the optimum level of output is nothing other than what every profit-seeking monopolist would strive for, given the B- and TC- functions. As explained previously though, the (partial) equilibrium outcome of monopolistic market will in general disturb the Pareto optimality of the associated outcome for the economy as a whole. For full optimality the monopolist or bureau's output should be so chosen that price and MC are equal ('marginal cost pricing', cf. Henderson and Quandt, 1971: 266–76). So, the truly optimal level of output, x_{OPT}, occurs where $p_x = MC$ (formulas (6) and (10) above respectively):

FIGURE 2.1

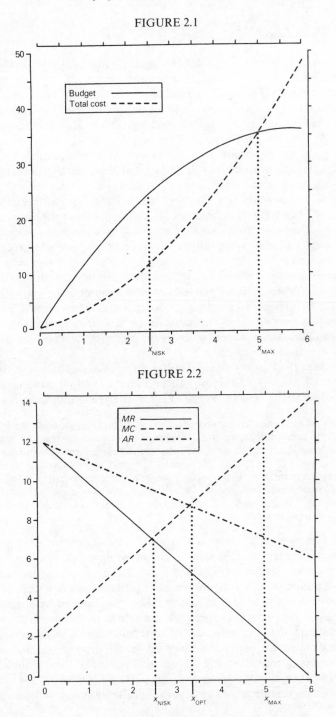

FIGURE 2.2

$$(12) \qquad x_{\text{OPT}} = \frac{a - c}{b + 2d}$$

As can be seen from formulas (11) and (12) and is also illustrated in Figure 2.2, the Pareto-optimal level of output x_{OPT} is always somewhere between Niskanen's optimal level, x_{NISK}, and the maximum level of output, x_{MAX}. Niskanen's conclusion that the budget maximizing bureau's output (and budget) is too large, still holds true, then, when Pareto optimality is the point of reference.

Part of the confusion as to the definition of an optimum level of output is most probably due to the fact that Niskanen argues that price has no operational relevance for a bureau, as it does not offer its services at a per-unit rate. This argument is hardly compatible with the idea of a budget-output function, which implies that the Government would be able to state exactly how much more money it would be prepared to spend when output was raised from any arbitrary x_0 to $x_0 + 1$. It is also not clear how this argument of non-operational relevance for the price concept, could be combined with the representation of a bureau as a perfectly price-discriminating monopolist. It is true that Niskanen's optimality concept and the concept of Pareto optimality are one and the same for such a model, since then the demand function is indeed given by the Marginal Revenue and not by the Average Revenue curve.

Rather than to say that price has no operational relevance for a bureau it is claimed that output and level of output have no such relevance. Even Niskanen himself seems to have doubts as to that:

> Bureaucrats and their sponsors do not, in fact, talk much about output — in terms of military capability, the value of educational services, the number and condition of the poor, etc. Most of the review process consists of a discussion of the relation between budgets and activity levels, such as the number of infantry divisions, the number of students served, the number of the poor served by a program, etc. The relation between activity level and output is usually left obscure and is sometimes consciously obscured. (Niskanen, 1971: 26)

The notion of a bureau as a single and independent monopolist becomes rather strange, since it might be expected that the many bureaux are competing for as large as possible a part of the total budget of the ministry. In this way there arises a picture which is quite different from that of the bureau as a monopolist, as sketched by Niskanen. Indeed, some game-theoretical model would be required to analyse the interaction patterns between the different bureaux. Consequently, even if budget maximization were truly the objective of each and every senior bureaucrat, then due to interaction none of them would ever completely realize this goal.

A final question which deserves some attention is, which goods or services should or could be supplied by profit-seeking firms and which by bureaux? Niskanen says that bureaux specialize in providing goods or services for which market price would be an insufficient indicator of their 'social' value. That is, goods or services with external or public aspects (Niskanen, 1971: 18). But as we have noticed before most goods have both private and public characteristics, so the real problem arises when some good or service is 'public' enough to justify public provision. Unfortunately, this is a problem of which Niskanen also has to admit that it still has to be solved. If so, then by whom is a budget-output function determined and how can an output be called too large or too small?

Neoclassical theory and public resource allocation: evaluation

The preceding sections have discussed three ways in which the neoclassical analytical framework has been used to tackle problems related to public resource allocation. Certainly in retrospect the first of these approaches, the study of potential conflict between individual interests and the outcomes of voting rules, seems the most practice-oriented and to some extent also the most successful. Indeed, despite the fact that the main formal result in this area consists of a proof that no democratic voting procedure is fully strategy-proof, for all practical purposes it can be claimed that under most of these procedures virtually no possibilities for profitable cheating do exist. The only drawback to this study of strategic voting was that the impossibility of cheating could be made intuitively clear but not formally proven. In fact, that inability to formally prove what is intuitively clear, is due to a much more general problem associated with the neoclassical analytical framework. Its inability to deal effectively with situations where individuals or agents have incomplete information about each other's preferences or interests and, therewith, likely behaviour.

The trouble with these economic mechanisms are manifold but two of them are particularly outstanding. Firstly, the necessary co-ordination between individual messages can only be achieved, so it seems, by some dynamic trial-and-error process, but it is not at all clear how such a process should or even could work. Secondly, even if it were taken for granted for a moment that the first problem could be solved, then it is still true that we have created optimal allocation mechanisms for ideal type goods, namely pure private goods and pure public goods. There is no instrument or criterion in neoclassical theory by which it can be decided whether some good should be considered public or private.

All results as to the Pareto optimality of outcomes for the above mentioned economic mechanisms depend, implicitly, on the assumption that production and supply of (pure) public goods is not vitally different from that of (pure) private goods, which is, of course, perfectly competitive! Undoubtedly, one of the merits of Niskanen's analysis of bureaux and bureaucratic behaviour has been that it has focused attention on difficulties which may arise with the supply of public goods. On the other hand, he has contributed to the existing confusion in this area by taking for granted the optimal solution to the aggregation of individual preferences problem.

In review the most important and recurrent question which has not been answered by any of the three approaches to the problem of public resource allocation, and which most probably *cannot* be answered by any neoclassically based analytical framework, is that of *agenda-building* in the widest possible sense. As has been shown in the section describing voting procedures, that if there is any room for manipulation by individuals it is not during the formal voting stage but at the preceding lobbying and agenda-building process. Similarly, even if the so-called economic mechanisms worked perfectly, an extra person would still be needed to decide whether some good should be allocated privately or publicly. Finally, how can it be said that a bureau's output is too large, if we do not even know why the output is as it is?

Information appears to be the magic word in this context, so perhaps for a sensible analysis of political processes the static concepts of neoclassical economics should be supplemented with some more dynamic concepts from information theory.

Notes

1. In the doctrine literature the transition is often ascribed to the 'Marginalist Revolution', but, first, there was no abrupt change of power, and, second, marginality was only an instrumental concept. 'Marginal utility analysis introduced the marginal concept as an instrument of maximization analysis.' (Hutchinson, 1953:16) Compare also Samuelson in his Nobel Prize Lecture, 'The very name of my subject, economics, suggests economizing or maximizing . . . so at the very foundations of our subject maximization is involved' (Samuelson, 1972:249).

2. For example, Jevons, one of the founders of neoclassical economics (besides Walras and Menger), announced in the first chapter of his *Theory of Political Economy*, 'My theory of Economics, however, is purely mathematical in character. The theory consists in applying the differential calculus to the familiar notions of wealth, utility, value, demand, supply, capital, interest, labour, and all the other quantitative notions belonging to the daily operations of industry. As the complete theory of almost every other science involves the use of that calculus, so we cannot have a true theory of Economics without its aid' (Jevons, 1879: 3–4).

3. Note that the more recently developed technique which appears to provide such a criterion, viz. *cost-benefit analysis*, is based on the assumption that any dollar has the same utility value for everybody.

4. Compare Hahn (1982: 746).

5. The exceptional case is the perfectly discriminating monopolist, i.e. a monopolist who is able to subdivide his market to such a degree that he sells each successive unit of his commodity for the maximum amount that consumers are willing to pay. This kind of monopolist equates marginal price to Marginal Cost for maximization and is therefore

an exception to the rule that imperfect competition is Pareto non-optimal.

6. In this example the dominant strategy equilibrium outcome is also Pareto-optimal, but this is not necessarily so as the well-known Prisoner's Dilemma game illustrates.

7. This behavioural assumption, as well as the Nash equilibrium concept itself, proved originally due to Cournot.

8. For the purposes of this section it suffices to consider those goods as public whose provision is of (some) interest to many or most people in society.

9. For a more detailed discussion of the sufficient condition for manipulability, cf. de Bruin (1985).

10. The Gibbard–Satterthwaite Theorem implies that there does not exist a dominant strategy equilibrium for every preference profile. That is, there are situations in which neither the sincere announcement of one's preferences nor any insincere revelation is a dominant strategy.

11. $x\,y\,z$ is shorthand for: x strictly preferred above y, y strictly above z, and x strictly above z.

12. This solution is, of course, rather arbitrary, but any alternative possibility entails some variant of the described problems.

13. Compare Samuelson (1954 and 1969).

14. This tax function is actually due to Walker (1981) and not to Groves and Ledyard. I have chosen this function because it seems a more simple one.

15. The index should be read 'modulo n' i.e. $n+2=2$, $n+1=1$, etc.

16. In addition, the system of representation is another important source of simplification. Not all members of the politico-economic system, but just a very small subset of representatives, are voting.

17. There is one exception, for the perfectly discriminating monopolist the demand function is given by his MR-curve (see footnote 5). This special case is also referred to later in this section.

References

Arrow, K.J. (1959) 'Toward a theory of price adjustment,' in M. Abramowitz et al. *The Allocation of Economic Resources*. Stanford University Press, pp. 41–51.

Arrow, K.J. (1970) 'Political and economic evaluation of social effects and externalities,' in J. Margolis (ed.) *The Analysis of Public Output*. New York: National Bureau of Economic Research, pp. 1–23.

Blin, J–M and M.A. Satterthwaite (1979) 'Strategy-proofness and single-peakedness,' *Public Choice*: Vol. 26, pp. 51–8.

Bowen, H.R. (1969) 'The interpretation of voting in the allocation of economic resources,' reprinted in K.J. Arrow and T. Scitovsky (eds), *Readings in Welfare Economics*, London: Allen and Unwin, pp. 115–132.

Clarke, E. (1971) 'Multipart pricing of public goods,' *Public Choice* vol. 11, pp. 17–33.

de Bruin, G.P. (1985) 'On voting procedures for decision-making on public goods,' *European Journal of Political Research*.

de Bruin, G.P. (1986) *Decision-making on Public Goods*, Ph.D. thesis University of Amsterdam.

Gibbard, A. (1973) 'Manipulation of voting schemes: a general result,' *Econometrica*. Vol. 41: pp. 587–601.

Groves, Th. (1973) 'Incentives in teams,' *Econometrica*. Vol. 41: pp. 617–31.

Groves, Th. and J. Ledyard (1977) 'Optimal allocation of public goods: a solution to the "free rider" problem,' *Econometrica*, Vol. 45, pp. 783–809.

Groves, Th. and J. Ledyard (1980) 'The existence of efficient and incentive compatible equilibria with public goods,' *Econometrica*, Vol. 48, pp. 1487–506.

Henderson and Quandt, 1971

Hahn, F. (1982) 'Stability.' in K.J. Arrow, and M.D. Intriligator (eds), *Handbook of Mathematical Economics*, Vol. 2. Amsterdam: North-Holland, pp. 745–93.

Hutchinson, T.W. (1953) *A Review of Economic Doctrines, 1870–1929*. Oxford: Clarendon Press.

Jevons, W.S. (1879) *The Theory of Political Economy*. London: Macmillan.

Johansen, L. (1977), 'The theory of public goods: misplaced emphasis?', *Journal of Public Economics*, Vol. 7: pp. 147–52.

Niskanen, W.A. (1971) *Bureaucracy and Representative Government*. Chicago: Aldine-Atherton.

Samuelson, P.A. (1954), 'The pure theory of public expenditure,' *Review of Economics and Statistics*, Vol. 36: pp. 387–9.

Samuelson, P.A. (1969), 'Pure theory of public expenditure and taxation,' in J. Margolis and H. Guitton (eds), *Public Economics*. London: Macmillan. pp. 98–123.

Samuelson, P.A. (1972) 'Maximum principles in analytical economics,' *American Economic Review*, Vol. 62: pp. 249–62.

Satterthwaite, M.A. (1975) 'Strategy-proofness and Arrow's conditions: existence and correspondence theorems for voting procedures and social welfare functions,' *Journal of Economic Theory*. Vol. 10, pp. 187–217.

Schumpeter, J.A. (1974) *Capitalism, Socialism and Democracy*. London: George Allen and Unwin.

Shubik, M. (1959) *Strategy and Market Structure. Competition, Oligopoly, and the Theory of Games*. New York: John Wiley (with introduction by O. Morgenstern).

Streissler, E. (1973) 'To what extent was the Austrian school marginalist?' in R.D. Collison Black et al. (eds), *The Marginal Revolution in Economics*. Durham, NC: Duke University Press. pp. 160–75.

Tideman, T.N. and G. Tullock (1976) 'A new and superior principle for making social choices.' *Journal of Political Economy* Vol. 84: pp. 1145–59.

von Neumann, J. and O. Morgenstern (1967), *Theory of Games and Economic Behavior*. New York: John Wiley.

Walker, M. (1981) 'A simple incentive compatible scheme for attaining Lindahl allocations,' *Econometrica*, Vol. 49, pp. 65–71.

3
Bureaucratic decision-making and the growth of public expenditure

Rune J. Sørensen

Introduction

This chapter is confined to a theoretical analysis of the process of public budget making. It reviews the two major approaches to the process, the incremental model and the public approach.[1]

The *incremental* theory builds on the works of Simon (1945) and Lindblom (1953). Wildavsky (1964) suggests that the complexity of budget making, limitations of knowledge, time and and resources, lead decision makers to 'satisfy' rather than to maximize'. They focus on marginal adjustments in last year's budget, making it a major determinant of next year's appropriations. Decision makers at higher administrative or political levels concentrate their efforts on the increments of requested or recommended expenditure growth. The incremental model proposes that relationships between the participants are stable.

The second group of theories can be labelled *budget-maximizing* bureaucrats. These theories are closely linked to the works of Niskanen (1971, 1975). Each bureau maximizes its appropriations knowing the demands of its sponsors. The costs of supplying the good is kept as a bureaucratic secret. Niskanen (1971) proposes public spending to be higher than the social optimal.

The argument to be advanced here suggests, on the one hand, that the incremental theory lacks sufficient capacity to generate a specific hypothesis. On the other hand, the static Niskanen-type of theory appears to be too abstract for empirical analysis, nor does it explain budget change. One possible answer is a rational choice theory addressing budget change. The final section of this chapter takes a preliminary step in this direction.

Incrementalism: the lack of specific propositions?

The core assumption of incremental theory is 'bounded rationality' or 'satisfying'. Building upon the contributions by Simon (1945) and Lindblom (Dahl and Lindblom 1953), Wildavsky argues that:

> Budgeting is incremental, not comprehensive. The beginning wisdom about an agency budget is that it is almost never actively reviewed as a whole every

year. Instead, it is based on last year's budget with special attention given to a narrow range of increases or decreases. (Wildavsky, 1964, 1979: 15)

In later quantitative studies (Davies, Dempster and Wildavsky 1966) the incremental propositions have been tested. The budgetary process was modelled by means of equations relating approved appropriations to recommended and requested budgets at lower levels and to last year's appropriations. The empirical support is quite impressive in the sense that last year's budget is a good predictor for this year's and in the sense that the parameter estimates took reasonable values. Again, the authors claim that the incremental propositions are supported.

We shall not discuss the testing of the various incremental hypotheses in any detail. Suffice to say that the testing has been subject to extensive criticism, such as Wanat (1974), Danziger (1978), Padgett (1980), Natchez and Bupp (1981), Lane et al. (1981) and Sharpe and Newton (1984). Whether or not the process of budget making is an incremental one is not entirely resolved.

At the theoretical level, one may question the consistency of the incremental theory. Firstly, even if relationships between the participants in the budgetary process are stable, the theory does not explain why a particular equilibrium solution has been obtained. Explaining that process as an incremental one does not explain the size of the agency's increment. Furthermore, deviations from the stable pattern are analysed as 'shift points'. These remain unexplained in the theory. The reason could be that the assumption of bounded rationality does not, by itself, explain the outcome of the budgetary process. Therefore, it is arguable that the incremental theory does not provide any explanation of government growth.

Secondly, the incremental critique of economic welfare theory and comprehensive programme budgeting is well taken. It is also accepted that the participants in the budgetary process restrict their attention to marginal adjustments to requested and recommended budgets and to incremental changes compared to last year's budget.[2] However, such a view on public budgeting does not logically exclude the assumption of rational behaviour at agency level. The individual agent or participant may be able to pursue fairly simple goals related to the budgetary process, even if we realize that comprehensive maximization of the welfare function is unrealistic. The incremental interpretation of budget making is not inconsistent with rational choice at the micro level.

Thirdly, the incremental theorists often argue in terms of implicit rational interaction. The agency anticipates reaction at higher levels, or compensate for cuts made earlier in the process. This seems to be the case for the classical formulations by Wildavsky (1964) as well as later formalized modelling (Danziger 1978, Cowart and Brofoss 1979).

However, it is very difficult to see how such propositions can be derived from the assumption of bounded rationality only. It appears that some more specific assumptions have to be made regarding the preferences of the participants and their ability to pursue their interests, in order to generate such an hypothesis.

Thus, the major limitation of incremental theory is the lack of specific assumptions to generate precise propositions. These have to include assumptions about the preferences of the participants as well as about the institutional features. Perhaps *public choice* has the answer to these problems?

The Niskanen approach:
too restrictive assumptions?

It is probably fair to say that political scientists view the Niskanen model with a substantial amount of scepticism. There is the view that the conventional public choice assumptions do not capture 'real world' politics. The emphasis on selfish maximization appears exaggerated, compared to the importance of professional commitments and even altruistic preferences.

The model predictions have not been subjected to extensive empirical testing. This is partly due to the problem of measuring the output of public bureaucracy and the political or social demands for bureau output. Most authors seems to agree that the Niskanen propositions have received mixed empirical support. (Conybeare, 1984: 486). To some extent this bias is rooted in the micro-economic apparatus commonly used to analyse processes of exchange at the market place. The application of these models can take the analysis into a world of abstractionism in which essential parts of the political and institutional setting are ignored.

The normative message from public choice is derived from comparing the politico-bureaucratic organization with the market system, usually concluding against the first. It is commonly recommended that market-like processes, such as competition, should be introduced into the public sector. Of course, the justification behind such suggestions is heavily dependent on the behavioural and institutional assumptions of the theory. This point is returned to in section four.

On the other hand, it should be remembered that the Niskanen model is an extremely simple one. Only two agents are the building blocks, the bureau and the sponsor. Both maximize utility, the sponsor maximizes some type of consumer surplus, while the bureau maximizes its budget. Assuming that the bureau keeps the information of the true costs of public production as a professional secret, Niskanen can deduce powerful implications.

Although simplicity is a scientific merit in itself, one should investigate whether the analysis of politico-bureaucratic interaction

ought to be remodelled in other directions. Also whether the implications are sensitive to minor modifications in the original assumptions.
Dialogue regarding the Niskanen model has centered around these
points. Attention should now be turned to some of the important
aspects of this debate.

Firstly, the assumption of budget maximization has been extensively
discussed (Niskanen, 1971: 28). On one hand, it has been argued that
the assumption can be justified on grounds other than purely private
and egoistic ones. It is the intrinsic nature of their work tasks which
lead bureaucrats to seek to expand their budgets, particularly information on expenditure needs. This has been well documented by
various authors such as Wildavsky (1964: 19) and Kristensen (1980:
255). Downs suggests that:

> . . . their views are based upon a 'biased' or exaggerated view of the
> importance of their own positions 'in the cosmic scheme of things'. These
> factors also cause occupants of many positions to behave like advocates,
> even if their psychological inclinations tend toward other types. (Downs,
> 1967: 107)

Although we accept that many bureaucrats are devoted to increasing
their appropriations, other types of preferences have been taken into
the analysis. It has been argued that 'slack' should be taken into the
bureaucrats' preference function (Migue and Belanger, 1974; Miller,
1977, Moene, 1984). Furthermore, it is less reasonable to explain the
behaviour of treasury bureaucrats or chief municipal administrators in
terms of budget maximization. These agents should be explicitly
included in the analysis, probably under the assumption that they
prefer a lower level of spending than do politicians and other
bureaucrats. Finally, one may well ask whether the agency head has
some consideration for the public sector as a whole, a point to which
we shall return.

Secondly, it has been argued that the politician (or 'sponsor' in the
classical formulation) plays an unrealistically passive role in the
model. Others such as Breton have suggested that a rational sponsor
would use control to the point where the marginal value of control
equals the marginal cost. Therefore, the model exaggerates the ability
of the bureau to keep the costs of production as a bureaucratic secret,
and expand the budget above the social and political optimum. This
argument, however, does not specify the institutional controls to be
employed. The marginal gain of control is usually unknown *ex ante*.
Although the assumption of a passive sponsor seems unjustified, it is
not quite appropriate to introduce the sponsor as an active agent in the
model.

Niskanen (1975) refined his original model by explicitly introducing
the Downesian assumption that politicians maximize re-election
prospects. Some new institutional details were also taken into the

model. Niskanen observed that '. . . a committee, not the whole legislature, conducts the review process for each bureau,' and '. . . most committees are dominated by legislatures who have higher demands for the services reviewed than the median demand in the whole legislature, and the committee decisions are very seldom amended or reversed by the whole legislature' (Niskanen, 1975: 624–5).

Within the new model, politicians can allocate their limited time between external 'advertising' and internal bureau-monitoring. As the politician maximizes the probability of re-election, Niskanen argues that monitoring is the less attractive activity.

> . . . the monitoring function, however, is a public good within the legislature; the benefits of monitoring accrue to the whole population as a function of their tax-costs. This creates a substantial 'free-rider' problem internal to legislatures and the expectation that monitoring activities will be under-supplied. (Niskanen, 1975: 626–7)

Thus, Niskanen (1975) reformulates the original proposition suggesting that budget-maximizing agencies, high-demand committees and insufficient monitoring lead to excessive public budgets.

Thirdly, bureaucrats possess an effective monopoly over information about production costs. The bureau also knows the political demand for its product. Thus, it can choose the budget output combination on the demand schedule which maximizes the agency budget. Modifications to these assumptions may change the conclusions.

Miller and Moe (1983) suggest another type of process in which the legislature forces the bureau to 'go first' in transmitting cost information. The 'demand-concealing' situation can lead to optimal budgets, whereas Niskanen's assumption of a 'demand-revealing' sponsor leads to excessive budgets (Miller and Moe, 1983: 305).

Along similar lines, Moene (1984) demonstrates how the Niskanen propositions can be completely reversed, making slightly different assumptions about information and preference-functions.[3] For example, assuming that the sponsoring institution knows the fixed costs of production, but relies on reported variable costs, Moene finds the likely solution to be an underexpansion of the bureau. Or, assuming that the bureau is free to determine its level of output *given* a particular budget, while the sponsor anticipates the bureau's responses, the activity level can be lower than socially optimal.

Finally, the model is a *static* one. Budget making is modelled as a process of once and for all cost-benefit calculus. This implies that the Niskanen-propositions do not provide any explanation of expenditure growth (Miller and Moe, 1983: 297). In this respect, the incremental theory and the static equilibrium analysis generate *alternative* rather than *competing* hypotheses, with the theories attempting to explain different phenomena. This appears to be sufficient justification to introduce the rational choice approach to the domain of incremental analysis. Such a model could be a more productive one in terms of realistic assumptions and (empirical) testability. Of course, this remains to be proven!

Towards a theory explaining
budget strategies

This chapter will now examine the public choice analysis of budgetary change within the public sector, thereby confronting the incremental model directly with the assumption of rational behaviour. It is reasonable to discuss the differences between the two models; furthermore, that of budgetary growth can be interpreted both within a hierarchical decision-situation and as a collective action problem. The three basic variables (1) – (3) in the analysis are:

W_t : The appropriation requested by the agency in year t

Z_t : The appropriation passed for the agency by the political body in year t

(1) $V = Z_t / Z_{t-1}$ Approved budget growth for the agency

(2) $X = W_t / Z_{t-1}$ Requested budget growth by the agency

(3) $Y = Z_t / W_{t-1}$ Proportion average requested growth accepted as approved growth by political body

Per definition, approved budgetary growth can be expressed by:

(4) $V = X*Y$ Approved budgetary growth

The bureau growth rate is the product of the agency's acquisitiveness (X), the political response (Y). Assuming initially that the bureau maximizes budget growth (V), what is the optimal level of requested budgetary growth?

Within the _incremental_ approach, a set of simple rules is the basis for decision-making. Earlier we have argued that the incremental theory has little to say about the design of these rules, apart from the fact that they represent stable relationships between the participants and marginal adjustments.

Some of the incremental models imply that the political responses are assumed to represent fixed levels of Y, that a fixed level of requested growth is accepted as approved growth. Of course, this assumption is hardly consistent with budget maximization, i.e. the bureau can attain any level of growth by asking for a sufficiently high budgetary growth. On the other hand, some incrementalists, such as Wildavsky, have argued that agencies requesting huge increases will be severely cut.

We have seen that most of an agency's budget is a product of past decisions. Beyond this area is one of discretion in which budget people cannot get all they want, but want to get all they can. Moreover, asking for too much may prejudice their chances of realizing a lesser amount. (Wildavksy, 1979: 24)

This formulation can be interpreted as a hypothesis that bureaux forward optimal requests, assuming some kind of political response function. The observation that political sponsoring institutions change budgetary requests marginally is, of course, in accordance with this model. Furthermore, the fact that the interaction between the participants involved in budget making is stable, inconsistent with the rational choice interpretation of budgeting, can mean that the stability is due to stable preferences and institutional patterns.

What is needed is an explicit analysis of the political cut-back function. An analysis parallel to the demand function in the traditional static equilibrium approach. We need to establish a political preference function.

First of all, we can assume that the political authorities prefer a budget growth V^*. Less would mean too low a growth of public services, and more would imply that other agencies got less, or that the budgetary deficit would be intolerable. However, the sponsor would probably avoid cutting the agency request too much. In other words, we assume the politicians to prefer higher levels of Y. This is particularly relevant when public attention is focused on changes in appropriations rather than levels of spending, when agency proposals are public, when bureaux can defend their requests in public, and when the political opposition is likely to take advantage of budgetary cut-backs on agency requests. Additionally, public budgeting is characterized by the problems of measuring agency output, difficulties of estimating the true costs of production, and evaluating the demand or needs for public services. The informational asymmetry of budgeting, so well spelled out in the Niskanen literature, indicates that politicians have a 'cut-back aversion'. The political preference function could be written:

(5) $W = W(V,Y)$ with Max $W = W(V^*,Y)$ and $W_Y > 0$ for $V < V^*$

Political preference function

It is reasonable to interpret V^* as the social optimal growth rate.

Once having established the political preference function, it can be assumed that the agency prefers a growth rate V^{**}, greater than politically and socially optimal:[4]

(6) $U = U(V)$ with Max $U = U(V^{**})$ $U_V > 0$ for $V < V^*$

Agency preference function

Finally, we assume that the bureaux make the first draw, that is take the initiative by requesting an increase or decrease in appropriations. The bureau knows the preferences of the political authorities (i.e.

'demand revealing'), and vice versa. The agency will pick the alternative (measured by X) maximizing budgetary growth (assuming V less than V^{**}). Figure 3.1 illustrates the situation:

FIGURE 3.1
Budgetary interaction between the agency and the political body

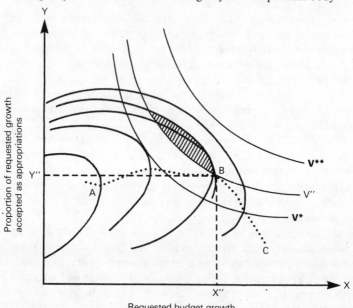

Requested budget growth

Figure 3.1 provides the iso-growth curves V^* and V^{**} in the growth (X) — acceptance (Y) diagram. The dotted line A–B–C represents maximum utility for the political body at different levels of requested budget growth (X). It is partially located above the V^* curve. The point B represents the tangent between the dotted response curve and the iso-growth curve V''. Thus, the bureau will request a budget growth X'', the sponsoring institution will respond by accepting the proportion Y'', yielding the growth rate V''. In accordance with the Niskanen proposition, the budget–growth exceeds the social optimum.

The shape of the response function A–B–C is of some importance in this model. Depending on the actual preference function W, it may rise or decline with increasing levels of X. (Remember that cut-backs increase the lower value on Y.)

The outcome is not Pareto-optimal for the participants. The hatched area symbolizes the set of Pareto improvements. If the agency and the sponsoring institution agree to a solution with lower requests and cut-backs, both would gain compared to the non-co-operative solution. The outcome would imply a higher growth of spending. Of course, the co-operative agreement generates a greater social loss than the non-co-operative outcome. The model indicates that it is socially preferable to organize budget making as a non-co-operative game in which politicians and bureaucrats make their decisions autonomously.

In the previous section, it was suggested that the Niskanen model should include an explicit analysis of the *bureaucratic watch dog*, such as the treasury, financial committees and chief municipal administrators. They review the agency proposals before the requests are handled by representative political bodies and are primarily concerned with the balancing revenues and expenditures. Compared to other players in the budgetary process, we can safely assume that they would prefer a lower agency growth rate.

How should this missing link be incorporated in the formal analysis? Perhaps the preceding model can by applied with two minor modifications.

Firstly, assume that the political preference function (5) is decreasing in Y. Y is now defined as the proportion of the treasury proposal X accepted as a final appropriation. This implies that the politicians prefer not to increase appropriations above the recommended growth-rate. Secondly, the treasury preference function resembles the agency function (6), except for the fact that the preferred growth rate V^{**} is lower than the political and social optimum.

What is the outcome of the interaction between the treasury bureau and the political agent? Because the political response function lies below the iso-growth curve V^*, the treasury would act to minimize budget growth, and recommended budget growth X would be located at the point on the reaction curve producing the lowest possible growth. Analogously to the above model, the equilibrium growth rate is lower that socially and politically preferable.

Bargaining is probably more frequent between the treasury and the politicians than between the ordinary bureau and the political body. Negotiations between the financial agent and political body are likely to cause lower budgetary growth rates. Pareto-improvements imply that the treasury recommends higher growth-rates, while political institutions more or less accept these proposals.

The final analysis of budgeting would require a simultaneous analysis of agency requests, treasury recommendations and political appropriations. The partial reasoning presented here can throw light on some of the institutional details of public budget-making.

Assume that the bureau requests are kept secret, in the sense that they are only used to elaborate the budget at the administrative level. Thus, the vote-maximizing politician with an aversion to cutting, is isolated from the agency requests. The politicians would not know the proposals at the agency level. Therefore, the interaction between the treasury agent and the political body will dominate final budget making. Such an organization of the budgetary process would imply a lower budget growth, compared to a situation in which the political body knew both the agency requests and the treasury recommendations.

In Norway, the agency requests are kept secret at *central* government level. Politicians in parliament do not know the administrative proposals. Parliament handles the budget on the basis of a proposal from cabinet in close co-operation with the treasury. Thus, the latter model seems to apply for the national level. At the *local* level, the budget process is much more public. Representatives of the local councils (as well as mass media) know the bureau requests. Interaction between agencies and politicians appears to play a more prominent role in local government. The Niskanen type of interaction is of greater relevance to local budget making. However, whereas the central level is free to increase public revenues, the municipalties and counties in Norway are faced with almost fixed level of revenues. Local government must present balanced budgets, they depend on large transfers from the central level and the local tax revenues are restricted by an upper percentage on net personal earnings. Therefore, the expenditure based budget process at local level is balanced by restrictions on the aggregate growth of spending.

Although the hierarchical aspect is the central concern and assumption for theories of budget making, it can be useful to take a look as the interaction between bureaux as well. This appears to be particularly relevant in loosely organized bureaucracies in which the powers of the sponsoring institution are quite limited, as seems to be the case in the original Niskanen model.

Initially a new preference function for all agencies in the organization is suggested, again assuming that the bureau maximize budget growth. Additionally, it is assumed that the agency prefers a balanced aggregate growth, since an excessive growth of public spending may harm bureaucratic interests as well. Firstly, at the central government level, rising expenditure can cause reduced take home pay, higher inflation and lower economic growth. Secondly, at local level, policies which are too expansionary will lead to a deficit in the accounts which must be financed by next year's budget. Thus, too high aggregate growth will lead to cut-backs later on, a situation the agency head would wish to avoid.

The new bureau preference function would have two arguements yearly agency budget growth and the aggregate growth of public spending. The optimum size of the latter variable is determined by the preference for stable expenditure growth. This would create a *collective action* problem at agency level very much analogous to the monitoring problem discussed by Niskanen (1975). The external effects generated by the acquisitiveness of an individual agency could lead to an excessive aggregate growth, suboptimal to all agencies. It is also to be expected that an organization containing a large number of small bureaux would have more aggressive budgeting behaviour than the bureaucracy with a smaller number of large departments. This is the common logic of collective action (Olson, 1965).

Niskanen (1971, 1975: 636; 1979: 524) suggests that public spending could be reduced by increasing the number of bureaux and introducing *competition* to government bureaucracy. The present analysis suggests the opposite proposition, that integrating small agencies into larger departments would reduce the acquisitiveness of bureaucracy.

The collective action situation can also be exploited in other ways. The treasury, or corresponding department, compile estimates of next year's growth of revenues. By (mis-)informing the agencies that next year's revenue growth will be relatively low, the treasury can induce the bureaus to suggest lower budget proposals.

Finally, to the extent that the bureau head prefers moderate and balanced aggregate growth, one would expect the agencies to accept the cuts made at higher administrative and political levels. In fact, the budgetary process may contribute to the realization of the agency's collective interests. Thus, the conflict between the bureau and the sponsoring institution is less acute than in the models discussed earlier.

Conclusions

This chapter has attempted to analyse whether bureaucracy operates independently of the sponsoring institution, the politicians; whether the bureaucrats are able to serve their own interests rather than the preferences of the political body; and the degree to which we can model the growth of public spending in terms of the interaction between bureaucratic agencies and political institutions. The incremental theory has little to say about these questions. The static Niskanen model does not directly focus on budget change and it employs certain assumptions which should be relaxed.

Propositions derived here do not support the general thesis that bureaucracy causes excessive growth of government. Our presumption will be that bureaucracy *may* pursue inflated budgets and that they *may* succeed or fail. The possibility that bureaucratic involvement in budget making can produce socially optimal growth of spending, or suboptimalities in both directions, cannot be excluded.

It has been tentatively established that some institutional pre-conditions need to be present for these cases to occur. There is a lot of work to be done in modelling budget making as a simultaneous process, linking the model to institutional assumptions and testing the propositions derived.

Notes

I am grateful for comments from Jon Hovi and Karl Ove Moene at the University of

Oslo, and for the useful criticism by the ECPR research group 'Bureaucracy Behaviour and Public Resource Allocation'.

1. The theory of *bureaucratic voting* assumes the political preferences of public employees to differ from the preferences of the electorate. A common hypothesis suggests that bureaucrats prefer higher growth of public spending and public employment. In public choice literature, bureaucratic preferences are linked to the benefits generated by public sector growth. Additionally, public employees commonly have high participation rates in elections, protest movements and political assemblies. Therefore, the size of bureaucracy has impact upon the growth of government.

A mixed set of theories argue that the *productivity* of the public sector is lower than that of the market sector. This is partly due to differences of technology, and partly to weaker incentives to increase productivity in the public sector.

2. Incrementalism can be interpreted as a method for decision making and as a model describing the relationship between the participants in the budget process. The first is called 'decision-incrementalism', the latter is called 'process-incrementalism' (Davies and Wildavsky, 1979). The focus is primarily on the latter interpretation.

3. Following Migue and Belanger (1974), Moene (1984) employs an agency preference function with two arguments, the level of production and budgetary slack.

4. Wildavsky (1964, 1979: 19) suggests that 'It is usually correct to assume that department officials are devoted to increasing their appropriations'. Thus, the assumption of budget maximization has been justified in the classical 'The Theory of the Budgetary Process' as well as in public choice literature.

References

Borcherding, T.E. (1977) *Budgets and Bureaucrats*. Durham NC: Duke University Press.

Brofoss, K.E. (1985) 'En beslutningsstrategisk analyse av statsbudsjettarbeid', i Hansen, T. *Offentlige budsjettprosesser*. Oslo: Universitetsforlaget.

Conybeare, J.A.C. (1984) 'Bureaucracy, Monopoly and Competition: A critical analysis of the Budget-Maximizing Theory of Bureaucracy', *American Journal of Political Science*, 28, pp. 479–502.

Cowart, A. and K.E. Brofoss (1979) *Decisions, Politics and Change*. Oslo: Universitetsforlaget.

Dahl, R. and C.E. Lindblom (1953) *Politics, Economics and Welfare*. Chicago and London: The University of Chicago Press.

Danziger, J.N. (1978) *Making Budgets: Public Resource Allocation*. London and Beverly Hills: Sage.

Davies, O.A., M.A.H. Dempster and Aa. Wildavsky (1966) 'A Theory of the Budgetary Process', *American Political Science Review*, LX, s.347–96.

Dempster, M.A.H. and Aa. Wildavsky (1979) 'On Change: Or, there is No Magic Size for an Increment', *Political Studies*, 32, pp. 371–89.

Downs, A. (1967) *Inside Bureaucracy*. Boston: Little, Brown and Company.

Dunleavy, P. (1985) 'Bureaucrats, Budgets and the Growth of State: Reconstructing an Instrumental Model', *British Journal of Political Science*, 15, pp. 299–328.

Guy Peters, B. (1981) 'The Problem of Bureaucratic Government', *Journal of Politics*, 43, pp. 56–82.

Kristensen, O.P. (1980) 'The logic of political-bureaucratic decision-making as a cause of governmental growth', *European Journal of Political Research*, 8, pp. 249–64.

Lane, J.-E., A. Westlund and H. Stenlund (1981) 'Analysis of structural variability in budget-making', *Scandinavian Political Studies*, 4, pp. 127–49.

Migue, J.L. and G. Belanger (1974) 'Towards a General Theory on Managerial Discretion', *Public Choice*, 17, 27–44.

Miller, G.J. (1977) 'Bureaucratic Compliance as a Game on the Unit Square', *Public Choice*, 29, pp. 37–51.

Miller, G.J. and T.M. Moe (1983) 'Bureaucrats, legislators and the size of government', *American Political Science Review* 77, pp. 297–322.

Moene, K.O. (1984) 'Types of bureaucratic interaction', *Memorandum* 20, Department of Economics, University of Oslo.

Mueller, D. (1979) *Public Choice*, Cambridge: Cambridge University Press.

Natchez, P.B. and I.C. Bupp (1981) 'Policy and Priority in the Budgetary Process', *American Political Science Review*, 67, pp. 951–63.

Niskanen, W. (1971) *Bureaucracy and Representative Government*. Chicago Aldine: Atherton.

Niskanen, W. (1975) 'Bureaucrats and Politicians', *Journal of Law and Economics*, 18, pp. 617–43.

Olson, M. (1965) *The Logic of Collective Action* Cambridge, Mass.: Harvard University Press.

Padgett, J.P. (1980) 'Bounded Rationality in Budgetary Research', *American Political Science Review* 74, pp. 354–72.

Simon, H. (1945) *Administrative Behaviour*. New York: The Free Press.

Wanat, J. (1974) 'Bases of Budgetary Incrementalism', *American Political Science Review* 74, pp. 354–72.

Wildavsky, Aa. (1964, 1979) *The Politics of the Budgetary Process*. Boston: Little, Brown and Company.

4
Ill-structured problems, informal mechanisms, and the design of public organizations

Donald Chisholm

Is it not good that a brain should have its parts in rich functional connection?
No — not in general; only when the environment itself is richly connected. When the environment's parts are not richly connected (when it is highly reducible, in other words), adaptation will go on faster if the brain is also highly reducible, i.e., if its connectivity is small. Thus the degree of organization can be too high as well as too low. . .

W. R. Ashby, 1962

Introduction
This chapter offers a point of view on public organizations, a way of looking at them that may shed some new light on old problems, in particular the problem of how to design them to co-ordinate behaviour effectively under a variety of circumstances. Given the many contemporary dissatisfactions with the performance of public organizations, especially bureaucracies,[1] this is more than a flight of intellectual fancy and quite practical consequences flow from the argument.

With Weber (1964), bureaucracy (and more generally, all forms of public organization) is viewed as a rational device for the achievement of collective ends,[2] but it is not proposed to consider it here as *the* rational device. Whilst recognizing that formal organizations such as bureaucracies have attendant problems, i.e. goal displacement, occupational psychosis and trained incapacity to think, which intrude on their rationality, and that there exist other powerful and useful ways of looking at bureaucracy, for example as political coalitions,[3] information processing systems, control devices, or cultural systems, — public organizations are treated here as analogs to individual human processes of problem solving.[4]

This approach appears to have several virtues. That there are genuine similarities between organization and cognition there is no doubt. There is ample precedent in the works of Dewey, Simon, Landau, and March, among others, for doing so. Organizations as assemblages of means-ends chains are directly analogous to the means-ends chains constructed by individual human problem solvers.

Connecting problem solving processes with public organization should reveal some new attributes of organizations or disclose old ones in a new light, thereby adding to the corpus of our knowledge (Landau, 1979).

The intent in this chapter is to revise conceptions of public organizations and to generate some new hypotheses about ways of organizing. In this sense there is less interest in delivering a finished rationale for a particular way of organizing than to ask what would follow, what might be learnt, if organizations are thought of in a particular way. By envisioning public organizations as problem solving processes an analogy is arrived at whose utility depends solely on its contributions to improving understanding.

While treating public organizations as rationale devices, following Newell and Simon (1972) and Simon (1985) a substantive, as opposed to procedural,[5] conception of rationality is employed. From this perspective rationality is judged in an *ex post facto* manner, asking, did the approach lead to the desired results, rather than were certain procedures followed? Behaviour is rational or adaptive if it is 'appropriate to the goal in the light of the problem environment; it is the behaviour demanded by the situation' (Newell and Simon, 1972: 53). No particular organizational design is identified with rationality; the rationality of any organization is judged by the results it produces. Results are emphasized over form. Neither apparent neatness or apparent messiness are appropriate criteria for judging the 'goodness' of an organizational arrangement.

Using this substantive view of rationality and treating organizations analogously to problem solving processes frees us from placing intrinsic value on any one form of organization. It redirects our focus to the links between the characteristics of the situation and particular organizational designs. Thus, we view Weber's bureaucracy not as the ultimate organizational rationality, but as a form that was better adapted to the particular problems of a specific time and place than alternative forms, and which may be less effective under other conditions.[6]

Moreover, treating organizations as analogous to problem solving processes permits the introduction of a temporal element into the analysis. By viewing public organizations as concrete manifestations of public policies, and public policies are treated

> . . . as working hypotheses, not as programs to be rigidly adhered to and executed. [Then] they will be experimental in the sense that they will be entertained subject to constant and well-equipped observation of the consequences they entail when acted upon. (Dewey, 1927: 202–3)

Then it is also well to consider public organization as hypotheses, to be treated experimentally and evaluated in light of their capacity to produce desired goals. As new information comes to light about organizational designs more effective under the same problem environment than existing designs, or as relevant conditions of the problem environment change, we should freely entertain altering organizational arrangements (Landau, 1973; Wildavsky, 1972).

Finally, the perspective is taken that it probably is not sensible either to assume that for any problem environment there is an optimal (in terms of efficiency or any other criterion) organizational design (problem solution) or to conduct a search for one. Instead there are at the least several designs which may be satisfactory. Either the search can be stopped as soon as a single satisfactory design is found, or other criteria can be used to choose among multiple satisfactory designs, should we enjoy that luxury.[7]

Ill-structured problems and organized complexity

Since organizations are being treated as problem solving devices, and the approach taken depends on the sort of problem faced, the first step is to distinguish among the myriad problems faced by public organizations in a way which facilitates connecting problem type with organization design. Fortunately, Simon (1973) has done so in a discussion of artificial intelligence programmes, differentiating between 'ill-structured' and 'well-structured' problems.[8] Ill-structured problems range from designing and constructing a new kind of warship to writing a fugue. Structure is a function of knowledge and understanding. In fact,

> ... definiteness of problem structure is largely an illusion that arises when we systematically confound the idealized problem that is presented to an idealized (and ultimately powerful) problem solver with the actual problem that is to be attacked by a problem solver with limited (even if large) computational capacities. (Simon, 1973: 186)

Problems only become well structured when it is possible to impose a structure on them. 'Much problem solving effort is directed at structuring problems, and only a fraction of it at solving problems once they are structured' (Simon, 1973: 187). Applying these concepts to public organizations, the key issue becomes how to design organizations to solve problems rather than their effective operation once designed. Bureaucracies are effective only when confronted with problems which are already well structured. Their forte is computation of solutions for well-structured problems. Neglect by managers of the difficulties attendant on making decisions on ill-structured problems in favour of concentration on routine operating decisions 'may well cause organizations to pursue inappropriate courses of action more efficiently' (Mintzberg et al. 1976: 246)[9].

Weaver (1948) has argued that sciences, such as physics, are equipped to understand recurrence of similar problems. Physicists and mathematicians have developed powerful techniques of probability theory and statistics to contend with what Weaver calls problems of 'disorganized complexity' (Weaver, 1948: 537). A problem of disorganized complexity is one in which

> the number of variables is very large, and one in which each of the many variables has a behavior which is individually erratic, or perhaps totally unknown. However, in spite of this helter-skelter, or unknown, behavior of all the individual variables, the system as a whole possesses certain orderly and analyzable average properties. (Weaver, 1948: 538)

However, an entire range of problems does not exhibit these properties. 'They are all problems which involve dealing simultaneously with a sizable number of factors which are interrelated into an organic whole. They are all . . . problems of 'organized complexity' (Weaver, 1948: 539) in which the variables are all interrelated in a complicated, but not random, fashion. These problems 'cannot be handled with the statistical techniques so effective in describing average behavior in problems of disorganized complexity' (Weaver, 1948: 540). Most problems confronted by contemporary social, economic, and political systems possess characteristics of organized complexity.

In one sense the logical response to organized complexity would be to centralize and consolidate public organizations in such a way as to take into account the various interrelationships. The key difficulty is then to discover the structure of those interrelationships and match the design to them.

In fact, it is not stretching the point to suggest that the major problem in the design of organizations is to assess the connectivity or interdependence of the various components of the problems the organization is intended to confront. Decisions made on appropriate division of labour, lines of authority and span of authority all pivot on the answers to several questions about interdependence. Which components are interdependent? What is the extent of that interdependence? What sort of interdependence is it?[10] However, the more immediately germane question is; do we know enough to answer those questions or can we find out within constraints of time and resources?

Administrative reforms of the American Progressive movement, along with bureaucratization more generally, and recently the various approaches to policy analysis such as PPB, PERT, MBO, ZBB, and now strategic planning, which can be grouped under the heading of systems analysis, answered the last question in the affirmative. The first two questions were answered, respectively, most and extensive. From this vantage point, failures of organizations and policies derive from the consideration of key factors in isolation and neglect of their myriad interrelationships. We either faced well-structured problems or could readily discover their structure.

In keeping with the larger Progressive movement, Stephen Leacock argued in favour of centralization for the United States government, since

> The federal relation between, let us say, the New York and Massachusetts of one hundred years ago rested upon an actual physical and economic separation: the federal separation of Ohio and Indiana, or of the two halves of Dakota today rests upon nothing but a form of constitutional contrivance at variance with the industrial life of the community. (Leacock, 1909: 40)

Interdependence had increased without an accompanying alteration (toward centralization in this case) of the government structure. Integration of the transportation industry (the railroads), concentration of capital, and organization of labour into 'vast groups representing the economic solidarity of the nation' were completely disconnected from the boundary lines of the state (Leacock, 1909: 43). His presumption was increased organized complexity. The answer was increased centralization of public organizations.[11] Just as physics dealt effectively with simple complexity using two or three variable equations, so was bureaucratic organization a relatively effective way of handling the simple problems of the late nineteenth century.

More recently systems analysis has led to the assumption of the practical possibility of understanding organized complexity through the use of more effective and more powerful analytic tools, such as computer simulations, and through the use of educated intuition. To some extent these attempts have proven successful.[12] However, they have often resulted in tying once separable problems more closely together, thus increasing the cognitive complexity of the problems confronted.

It would seem that through its language and emphases, systems analysis may have shown the world as more closely related than it really is. If we must make any assumptions about interdependence, it would probably be more accurate if we assumed lower levels rather than higher, since

> Hierarchic systems are . . . often nearly decomposable. Hence only aggregative properties of their parts enter into the descriptions of the interactions of these parts. A generalization of the notion of near decomposability might be called the 'empty world hypothesis' – most things are only weakly connected with most other things. For a tolerable description of reality only a tiny fraction of all possible interactions needs be taken into account. (Simon, 1969: 110)

This suggests error in the conventional tendency to impute high levels of interdependence to the parts of system on an *a priori* basis: even most complex systems are nearly decomposable. And the extent and contours of system interdependence are not to be assumed, they are empirical questions.

Centralized, formal organizations such as bureaucracies are intended to handle co-ordination among earlier problems (decomposition created by division of labour and specialization) where the structure of the larger problems, of which they are components, is well understood, e.g, they are well-structured problems. Such mechanisms are, however, not suited to handling ill-structured problems where the pattern of interdependence among the components is not well understood.

In fact, more often than not problems of organized complexity facing public organizations are 'ill-structured', as opposed to 'well-structured.' It is not exaggeration to suggest that most important decisions made in public organizations lie closer to the ill-structured than the well-structured side. As more and more problems have been moved from the private sector to the public sector, the percentage of ill-structured problems faced by public organizations has increased dramatically. Where standard forms of bureaucratic organization worked readily for simpler problems, they are now inappropriate and inadequate to the demands imposed by problems of environmental protection, urban renewal and the elimination of poverty, to name but a few.

Structure is a function of knowledge and understanding. Problems only become well-structured when it is possible to impose a structure on them. Hierarchical co-ordinative arrangements can only follow the attainment of hierarchies of knowledge. To do otherwise results in the problems associated with premature programming (Landau and Stout, 1979). Hierarchical public organizations, such as bureaucracies, and systems analysis approaches may serve only to increase the difficulty of solving any particular problem having characteristics of organized complexity.

Ill-structured problems only begin to acquire structure when they are decomposed into various problems of component design, that is, a series of smaller problems that can be well-structured. This results in a problem 'well-structured in the small, but ill-structured in the large' (Simon, 1973: 190). Smaller problems that are capable of comprehension are isolated and the larger problem, environment, treated as ill-structured. The larger problem is solved by confronting each component individually rather than in parallel. While this approach increases the probability that 'interrelationships among the various well-structured subproblems [will] be neglected or underemphasized' (Simon, 1973: 191), there are ways of dividing the whole problem into parts that do 'less violence to those interactions than other ways of dividing it' (Simon, 1973: 191).[13] The major difficulty is discovering how to make those divisions.[14]

Thus, the concept of decomposition serves a dual purpose. It suggests not only a way of thinking about the extent of linkages (relatively minimal) among the components of a system possessing the properties of organized complexity, but a process for moving from ill-structured to well-structured problems.

Some radical proposals

In light of what has been said above, several what might be considered by some students of classical (or even the 'new') public administration as rather radical guidelines for the design of public organizations, are now proposed. The first is that more time and resources are spent on structuring problems. The second is that decentralized forms of public organizations are employed where it is appropriate to do so. This can be determined by no less than careful investigation of the interdependence in a problem environment or set of environments. Moreover, given the 'empty world hypothesis', where the structure of the problem is not known this rule of thumb should be followed; use no more co-ordinating apparatus than is absolutely necessary to bring about a satisfactory level of co-ordination.[15] That is, make a presumption in favour of lower levels of interdependence rather than higher, in order to avoid minimize cognitive complexity.[16]

The proposal is not simply to decentralize a formal organization, with its components still linked formally and contained within the confines of a single organization.[17] Nor is a market system proposed. Rather, the proposal for any problem environment is series of formally independent public organizations to handle the smaller well-structured problems, linked through informal channels,[18] conventions, and contracts to handle the larger problem which remains ill-structured.[19] Once a large, ill-structured problem has been decomposed into smaller well-structured problems that can be effectively handled by bureaucratic forms of organization, interdependence among the components, e.g. the smaller well-structured problems, is addressed by informal mechanisms. The goal is to permit the decomposition of the larger problem environment in order to take advantage of bureaucratic efficiencies, without ignoring the connections among those problems on the one hand or imposing a structure on them on the other.

Furthermore, since learning about interdependence (e.g. the structure) in any particular problem is on the basis of trial and error, whatever mechanisms are used to solve the problem in the interim, prior to the development of knowledge sufficient to structure the problem, should be easily changeable and flexible enough to accommodate unforeseen difficulties before changes can be made. Formal arrangements suffer from goal displacement and institutionalization, but informal mechanisms are much less prone to these difficulties. They are created on an as needed basis and endure while their utility as problem solving devices lasts.

While this approach is compatible with theories of 'mutual adjustment', it focuses on the mechanisms which permit and facilitate co-ordination rather than commonalities of interest and processes of negotiation, etc. In the same way, it complements rational choice theories of organization by emphasizing the factors which provide the ability and opportunity to co-ordinate, rather than on whatever motivations to co-operate may exist.

Three informal mechanisms provide ways of coping with interdependence among organizations which confront well-structured components of a larger ill-structured problem: channels of communication, norms or conventions governing behaviour, and contracts.

Informal channels between pairs of individuals make possible communication between organizations, where communication is understood to include exchange of positions, technical information and actual negotiation of specific sorts of agreements and contracts. Informal channels provide the actual devices by which communication takes place, they supplement and, in many cases, supplant formally arranged channels for communication. They permit secrecy and the exchange of sensitive information.

Informal channels rest not on formally designated liaisons, but upon foundations of trust and reciprocity between two individuals who have interacted over a period of time. They are developed on an as needed basis as problems of interdependence arise which require some kind of co-ordination among formal organizations, and come into play only as they are needed to conduct business. As conditions change and they become obsolete or irrelevant, they are not retained as are formal devices. They wither away and are replaced by informal channels more appropriate to the problems at hand.

Informal channels may be rather specialized, either on the basis of problem addressed or type of communication transmitted. Also, informal channels may address a range of problems, either those extant at one point in time, or a series of problems as they arise over time. The evidence for their flexibility is rather impressive, in direct contrast to formal channels. Where problems are ill-structured such flexibility is critical. It permits rapid adjustment of organizational mechanisms as knowledge advances, and problems move from ill- to well-structured.

Moreover, and this is a key point, informal channels are developed by many participants at many different times. They thus require only a tiny fraction of the knowledge, or structure for problems, necessary to the success of formally designed centralized organizations such as bureaucracies. Each participant need know only about the specific problem he confronts at the time. A corollary of this is that informal channels involve only the persons actually relevant to the solution of a problem. Their contours are dictated by the character of the problem, not by the requirements of centralized control. This facet of informal channels results simultaneously in minimizing the cognitive complexity of any particular problem and in reducing the number of participants necessary to the successful resolution to that problem. On the one hand, reliance on informal channels to cope with ill-structured problems is a radical form of decomposition, which seeks to minimize the complexity faced by any single decision maker. On the other hand, it is a radical form of decentralization of authority which permits the fullest exercise of individual expertise, judgement, and intuition. Both aspects should facilitate the solution of those problems.

Informal channels also, in some real sense, make possible development of the other two mechanisms. Over a period of time, informal exchanges between two individuals result in the build up of the mutual trust and respect which facilitate informal agreements and contracts. Close contact in series of interactions also makes likely the development of shared norms of behaviour.

Informal conventions or norms, whether left implicit or made explicit, cope with interdependence by co-ordinating behaviour in several ways. They form general foundations for more specific sorts of agreements or contracts. They make possible the narrowing of differences among independent participants, thereby facilitating subsequent agreements or contracts. They may also substitute quite effectively for explicit, specific agreements as a means of co-ordinating behaviour. If behaviour of members of formal organizations is achieved by the provision of common decision premises by a central authority (Simon, 1957), informal norms conventions achieve the same co-ordination for the same reason in the absence of a central authority.

Whatever the source, conventions and norms show a striking capacity for co-ordinating behaviour in the absence of a formal structure. In interorganizational committees which have been observed, informal procedures developed rapidly, effectively co-ordinating very specific forms of behaviour and were taught readily to newcomers (although sometimes with more than a hint of coercion), thus providing striking confirmation in the context of administrative organizations for the findings of Fenno (1973) on Congressional committees. Such informal norms proved remarkably well adapted to solving the particular problems faced by those involved.

Informal agreements or contracts provide more specific forms of co-ordination than conventions or norms, but retain a remarkable degree of flexibility and capacity to cover problems which were not anticipated when they were arranged. Frequently such contracts are left at the level of oral agreement, for the explicit reason that committing them to paper may rob them of their principal virtue of flexibility, and worse perhaps, put them at the mercy of legal counsel.

Nonetheless, research has shown no evidence that such agreements were ever unilaterally abandoned, even though their legal standing may have been questionable. This generalization includes informal agreements which governed the transfers of millions of dollars between competing organizations. Finally, these agreements have proven quite stable, in some cases surviving turnover in the individuals who originally negotiated them.

Some probable objections to the proposals

Several objections to these proposals may be foreseen. Given the evidence for bureaucratic territoriality and imperialism, it may be unreasonable to expect multiple, independent public organizations to work out solutions to problems that concern them severally. It is unrealistic to rely on 'informalities' to achieve co-ordination, because they develop only spontaneously and naturally and therefore remain unreliable, serve only personal or group ends, are antithetical to larger organizational ends or, at best, serve them only tangentially or incidentally. Finally, informalities do not possess either the neatness of form of bureaucratic structures, nor do they deliver the apparent certainty of the latter.

In recent years, public choice theorists have confronted problems of co-operation and co-ordination among independent self-interested participants. Whilst formerly too simplistic to shed much light on the complex interactions of organization members, both in the problems they chose to address and the factors they elected to include in their formulations, theorists such as Axelrod (1984) and Hardin (1982) have developed theories which are very useful for addressing the problems in this chapter.

Axelrod (1984), using what must be the limiting case (enemies opposing each other in battle), has demonstrated the strong probability that co-operation (co-ordination) among independent actors will evolve if certain minimal conditions are met. He assumes no more than self-interest as a motivating force since it 'allows an examination of the difficult case in which co-operation is not completely based upon concern for the others or upon the welfare of the group as a whole' (Axelrod, 1984: 6).

In Axelrod's formulation (as in the world public organizations inhabit) actors are assumed to interact an indefinite number of times, so that none may be sure when their last interaction may occur, meaning that decisions affect not only the solution of the problem immediately at hand but those of problems coming later. This is a point soon learned by any newly elected Congressman. The key is to enlarge the 'shadow of the future'. Axelrod's formulations also support the contention that informal conventions, at least, may be explained not as spontaneous, unconscious developments, but as conscious, self-interested constructions.

Thus, informal conventions may arise in the absence of some larger common interest among those involved, without motives of altruism on their part and without trust as a foundation, even where those involved are actually enemies. How much more certain co-ordination will be under more favourable circumstances, i.e., where they are part of a common professional culture, located with common larger governmental entities, etc.

The term 'informal mechanisms' has been used quite consciously, to convey the truly artificial character of these devices. They are not part of a 'natural system' which somehow arises, as opposed to an 'artificial system' of organization, as Thompson (1976) has suggested. They are not somehow organically generated, although their apparently spontaneous generation might appear to indicate otherwise. While they lie outside the formal structure (if indeed one exists at all), they are no less artifices designed and intended to solve problems. Individuals are motivated to create informal mechanisms because they help them to contend with the uncertainty created by interdependence of their organizations with other organizations, e.g. organized complexity. Informal mechanisms help those individuals to structure the problems they face.

Hardin (1982), in a discussion of 'contract by convention,' argues that informal conventions can arise out of the self-interest of the actors involved, and once they exist, are honoured because again it serves their self-interest, in particular, because conventions lead to expectations about each other's behaviour, 'and because we have expectations, we suffer costs if we do not live up to them.' (Hardin, 1982: 175). Establishing conventions within a group gives the members 'power to sanction each other's violations of the convention' (Hardin, 1982: 177). Like Axelrod (1984), Hardin attributes the power of convention to order behaviour, to the continuing exchange in ongoing relationships.

That informalities serve only personal or group ends, typically in opposition to larger organizational goals, was a commonly accepted finding of the Hawthorne studies. That informalities might facilitate larger organizational goals, although only incidentally, was a well-argued conclusion of Barnard (1971). However, the writer's research (Chisholm, 1984) indicates that informal channels, normal conventions, and contracts are not only self-consciously rational adaptations to problems, they are also developed with the explicit intention meeting larger organizational goals. This suggests that placing confidence in informal mechanisms as primary devices for problem solving and co-ordination would not be in error.

Finally, while the outward messiness and lack of *a priori* certainty inherent in informally co-ordinated multi-organization systems is likely to make them unattractive to those who follow a procedural concept of rationality,[20] on the basis of substantive notion of rationality there can be little argument against them. Informalities are tremendously effective mechanisms for co-ordinating bureaucratic organizations in the face of ill-structured problems. The rationality of such systems must be judged not on appearance but on the results they produce.

Creating favourable conditions for informal co-ordination

There is an organizational system which happened to develop in a particular way without conscious effort on the part of a central agency or agent to make it look that way, but whose characteristics could without doubt be replicated in analogous problem environments by conscious effort and design.[21] This is simply to say that while informalities cannot be centrally designed, the development of informal mechanisms should not be left purely to serendipity. Factors which facilitate their development can be readily identified, and the conditions which favour those factors created. Thus, the task shifts from one of attempting to structure the larger ill-structured problem to one of creating conditions favourable to the development of informal mechanisms which can cope with that ill-structured problem. Structure can then be imposed over time.[22]

Assuming some level of motivation significantly above zero, factors affecting the probability of the development of informal co-ordinative mechanisms are ability and opportunity. These factors may be addressed at three levels of analysis; the individual, the organization, and the larger organizational system.

The properties of the larger system of bureaucratic organizations in a given problem environment are considered first. Opportunity for contact between individuals from different organizations must exist before informal channels can develop. Formally contrived co-ordination activities, such as interorganization committees, provide this opportunity. The value of such contacts frequently overshadows any immediate substantive results, and so such bodies might be established not with the intent of actually co-ordinating, but for the purpose of providing opportunities for informal channels to develop.

An equally important factor is the movement of personnel among organizations. While high rates of turnover at single organizations are typically considered something to be avoided, in moderate amounts they prove remarkably effective in promoting an informal system of relationships.[23] As individuals move from one organization to another, they carry with them an intimate knowledge of the formal structures and informal decision premises and processes of their former organizations. When situations arise regarding communication or negotiation with their former organization, they know who to talk to and how to achieve results.

Furthermore, when people move they carry to their new organizations existing patterns of doing things, existing decision premises, ranging from specific technical procedures to more general views of the world. Thus, one result of turnover is to spread common decision premises, contributing to greater influence of informal conventions and norms and narrowing the gaps organizations must bridge to come to specific agreements. Rather than attempt to minimize turnover, we might wish to create a situation where it can take place readily.

From properties of the organizational system in a problem environment, consideration must now be given to properties of individual organizations. These affect both the opportunity and ability of their members to develop informal channels and ultimately the conventions and agreements which provide co-ordination. An organization's managers are one factor. Do they permit, or perhaps directly encourage, their personnel to develop informal channels with others outside the organization, or do they stand in the way of such contacts? Such willingness appears to be a function of attitudes about the character of organization (is it a formal structure or people?), concern about informal channels undermining a manager's authority, and managerial style (making all decisions versus giving subordinates discretion). Managerial opposition or support alters the cost to individuals of making informal connections. It also affects the value of the individual as an informal contact to others outside the organization. Educating managers, by demonstrating the advantages which will accrue to them by doing so, to place their subordinates intentionally in situations where there is potential for making contacts and to give those subordinates discretion to make commitments for the larger organization, should increase the probability that informal channels will develop.

Another aspect of individual organizations which facilitates the development and maintenance of informal ties is adequate staffing. Time and effort is required to develop and maintain informal channels. A staff of sufficient size to permit specialized attention to particular problems appears to be essential. Thus, adequate funding for such purposes should be given careful consideration.

Finally it is necessary to consider personal attributes which facilitate the development of informal channels, the individual's personality and attitudes, along with membership of professional organizations and social groups. Attitudes about the sanctity of formally prescribed ways of doing things affect one's ability to act informally. Some people treat formal rules as objects of worship, others take satisfaction in circumventing formal procedures. The latter are more inclined to develop informal relationships with others outside their own organization. Furthermore, ease in dealing with others and good interpersonal skills also increase the likelihood of developing informal ties. Thus, hiring practices and employee training programmes may be structured to emphasize attitudes which facilitate informality and good interpersonal skills. This is probably easier stated than accomplished.

More readily manipulated are employee memberships in professional organizations and other social groups. Such memberships have several effects. They improve the probability that a person will meet members of other organizations in the problem environment. They also increase the likelihood that individuals will identify with one another through the development of common social activities and will share values, thus paving the way for informal channels, norms, and agreements. It is a relatively simple matter to encourage employees to join such professional associations and to provide the time and resources for them to do so. Consideration may also be given to creating locally focused (e.g. within the problem environment) associations where they do not already exist.

Even though informal mechanisms are the cumulative results of many individual decisions, and they cannot be comprehensively planned and executed in the same manner as formal devices, conditions (which affect ability and opportunity) can be created which favour their development. Insofar as we seek to rely on informal mechanisms to cope with the larger, ill-structured aspects of a problem environment, the creation and manipulation of these factors become essential to the solution of such problems.

Conclusion

Thinking of public organizations as rational problem-solving devices, where rationality is viewed in substantive terms, and means are adapted to ends but constrained by knowledge of the structure of the problems faced, leads us to evaluate the design of those organizations very carefully. Bureaucratic forms are suited only to a increasingly narrow range of problems which can be called well-structured. From this perspective, bureaucratic failures and ineffectiveness come more from inaccurate assumptions about knowledge and the imposition of inappropriate designs for problem solving which follow from those assumptions, than from problems of implementation, failures in control, goal displacement, or bureaucratic politics.[24]

Simon's distinction between well-structured and ill-structured problems, in concert with his arguments about decomposition of complex systems and his 'empty world hypotheses', permits us to develop a scheme for choosing among alternative organizational designs. Formal, hierarchical designs are reserved for that class of problems where the structure is well understood, i.e. we know the extent and character of the connectivity of the components. Ill-structured problems require loosely coupled, flexible, and adaptive designs which are capable of adjusting to changes in knowledge about the structure of those problems, and which permit the exercise of expertise, judgement, and intuition on the part of decision makers. By decomposing larger problem environments into their components, which are more readily understood (e.g. structured), the problem becomes well-structured in the small, permitting us to employ standard bureaucratic forms and their efficiencies for those component problems, while the problem remains ill-structured in the large. For co-ordination and solution of the larger ill-structured problem, it is suggested that we rely upon informal mechanisms (namely, channels, conventions, and contracts), thus creating an intentionally hybrid decentralized system of formal and informal structures. By their special characteristics, informal mechanisms are better able to cope with ill-structured problems. They require the participation only of those persons necessary to the solution of the problem, and place decision-making authority in the hands of those most qualified. However, rather than trust to good fortune for the creation and maintenance of informal devices, some conditions have been suggested which facilitate them and which may themselves be created.

Thus, when faced with the need to solve a large, ill-structured problem, several steps are appropriate. Decompose the larger problem into its constituent parts. Insofar as those components are well-structured, use standard forms of bureaucracy to deal with them. Co-ordination of the interconnections of the components is then left to informal mechanisms which are developed on an as needed basis. The central issue for informal mechanisms is not their design, but creating the conditions which facilitate their development by a multiplicity of actors making a myriad of individual decisions.

Notes

1. In this chapter, 'bureaucracy' is used in its narrow technical sense, following the characteristics described by Weber (1964).

2. State intervention through public organizations may occur for two reasons: the provision of public goods and to take into account externalities of behaviour of individual participants. Both require the co-ordination of behaviour, but it is primarily the latter with which this chapter is concerned.

3. For a formal model of a political coalition approach, see Chisholm (1986).

4. In fact, Garlichs and Hull (1978) have argued that 'problem-solving capacity is analytically distinct from control capacity', going so far as to suggest that 'within certain limits, control capacity and problem-solving capacity are inversely related' (Garlichs and Hull, 1978: 164).

5. Micro-economic models of behaviour are one example of a procedural view of rationality.

6. Similar arguments have been made from other vantage points by Thompson and

Tuden (1964), Braybrooke and Lindblom (1970), Thompson (1967), and Landau and Stout (1979).

7. Simon (1975) refers to such choices as matters of 'style'.

8. Simon contends that it is 'impossible to construct a formal definition of "well-structured problem." '. [Being] content simply to set forth a list of requirements that have been proposed at one time or another as criteria a problem must satisfy in order to be regarded as well-structured.

(i) There is a definite criterion for testing any proposed solution, and a mechanizable process for applying the criterion.

(ii) There is at least one problem space in which may be represented the initial problem state, the goal state, and all other states that may be reached, or considered, in the course of attempting a solution of the problem.

(iii) . . . all transitions from one considerable state to another [can be represented].

(iv) Any knowledge that the problem solver can acquire about the problem can be represented in one or more problem spaces.

(v) If the actual problem involves acting upon the external world, then the definition of state changes and of the effects upon the state of applying any operator reflect with complete accuracy in one or more problem spaces the laws (laws of nature) that govern the external world.

(vi) All of these conditions hold in the strong sense that the basic processes postulated require only practicable amounts of computation, and the information postulated is effectively available to the processes, i.e. available with the help only of practicable amounts of search. (Simon, 1973; 182–3)

See also Reitman (1964).

9. Mintzberg, et al. (1976: 246) describe 'unstructured' decision processes as 'processes that have not been encountered in quite the same form and for which no predetermined and explicit set of ordered responses exists in the organization'.

10. Some efforts have been made to distinguish different kinds of interdependnece in the organizational context, notably Thompson (1967). While recognizing the importance of this question to the design of appropriate decision processes and organizational arrangements, for simplicity's sake it is left outside the scope of this chapter.

11. Note that the President's Commission on the Space Shuttle disaster came to the conclusion that the conditioning factor in the accident was a problem of authority in NASA which could be remedied only through centralization.

12. Steinbruner's (1974) cybernetic theory of decision is another attempt to deal with problems occasioned by organized complexity, but retains both centralized and formal characteristics.

13. Alexander has made one of the few attempts to provide a generalized method of decomposing complex problems in a discussion of urban design problems, but it does not appear that his efforts were entirely successful (Alexander, 1979: Chapter 6).

14. Although the question as posed in the abstract is how to design an organizational system to reflect the character of the problems it must confront, rarely has the opportunity to design organizations from scratch arisen. More often the choice is how to modify an existing organizational design, which seems no longer (if indeed it ever did) to handle effectively problems of interdependence. Thus, rather than attempting to decompose the system by starting over, there is at least some benchmark in the present organizational arrangements from which to begin. Presumably the existing arrangements represent a body of knowledge, however imperfect, about the decomposition of the system which has been accumulated over time on a trial and error basis.

15. Aside from minimizing cognitive complexity, Alexander has argued persuasively that the success of some organizational systems derives from the fact that the 'system is so organized that adjustment can take place in each of (its) subsystems independently of the others' (Alexander, 1979: 65).

16. The writer's research (Chisholm, 1984a) showed that what appeared on the surface to be an extraordinarily complex set of interdependencies among multiple organizations in a single problem environment, upon closer inspection could be readily analysed as a series of bilateral interdependencies whose solutions could proceed independently from each other. In other words, the system was eminently decomposable.

17. The discussion which follows is based upon research reported in Chisholm (1984a). The public transit systems of the San Francisco Bay Area and the Washington DC Metropolitan Area formed the empirical basis for the study.

18. Like 'ill-structured problem', 'informal' is a residual term, defined largely in terms of what it is not. Informal mechanisms are not formal, where formal is understood to include legally designated structures and processes of organizations. Since informalities are not written down and do not appear on organization charts they can only be observed as behaviours, or their existence inferred from the observation of behaviours.

19. In concept at least, there is some point at which connectivity (and knowledge of it) reaches a level where it makes sense to formalize ties among the components. Such a point is difficult to establish on a priori basis but can be noted in practice.

20. For a discussion of the motivations behind drives for certainty and the attractiveness of centralized co-ordination mechanisms, see Chisholm (1984b).

21. Refers to the San Francisco Bay Area public transit system, which is comprised of six major publicly owned transit operators, and a host of smaller operations, all of which are operated as standard bureaucracies, but whose interconnections are handled through informal mechanisms.

22. Hardin (1982: 209) notes that 'often what the members of a group can do almost instinctively is likely to be both a more efficient and a more coherent guide to action than what they might be able to agree upon after extended discussion.'

23. With the caveat that personnel move from one organization to another within the same problem environment, not out of the system entirely.

24. This is the central thesis of the very persuasive argument made by Landau and Stout (1979) in somewhat different language.

References

Alexander, C. (1979) *Notes On the Synthesis of Form*. Cambridge, Mass.: Harvard University Press.

Ashby, W. R. (1962) 'Principles of the Self-Organizing System' pp. 255–78 in H. V. Foerster and G. W. Zopf (eds) *Principles of Self-Organization*. New York: Pergamon Press.

Axelrod, R. (1984) *The Evolution of Co-operation*. New York: Basic Books.

Bernard, C. (1971) *Functions of the Executive*. Cambridge, Mass.: Harvard University Press.

Braybrooke, D. and C. E. Lindblom (1970) *A Strategy of Decision: Policy Evaluation As a Social Process*. New York: The Free Press.

Chisholm, D. (1984a) 'Informal Organization and the Problem of Coordination'. Unpublished doctoral dissertation, University of California, Berkeley.

Chisholm, D. (1984b) 'Coordination as Moral Imperative, Coordination As Instrument'. Paper prepared for delivery at the 1984 annual meeting of the American Political Science Association.

Chisholm, D. (1986) 'Organizational Adaptation to Environmental Change', IGS Studies in Public Organization 86–1. Berkeley: University of California.

Dewey, J. (1927) *The Public and Its Problems*. Denver: Alan Swallow.

Fenno, R. F. (1973) *Congressmen in Committees*. Boston: Little, Brown.

Garlichs, D. and C. Hull (1978) 'Central Control and Information Dependence: Highway Planning in the Federal Republic of Germany'. pp. 143–65 in K. Hanf and F. W. Scharpf (eds) *Interorganizational Policy Making: Limits to Coordination and Central Control*. London: Sage.

Hardin, R. (1980) 'Rationality, Irrationality and Functionalist Explanation'. *Social Science Information*, 19, pp. 755–72.

Hardin, R. (1982) *Collective Action*. Baltimore: Johns Hopkins University Press.

Landau, M. (1973) 'On the Concept of a Self-Correcting Organization.' *Public Administration Review*, 33, pp. 533–42.

Landau, M. (1979) *Political Theory and Political Science*. New Jersey: Humanities Press.

Landau, M. and R. Stout (1979) 'To Manage Is Not to Control Or the Folly of Type II Errors'. *Public Administration Review*, 39, pp. 148–56.

Leacock, S. (1909) 'The Limitations of Federal Government'. *Proceedings of the American Political Science Association*, 3, pp. 37–52.

Mintzberg, H., D. Raisinghani, and A. Thoret (1976) 'The Structure of "Unstructured" Decision Processes'. *Administrative Science Quarterly*, 21, pp. 246–75.

Newell, A. and H. A. Simon (1972) *Human Problem Solving*. Englewood Cliffs: Prentice-Hall.

Reitman, W. (1964) 'Heuristic Decision Procedures, Open Constraints, and the Structure of Ill-Defined Problems'. pp. 282–315 in M. W. Shelly and G. L. Bryan (eds) *Human Judgements and Optimality*. New York: John Wiley.

Simon, H. A. (1957) *Administrative Behavior*. New York: The Free Press.

Simon, H. A. (1969) 'The Architecture of Complexity', pp. 84–118 in H. A. Simon, *The Sciences of the Artifical*. Cambridge, Mass.: M.I.T. Press.

Simon, H. A. (1973) 'The Structure of Ill-Structured Problems'. *Artificial Intelligence*, 4 pp. 181–201.

Simon, H. A. (1975) 'Style in Design'. pp. 1–10 in J. Arches and C. Eastman, (eds) Proceedings of the 2nd Annual Environmental Design Research Association Conference, October 1970. Pittsburgh: Carnegie-Mellon University.

Simon, H. A. (1983) *Reason in Human Affairs*. Palo Alto: Stanford University Press.

Simon, H. A. (1985) 'Human Nature in Politics: The Dialogue of Psychology with Political Science'. *American Political Science Review*, 79, pp. 293–304.

Steinbruner, J. D. (1974) *The Cybernetic Theory of Decision*. Princeton: Princeton University Press.

Thompson, J. D. (1967) *Organizations in Action: Social Science Bases of Administrative Theory*. New York: McGraw-Hill.

Thompson, J. D. and A. Tuden (1964) 'Strategies, Structures, and Processes of Organizational Decision' in H. J. Leavitt and R. Pondy (eds), *Readings in Managerial Psychology*. Chicago: University of Chicago Press.

Thompson, V. (1976) *Bureaucracy and the Modern World*. Morristown: General Learning Press.

Weaver, W. (1948) 'Science and Complexity'. *American Scientist*, 36, pp. 536–44.

Weber, M. (1964) *The Theory of Social and Economic Organization*. Edited with an introduction by T. Parsons. New York: The Free Press.

Wildavsky, A. (1972) 'The Self-Evaluating Organization'. *Public Administration Review*, 42, pp. 509–20.

II
EMPIRICAL STUDIES

5
Testing theories:
the contribution of bureaumetrics

Andrew Dunsire

Introduction

Bureaumetrics is the quantitative organizational analysis and comparison of government departments and agencies — 'bureaucracies' as
popularly understood. If one characteristic of bureaucracy is said to
vary with another, if bureaucracies are held to differ on some
characteristics from organizations of other kinds, or if bureaucracies
are asserted to change over time in a characteristic way — bureaumetrics attempts to quantify the asserted relationship. It is not content
to theorize about the logic of the situation, what 'must be the case'
given this and that premise, nor even to show causal connections, to
build a model with the directional arrows entered. It wishes to measure
the empirical variables of the situation, and to calibrate the strengths
of causal influences. In this respect, bureaumetrics stands in relation to
theory of bureaucracy as does econometrics in relation to theory of the
market.

How like one another *are* the departments of central government? In
what respects, if any, is it true that if you have seen one, you have seen
them all? What are the dimensions on which government agencies
vary? What factors, when comparing the performance of government
departments with one another, should be held constant? What factors,
in what strength, make it preferable to allot a particular governmental
function to one ministry rather than another (the 'allocation of
portfolios' problem)? When is 'the larger the better' true, and in what
circumstances is small beautiful? Is there one internal configuration or
management structure in a bureaucracy that is better than another for
certain tasks, or in certain environmental conditions? Is it true that
bureaucrats always maximize their budgets? What exactly happens
when reorganizations are decreed? What are the detailed effects upon
different government departments when cuts in staff and/or budget
are imposed?

There are plenty of theories and suppositions about each of these questions and it cannot be pretended either that quantitative analysis 'solves' them, or that obtaining the requisite figures is free of difficulties both theoretical and practical. These are the kinds of questions which the method of bureaumetrics addresses, the research on which is reported here, albeit briefly and summarily. Questions of output measurement and performance have yet to be tackled.

Methods

The choice of principal data-collection method was made before the research began, for two main reasons. Firstly, one of the prime tasks was to provide what was lacking in previous descriptions of British central government: a map of the entire field, a survey of *all* government departments. Such a wide scope obviously cut out all the more labour-intensive methods, and pointed to the use of documentary sources wherever possible. Secondly, a research project which depends upon interviewing or sending long questionnaires to busy public officials is not going to be welcomed by them (and may not get a research grant in the first place). However, the same public officials, conscious of how much information they already compile and publish on all kinds of things, will very likely warmly welcome a project which proposes to actually use some of this readily available data, and may prove very helpful in elucidating it and even supplementing it. Both considerations indicated the full exploitation of already published sources of information, before falling back upon direct enquiry of any kind.

The available data used represented three main kinds. The first category is officially published handbooks and documents issued annually or at regular intervals, purchasable by anyone from (in Britain) Her Majesty's Stationery Office, (HMSO) the Government Bookshop. These included the Estimates of Expenditure presented to the House of Commons each year (by 'expenditure programme' rather than department by department), and the Appropriation Accounts; the *Civil Service Yearbook*, listing all civil servants of the rank of Assistant Secretary and above, by department and by official duties; another yearbook called *Civil Service Statistics*, presenting various statistical tables and analyses; the daily official reports of proceedings in Parliament, minutes and reports of Parliamentary committees, reports and papers presented to such committees and published; and so on. The second category comprised occasional or irregular publications of broadly the same sort, including books and documents published by individual departments, material drawn from occasional articles in official periodicals such as the Treasury's *Economic Progress Report* or the former Civil Service Department's *Management Services in Government*, and from unofficial sources such as the bulletins of the main civil service unions; newspaper journalism and academic journal articles; and so on. Into the third category came officially collected but restricted circulation materials, centrally stored, and made available to us under suitable guarantees, or 'edited' and 'doctored' to remove any sensitive material. These included the record called 'Staff in Post' produced by the Management and Personnel Office, some printouts from the Treasury's Financial Information Systems computer records, and individual answers to specific queries. In this category also came documents submitted to Parliamentary committees but not published, and deposited in Parliamentary libraries. The bulk of the analyses, however, depend upon the publicly available materials in the first category.

Two other methodological problems may be touched on here, the definition of the 'field', and the definition of the 'unit of analysis'. A researcher setting out on a survey has to decide whether he is going to attempt a 'census' approach, describing the entire population of whatever he is interested in (say, as in this case, British central government departments) on a chosen dimension or dimensions; or whether he is going to select a sample for detailed study, with inferences following about the population as a whole. This first project chose to include *all* central departments in the survey, for three reasons. Firstly, a sample needs a sampling frame, a way of making sure the sample is representative in either a structured or a random fashion. For the population selected, no sampling frame existed and indeed, it became an objective to provide one for future researchers. Secondly, a full survey would enable a fresh look to be taken at the classification of subjects, on multidimensional scales, without pre-conceptions of what groupings to expect. Thirdly, the disparity between the 'whole population' and a statistically reliable sample was relatively small — any sample should have not less than about thirty elements, while however it was counted the selected population did not have more than about seventy units. It therefore seemed worthwhile to go for the census approach.

Having made this decision, it might then seem simple to construct a list of all the units to be included. In many countries, central government departments are few, legally defined and frequently named in statutes. Here the problem for the researcher is not so much the definition of a department as the decision whether to analyse at whole-departmental level, or the first level of 'decomposition', the subdepartment level, or somewhere below that, multiplying the number of units of analysis by three or four for each step downwards in the hierarchy, thus enabling much finer discriminations. It was anticipated that the main difficulty would be finding the data, unobtrusively, for units 'below' whole-department level. But in fact it became necessary to first tackle (since the survey was in Britain) the problem of how to define a 'central government department'. There were no fewer than eleven or twelve different lists of 'departments', each supposedly complete, each as 'official' as the next, and varying greatly in length, from below thirty to over seventy. Many bodies treated as separate departments for some purposes are not so treated for others, for example, a group of about twenty state museums. We settled on one of the longer lists, a parliamentary one denominating units which separately account for their expenditures and containing sixty-nine names. This gave a reasonable certainty of being able to aggregate, to match other lists, rather than having to try to break given figures down. Again, not all 'departments' in Britain are 'ministries', directly under the control of a Minister. Some are under ministerial control at one remove, some are relatively autonomous. The implications of this constitutional status difference needed exploration.

The other point about *level* of analysis — whether significant differences in the characteristics of the parts of an organization are being masked and hidden, if data is only collected about the organization as a whole — remains. Its importance in this project was investigated, and in later projects subdepartmental units have occasionally been adopted as the unit of analysis, but it gets progressively more difficult to do by unobtrusive methods.

Indices

Despite being limited, by and large, to published information, it is true to say that the survey took in as many tables as could be found of the required form. That is, the sixty-nine agencies down one edge and columns of figures opposite — whatever the figures represented. There was, it was felt, always some way to make use of them. Investigations were greatly influenced by the existing organizational analysis literature (even though it mainly dealt with other types of organization than government departments) and the conventional dimensions for data collection about organizations were size, internal structure, technology or type of work process, and type of environment. These concepts were adapted to the bureaucratic setting, with the addition of one other, the concept of 'political salience'. It was thought it might be an important thing to know about a government department, how politically sensitive its work is, and investigators expected to find two kinds of political salience: political exposure, and political weight or 'clout'. A government department high on exposure might be often in the public eye, but not necessarily as influential in the inner counsels of government as some others, whose weight was thrown about behind closed doors.

For each of these concepts or dimensions it was necessary to find or devise a number of individual aspects to be measured. Size, for example, can be thought of as number of staff, number of pounds of annual budget, number of clients served, transactions effected, or area covered by plant and buildings, and so on. Also an organization which is large on one measure may not be as large on another. For one reason and another only two measures of size have therefore been used: staffing and spending.

The 'internal structure' of an organization is a much more complex notion. It is most often used, perhaps, to complement 'process', structure being the framework, fabric or vehicle within and through which the work flows and inputs are processed into outputs. Sometimes structure is equated with 'management structure'; the organization chart, or distribution of responsibilities for distinct tasks and functions. Some authors include in the structure of an organization all its 'designed' features, including manuals of procedure and decision processes, and some will use structure as a synonym for 'pattern' when describing behaviour in organizations. However, a very limited view of what structure means had to be taken, dictated largely by the data gathered. Basically this meant, the number and relative distribution of 'parts' of various kinds, the 'shape' or the organization, as determined by the number of levels in its hierarchy and its 'population' at each of these levels; its degree of specialization, indicated by the numbers of distinct *kinds* of parts; the relative numbers of different occupational groups in its staff; and the degree of its dispersion — the relative importance of its regional or local office network. For the dimension of 'structure' eighteen measures were devised in this way, stringing out the sixty-nine departments along each (Hood and Dunsire, 1981).

The 'environment' in which an organization operates is a necessary aspect of its description, and may have an influence on its 'shape' or other structural manifestation. One element in the environment of a government department is its 'political salience', already mentioned. No fewer than thirty different measures of this were taken, though not all were continued with. They ranged over the number and size of parliamentary bills introduced annually, the number of ministers attached to the department, the number of debates on the department's business engendered, the number of mentions of the department on the front page of *The Times* during a sample period, the number of Parliamentary Questions asked, the average increase in the department's budget over a period of years, the number of complaints to the Ombudsman about a department's work, the number of reports and official papers produced by each department, and so on. To reproduce this list would probably be unhelpful and anyone trying to replicate this study in another context would have to devise their own (Hood and Dunsire, 1981: 88).

Other aspects of 'environment' measured included the *predictability* of the financial environment (whether or not next year's expenditure can be more or less accurately calculated); the *self-sufficiency* of a department (how far they are totally dependent on parliamentary votes of taxation, or have their own sources of revenue); the degree of *linkage* with other departments, *nodality* — (how far the environment of a department consists of other departments, or is relatively isolated); the *type of clientele* (customers are individual citizens, other departments, other corporate bodies, overseas) and so on. Ten measures of environment were devised under these heads.

For 'technology', the existing literature was of very little help and almost everything had to be invented. In particular, it was necessary to move from thinking in terms of 'internal processes' or techniques (parallel to techniques of manufacture in industrial organizations) to thinking in terms of 'external techniques', or modes of delivery — parallels with retail and distributive trades rather than with manufacturing. For the more conventional 'work process' understanding of 'technology', data was collected on the number of computers installed (this was, of course, in 1976–7) and their cost; also the proportion of gross budget that each department spent on plant, machinery and vehicles — their 'hardware'. For 'external technology', the department's degree of 'regulativeness' was measured, how many statutory instruments and orders it issued in a year; how much it went in for propaganda and persuasion as its mode of achieving its ends; how much it spent on obtaining information (research and development); and a composite index which was called 'resource mix' — how much of its budget each department spent on salaries for its own staff, on lending and investment, on purchasing goods and services, on grants and other payments; and how much of its income it earned though sales and other receipts. These gave thirteen variables by which to measure 'technology'.

This work produced a total of seventy-three variables on which to string out the sixty-nine organizations. But such numbers are too large to grasp, or to see patterns in very easily. Even ten measures for a single dimension are rather many. A way has to be found of representing how the items under investigation differ from one another on, say, political salience or technology, without simply presenting the data on twenty or thirty measures. This is the purpose of constructing *indices* for each of the major dimensions in which one is interested and there are two broad ways of setting about it. The researcher can look hard at the variables, using previous knowledge and experience and intuitive judgement, and group the variables into, say, four or five conventionally recognized categories. Thus under 'structure' might be aggregated variables under heads like 'managerial structure', 'grading structure', 'territorial structure' and so on. Or else, the researcher can decline to impose pre-existing categorizations in that way and, as it were, ask the data how *it* sees its 'natural' aggregations, by using mathematical techniques like factor analysis and principal components analysis. In this case the second approach and latter technique were employed.

Principal components analysis uses a computer to assess the total variance in the data, that is the spread of difference among the items on all the variables, to see which set of variables seems to be responsible for the greatest amount of that variance (the first component), and then what accounts for the largest proportion of the variance not accounted for by the first factor, and so on. It is seldom useful to proceed beyond four or five such succeeding factors.

On environment and type of work four indices were found which do not much resemble the labelling of the original variables and are all aspects of finance in the departments. They are (1) 'Financial mix'; (2) 'Self-sufficiency in finance'; (3) 'Financial interrelatedness'; (4) 'Financial uncertainty'.

It was these indices, and not the original variables, which were then used to test various hypotheses about the relationship between departments and between each dimension and the others, in the 'cross-sectional' studies that will be described below. These cross-sectional studies brought quantitative analysis to bear on a population of organizations sharing some characteristics (all British central government departments) and contrasting on a number of other characteristics, at a single point in time (the year 1976/77 for most purposes). For the longitudinal studies which were carried out some years later (also described in brief below), a much simpler research design was used, involving only a handful of relatively 'raw' variables. Figures for 'top staff' or 'mandarins', percentage of total staff in a department represented by those in the rank of under secretary and above; for 'middle staff' assistant secretary and down to higher executive officer (from these could be derived the percentage of 'bottom staff' and hence the overall 'shape' of the department); for 'administrative grades' (people of all ranks but not specialized by profession or occupational category) as proportion of total staff — this figure and its reciprocal can provide a broad indication of the 'generalist/specialist' balance in a department; for 'salary costs' as a percentage of the departmental budget — this figure can indicate the degree to which a department's technology is 'bureaucrat-intensive', or conversely, operates more in a 'money-shifting' mode. Finally two measures of relative size, departmental budget as percentage of Government budget, and departmental staff total as against Government staff total. These relatively simple indices can given a good 'outline' understanding of the major differences between departments, and make comparisons over a number of years more feasible within the research resources and time available, than would have any attempt to replicate the richer details of the cross-sectional analyses. The period covered was for most purposes 1972–84.

Applications

Cross-sectional studies: testing contingency theories

The 'contingency theory approach' was for a long time the 'dominant paradigm' of organizational analysis (see, for example, Blau and Schoenherr, 1971; Hall, 1972; Pugh and Hickson, 1976). The approach begins from what may be called the 'structure/performance hypothesis', which postulates that there is for any organization a structure which will maximize its performance (or, more generally, that structure affects performance). It then proceeds to ask what attributes or characteristics of an organization influence its structure or internal configuration. If certain things are known about an organization, can predictions be made about what structure it will have? Through the pioneering work of people like Trist and Bamforth (1951), Joan Woodward (1958) and Burns and Stalker (1961) in Britain, and Walker and Guest (1952), Thompson and Bates (1957), and Udy (1959) in the United States of America, the governing factors came to be conventionally listed as size, environment, and technology (as already mentioned). A considerable body of work has been done by scholars in this field, impossible to list here, and of course the approach has not been without its critics (Clegg and Dunkerley, 1977).

Perhaps the most generally familiar propositions of contingency theory are that the 'one best way' military-type structures of the Scientific Management theorists never really applied to anything but the assembly-line type of manufacturing technology. That, for example, petrol refining and chemical manufacturing require a quite different management structure (and industrial relations practices); that firms in a stable or traditional industry like textiles develop managerial practices quite different from those in a volatile, rapidly developing industry like electronics ('mechanistic' and 'organic' styles); that as firms grow in size, a greater and greater proportion of their attention has to be given to co-ordination and control (leading to disproportionate increase in managerial and administrative staffs). The focus of interest, as can be seen from these examples, was in manufacturing industry; and although there have been several studies in other sectors, and some (notably the 'Aston' studies, reported in Pugh and Hickson, 1976; Pugh and Hinings, 1976) spanned not only different sectors of 'private' organizations but also the 'public sector', there was no previous study of the population of central government departments upon which to draw for concepts or measures. Accordingly existing terms had to be adapted as best they could, and used with the data available to explore the applicability of these theories to this field.

From one point of view, there is no *prima facie* reason to suppose that government departments are not organizations like any others, and so susceptible to the same kind of analysis as firms, or local authorities or insurance offices. If there *is* a relationship between size and structure, or environment and structure, it should surely become manifest in government departments as elsewhere. There is plenty of *variety* among government departments in Britain. They vary in size from the Ministry of Defence with over a quarter of a million civil servants (not counting the armed forces) to the Privy Council Office and several others with a few score; in volatility of environment from the Foreign and Commonwealth Office to the various official registries; in administrative technology from the highly-bureaucrat-intensive Inland Revenue Department (spending over 80 percent of outgoings on salaries) to the 'money-moving' departments like the Scottish Office and the Welsh Office (spending less than 3 percent of outgoings on salaries). Is it not mere commonsense to expect that departments with such different kinds of job to do, and working in such different environments, will take up different internal forms?

On the other hand, there *are* some reasons to suppose that government departments are *not* organizations like others, and reasons to expect their internal forms not to respond to contingencies of technology and environment as others do. These will be dealt with in more detail after a look at the findings.

The starting point was size, and the search for relationships between the two measures of size (staff and budget) and each of the five structural indices in turn (complexity; senior and executive staff; administrative component; concentration and fringe bodies; span of control of chief executive). The overall picture *was* broadly compatible with orthodox contingency theory expectations. 'Complexity' was very strongly related to the two size measures, and 'complexity', as an index, combined a larger number of structure variables.

Two findings were less expected. The first was that *only* complexity was strongly related to size, the other four were not. The second was that the relationship between size and complexity applies more weakly as agency size decreases — the smaller the organization, the less surely its structure can be predicted from its size.

Now a traditional scientific management analyst would have no difficulty in explaining the lack of relationship between span of control of chief executive and organization size. That, he would say, obeys its own laws, and is relatively constant whatever the size of firm, and so on, and the findings also agree. It is not so easy to explain, however, why shape (proportions of top, middle, and bottom staff) do not respond to change in size, for it is by no means the case that shape is relatively constant — it varies considerably among the sixty-nine departments. But size does not predict shape (a finding consistent with the results of Kaufman and Seidman, 1970, in US government agencies). Similarly, the lack of relationship between size and administrative component is a surprise, since whether one follows

Terrien and Mills (1955), Mason Haire (1959) or Parkinson's Law (1958) (who all suggest that administrative component increases disproportionately with growth in size), or more recent studies which have found a negative correlation (administrative component decreases with growth — Anderson and Warkov, 1961; Holdaway and Blowers, 1971; Blau and Schoenherr, 1971; Hall, 1972; Heydebrand, 1973), a relationship should have been found one way or the other.

The other finding, that the relationship between size and 'complexity' is stronger in the big departments than it is in the smaller, goes counter to some other organizational analysts' results (Child, 1977; Hall, 1972). It too does not have an easy explanation. It is not that the smaller organizations are found to be 'simpler' (scoring less on complexity) than the larger. That is exactly what a strong relationship between size and complexity would mean, if it applied in all size ranges. It is rather that the relationship is still there, in the aggregate analysis, but less strongly, and more cases would be found of the opposite in the smaller ranges.

These results have a bearing on the debate on whether 'big is beautiful' in administrative terms. In the 1960s and early 1970s in Britain, administrative reformers in Government circles believed in the virtues of great size — economies of scale, greater co-ordination, better overview of problems, less interdepartmental politics. Then the pendulum swung, and it was believed that large departments overload ministers, that co-ordination in fact gets more difficult, that large organizations are inevitably top heavy. Now, perhaps, neither view obtains, and it is seen that it cannot be size alone that brings such problems. There are relatively large departments in terms of staff size, such as the Inland Revenue, which are not thought to be in any way managerially difficult, and departments only a third of its size (like the so-called 'giant' Department of Trade and Industry) which were dismantled for managerial and political reasons that cannot have been linked to size as such, but perhaps to variety of functions.

The survey looked into the question of the workload of ministers and top civil servants (mandarins) in departments of different size. It was found that the political salience of departments (as measured by indices embracing such variables as parliamentary questions, debate subjects, number of draft statutes introduced, and so on) was loosely related to size. But there were correspondingly larger numbers of ministers to carry this political load. The other aspect of ministerial workload is control of their civil servants; if in the process of growth the number of mandarins grows faster than the number of ministers an 'overload' will occur. However, no clear relationship was found between size of department and minister-to-mandarin ratio although there may be a very slight tendency to overload in this sense with increase in size, but nothing marked. Nor did a stronger relationship emerge in any of the other measures of political workload with size. Not that the workload of all ministers is made up in the same way. Defence ministers, for instance, are more lightly-loaded in parliamentary terms than many of their colleagues in other large departments, but they are fewer in relation to their mandarins than these colleagues. Northern Ireland Office ministers were equal in number to Defence ministers, though supervising one-fiftieth of the number of mandarins, for their bed of nails is of a different kind.

Let us turn now to see whether structure, in the selected population of organizations, is predicted by *environment* or *technology*. As stated previously, close relationships found between a firm's business environment (as measured by the kind of market it was in, rapidity of product change, and so on) and its style of management structure helped to launch contingency theory (Burns and Stalker, 1961; Lawrence and Lorsch, 1967). Indices of a British government department's financial environment were devised which might be thought a close approximation to that type of variable; financial uncertainty, financial inter-relatedness, and financial self-sufficiency. However, no relationship worth noting between any of these indices and the indices of structure was found. Niskanen (1971) postulated a strong relationship between bureaucratic financial self-sufficiency and structure, as compared to financial dependence, but the survey did not find any.

The other composite index in this group, labelled 'financial mix', was of a somewhat different kind and related more to the variables for 'external technology' though the distinction is not hard and fast. Here a strong relationship was found between 'financial mix' and 'complexity', but it was also clearly related to size. The same was true if some individual measures of technology were taken: and there were no correlations that were not also related to size. Does this mean that size is the basic determinant of structure, as the Aston group concluded (Pugh and Hickson, 1976)? It would not appear so. Exercises in multiple regression and other techniques simply showed that three of the indices, total staff, general parliamentary salience, and financial mix, could all predict the structural index 'complexity' quite well on their own, but that they were also strongly related to each other. So it was difficult to isolate one of them as the best predictor of structure (see discussion in Hood and Dunsire, 1981: 127–32).

It was said earlier that there were some reasons why one might *expect* government departments not to follow the patterns that contingency theory suggests. It is important to see all of the above analysis in the light of these reservations. There are three, called the 'iron grid effect', the 'holding company effect', and the 'non-standard measures effect' described very briefly as follows.

The iron grid effect refers to the possibility that 'adaptation' of internal structure in government departments to influences of environment or technology may well be made impossible by strongly-held expectations, backed up by centrally-imposed regulations and size-related allocation rules. That is, that internal structure in government departments is *uniform*. The civil service may be a non-responsive set of organizations in structural terms and some observers say this is precisely what is wrong with it, the reason for what they see as its unsatisfactory performance. It is akin to Meyer's 'iron law of structural inertia' (Meyer, 1977). Bureaucratic organizations have put themselves in a straitjacket.

The second possible explanation of the lack of relationship between structure and type of work/environment in government departments is that the government department as such is not always, or even not often, the appropriate unit of analysis to show the effects sought. Adaptation may indeed occur, but be masked by the way the figures are collected. If a unit responds in its structure to changes in setting and in task, then in many cases the unit which would sense these changes is not the department as a whole, but a subdivision of the department, at first, second, or perhaps even third level of decomposition. The result would be a large number of adaptations inside one department, of which much would go unremarked at whole-department level. In business terms, one would not expect a 'holding company' type of structure to adapt but would look for adaptation in the individual 'profit centres'.

This is a plausible theory, and when sample checks were run on the various sectors of large departments like Defence, Environment, and Health and Social Security, it was indeed found that large variations occurred in several structural measures among units of the same department. Within the data to hand, a test was devised for the holding company effect by looking at structure/environment/type of work relationships at different size ranges, on the hypothesis that the smaller the organization, the more homogeneous it is likely to be, in type of work and environment, and the less likely is any relationship to be masked by a holding company effect. But no more evidence was found of an impact of environmental/type of work upon structure in the smaller organizational ranges than in the larger (neither did Blau et al., 1976). In fact, as noted above, such relationships as were found between size and complexity, got weaker in the smaller ranges. The opposite of what might be expected if the holding company effect was operating.

The third possible explanation for lack of correspondence between the survey's findings and those of earlier workers in other organizational settings is a matter of the measures used. Partly because of the inherent differences between government departments and other types of organization, and partly because of the limitations of the survey's research methods, the conventional contingency theory measures of structure, and of technology in particular, could not be used. Thus, while the 'spirit' of the exercise was by and large the same, the measures used in this study are 'non-standard', and so not strictly comparable with other work. Certainly this work cannot be said to be a replication of other work. The findings, accordingly, are not strictly comparable either.

This exercise in testing contingency theories by bureaumetric methods, therefore, has yielded uncertain results. It can be shown that in British government departments a number of measures of administrative structure, political salience, financial environment and type of work or technology are all related to size, and that there are not very clear relationships between any of these that are not associated with size. But it is perhaps just as important to know that some characteristics of administrative structure are not related to size, and apparently not related to anything else either. The shape of the department in terms of staff in top, middle and bottom grades, the size of the administrative component, the number of fringe bodies and the degree of concentration/dispersion territorially, and some others all remain unexplained by anything the survey applied as suggested by contingency theory. There is a high degree of what Child (1972) calls 'strategic choice', in the sense that size, financial structure, political salience and the other factors appear to have no determinate or automatic constraining effect on many aspects of structure in government departments as they are now. This conclusion holds whether it is thought of as a good thing or a bad thing.

As for contingency theory itself, the only conclusion from the testing must be that the results are inconclusive. Contingency theory is neither finally upheld nor finally undermined. Perhaps more doubt has been thrown on its universality. But contingency theory no longer holds the sway it did among organizational analysts in any case.

Mapping and categorizing

All the analysis so far has been on an aggregate basis, exploring the relationships between one continuous variable and another for a given statistical population. That is, one says of a population (in this case, of government departments) that there is such and such a relationship between size and complexity, for example, in that population. That says nothing specific about any particular member of the population; it only tells us about patterns in the population as a whole (or, if the research is longitudinal, about trends of change in the population). The particular characteristics (or *character*) of the individual department are unobservable in the analysis and what is known, is known about the set of departments. That may be valuable knowledge. The finding that there is no relationship in British central government departments between overall staff size and the number of mandarins, for example, contrary to what might be assumed, is at least interesting and may avert error.

But bureaumetric data may also be used in another way, to focus attention on each individual department, to ask what its characteristics are, to locate it in relation to others, and put it into categories, or families. Most people are aware that government departments differ from one another. Contrary to a fairly universal disparaging stereotype, they are not identical, equally filled with equally faceless bureaucrats. There are large departments and small departments; departments almost entirely located in the capital city and departments with offices all over the country; getting departments and spending departments; departments concerned with internal matters and departments concerned with foreign affairs; law and order departments; economic departments; social departments and so on. This list of distinctions could easily be doubled without becoming in the least esoteric and these classifications are made and understood by ordinary citizens. If you ask, "What kind of a department is the department of X?", the answer will involve placing the department of X on one or more of these dimensions of difference.

Systematically classifying government departments in multidimensional space, in order to furnish a more formal and rigorous map of the bureaucratic terrain than can be intuited by even the most senior and experienced 'old hand' in Whitehall-watching, was the second main exercise in bureaumetrics which the University of York team undertook. Using the term 'map' pushes the metaphor to its limits, because a conventional map describes a given terrain in two or at most three dimensions, whereas current research was talking in terms of seventy or more dimensions, or a smaller but still large number if use is made of the 'composite indices' whose construction has already been explained. It was, therefore, decided to shift to another metaphor, the detection of 'family likenesses', on the analogy with human experience, that members of the same family (even the extended family) can display remarkable variety on any one characteristic, whether of appearance or behaviour, and yet betray a recognisable likeness to one another in general.

So the questions to ask of the data became, not 'is variable A related to variable B in this set of organizations (as it appears to be in other sets)?', but 'is department X more like department Y than department Z?' or, 'which departments are at the extremes of any particular scale?', and 'taking all scales together, which departments belong together?'. To answer questions like these, statistical techniques were needed that will operate on the data independently of conventional classifications and uninfluenced by preconceptions of what 'putting like with like' implies.

One such technique is 'Cluster Analysis'. In conventional classification, one begins with a set of categories whose 'meaning' is defined, and any problems arise from the difficulties of assigning cases to categories. In certain circumstances, further techniques (such as discriminant analysis) can be used to improve the 'fit' of the categories to the cases. But cluster analysis, by contrast, does not begin with a set of categories at all. The computer, as it were, tells us what the groupings or clusterings are, by constructing a multidimensional space and then noting which cases in this space are close to one another (think of clusters of stars in the heavens, although that of course is only three-dimensional space). The problem for the researcher is then to try and grasp what it is the computer is fastening on to, what properties each cluster shares, in order to label intelligibly the categories thus elicited.

Cluster analysis exercises were carried out in the three main conceptual areas already described: administrative structure, political salience, and environment/type of work. A fourth one was also introduced, using some of the indices which had been constructed rather than the raw variables, to explore the extent to which departments clustered consistently from one conceptual area to the others and whether an overall pattern might be seen.

Some of the clusters proved quite interesting. One such cluster was a group of small, self-financing, non-ministerial departments (i.e. not headed by a Minister of their own), including the Office of Fair Trading, the National Debt Office and the Public Works Loan Board. Another contained the parliamentary offices, the record offices and the national museums, an intuitively acceptable grouping that seems to come together on account of their small size, low structural complexity, lack of any important self-financing component in their budgets, and the relatively low proportion of administrative staff. But a third cluster is both what might be expected and at the same time, quite remarkable. It comprises the major Scottish Office departments, plus the Cabinet Office. (In a second analysis by a different method, for checking purposes, the Cabinet Office moves out and the major Scottish Office departments cluster all on their own.) What could be more natural? The interesting point is that the computer did not *know* that these departments were Scottish and could not have isolated them because of that. They come together because they all have a high proportion of senior and executive staff, score low on financial structure and financial uncertainty, and have relatively few first-level commands. They just happen to be more like each other than they are like any UK-wide or England-and-Wales department (except the Cabinet Office).

How do these findings about the 'families' into which British government departments fall compare with other people's categorizations? The most common 'conventional' categorizations of British central government departments are (a) into 'giant' departments and the rest, and (b) by 'major function', or what is called distinction by policy field, into e.g. law and order, financial, social, and so on. The questions then are whether these analyses pick out the 'giants' from the rest, and the extent to which the groupings can be construed as policy fields.

The 'giants' in British terminology are the departments which were created in the 1960s and 1970s in pursuit of a policy of merging cognate departments under one administrative roof for better co-ordination. There were originally four of these; Defence, Health and Social Security, Environment and Trade and Industry (the last was never particularly 'giant' in size but it was formed by merger of previously distinct offices). Of these, Defence and DHSS do indeed stand out from the rest in our analyses. They form 'clusters of one' on both structure and environment/type of work dendrograms. The Department of the Environment, on the other hand, shares its salient characteristics with other departments (notably MAFF), and does not stand out particularly. The old Department of Trade and Industry was split up again in 1974, into four separate departments (Trade, Industry, Energy, and Prices), and entered the analyses in that form. It is of interest that Trade, Industry and Energy are members of the same cluster by structure and also by political salience, but they go separate ways on environment/type of work. They all come together again in the composite dendrogram, however (and possibly Prices would too, but for its budgetary eccentricity). It is only possible to speculate that something similar might be found if the other giants could be dissected in that way.

For the present purpose, perhaps the clearest presentation of a categorization of government departments by substantive policy field was that of a former Head of the Home Civil Service (Armstrong, 1970), who grouped central government into five substantive sectors, territorial departments, and central departments. Not all of the survey departments appear in the Armstrong classification, but grouping the major departments into his categories would produce the following:

Sector 1 (Overseas and Defence)	FCO, MOD, ODM
Sector 2 (Financial, Economic, Industrial)	Treasury, Trade, Industry, Energy, Prices, Employment, MAFF
Sector 3 (Physical)	DOE
Sector 4 (Social)	DES, DHSS
Sector 5 (Law and Order)	Home Office, Lord Chancellor
Central departments	Treasury, CSD, Cabinet Office, Privy Council
Territorial departments	Scottish Office departments, Welsh Office, N. Ireland Office

Comparing these sectors with the survey groupings, it is clear that there is not much congruence. The three 'Overseas and Defence' departments never fall into the same cluster in any of the survey analyses, and even pair by pair, they come together infrequently and only with others. Armstrong's Sector 3 is now one department, though it was not in 1970. The two Sector 4 departments never appear in the same cluster, nor do the two Sector 5 departments (the law and order sector). Only the second sector, financial, economic, industrial, can be said to work quite well as an empirical cluster, although all seven departments never actually cluster together. Trade, Industry, Energy and MAFF are grouped and fall into the same neighbourhood as Employment. All five cluster together in political salience, and Trade and Treasury also appear together once or twice.

Armstrong's 'central departments' appear in the same cluster only in the political salience analysis, otherwise they are fairly well scattered. The Treasury does not appear in the same cluster as CSD, or the Cabinet Office, or the Privy Council Office, and none of the last three appears with another except in the large catch-all cluster in political salience. The territorial departments never appear together in a cluster either, though all the Scottish departments notably do, and on the neighbourhood map the Welsh Office is linked in with the Scottish departments (but the Northern Ireland Office is not in the network at all).

The evidence from this particular comparison is that Armstrong's 'policy field' classification does not reflect to any significant extent any underlying affinities among departments in terms of administrative structure, political salience, or environment and type of work. What of the alternative possibility, that 'policy field coherence' can nevertheless be seen in the clusterings revealed in the survey's analyses? Well, one could point to the consistent clustering together of the museums, which with one exception fall in the same group in all four analyses and possibly to the way that Defence emerges as *sui generis*. Although the Scottish departments do cluster, somewhat surprisingly, 'Scottishness' is dubiously a 'policy field' matter since these departments straddle all 'fields'. But outside these possibilities, the evidence for a connection between policy field distinctions among central government departments and the kinds of distinctions being investigated is almost entirely lacking.

That is not to say that policy field classifications have somehow been discredited. They will remain the basis of everyday operational groupings of departments for most people's purposes, probably. But multidimensional analysis may have alerted people to an alternative that might not otherwise have occurred to them. It has shown that there is fairly strong empirical support, stable through several independent analyses, for a conclusion that departments in British central government are of three main types.

1. Departments headed by a minister, financially and structurally complex and politically salient, divided again into large and medium-sized if required.

2. Small non-ministerial administrative departments, divided again into tax-financed and self-financing.

3. The 'fringe', comprising the museums, record offices, and parliamentary offices.

Outside those patterns, the Ministry of Defence is in a category of its own and there are some grounds for regarding the Scottish Office departments (quite apart from any Scottishness) as a distinct type when seen 'in the round'. These categories are not perhaps very startling. But this, after all, has been a first venture, and mainly to explore the potentialities of the techniques. Some small part of these analyses may bear closer study and expansion, for particular policy purposes.

These were exercises in what might be called 'pure bureaumetrics'. Some 'applied bureaumetrics' studies of the cross-sectional kind were also carried out, looking into the 'allocation of portfolios' problem, exploring the properties of agency type, and making a closer study of the Scottish Office in the UK context (see Hood and Dunsire, 1981: Part III). But for the present account it is now time to turn to longitudinal applications of the bureaumetrics techniques.

Longitudinal studies:
testing theories of bureaucratic behaviour
So far time-series have been employed not so much to refine the findings of cross-sectional analyses as to test with empirical data a number of common assertions about trends and behaviour patterns in this area of bureaucratic structure and practice. For these purposes a much reduced number of both units and variables can provide evidence of good quality. A population of about twenty-seven departments is now being used (the major ones, omitting the 'fringe') which still gives a wide range of size and other characteristics and a list of variables in single figures. The span of years being worked with was also pragmatically chosen. 1972 saw the inauguration of a new series of one of our major sources, and several others were revised at about the same time, so that 1972-to-the-latest-available-table is our timespan for many investigations.

The first of these to be reported here concerns what is often referred to as the 'economic theory of bureaucracy'. It is as it were an article of faith among many economists (following Tullock, 1965; Niskanen, 1971) that bureaucrats are 'economic men' just like businessmen, maximizing their personal advantage through their operations, though not in the market and not in terms of financial gain only, but in the bureaucratic setting (what might be thought of as the 'policy market'), and with pay-offs in intangibles such as power and prestige as well as salaries and perquisites. It is a large theme, and only a part of it was tackled; the assertion/assumption that bureaucrats are budget-maxi-mizers, that bureaucrats reap utility from a large budget (see Niskanen, 1971; Wagner, 1973; Williamson, 1975; Pommerehne and Frey, 1978; Hall, 1980: 216; Kristensen, 1980; Jackson, 1982: 124). An increase in budget is sought by bureaucrats because some part of any increase can be converted into private benefits (e.g. the possibility of enlarging one's staff, or of general expansion raising the possibilities of promotion, additional equipment or travel, and so on). Conversely, budget cuts are resisted because of the private disamenity that will accompany a reduction in spending on public objectives. Within budgets, 'rational' self-regarding bureaucrats, presented with any chance to argue for more 'bureaucrat-intensive' methods of service-delivery as against 'money-moving' and less bureaucrat-intensive methods, will always press for the former because of the greater possibilities of private conversion.

These theories are not alleging widespread *corruption* in public services, rake-offs, kickbacks, bribes and similar venalities and crimes (if such exist, they are not defended). Rather the tone is one of world-weary realism. Let us recognize that bureaucrats are human and that they live by the same kind of lights as do the rest of us. The economic appreciation of bureaucratic motivation has 'passed into the language', we *all* now know that the enormous success of the television comedy programme *Yes, Minister* arises from its articulating, through humour, truths which would not be countenanced as objective description, as when the fictitious Permanent Secretary, Sir Humphrey Appleby, says:

> The Civil Service does not make profits or losses. *Ergo*, we measure success by the size of our staff and budget. By definition, a big department is more successful than a small one . . . this simple proposition is the basis of our whole system. (Lynn and Jay, 1981: 57)

British non-economist commentators tend to take one of two lines of criticism of all this. The first points to some well-known differences between the bureaucratic milieux in Britain and in the United States. The latter is much more decentralized and business oriented anyway, the former tightly knit and controlled, with the higher ranks socialized into an ethos that stresses service-wide standards and places higher value on administrative operations that are 'lean' than on bureaucratic 'bloat' (Self, 1972; Kogan, 1973; Young, 1974). In the British civil service, promotions at higher levels are centralized and conditions of work (including accommodation and floor-space, furniture and fittings) are laid down by well-policed rules and staff complement and salary levels are not at the discretion of bureau chiefs. Some of the most prestigious and (to the ambitious) most desirable departments in

British central government have relatively small budgets and staffs, e.g. Treasury, Cabinet Office. Not even the most acerbic permanent secretary in real British life would be likely to agree with Sir Humphrey that the key to advancement in the higher reaches of the British civil service lies in simply raising your budget higher and higher. Some would say that the self-regarding British civil servant is more likely to *avoid* budgetary and other growth if he can, as being irreconcilable with 'on-the-job leisure', from which the bureaucrat may also derive utility (Leibenstein, 1976: 95–117; Jackson, 1982: 133; Peacock, 1983: 128).

The other line of criticism of the theoretical 'economic' model of bureaucratic behaviour accepts that British civil servants resist cost-cutting and staff-saving exercises, but holds that this is accounted for less by the maximizing of private benefits by individuals than by collective preservation of the civil service's autonomy, a defence mechanism and closing of ranks against threats to their way of life and accustomed modes of operation. Hence the fate of successive attempts to introduce business efficiency methods into central government departments (cf. Chapman, 1978; Hennessey, 1984; Fry, 1985).

There are two difficulties in tackling the question as to whether expansion of the British government's budget as a whole has brought identifiable benefits to the civil service as such. One lies in how to measure such benefits, and track down the evidence. The other lies in controlling the changing value of the money in which government budgets are expressed, over any period long enough to provide satisfactory answers. For the first difficulty, survey solutions were governed by the data it proved possible to collect by unobtrusive methods and settled for indices of (a) total civil service staff; (b) top staff (under secretary and above); (c) numbers of personal secretaries to top staff; (d) numbers of administrative staff — the 'generalists' of all ranks, from top to bottom. If directing officials are benefiting in other than a criminal way from increase in budget, it was reasoned, this ought to show up somewhere in these figures.

As for the second difficulty, recent work has shown that the general consumer price index may not accurately measure change in the prices of the mix of purchases that government typically makes (Beck, 1976; Heald, 1983; 179–80: Alt and Chrystal, 1983: 188–9). So converting the actual value of government spending in current cash terms to constant-price values may give different results depending on the deflator used. To guard against this four different official price indices were used (the retail, producer, and pensioner price indices published in the Treasury's publication *Economic Trends*, and an implied index of costs and prices for government final consumption published in the annual *National Income and Expenditure*), and found to be so highly correlated that any one of them could be used. Figure 5.1 shows two curves for government expenditure. The heavy line is actual spending by central government departments in cash terms. The dashed line shows what total government expenditure would have been if it had been subject to no policy change whatsoever since the base year and had simply risen in line with inflation as measured by Retail Price Index (RPI) (this line is, of course, simply the rise in RPI itself).

FIGURE 5.1
Central government spending and RPI

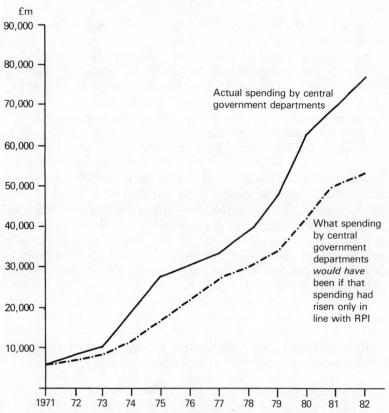

Source: Appropriation Accounts; Economic Trends.

It can be seen that the budget rose appreciably in real terms. Whereas between 1971 and 1982 (the latest year for which figures were available) RPI rose just over 300 percent, government spending as deflated by the same index rose about 444 percent, an increase in real value of around 36 percent. Was part of that increase channelled into benefits for bureaucrats, as measured by the indices listed earlier? Table 5.1 gives the figures.

TABLE 5.1
Selected civil service staff categories, 1972 to 1983

Year (1)	Total CS staff (2)	Top staff (ranking U/S and above) (3)	(3) as % of (2) (4)	Personal secretaries (5)	(5) as % of (2) (6)	Administration group staff (7)	(7) as % of (2) (8)
1972	701,896	723.0	0.10	4,581	0.65	220,654	31.4
1973	692,656	771.0	0.11	4,025	0.58	230,654	33.2
1974	694,384	817.0	0.11	3,941	0.56	262,727	37.8
1975	693,921	761.5	0.10	3,883	0.55	267,822	38.5
1976	745,120*	774.0	0.10	4,811	0.64	251,851	33.8
1977	746,161	788.0	0.10	4,837	0.64	252,747	33.9
1978	737,984	813.0	0.11	4,810	0.65	251,758	34.1
1979	733,176	814.0	0.11	4,772	0.65	250,908	34.2
1980	707,620	813.0	0.11	4,776	0.67	240,137	33.9
1981	695,070	770.0	0.11	4,785	0.68	238,297	34.3
1982	675,424	736.0	0.10	4,700	0.69	236,274	34.9
1983	652,534	694.0	0.11	4,624	0.70	231,662	35.5

Sources: (2) *CS Statistics*; (3) *CS Statistics*; (5) HM Treasury; (7) HM Treasury.
*this big surge reflects the re-inclusion of about 21,000 MSC staff in the civil service manpower figures.

In so far as the theoretical expectation is that some of the growth would be siphoned off into general expansion of the civil service, it does not appear to be borne out. Although there were fluctuations, total staff *fell* over the period. Of course, we do not know that the environment was constant, or that technological changes would not point to an even greater fall than actually occurred. But as things are, there is no correlation between numbers of civil service staff and size of central government's budget (whether in current or in constant prices) over the period examined.

Bureaucratic surplus, however, may have been extracted in other ways than increase in overall numbers. Perhaps, within a stagnant total, there were more 'chiefs' and fewer 'indians', or perhaps (as Peacock has suggested, 1983: 128) the opportunity was taken to increase the proportion of administrative grades relative to the rest. But Table 5.1 does not offer much support for the first of these possibilities. The proportion of chiefs to 'indians' fluctuates within a very narrow band and for all practical purposes is constant. This in itself bears out one of the assumptions of the economic theorists, that

the number of subordinates per supervisor is rather rigidly fixed in the public administration hierarchy, [and so] the more members a government department has, the more superior positions there are and the larger the absolute number of administrators with (relatively) high incomes. (Pommerehne and Frey, 1978; 99)

It becomes apparent that the ratio of subordinates to supervisors *is not* rigid, as may be seen when considering the matter department by department. Clearly however, the chiefs in this instance failed to follow the logic through, for although they *did* manage a small proportional increase in the number of administrative grades, relative to total staff, they did not seem to reap personal advantage from it.

Perhaps they took the surplus out in the way of 'perks' rather than posts? In the British civil service perks are relatively scarce, compared with the company cars, privileged stock-options and so on which are typically enjoyed by executives of private sector companies. Knighthoods, other 'gongs' and the chance of lucrative directorships on retirement at sixty or resignation earlier, bear no logical relation to size of either budget or staff. One of the relatively few perks officially available to top civil servants during their service, again, much more rarely than in the private sector, is the assignment of a personal secretary.

Table 5.1 indicates that numbers of personal secretaries did indeed go up during the period, absolutely and in relation to the number of civil servants generally (though it fell slightly in relation to the number of administration group staff, down from 2.076 percent to 1.996 percent). So it is just possible that senior civil servants did use the high degree of discretionary power the theory says they derive from 'information-impactedness' (Williamson, 1975), to get themselves a few more personal secretaries.

Alternatively, the reason could be entirely different. Perhaps the bureaucratic surplus was not extracted in the form of more civil servants, more top jobs or perks, but in salary increases and rises in pay-related benefits such as pensions. That would, after all, be the most straightforward way of using power, individually or collectively. Budget/utility theories of bureaucracy do not specify precisely how this should be expected to operate, so four extreme hypotheses were proposed about the ways in which real increases in central government's budget might be related to changes in civil service pay costs, to see which came closest to what actually happened. The hypotheses were as follows:

Hypothesis 1
The *whole* or a large proportion of any real increase in government's budget is appropriated in the form of pay and/or pay-related perks for the civil service.

If all real budgetary increases were spent in this way, over time it would result in an increase in the proportion of the total government budget devoted to pay and pay-related perks.

Hypothesis 2
As government budget changes, a constant proportion of it is devoted to

pay and perks, following the old 'poundage' principle once used for paying tax collectors.

If this were the case, rational, self-interested bureaucrats would still be strongly motivated to seek increases in budget, since they would share *pari passu* in any such increase. Consequently, it would be found that the pay and perks of civil servants constituted a more or less constant percentage of the total central government budget, as the latter changed.

Hypothesis 3
there is *no* increase (but also no decrease) in the real level of pay and pay-related perks of the civil service as the real level of central government's budget rises.

Here it would be found that the level of pay and perks remained constant in relation to RPI, though not necessarily in relation to the government's budget, as the latter changed.

Hypothesis 4
the real level of civil service pay and pay-related perks *falls* while the real level of government's overall budget rises.

In this instance, pay and perks would fall in relation to RPI.

Figure 5.2 shows two fine lines and a heavy line. The higher fine line indicates what spending on civil service pay and perks would have been over the period 1971 to 1982 if it had remained proportional to total government budget as at 1971 (the outcome would not be materially different if the year 1972 or 1973 were taken as the base). This line therefore represents *Hypothesis 2* and a level of spending anywhere above it on the graph would be consistent with *Hypothesis 1*. The lower of the two fine lines indicates what spending on pay and perks over the period would have been had it remained in line with the rise in the RPI since 1971. It therefore represents *Hypothesis 3* and a level of actual spending anywhere below that line would be consistent with *Hypothesis 4*.

The heavy line in Figure 5.2 shows what the total amount spend on civil service pay and pay-related perks actually was, as estimated by official sources. Clearly both the first and the fourth hypotheses are rejected by the facts (although the graph cannot show, because it is designed to cover the period as a whole, that *Hypothesis 4* would apply in some individual years). As can be seen, the observation of what actually happened in this period falls somewhere between the second and third hypotheses. Pay rose by less than would have been necessary to keep it in proportion to real increase in government spending, but by more than would have sufficed simply to keep it in line with inflation. Thus, some part of the increase in budgets can be said to have gone to improving civil service pay levels. Whether that part was large enough

FIGURE 5.2
Estimates for the total cost of the civil service (including pensions)
1971 to 1982

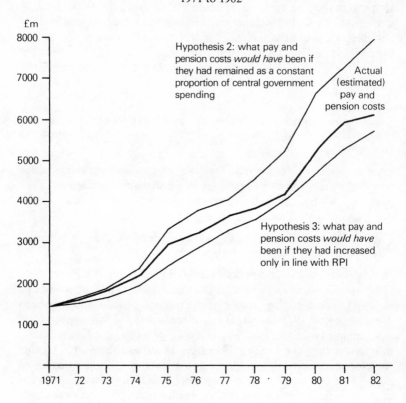

Source of data: Economic Trends; Memorandum by the Chief Secretary to the Treasury on the Supply Estimates.

to sustain the economic theory of bureaucratic behaviour, or merely to avoid its complete rejection, is a matter of opinion.

Looking at civil service pay costs over the period in per capita rather than aggregate terms, a rather higher rate of increase is shown, because of the fall in total staff numbers. However the observed pattern still lies between *Hypothesis 2* and *Hypothesis 3*, rising more than the RPI but proportionately less than the overall budget.

Two other points might be made before turning to the department by department analysis. Firstly, what is postulated of bureaucratic behaviour by the budget/utility link theories is postulated *a fortiori* of top civil servants, the chiefs, who are assumed to be the closest to budget-making, the most powerful in terms of their control over information and so the most able to reap self-regarding benefits from a bureaucratic surplus. It is significant therefore that, although civil service pay in general (excluding superannuation) rose by 336.5 percent in the period under review against a rise in RPI of 300.8 percent, the pay of under secretaries rose by 224.9 percent, that of deputy secretaries by 191.3 percent and that of permanent secretaries by 136.9 percent (official sources). Either these people are not motivated in the way the theories assume, or they are extraordinarily inept in looking after their own interests.

The second point to be made is that although per capita pay in the civil service, if superannuation benefits are included, did rise over the period 1973 to 1982 (a convenient period for the comparison, though 1970 to 1982 would give the same result) by between 1 and 2 percent in real terms, real per capita earnings (disregarding pension provisions) in all industries and service in Great Britain rose by just over 9 percent (data from *Department of Employment Gazette*, December issue 1980 and 1983: Table 5.6). If civil service superannuation is omitted, civil service per capita pay *fell* by over 6 percent. This too is something of a problem for the economic theories of bureaucracy, which tend to assume that civil service salaries, lacking the hard discipline of the market, are always cushioned against falls relative to the private sector.

Thus one would have to conclude that economic theories of bureaucratic behaviour are at best not very good at predicting the relationship between rise in overall budget and private benefits gained by civil servants in Britain, at least as shown by aggregate civil-service-wide figures. Are they perhaps better at departmental level?

One advantage of operating at department by department level is that it avoids the need to deflate actual spending totals, whether for the department or for the government as a whole. By determining the proportion of total government expenditure which each department disposes of, and ranking departments in that order, it is possible to note whether a department rises or falls in the 'league table' of spending. It is also possible to see whether one that rises in the budgetary league also rises in some other league table representing appropriated 'private' benefits, and correspondingly, departments which lose rank position in budget terms also decline in other rankings. If that were to happen, it would provide clear underpinning for conventional economic theories of bureaucratic behaviour.

Ten individual departments which existed in more or less unchanged form over the decade 1972 to 1982, were selected and as well as being ranked by budget share for each year, they were also ranked by share of total civil service staff, and share of 'top staff' (as before, personnel of the rank of under secretary and above). Incidentally, it was noted again, as in the earlier cross-sectional study, that ratio of top staff to total staff is not a civil service constant, but differs markedly from

TABLE 5.2
Four types of relationship between share of central government budget, share of civil service 'chiefs' and share of total civil service staff — 10 departments 1971–82

| | | Correlation with share of central government budget | | |
| | | Share of total CS staff | Share of total CS 'chiefs' (a) | |
Group	Department			Comment
1	DOE	r = 0.8***	r = 0.8**	Increase in share of total civil service staff
	Sc. Office	r = 0.6*	r = 0.8**	and share of civil service 'chiefs' relates
	W. Office	r = 0.7**	r = 0.7*	to increase in share of central government budget
2	DHSS	r = 0.8***	n.s	Increase in share of total civil service staff
	MAFF	r = 0.8***	n.s.	(but *not* share of civil service chiefs) relates
	HO	r = 0.8**	n.s.	to increase in share of central government budget
3	Treasury	n.s.	r = 0.8***	Increase in share of 'chiefs' (but *not* share of total CS staff) relates to increase in share of central government budget
4	MOD	n.s.	n.s.	*Neither* share of total civil service staff
	Employment	n.s.	n.s.	*nor* share of civil service chiefs is related
	DES	n.s.	n.s.	to share of central government budget

Source of data: *Appropriation Accounts; Civil Service Statistics*; HM Treasury.

Significance levels: *p = 5 percent **p ⩽ 1 percent ***p ⩽ 0.1 percent n.s. = not significant
(a) Total figures here refer to the totals for the 34 biggest central government departments over the period 1971–82; a few very small departments (museums, registry offices, etc.) are excluded.

department to department. It was also found that within a particular department the ratio can change over time. In six of these ten departments over the period, top staff numbers increased by a smaller percentage than did total staff, so that the proportion of chiefs fell. In the other four departments, there was no clear relationship at all between changes in total staff and changes in top staff.

To return to the comparative ranking exercise, Table 5.2 presents the findings. The relationship between share of budget, share of total staff, and share of top staff is clear, for some departments. The three departments in Group 1 in the table might be said to conform to the predictions of conventional budget/utility theory. However, an equal number of departments (Group 4) show no statistically significant relationship among the three items and so might be said to contradict the theory. The remaining departments (Groups 2 and 3 in the table) show significant relationships between changes in budgetary share and changes in *either* total staff share *or* top staff share (but not both). The picture does not change in principle (although one or two departments shift groups) if one uses absolute figures instead of proportions of total. It can be said, as a general and robust conclusion, that *some* departments show a significant relationship between an increment in budget and an increase in what could be regarded as bureaucratic benefits, but that in a roughly equal number of cases, no such relationship can be detected.

Looking at expenditure on *salaries* (excluding superannuation costs) as percentage of gross actual spending in the decade, some departments reproduce the aggregate-level picture of a slight fall in the proportion of pay costs to total spending (and this seems to happen irrespective of whether departments have climbed or fallen in the budget league), while other departments show an increase in that proportion. Once again, whether or not the predictions of the theory of bureaucratic behaviour are realized seems to depend upon the department chosen for analysis.

The conclusions from this exercise, both at aggregate or macro-level and at departmental or meso-level, were accordingly that the economic theories of bureaucratic behaviour cannot be set aside altogether, but that neither can they be relied on as they stand now. There is, after all, an alternative explanation which would better account for *everything* that has been found, namely, that the disposition of such bureaucratic benefits as senior posts, personal secretaries, pay rises and staff increases in general, is a consequence of *specific policy decision* — which might or might not be related to budgetary changes, according to circumstances. (The problem with *that* explanation is that it will explain *anything*.)

The findings about budget/utility theory might be interpreted in two ways. Firstly, they might be read as a special case, since only the British central government scene — which may be asserted to be rather peculiar, in the broader world of bureaucracies — has been looked at. Secondly, they might be read as indicating rather that the theory simply needs refinement, it is, as it were, *bound* to be true, so long as you specify the situation sufficiently. This research, moreover, indicates the necessary lines of development. An improved budget/utility theory will have to be able to move away from the simple equation of *any* budgetary expansion with *all* bureaucratic utility and specify, on the one hand, what *kinds* of budgetary increase might lead to higher extraction of bureaucratic surplus (for instance, even large increases arising from demand-led transfers such as welfare benefits are unlikely to generate as much surplus as increases in smaller but highly discretionary funds). On the other hand, what *kinds* of utility are likely to be extracted (augmentation of staff, more promotion, more leisure, etc.) in what circumstances, and to what degree. In other words, if an economic theory of bureaucracy is to be worth anything, it has to be more like a good economic theory of the market, which can predict what degree of 'consumer surplus' to expect in different market conditions. It might then be able to explain why bureau chiefs in

Britain, with all the power and political resources they are usually said to possess, have been so singularly unsuccessful in the period under review in translating budgetary growth into increases in take-home pay for themselves. It might explain why budgetary increases appear to be associated with bureaucratically appropriable benefits in some departments, but not in others.

This analysis has not shown that such an improved budget/utility theory is in principle possible, or impossible. Nor has it shown that a worthwhile theory would be worth developing; merely that if such a theory is to be used, it would be better for it to be a good one.

Testing theories of reorganization

Administrative reform or bureaucratic reorganization has a long history and mounds of literature (for reviews, see Caiden, 1970; Leemans, 1976; Chapman and Greenaway, 1980; Pollitt, 1984). As Leemans pointed out (1976: 50) fashions change concerning what should be reformed. At one time, stress is all on change in *structure*, under the influence of some version of the structure/performance hypothesis. At another time, the emphasis is on selecting, training and motivating the right *people*, under the influence of 'human relations theory' and organizational psychology; and at another, all problems are to be solved by new *procedures*, from Organisation and Methods in the early days, through output budgeting and Programme Analysis and Review to the latest in Whitehall gadgetry, FMI (financial management initiative), under the influence of economics and business management. It is fairly general amongst academic commentators on this subject now to treat all proposals for administrative reform with scepticism, and to point out that no one seems much interested in follow-up studies, to see whether the changes made have produced the effects promised. The political pay-off is frequently taken at the 'front end', in the trumpeted inauguration of the reform, but for most of those involved, it may be better never to know whether it worked or not.

In Whitehall between 1971 and 1984 there were ten cases of what might be called 'bureau-shuffling' — mergers and splits, two departments becoming one, or one becoming two (or more). Usually the reasons given referred to changes in policy emphasis, or administrative coherence, or in one case, ministerial overload. Pollitt (1984) has provided an analysis of the events and their setting. What the survey set out to do was a limited exercise in evaluation, to explore through its bureaumetric variables some of the more readily-measurable consequences of these Whitehall changes. The ten cases are listed in Table 5.3.

The initial investigation looked at the possibility that mergers take place between departments that are like one another, and demergers occur when sectors of a department are, or have grown, dissimilar. Often the ostensible reason for reform is to 'put like with like', though it is usually *policy coherence* that is in mind. If civil service reductions are in train, it may be thought necessary to combine responsibility for cutting budgets with responsibility for cutting staff numbers. Alternatively, ministers may believe that an export drive will be facilitated by bringing together trade promotion and industrial sponsorship and so on. It could, however, be that policy field coherence is itself an index for a more general administrative similarity. On the commonsense assumption that what you are trying to do influences the tools you use and the people you employ, it would not be unexpected to find departments broadly similar as administrative operations attracting each other policy-wise and departments composed of dissimilar elements being put under strain, resulting eventually in fission.

Six indices, as described earlier, were used, *top staff* (grades down to under secretary as percentage of total staff); *middle staff* (grades from assistant secretary down to higher executive officer and equivalent as percentage of total staff) — these two indices, together with the remainder of bottom staff, describe the shape or staff configuration of the department; *administrative staff* as percentage of total staff (the

TABLE 5.3
Mergers and demergers in Whitehall 1971–84: ten cases

Mergers
1 Department of Prices and Consumer Protection with the Department of Trade, 1979 (Pr and Tr)
2 Ministry of Overseas Development (ODM) with the Foreign and Commonwealth Office (FCO), 1979
3 Department of Education and Science (DES) with the Office of Arts and Libraries (OAL), 1980/81
4 HM Treasury and part of the Civil Service Department (CSD), 1981
5 The Lord Chancellor's Office with the Office of the Public Trustee (PTO), 1982
6 The Department of Trade with the Department of Industry (DoI), 1983

Demergers
7 The Department of Trade and Industry into the Department of Industry, the Department of Trade, the Department of Energy, and the Department of Prices and Consumer Protection, 1973 (DTI, DoI, DTr, DEn, Pr)
8 The Foreign and Commonwealth Office into the FCO and the Ministry of Overseas Development (ODM) in 1974
9 The Department of the Environment (DOE) into DOE and the Department of Transport (DOT), 1976
10 The Department of Education and Science (DES) into DES and the Office of Arts and Libraries, 1979

Note: For some purposes case number 6, the remerger of Trade and Industry, was too recent to be included in the analysis.

balance of generalists and specialists, very broadly considered); *salary costs* as percentage of total budget (indicates degree of 'bureaucracy-heaviness', as compared with 'money-shifting' styles of operation); *departmental budget* as percentage of total Government budget (relative financial size); and *departmental staff* as percentage of total government staff (relative staff size). Because the remerger of Trade with Industry in 1983 was only taking place while the work was being done, that case was excluded from this analysis.

The most cursory glance at the data found in Table 5.3 throws doubt on the theory. Take the two Foreign and Commonwealth Office FCO cases. The Overseas Development Ministry ODM split off in 1974, and merged again in 1979. This part is three or four times the size of the rest of FCO in staff, is three or four times more 'bottom-heavy' in shape, considerably more 'generalist', and about forty times more 'money-moving' in administrative style. It seems clear that as administrative operations, FCO and ODM would never have attracted one another into a policy-field merger. Indeed, it might even appear that (as in magnetism proper) it is *unlikes* which attract one another. Except for that unlooked-for possibility, the better hypothesis must be that policy-field coherence is independent of administrative operational similarity.

However, what was more interesting were the *effects* of such reorganizations, rather than the reasons for them. Undoubtedly the best way of comparing effects would be to measure outputs before and after the events, but as is well known (cf. Heald 1983) measuring the outputs or performance of government departments is as yet a very difficult matter, especially if one wishes to do it comparatively. What had to be done here was to make the somewhat heroic assumption that output did not change on reorganization, and focus instead on *input*. Three principal hypotheses were explored regarding the impact of bureau reorganization on inputs:

(a) change in *scale* creates administrative economies or diseconomies;
(b) reorganization always produces cost escalation;
(c) reorganization in practice has little observable effect on bureaucratic structure and working.

Adam Smith (1762; 1776) was not the first to point to the 'economies of scale' — the idea that inputs need not grow as fast as outputs as the scale of production is increased. Administrative reformers in the 1960s and early 1970s were generally persuaded that increase in size could bring administrative advantages, in the ability to increase specialization of staff and yet keep them busy, to keep down training and other overheads, and the like. Others, however, leant the opposite way — larger enterprises become harder to co-ordinate and control, develop tendencies to X-inefficiency, and take too long to notice and correct their mistakes.

There is also the time factor. Diseconomies that appear in the short run might only be preliminary to greater economies later. People take time to 'settle in and bed down'. Or alternatively, there might be short-term 'honeymoon effects' that soon dissipate.

It was not felt that there could be a lot of scope for economies or diseconomies of scale to operate in the period under study, because for Whitehall as a whole, there was no evidence of an increase in *concentration* ratios — bigger departments getting bigger and small departments getting smaller. The nine largest departments in staff size accounted for about the same proportion of total staff throughout the period (*c.* 85 percent); the nine biggest spenders (not the same nine departments) likewise in share of total budget, and at the same level (between 86 percent and 89 percent). However, that could mask considerable differences between departments and certainly, there had been changes in scale, as departments merged and split. Assuming constant output, were there discernible economies in inputs, or the opposite, as measured by indices of top staff, specialist ratio, and so on?

The data was too detailed to present here (see Hood, Huby, Dunsire, 1985). Suffice it to say that no clear evidence was found of *dis*economies of scale in proportions of top staff and middle staff. Top management and middle management do not grow in relation to the total after mergers, as might be expected if larger scale means disproportionate increases in difficulty of managerial control. However, there do not appear to be any economies of scale either, in merged departments even if one discounts the first disruptive year or two. In some departments top staff proportion falls immediately but rises later. FCO/ODM shows a slight gain in top staff on merger, and a slight overall *fall* on demerger — the opposite to what one might expect. Changes in other indices appear *before* the event rather than after it, or simply continue a trend. The idea that mergers will lead to the more efficient use of ancillary staff and experts, and that the reverse will occur with demergers, gains no support either. Certainly, there are no dramatic 'before' and 'after' metamorphoses that leap out from the figures.

What of the second hypothesis, the wry expectation that whenever anything is reorganized, it becomes more expensive? The British taxpayer has got used to this, in relation particularly to the sweeping reforms of local government, the National Health Service, and the water industry in the 1970s and indeed, there are plenty of reasons why the phenomenon might occur. Severance and redundancy payments, perhaps; a tendency to 'level up' rather than down on facilities, grade-equivalents and the like; costs of rebuilding headquarters to accommodate merged staffs; more planners, advisers, personal assistants, public relations people, and other non-line appointments and, often remarked, relatively huge increases in salaries of top staff to 'compensate' for increased responsibilities. Some of these increases are less plausible in central government reorganizations, where salaries and appointments are rigidly controlled, but maybe other such effects occur there.

What actually happened, in the nine cases under review? Here again, no evidence of inexorable cost escalation was found. A department's share of total government expenditure does not rise appreciably after a reshuffle. Indeed, if anything, budget share *decreased* slightly (with two exceptions, one a rise, the other neither rise nor fall). Similarly, staff numbers did not rise. As a proportion of total civil service staff, staff size in reorganized departments typically seems to *fall* following mergers (one exception), and to fall slightly or remain steady in demergers. The caricature of reorganizations as inherently leading to budget creep and bureaucratic bloat cannot be sustained on this evidence (bearing in mind that constant output is assumed and productivity cannot be measured).

So to the third hypothesis, which has been formulated (by Meyer, 1977) as the 'Iron Law of Inertia'. The Law has several variants (Wallace, 1975: 23; Rourke 1976: 29), and many exponents. At its simplest, it states that structural reforms are 'skin-deep'; they change names and titles at the highest level, but at the next level down everything goes on as before. This hypothesis assorts well with the assertion that 'bureau-shuffling' is *political theatre*, a matter of personalities and power games among Ministers, absorbing to political journalists and commentators, but not actually of much consequence for what government achieves, or how it achieves it. Pollitt (1984) attributes most departmental reshuffles to considerations of high policy, party-balance and image-construction, not administrative effectiveness.

The Iron Law of Inertia argument is that when politicians play bricks with government bureaux for good or bad reasons, the bureaux, as going concerns, typically change hardly at all. There is plenty of administrative science anecdotal evidence (for example, see Barker, 1970: 7; Dunsire, 1961: 155; Thoenig and Friedberg, in Leemans 1976). Thoenig and Friedberg describe the merger of the Ministries of Public Works and Housing in France in 1966:

> The sectional directorates remained untouched, and only the Personnel and Budget Directorates of the two former Ministries were merged. Otherwise every service remained the same, with the same people and the same tasks: juxtaposition rather than integration. (Leemans 1976: 327)

The extent to which current data bore out the 'Iron Law' was explored, as expressed in these two hypotheses:

1. Changes in distribution of internal portfolios as a result of a

reorganization event (merger or demerger) will leave organizational pattern at the first level of decomposition (alternatively, at the second level of decomposition) unaffected.

2. The top directorate in the department(s) after merger or demerger will show continuity.

What 'first level of decomposition' means, as already noted, is the number of commands or administrative jurisdictions on the hierarchical level immediately below the top civil service or permanent (as distinct from political or ministerial) level in the department. The second level of decomposition is, correspondingly, the next step down in the hierarchy. Pure inertia would imply that the structure at the first (sub-Ministry) level remained exactly the same before and after reorganization, perhaps with the exception of finance and personnel branches (as in Thoenig and Friedberg's case). However, that would be unusual, for in the normal course of things government departments change internal portfolios a little year by year; then, a change a couple of years after a reorganization event might be a delayed response. Judgement is required. But the main discriminator, as to whether in mergers the first-level units are integrated (whole, or piece by piece) or are merely juxtaposed side by side, is not too difficult to apply; correspondingly in demergers, the continuance of 'going concerns'.

The data here is not statistical, and difficult to present in a treatment of this length. But it is clear enough that the inertia hypothesis is upheld in five of the cases and not upheld in the other five.

In the Department of Trade and Industry (DTI) demerger of 1974 (a split into four distinct ministries — Industry, Trade, Energy, and Prices) not one of the new ministries was formed by the budding-off of a sub-Ministry, entire and sole, as a going concern. Trade was closest but it included Shipping and Civil Aviation from another sub-Ministry (which itself disappeared as such). The new Energy department had originally been only a segment of a sub-Ministry in DTI, and was enhanced by sections from other sub-Ministries. Prices was an even smaller segment of a sub-Ministry, and waxed for a year or two on its own until the change of governing party in 1979 killed it altogether. So in the DTI demerger, going concerns were broken up and swallowed up, at sub-Ministry level. The same kind of story can be told of the splitting up of the Civil Service Department, and in the hiving-off of Transport from the Department of the Environment. In each case, units were transferred which were only parts of sub-Ministries and parts of *second*-level units — i.e. were units at the third level of decomposition. The inertia hypothesis was poor at predicting what happened, some bureaux did indeed move in and out of ministries unscathed, but others suffered insult or injury by being swallowed up or broken up.

Some instances of 'fireproof' bureaux emerged, however. A bureau from the Trade sub-Ministry of DTI, concerned with industrial property, insurance, company law and insolvency, persisted totally unchanged throughout the existence of the separate Department of Trade, without even a change of incumbent head, and emerged intact into the reconstituted DTI in 1984. Other bureaux persisted, but acquired or lost tasks. But more striking than these tales of second-level survival through storm and strife, is the imperturbability of the entire ministry of ODM through repeated merger and demerger with the FCO (those which come into our period were by no means the first in the department's history). Here, the juxtaposition thesis is convincingly supported. The two entities, FCO and ODM, come together and are sundered as entities, with hardly a sign of integration or proliferation attributable to merger or demerger as such.

The smaller reorganization events on this list were like FCO/DOM rather than DTI; minuscule transactions in comparison, but for what they are worth, showing nothing but juxtaposition.

Hence the answers to the finding on the inertia hypothesis, as tested on these internal reshufflings, must be yes and no. But, it could be said, the hypothesis might fare better at the *third* level of decomposition even where mergers and demergers do not take place cleanly along existing split-lines at sub-Ministry or bureau level, perhaps they do at a lower level. However, it was found that some of the changes moved pieces at even lower levels than that. In any case, saving the hypothesis by this means would render it vacuous and would merely say that there is a level at which civil servants' work is not affected by merger or demerger, without specifying that level, or the circumstances.

From the evidence, it would seem that inertia is more likely to apply the farther are the concerns at a bureau from those of ministers; the more it is dealing with a highly-specific clientele and long-established routines. But this is perhaps only to say that all policies change but some are less volatile, or stable, than others. The more there is a party-political interest, the more likely is a bureau to be split up or swallowed up. But that conclusion is far from watertight. For instance, one of the most persistent Industry bureaux was called Industrial and Commercial Policy.

Looking at the ten cases as a whole (six mergers and four demergers), it would seem that sometimes, at least at ministerial-level, cabinet-shuffling in Britain does have serious effects at administrative levels well below the superficial. This is still quite consistent, of course, with observations by individual civil servants that their daily work is affected but trivially (new headings on papers, etc.) — *so far as they can see*.

The hypothesis about continuity in top directing staff was tested by looking at whether the people at the helm in the departments created by the merger or the demerger had been already in a top or first-level post in the same department(s) before the event. The hypothesis was almost invariably supported. There was no example of a 'new broom' brought in from outside the Civil Service, or from a social background markedly different, to head a reorganized unit.

From the analysis as a whole, of this decade of administrative reorganization in British central government departments, considering the three principal hypotheses put forward (change in scale creates administrative economies or diseconomies, reorganization always increases costs, reorganization has little observable effect upon internal structure — the Iron Law of Inertia), the third seems the most applicable to the noted results, with some reservations only in the area of bureau-level reshuffles in some ministries. This conclusion can be interpreted in several ways. It might simply bear out the fundamental truth that you cannot alter the environmental and technological realities of service provision and delivery, in terms of requisite staff, skills, equipment, and routines, by redrawing departmental boundary lines. At operating levels, things are as they are because that is how they have to be.

Others might see the conclusion as evidence that you don't change bureaucratic behaviour by changing the command structure, only by changing the *rule* structure. The most obvious interpretation, on the other hand, might see the conclusion as further proof of the British civil servant's capacity to block innovation, resist change, and damp down any disturbance of comfortable habits.

Testing theories of what happens in fiscal crisis

Whether or not one puts it down to a 'crisis of capitalism' (O'Connor, 1973), there can be no doubt that a long period of government growth, culminating in what has been called the 'treble affluence' of the 1960s (Wright in Hood and Wright, 1981: 3; Rose, 1984: 219) is at an end, and that the later 1970s and early 1980s have been a time of cutback and retrenchment in public sector expenditure and staffing. This has produced a small literature of its own (Levine, 1978, 1981; Rose and Peters, 1978; Wright, 1980; Hood and Wright, 1981; Bramley and Stewart, 1981; Cohen, 1984; etc.) largely on the basis of short experience in individual sectors and theoretical generalizations. By now, public sector cutbacks have been in progress in Britain since the retrenchment imposed on the Labour government by the International Monetary Fund (IMF) in 1976 and since 1979 Britain has had a Conservative government pledged not only to reductions in public expenditure but also to a specific programme of staff reductions in the civil service. Bureaumetric techniques have been applied to a systematic assessment of what has been happening, on the basis of aggregate data of the kind described in the previous section, in central government departments.

Figure 5.2 has already made clear that during this period one is dealing *not* with massive cutbacks in central government expenditure in Britain, but rather, perhaps, with attempts to restrain inexorable growth. The first question asked was whether this restraint was imposed more or less equally 'across the board', or selectively. There are plenty of plausible reasons for expecting that the reflex impulse of bureaucracies faced with cuts will be to impose proportional reductions on each of their component parts. This is fair, it preserves parity of corporate esteem. It leaves undisturbed the budgetary configuration resulting from (often) decades of incremental budgeting and avoids the internecine battle that would follow any attempt to alter corresponding expectations. Besides, civil services have strong tendencies towards uniformity of structure, rigid personnel rules, and strong trade unions — all factors working against radical redeployment of resources. External lobbies which might tolerate piecemeal and minor reductions might mobilize in vehement protest against attacks on what they saw as their interests. Finally, timescale perceptions are important. If retrenchment is seen as a temporary 'belt-tightening', then the rational way to retain capability of future restoration of present levels of activity is to prune everything back a little without actually destroying capacity.

What actually happened? Seven annual observations (1976–83) over twenty-eight departments were used; except for one department (Health and Social Security (DHSS)) each department had a 'real' (inflation-adjusted) cut in budget in at least one year (DHSS had real *increases* in each year); five departments had one year of cut but then increased in each succeeding year; five had two years of cuts but otherwise increased in real terms in the other years; four were cut in three years; and the remaining thirteen were cut in four or more years out of the seven. Whatever the rationale behind the strategy, it was certainly not 'equal misery all round'. Nor is there evidence of 'equal misery' at first and selectively later. The picture is similar in respect of staffing: nine departments had staff cuts in all of the seven years under observation; six departments had staff cuts in six out of seven years; four in five; two in each of four years; three departments had staff cuts in three out of seven years, but one of those (DHSS) showed an overall increase over the period, as did the remaining four departments with cuts in only two years. The peak years for cuts in terms of the numbers of departments affected were 1980 and 1982 (twenty-three and twenty-six departments lost staff); in terms of total staff reductions, the peak years were 1980 and 1983.

By any measure, then, 'suffering' was by no means equally shared among Whitehall departments — selectivity operated. What, then, were the selection tactics? In the literature, one is led to expect two kinds of tactic. The first, that a department faced with cuts will protect what it sees as its main resources, at the expense of less vital activities (Hartley and Lynk, 1983); second, that those who wield the axe bring it down on everyone else before themselves. Consider each of these in turn.

The data permitted examination of three pairs of hypotheses concerning protection of principal resources, as follows:

1. and 2. Departments with a preponderance of generalists will protect the generalists: in cuts, the numbers of specialists will be reduced disproportionately and *vice versa* for departments with a preponderance of specialists.

3. and 4. Departments whose main functions are of a 'money-moving' kind, i.e. paying other people to do things, will protect their contract and grant funds. In cuts, salary costs will not rise as a proportion of total budget and *vice versa* for departments whose main functions are of a 'labour-intensive' kind, salary costs will not fall.

5. and 6. Highly-dispersed departments, or those with many branch offices, will not become more concentrated and *vice versa*, highly-concentrated departments will protect headquarters offices and degree of dispersion will not increase.

Five departments always had more than 80 percent of their staff in the administrative grades in these years: the Intervention Board for Agricultural Produce (administering the EEC farm subsidies), HM Customs and Excise, Export Credits Guarantee Department, Department of National Savings, Department of Employment. These can be called the 'generalist' departments. Five departments always had under 20 percent of their total staff in administrative grades: HMSO, Ministry of Defence (MoD) Home Office, FCO and Ordnance Survey department. These can be called the 'specialist' departments. The other eighteen departments were spread quite evenly between these two thresholds and will be left out of the analysis.

The data shows, whereas all the generalist departments became *more* generalist over the period (except for one which showed no change), the specialist departments were spread between three which showed increases in specialist-heaviness and two which showed decreases. Thus there is some support for the contention that generalist departments have protected their principal resource, while specialist departments have not tried, or have not managed, to do so.

The next pair of hypotheses would suggest that money-moving departments protect their cash, while 'do-it-yourself' labour-intensive departments protect their salary bill. Distributing the departments by the proportion of their total budget spent on staff salaries shows a very skewed pattern. A small number of departments are *very* 'salary-heavy' with the money collecting departments HM Customs and Excise and Inland Revenue, spending around 80 percent of budget, followed by a money storing department, National Savings, with around 40 percent and then a considerable gap to the spending departments proper, with only a few of them using more than 10 percent of their budget on salaries (MoD and FCO among them). At the other end are a group of departments regularly spending less than 2.5 percent of their total budget on staff salaries: Energy, Environment, the Welsh and Scottish Offices, Export Credits, and Industry. These last are the money-movers. But what the figures show is that practically all departments, whether labour intensive or money moving, showed decreases over the period in the proportion of budget spent on salaries. In a period of staff cuts, this was perhaps to be expected. Standardizing for extent of staff cuts might clarify the picture but at the time of writing this has not yet been done.

A department's 'degree of concentration' indicates the extent to which its staff is concentrated in one or two regions of the country or, on the other hand, dispersed so that it has staff in all or many regions. Distribution was fairly normal here: a few departments that are *very* 'HQ-heavy' (Treasury and Civil Service Department, the Scottish Office, and the Welsh Office — the latter two in Scotland and Wales respectively, the first two in the South East region, i.e. London in these cases); a cluster of fairly-concentrated departments; a cluster of fairly-dispersed departments; and three very highly-dispersed departments, 'branch-office-heavy' (Inland Revenue, DOE, DHSS). If, as the third pair of hypotheses suggests, highly-dispersed departments protect their branch office network during cuts, whether of budget or of staff, they should get *more* dispersed over the period. The three most highly-dispersed departments *did* get more dispersed — but unfortunately for the hypothesis, for two of them (Employment, and DHSS), the period was not one of cuts, whether in budget or staff. Similarly, highly concentrated departments should get *more* concentrated in a period of cuts. And indeed, two of the most highly concentrated (Scottish Office and Welsh Office) *did* get more concentrated. But one of them (Welsh Office) had staff *increases* over the period, not cuts. So the picture is not at all clear even at the extremes and it is less so among the rest of the departments. It cannot be said that either hypothesis is upheld.

There is, therefore, hardly any clear evidence that selectivity in making cuts has operated through tactics of protecting the principal resource at the expense of peripheral activities, with one possible exception: that highly-generalist departments did contrive to get more generalist in spite of cuts.

Consideration is now given to the evidence for the second possible tactic; that the axe-wielders protect themselves. Seven hypotheses were identified for testing, as follows:

1. The central controlling departments (Treasury, Civil Service Department, Cabinet Office) *improve* their position in the league tables of staff size and budget size.

2. The large departments stay large at the expense of the smaller departments (their share of total budget and staff increases).

3. Central government protects itself against the rest of the public sector (its share of total public spending increases).

4. Central government protects itself against the private or independent sector (expenditure on purchases and contracts decreases in relation to expenditure on civil service salaries).

5. Whitehall 'chiefs' protect themselves against 'indians' (departments increase in top and middle heaviness).

6. Full-time male 'bureaucrats' protect themselves (the proportions of specialists, industrial staff, part-time staff and women, decrease).

7. Headquarters protect themselves against the field (concentration increases).

Taking these in turn, briefly.

If it is going to be true that 'whoever suffers, it will not be the Treasury', then Treasury (and the other central controlling departments) should climb steadily in the rankings. In fact they did not do so. Treasury/Civil Service Department/Cabinet Office taken together had real budget cuts in three years out of the seven, and lost staff in six years out of seven. There is no evidence that the central controlling departments preserved their own positions at the expense of the rest of Whitehall.

Do the big boys always win? The big spenders, Environment, DHSS and Defence, each spend several times as much as their nearest rivals and collectively, they did increase their share of total government expenditure between 1976 and 1982 — from 62.7 percent to 65.2 percent. In fact, however, it was only DHSS which did so (23.9 percent to 34.1 percent). The other two suffered cuts like everyone else, Defence in one year, Environment in five out of seven years. In staffing, Defence outclasses all, being twice as large as the next biggest, DHSS, the runner-up to which is not Environment but Inland Revenue. Environment and Employment jockey for fourth and fifth place and the Home Office consistently lies sixth. Again the three largest had different fortunes. Defence went down from 36 percent of the total civil service to 32.2 percent, while DHSS and Inland Revenue increased — DHSS from 12.3 percent to 14.5 percent, IR from 10.6 percent to 11.3 percent. Defence had staff cuts every year, IR in three years out of seven, DHSS in no year. If the big boys always win, only the demand-driven Health and Social Security is a 'big boy'.

Does Whitehall look after itself at the expense of the local authority and public corporation sector? There is something in this. Between 1976 and 1983 central government expenditure went up by 143 percent, or 14 percent after adjustment for inflation. In the same period local authority expenditure went up by 107 percent which after adjustment is a *decrease* of 3 percent. The public corporation sector as defined in annual public expenditure terms does not mean the 'nationalised industries' as commonly understood, but such bodies as New Town Corporations, housing corporations and the like. Over these years their expenditure did not move steadily but, for what it is worth, comparing the first year with the last shows an RPI-adjusted decline of 53 percent. In another analysis, central government expenditures on local government associated purposes and public corporation associated purposes, when added together and compared with total central government expenditure, show a decline from 21.3 percent to 17.6 percent over the period. So there *are* grounds for holding that central government protects itself against the rest of the public sector.

. Does Whitehall also protect itself against the private sector? It would do this, in a time of retrenchment, if it ensured that cuts fell on expenditures which are *not* civil service-salary-related, before expenditures which are. If the 'budget/utility theory' already discussed is followed, that is what would be expected. But as noted above, not *all* expenditures are likely to be equally productive of 'bureaucratic surplus': DHSS's massive budget growth could be composed of increases in payments, not larger numbers of payments, which would expand the discretionary spending power of bureaucrats by very little.

So to maximize the chances of finding what is being sought, it is necessary to include only budget items which are highly discretionary and exclude transfers and subsidies. The figures for central government current and capital expenditures on *goods and services* and expenditure on research and development (which can be done 'in-house' or by external contract) were taken. The results showed that expenditure on goods and services increased between 1976 and 1983 by 34.8 percent, while salaries increased by only 2.1 percent (each figure corrected for inflation). Intramural Research and Development expenditure, RPI-adjusted, increased by 2.0 percent over the period, while extramural R&D increased by 14.0 percent. In neither case does the evidence support the hypothesis; i.e. Whitehall does not appear to protect itself against the private sector.

Does the 'top brass' come off best in periods of cuts? You will hear this (often bitter) allegation wherever staff and salary cuts are made. If the hypothesis is to be upheld, then as total staff numbers decrease the proportions of top staff and/or middle staff should increase, accompanying a larger decrease in lowest-level staff, or 'shop floor'. The figures for the set of departments under consideration were as follows. Between 1976 and 1983, total staff declined by 5.99 percent, top grades (under secretary and above) declined by 20.3 percent, middle staff by 8.24 percent and bottom staff by 6.16 percent. A clearer comparison, however, is increase/decrease in the *share* of each group and here top staff's share declined by 0.03 percent, bottom grades decline by 0.14 percent, while the share of the middle grades goes up by 0.17 percent.

There would be some justification, therefore, in saying that it is not *top* brass that comes off best, but middle management. When we replicated the exercise department by department rather than in aggregate, the same pattern appeared. Among departments whose total staff *increased* over the period (six departments), all six showed top staff declining in numbers, three showed middle staff increasing at the expense of bottom staff, and in the other three bottom staff increased at the expense of middle staff. Among departments showing an overall decrease in total staff (21 departments), as many had lost top staff as had gained top staff (in tiny numbers either way), but there was a marked transfer from bottom staff to middle staff in relative departmental configuration, only three departments going the other way. It is the *middle*-level staff who seem not to lose in time of cuts.

Does the civil service 'revert to type' in retrenchment? The common stereotype of the civil servant is that of a male clerk with job security and a pension. Therefore, if this kind of person looks after himself, we should expect to see the proportions of non-generalists, of industrial or manual staff, of part-time staff and of women, being reduced over the period. What happened? At first sight, it looked as if the administrators did protect themselves. The percentage of administrative grades plus secretarial grades went up from 37.74 percent of the total to 39.47 percent. However, if calculated as a percentage not of the entire civil service, but of the non-industrial grades only, the rise disappears and becomes a slight fall. Did the non-industrials, then, protect themselves against the industrials? This period must be set into its context, which is of a long-term decline of the proportion of industrial civil servants (43.5 percent in 1951, 40.9 percent in 1961, 28.9 percent in 1971, 21.9 percent in 1981), an average decline of about 7 percent per decade. So it would need a decline of more than about 5 percent in the seven survey years to beat 'par for the course'. In fact, industrials between 1976 and 1983 went down by just under 4 percent: a graph would show a *slackening* in the rate of decline of the industrials since 1976. Indeed, the civil service was more clerical and less manual in 1983 than it was in 1976, and even if this was only the continuation of a long-term trend, one might perhaps have expected the 'information revolution' and electronic offices to have had more effect on clerical numbers than they apparently have had.

The figures for part-timers are interesting. The proportion of the total *increased* from 1976 to 1980 and then fell, so that the proportion at the end of our period was almost exactly the same as at the beginning (2.85 percent). It is tempting to see this as indicating a switch in attitude to the cuts in general. Up to 1979, cuts could perhaps be seen as temporary and the fabric kept in place for future restoration (while meeting immediate calls for staff reductions) by replacing natural wastage of permanent staff by part-time appointments. By 1980, perhaps, this was seen as self-delusion.

Women non-industrial staff, as a proportion of the non-industrial total, show a steady if small *increase* year by year. If this trend continues until 1989 women will be in the majority in the non-industrial civil service. It cannot be said, therefore, on these figures, whether for the generalist/specialist balance, the non-industrial/industrial balance, the full-time/part-time balance, or the gender balance, over the period 1976–83, that the male career clerk protects his own interests.

Finally, do headquarters protect themselves at the expense of the field, in retrenchment? There might be some logic in this. By and large, it takes just as big an HQ unit to control a network of one hundred field offices as one of seventy-five or one hundred and twenty-five, therefore, if you need big staff cuts, they have to come from the field. But what figures we have do not support this thesis. The concentration index falls over the period, suggesting increased dispersion, not decreased. The region, which includes London where most headquarters are, had the biggest percentage reduction in staff in Britain.

Evidence that the axe-wielders in Whitehall cut everyone else before themselves is therefore singularly lacking, with one exception — it seems to have been true that central government imposed more cuts on local authorities and public corporations than it imposed on departments of central government.

The Treasury and Civil Service Committee of the House of Commons has been concerned to monitor cuts in civil service manpower, to gauge their effects upon services to the citizen. The Committee, at its own request and perhaps motivated by suspicions (or theories) about how cuts would actually be achieved, had been supplied each three months and year by year with figures showing differential cuts in the industrial (or manual worker) grades as compared with the non-industrial (white-collar) grades of the civil service; in regional and local office staffs as compared with headquarters staffs; in the highest ranks as compared with the lower ranks; and in the administrative and clerical grades as compared with professional and scientific etc. grades. These questions have been touched upon earlier in the chapter, for the longer period 1976–83, and do not need reiteration. Perhaps another set of figures, provided to the Committee at its request, illustrates their fear (or hypothesis) that the Government would try to mask the degree to which cuts were achieved not by increased efficiency (praiseworthy), or by privatization (to be expected, ideologically-speaking), but by cutting out services and lowering standards of service (politically vulnerable). So figures were requested and provided on *sources* of cuts in the following categories.

(a) (i) increases and (ii) decreases arising from change in workloads (including revised economic assumptions);

(b) carrying out work more efficiently by a major change in method;

(c) general streamlining (including lowering standards of service and other minor changes);

(d) increases arising from new activities;

(e) dropping or materially curtailing a function;

(f) privatization, including contracting-out;

(g) hiving-off to new or existing public body.

Here the categories into which increases of staff might fall are omitted — (a) (i) and (d) — and concentration is on the decreases.

The out-turn over the four years for the Civil Service as a whole is summarised in Table 5.4. If the Committee did have the fears (hypotheses, predictions) ascribed to them conjecturally above, as the basis for their requests for information, they seem to be well supported. In broad terms, four-sevenths of the total 123,000 staff savings over the period are accounted for by the two middle categories, i.e. 'general streamlining' (which includes the lowering of standards of service), and the dropping or material curtailment of functions. Most of the manpower, apparently, was saved because less was done and that was done less well (apart from possible minor savings from minor improvements in efficiency). One seventh arose from reductions in workload, by and large from a changing outside environment, including 'revised economic assumptions'. Only one-seventh came from increased efficiency through major changes in work method (including computerization). The final seventh came from privatization and hiving-off taken together.

Conclusion

Some of the *limitations* of bureaumetrics as an approach to the theory of bureaucracy may have become apparent in the course of this chapter, as well as its strengths. Quantitative analysis, putting numbers on factors, is not appropriate for all aspects of bureaucratic structure and processes. The 'unobtrusive measures' method of data-collection is not a *sine qua non* of bureaumetrics, but where relying principally on using already existing data sets, the tendency is to start from the numbers to hand or readily available, and then see what 'mileage' can be squeezed out of them. The longitudinal exercises reported in this chapter have based themselves on a quite small number of variables (seven, for many analyses). It is often surprising how much work a single index can be made to perform.

These and several other limitations, in principle and/or in practice, on the development of the bureaucratic approach tend in consequence, to narrow the range of theories that it can be applied to. However, just because a tool has a specialized range of uses there is no reason not to

TABLE 5.4

Manpower reductions by source category 1980–84:

numbers of staff and percent of total

	1980–81		1981–82		1982–83		1983–84		TOTAL 1980–84	
	Number of staff	as % of total	Number of staff	as % of total	Number of staff	as % of total	Number of staff	as % of total	Number of staff	as % of total
(a) (ii) change in workload	1,746.5	6.5	3,845	12.3	4,716	16.1	7,348	20.2	17,655.5	14.3
(b) change in methods	3,966.5	14.8	4,640	14.8	5,404	18.5	4,447	12.2	18,457.5	14.9
(c) general streamlining	12,188	45.4	8,526	27.3	6,831	23.4	6,891	18.9	34,436	27.8
(e) dropping functions	6,787.5	25.3	7,184	23.0	7,632	26.1	11,933	32.8	33,536.5	27.1
(f) privatization	1,571	5.8	6,046	19.3	4,029	13.8	2,655	7.3	14,301	11.6
(g) hiving off	601	2.2	1,008	3.3	600	2.1	3,162	8.6	5,371	4.3
TOTAL REDUCTIONS	26,860.5	–	31,249	–	29,212	–	36,436	–	123,757.5	–

Sources: HC 423, HC 46, 207/1982–83, 207/1983–84

(1) Seventh Report from the Treasury and Civil Service Committee, 1980–81, *Civil Service Manpower Reductions* HC 423. 13 July 1981.

(2) First Special Report from the Treasury and Civil Service Committee, 1982–83, *Civil Service Manpower Reductions*, HC 46. 15 November 1982.

(3) Report on Manpower Reductions in 1982–83 to the Treasury and Civil Service Committee. Third Annual Report, Management and Personnel Office. 207. No date.

(4) Report on Manpower Reductions in 1983–84 to the Treasury and Civil Service Committee. Fourth Annual Report, Management and Personnel Office. 207. No date.

make fullest use of it within that range. The stance is quite plain, where a theory about bureaucratic structure or process or behaviour is expressable in testable form (and if it is not, does it deserve to be called a theory?), then it ought to be so expressed; if a theory is expressed in testable form, it ought (sooner or later, by someone or other) to be tested; and if it is testable by the sort of quantified data approach that bureaumetrics can handle, then bureaumetrics ought to be brought into play. Only the edges of the universe of problems susceptible of this kind of treatment have been touched upon. Although this chapter has concentrated on the testing of other people's theories, it has noted where the exploration of quantified data can itself throw up theoretical puzzles, that need theorizing about and consequent testing, perhaps from different kinds of data (opinion or motivation survey, historical or legal analysis, etc.).

Again, in this chapter analyses at only two *levels* is reported, the macro- and the meso-levels, i.e. at whole-government level and bureaucracy by bureaucracy. Smaller units of analysis (*parts* of bureaucracies) are indicated as appropriate in some situations, though data gathering becomes more problematic. Then, in the other direction, there are possibilities of international comparisons, if sufficiently standardized data sets can be devised. Perhaps the most fruitful challenge before users of the bureaumetric approach (whether or not they see themselves as such) is the analysis of bureaucratic *outputs* as well as inputs like people and money. Although there is a growing literature on the difficulties of measuring bureaucratic outputs and many people are exploring the territory, it is treacherous country with little firm ground yet charted and few well-trodden paths.

What will have become clear, perhaps, is that when theories *are* tested by bureaumetric methods (or possibly by *any* of the methods of social science in general) the most frequent result is a negative one. Typically, the proposition is not upheld or only very weakly supported. This is unsatisfying because usually, in the nature of the process, nothing positive is put in its place. Empirical social science is better at knocking down ideas than at setting them up, at destructive rather constructive argument, or as Rein puts it (1976), research almost never proves the positive. Bureaumetrics is no exception. We have, it may be agreed, shown within the limits of our data that a fair number of theories about bureaucratic structure and behaviour, some quite important and influential, are not upheld by empirical investigation among British bureaucracies. That may be purely negative but it is not negligible. It is surely necessary to know whether assertions (confidently made on logical deduction from first principles, axioms, or experience) about what bureaucracies or bureaucrats are like, are or are not always true. If they are true only contingently then the directions of refinement of the theoretical proposition may be indicated. That is a not unworthy contribution.

Note

The research reported here was carried out in association with Christopher C. Hood of the University of Glasgow, and with the assistance of Ms K. Suky Thompson and Dr Meg Huby. The research was supported financially by the UK Economic and Social Research Council (awards HR 3871/1 and E 0023 2018), and in terms of advice and tables of statistics by HM Treasury and other departments of British central government, to whom we express our gratitude. All commentary and conclusions are the responsibility of the author.

References

Alt, J. and K.A. Chrystal (1983) *Political Economics*. Brighton: Wheatsheaf.

Anderberg, M.R. (1973) *Cluster Analysis for Applications*. New York: Academic Press.

Anderson, T.R. and S. Warkov (1961) 'Organizational size and functional complexity', *American Sociological Review*, 26.

Armstrong, W. (1970) 'The Civil Service Department and Its Tasks', *O & M Bulletin*, 25, pp. 63–79. Reprinted in R.A. Chapman and A. Dunsire (eds) (1971) *Style in Administration*. London: Allen and Unwin.

Barker, D. 'Mergers Leave Whitehall Cold', *The Guardian* 17 October 1970, 7.

Beck, M. (1976) 'The expanding public sector: some contrary evidence', *National Tax Journal*, 29, pp. 15–21.

Blau, P.M. and R.A. Schoenherr (1971) *The Structure of Organizations*. New York: Basic Books.

Blau, P.M., C.McH. Falbe, W. McKinley, and P.K. Tracy (1976) 'Technology and organization in manufacturing', *Administrative Science Quarterly*, 21.

Bramley, G. and M. Stewart (1981) 'Implementing public expenditure cuts', in S. Barret and C. Fudge (eds) *Policy and Action*. London: Methuen, pp. 39–63.

Burns, T. and G.M. Stalker (1961) *The Management of Innovation*. London: Tavistock.

Caiden, G. (1970) *Administrative Reform*. London: Allen Lane.

Chapman, L. (1978) *Your Disobedient Servant*. London: Chatto & Windus.

Chapman, R.A. and J.R. Greenaway (1980) *The Dynamics of Administrative Reform*. London: Croom Helm.

Child, J. (1972) 'Organizational structure, environment and performance — the role of strategic choice', *Sociology*, 6(1), pp. 1–22.

Child, J. (1977) *Organization: A guide to Problems and Practice*. London: Harper & Row.

Clegg, S. and D. Dunkerley (eds) (1977) *Critical Issues in Organizations*. London: Routledge and Kegan Paul.

Cohen, G. (1984) 'Cutting Public Expenditure: Proposition 13 in California', in D. Lewis and H. Wallace (eds) *Policies Into Practice*. London: Heinemann, pp. 93–108.

Dunsire, A. (1961) 'The Passing of the Ministry of Transport and Civil Aviation', *Public Law*, 150–64.

Fry, G.K. (1985) *The Changing Civil Service*. London: George Allen and Unwin.

Haire, M. (1959) 'Biological models and empirical histories of the growth of organizations', in M. Haire (ed.) *Modern Organization Theory* New York: John Wiley.

Hall, P. (1980) *Great Planning Disasters*. London: Weidenfeld and Nicolson.

Hall, R.H. (1972) *Organizations: Structure and Process*. Englewood Cliffs: Prentice-Hall.

Hartley, K. and E. Lynk (1983), 'Budget cuts and public sector employment: the case of Defence', *Applied Economics*, 15(4), pp. 531–40.

Heald, D. (1983) *Public Expenditure* Oxford: Martin Robertson.

Hennessey, P. (1984) *Routine, Punctuated by Orgies*. London: BBC.

Heydebrand, W. (1973) *Hospital Organization*. New York: Dunellan.

Holdaway, E.A. and T.A. Blowers (1971) 'Administrative ratios and organizational size: a longitudinal examination', *American Sociological Review*, 36.

Hood, C.C. and A. Dunsire (1981) *Bureaumetrics*. Farnborough: Gower.

Hood, C.C., M. Huby, and A. Dunsire (1985) 'Scale economies and iron laws: mergers and demergers in Whitehall 1971–1984', *Public Administration* 63 (1), pp. 61–78.

Hood, C.C. and M. Wright (eds) (1981) *Big Government in Hard Times*. Oxford: Martin Robertson.

Jackson, P.M. (1982) *The Political Economy of Bureaucracy*. Oxford: Philip Allan.

Kaufman, H and D. Seidman (1970) 'The morphology of organizations', *Administrative Science Quarterly*, 15.

Kogan, M. (1973) *Comment on Niskanen's 'Bureaucracy Servant or Master?'*. London: Institute of Economic Affairs.

Kristensen, O.P. (1980) 'The logic of political bureaucratic decision-making as a cause of government growth; or, why expansion of public programmes is a private good and their restriction is a "public good" ', *European Journal of Political Research*, 8, pp. 249–64.

Lawrence, P.R. and J.W. Lorsch (1967) *Organization and Environment*. Boston: Harvard University Press.

Leemans, A.F. (ed.) (1976) *The Management of Change in Government*. The Hague: Martinus Nijhoff.

Leibenstein, H. (1976) *Beyond Economic Man*. Cambridge, Mass.: Harvard University Press.

Levine, C.H. (1978) Symposium: 'Organizational decline and cutback management', *Public Administration Review*, 38(4).

Levine, C.H. et al. (1981) *The Politics of Retrenchment: How Local Governments Manage Fiscal Stress*. Beverly Hills: Sage.

Lynn, J. and A. Jay (1981) *Yes Minister*. London: BBC TV.

Meyer, M.W. (1977) *Theory of Organizational Structure*. Indianapolis: Bobbs-Merrill.

Niskanen, W.A. (1971) *Bureaucracy and Representative Government*. Chicago: Aldine-Atherton.

O'Connor, J. (1973) *The Fiscal Crisis of the State* New York: St Martin's Press.

Parkinson, C.N. (1958) *Parkinson's Law; or, The Pursuit of Progress*. London: John Murray.

Peacock, A.T. (1983) 'Public *X*-inefficiency: informational and institutional constraints', in Hanusch, H. (ed.) *Anatomy of Government Deficiencies*. Berlin/Heidelberg: Springer-Verlag, pp. 125–38.

Pollitt, C. (1984) *Manipulating the Machine: Changing the Pattern of Ministerial Departments 1960–83*. London: George Allen and Unwin.

Pommerehne, W.W. and B.S. Frey (1978) 'Bureaucratic behaviour in democracy: a case study', *Public Finance*, 33, pp. 98–112.

Pugh, D.S. and D.J. Hickson (1976) *Organization Structure in Its Context: the Aston Programme I*. Farnborough: Saxon House.

Pugh, D.S. and C.R. Hinings (1976) *Organization Structure: Extensions and Replications*. Farnborough: Saxon House.

Rein, M. (1976) *Social Science and Public Policy*. Harmondsworth: Penguin Books.

Rose, R. (1984) *Understanding Big Government*. London: Sage.

Rose, R. and B.G. Peters (1978) *Can Government Go Bankrupt?* New York: Basic Books.

Rourke, F.E. (1976) *Bureaucracy, Politics and Public Policy* (2nd edn.) Boston: Little, Brown.

Self, P. (1972) *Administrative Theories and Politics*. London: Allen and Unwin.

Smith, A. (1762) *Lectures on Jurisprudence*.

Smith, A. (1776) *The Wealth of Nations*. London.

Terrien, F. and D. Mills (1955) 'The effects of changing size upon the internal structure of organizations', *American Sociological Review*, 20.

Thoenig, J.C. and E. Friedberg (1976) 'The Power of the Field Staff: the case of the Ministry of Public Works, Urban Affairs and Housing in France', in Leemans (ed.) (1976), pp. 314–37.

Thompson, J.D. and F.L. Bates (1957) 'Technology, organization and administration', *Administrative Science Quarterly*, 5, pp. 485–521.

Trist, E.L. and K.W. Bamforth (1951) 'Some social and psychological consequences of the longwall method of coal-getting', *Human Relations*, 4, pp. 3–39

Tullock, G. (1965) *The Politics of Bureaucracy*. Washington DC: Public Affairs Press.

Udy, S.H. Jnr. (1959) *Organization of Work*. New Haven: Human Relations Area Files Press.

Wagner, R.E. (1973) *The Public Economy*. Chicago: Markham.

Walker, C.R. and R.H. Guest (1952) *The Man on the Assembly Line*. Cambridge Mass.: Harvard University Press.

Wallace, W. (1975) *The Foreign Policy Process in Britain*. London: Royal Institute of International Affairs.

Webb, E.J. et al. (1966) *Unobtrusive Measures: Nonreactive Research in the Social Sciences*. Chicago: McNally.

Williamson, O. (1975) *Markets and Hierarchies*. New York: Free Press.

Woodward, J. (1958) *Management and Technology: Problems of Progress in Industry*. London: HMSO.

Woodward, J. (1965) *Industrial Organization, Theory and Practice*. London: Oxford University Press.

Wright, M. (ed.) (1980) *Public Spending Decisions: Growth and Restraint in the 1970s*. London: George Allen and Unwin.

Young, R.G. (1974) 'The administrative process as incrementalism', *in Public Administration* (Social Services: A Third Level Course) D331, Block II, Part 3. Milton Keynes: The Open University Press.

The bureaumetrics projects: bibliography

Christopher C Hood, Andrew Dunsire and K Suky Thompson (1975) 'Dimensions of Difference between British Central Government Agencies'. Paper presented to a conference on Methodology of Study and Research in Public Administration, Free University of Amsterdam.

Christopher C Hood (1978a) 'Keeping the centre small: explanations of agency type' *Political Studies*, 26(1), pp. 30–46.

Christopher C Hood (1978b) 'The Crown Agents Affair', *Public Administration*, 56, pp. 297–303.

Christopher C Hood, Andrew Dunsire and K Suky Thompson (1978a) 'The concept and measurement of "political salience" in British government departments'. Occasional Paper 1. York: Machinery of Government Project. Institute of Social and Economic Research, University of York.

Christopher C Hood, Andrew Dunsire and K Suky Thompson (1978b) 'Measuring administrative structure in British central government'. Occasional Paper 3. York: Machinery of Government Project. Institute of Social and Economic Research, University of York.

Christopher C Hood, Andrew Dunsire and K Suky Thompson (1978c) 'Appropriateness of structure: prerequisites of prediction'. Paper presented to the conference of the European Group of Public Administration, Paris, June 1978. Occasional Paper 4. York: Machinery of Government Project. Institute of Social and Economic Research, University of York.

Christopher C Hood, Andrew Dunsire and K Suky Thompson (1978d) 'The Scottish Office in the UK context: some quantitative comparisons'. Paper presented to the Political Studies Workgroup on UK Politics, Strathclyde, August 1978. Occasional Paper 5. York: Machinery of Government Project. Institute of Social and Economic Research, University of York.

Christopher C Hood, Andrew Dunsire and K Suky Thompson (1978e) 'Describing the status quo in Whitehall: a prerequisite for the analysis of change'. Paper presented to the conference of the Public Administration Committee (JUC), York, September 1978. Occasional Paper 6. York: Machinery of Government Project. Institute of Social and Economic Research, University of York.

Christopher C Hood, Andrew Dunsire and K Suky Thompson (1978f) 'Measuring "environment" and "type of work" in central government departments'. Occasional Paper 7. York: Machinery of Government Project. Institute of Social and Economic Research, University of York.

Christopher C Hood, Andrew Dunsire and K Suky Thompson (1978g) 'Exploring the properties of "agency type" in British central government.' Occasional Paper 8. York: Machinery of Government Project. Institute of Social and Economic Research, University of York.

Christopher C Hood, Andrew Dunsire and K Suky Thompson (1978h) 'So you think you know what Government Departments are . . .' *Public Administration Bulletin*, 27, pp. 20–32, September 1978. Occasional Paper 2. York: Machinery of Government Project. Institute of Social and Economic Research, University of York.

Andrew Dunsire, Christopher C Hood and K Suky Thompson (1979) 'Des Structures Appropriées: conditions nécessaire à la prévision' *Revue Francaise d'Administration Publique*, 9; pp. 21–61, Jan–Mar.

Christopher C Hood (1979a) 'The "machinery of government" problem' *Studies in Public Policy*, 28 Centre for the Study of Public Policy, University of Strathclyde.

Christopher C Hood, Andrew Dunsire and K Suky Thompson (1979) 'Comparing the Scottish Office with "Whitehall": a quantitative approach' *British Journal of Political Science*, 9(3), pp. 257–80, July.

Christopher C Hood (1979b) 'Central non-departmental bodies and government growth'. Paper presented to the conference of the Public Administration Committee (JUC), York, September 1979.

Christopher C Hood and Eileen Sutcliffe (1979) 'The Faces of Bureaucracy', *New Society*, 50 (890), pp. 186–7, 25 October 1979.

Christopher C Hood and Andrew Dunsire (1981) *Bureaumetrics: the quantitative comparison of British central government agencies*. Farnborough: Gower.

Andrew Dunsire (1981) 'Measuring the Administration'. Paper presented at Centro di Formazione e Studi per il Mezzogiorno (FORMEZ), Rome, April.

Christopher C Hood (1982) 'Governmental bodies and government growth', in Barker, A. (ed.) *Quangos in Britain: Government and the Networks of Public Policy-Making* London: Macmillan, pp. 44–68.

Christopher C Hood (1982) 'Imperialismus des Rechnungshofes oder Briefkasten für Unruhestifter?" ZiF Forschungsgruppe 1981/82 Discussion Paper No 19. Bielefeld: ZiF 1982.

Christopher C Hood (1983) 'A Tale of Two Quangocracies: Members of British commercial public boards 1950–style and 1980–style' *Policy and Politics* 11: pp. 1–13

Christopher C Hood (1983) 'The Hidden Public Sector: the world of para-government organisations' *Studies in Public Policy*, No. 133, Centre for the Study of Public Policy, University of Strathclyde 1984.

Christopher C Hood (1984a) 'The Hidden Public Sector: the Quangocratisation of the World?' in F-X Kaufman, V Ostrom, G Majone (eds.) *Guidance, Control and Performance Evaluation in the Public Sector*. Berlin and New York: de Gruyter, 1986.

Christopher C Hood (1984b) 'PGOs in UK Central Government', paper prepared for the first meeting of ECPR Research Group on Para-Government Organisations, Augsburg, March 1985.

Christopher C Hood, Meg Huby and Andrew Dunsire (1984) 'Bureaucrats and budgetary benefits: how do British central government departments measure up?' *Journal of Public Policy*, 4(3), pp. 163–79.

Christopher C Hood, Meg Huby and Andrew Dunsire (1985a) 'Scale economies and iron laws: mergers and demergers in Whitehall 1971–84', *Public Administration*, 63(1): pp. 61–78.

Christopher C Hood, Meg Huby and Andrew Dunsire (1985b) 'From growth to retrenchment: a perspective on the development of the Scottish Office to the 1980s' in *Scottish Government Yearbook 1985*. Edinburgh: Paul Harris.

Andrew Dunsire, Meg Huby and Christopher C Hood (1985a) 'Whitehall in Retrenchment, Who Got Less, When, How, 1976–83. I: Equal Misery or Selective Cuts?', paper prepared for the Fifteenth Annual Conference of the Public Administration Committee (JUC), York, September 1985.

Andrew Dunsire, Meg Huby and Christopher C Hood (1985b) 'Whitehall in Retrenchment, Who Got Less, When, How, 1976–83. II: Plans and Outturns; an exercise in evaluation', paper prepared for Working Group No 6 of the Conference of the European Group of Public Administration (IIAS), Leuven, September 1985.

Andrew Dunsire, Meg Huby and Christopher C Hood (1985c) 'Whitehall in Retrenchment: Who Got Less, When, How, 1976–83. III: An exercise in vulnerability analysis'. In preparation.

6
British administrative trends
and the public choice revolution

Christopher Hood
(with Meg Huby and Andrew Dunsire)

The economics of bureaucracy:
administrative theory for a mass-tax society?
The purpose of this chapter is to explore the extent to which administrative trends in the UK over the past two decades or so seem to reflect a swing away from the normative principles of 'mainstream' public administration theory towards the normative principles commonly associated with the 'public choice' or 'economics-of-bureaucracy' approach to administrative theory.

Such an exploration can only be tentative and impressionistic, given limitations of data. Obviously, too, the validity or otherwise of a normative theory is not established by demonstrating whether real life trends are moving nearer or further away from what that theory would prefer to be the case. Establishing the direction of change can tell us something about the waxing and waning of administrative doctrines in public and political favour, but cannot falsify or validate those doctrines as such.

There are some prima facie grounds on which it might be argued that social trends in the UK over the past two decades or so might have moved the climate of opinion about public service provision towards the normative ideas associated with 'public choice'. In particular, changes in taxation might have served to increase sensitivity to the tax cost of public services and thus to make issues of waste and efficiency in public services (the central issue for economics-based theories of administration) more salient for the electorate at large. Throughout this century, the largest single source of tax revenue in the UK has been income tax (Hood, 1985), but the tax has changed from a tax on a minority of workers to a tax on almost all of them. In 1938 less than 20 percent of the UK labour force paid income tax. By 1968 over 80 percent of the labour force paid income tax and the figure has remained approximately at that level thereafter. (Figures calculated from Inland Revenue Statistics and from labour force statistics in Annual Abstract of Statistics.)

The proportion of the electorate paying income tax has thus risen enormously over the past half-century. Moreover, inflation and fiscal drag has meant that since the late 1940s, more workers have been exposed to tax for more of their earnings, with the income tax threshold falling as a percentage of manual workers' average earnings over that period (see Cmnd 9576, 1985, 10–11). Mass exposure to taxation has also been increased by inflation and fiscal drag in a progressive tax structure, raising social security taxes from 1948 onwards (Rose and Karran, 1983: 58; Table 3) and by a near-doubling of the proportion of married women in paid employment from just over 20 percent in 1951 to approximately 50 percent from the mid-1970s (figures from *Social Trends*, 1970–75) and the trend towards 'two-income families', which these figures represent, will tend to increase the exposure of families to income tax liability. All of these developments could be argued to lead to a reduction in voter incentive to support general tax-financed measures, sharply increased tax visibility among the population at large and a much larger constituency of interest in designing public services to eliminate waste and moral hazard.

This development alone might lead to changes in attitudes to public administration, in the direction of more criticism of bureaucratic waste, more questioning of the financing basis of public services and so on. And to the change to a mass-tax society can be added other, more imponderable, social developments; the waning of 'paternalism', the waxing of 'consumerism', the weakening legitimacy of producerism (particularly of labour unions, to which nearly 70 percent of workers in the public sector belong, as against less than 30 percent in the private sector. In a 1968 NOP poll, 50 percent of respondents denied that unions 'had too much power', but to an identical Gallup poll in 1979 only 15 percent denied the proposition). Such trends might be argued to be the sort of context in which faith in traditional public administration principles of large scale public bureaucracy as an efficient and fiduciary instrument of the public purpose (rather than an inherently wasteful and self-serving one), might start to falter.

The economics-of-bureaucracy challenge to traditional public administration doctrines

Over the past twenty years, the intellectual world of public administration has been revolutionized by the extension of public choice theory to questions about the organization of public services. The public choice approach is conventionally defined (Mueller, 1979: 1) as the application of the methodology and behavioural assumptions of economics to the subject matter of political science, and this term came to be applied to economics-based approaches to administrative analysis in the 1970s (an early reference for this usage is Ostrom and Ostrom, 1971). This now presents a serious challenge to 'mainstream' public administration ideas, which derive mainly from Continental European theory about bureaucracy, and are an intellectual product of law and political science. Mainstream theory focuses largely on public bureaucracy, locates administrative 'improvement' in the professionalization of administrative work within orderly hierachies, in the elimination of rivalry and conflict between public bureaucracies by rationalizing and broadening jurisdictions (see Ostrom, 1974).

The challenge to that approach is serious because public choice offers an alternative way of analysing public services which is more or less coherent and consistent, involving a common economics-based language and a broadly consumer-oriented approach to public service provision. As this book testifies, the public choice approach to public service organization has swept the halls of academe over the last two decades and its influence has gone wider than that. Ironically, such serious criticism of the approach as there has been, has largely been couched in the language and style of the public choice approach itself (e.g. Dunleavy, 1985). No strong intellectual defence of the 'old faith' against the new economics-based approach has yet appeared.

In common with more orthodox public administration theory, the economics-based approach to administrative theory is founded on the assumption that it makes a difference how public services are organized (Niskanen, 1975: 640). But that is all that the two approaches have in common. Both approaches can be presented in terms of more or less neutral and descriptive theory about the working of institutional arrangements. But it is their normative implications and the prescriptive doctrines bound up with them, which are of interest here. In general, the economics-based approach to administrative analysis embodies as distinct a set of prescriptive principles as the 'mainstream' public administration ideas which it challenges (though there are, of course, different strains and emphases within this approach). By and large, these reflect attempts to apply a competitive model to the operation of the public sector wherever possible. The normative implications for the organization of public services tend to include the following:

— a bias towards small-scale rather than large-scale enterprise in public service provision;

— a bias towards performance contracting rather than direct labour through open-ended employment contracts;

— a bias towards multiple-provider structures of public service provision (preferably involving rivalry among competing providers) rather than single-provider structures;

— a bias towards user charges (or at least earmarked taxes) rather than general tax funds as the basis of funding public services other than pure public goods;

— a bias towards private or independent enterprise rather than public bureaucracy as the instrument of service provision.

These biases are subject to the conventional 'other things equal' qualification. All rest on arguments concerning allocative and X-efficiency, matters on which traditional theorists of public bureaucracy, such as Max Weber, had nothing to say (Albrow, 1970: 64). It is, of course, this fatal defect of received public administration theory which has opened it up to the public choice attack. The main lines of the argument are by now familiar. They are summarized briefly below.

Economics-based ideas about public administration share with some 'new left' thinking a general preference for small-scale over large-scale public service organization. The argument goes that smaller scale organization can better reflect consumer preferences, and will tend to weaken producer power as against consumer power, since dissatisfied consumers can vote with their feet by moving elsewhere (Niskanen, 1971: 130). The ability of labour unions to disrupt public services in pursuit of benefits for producers may well be augmented where there is uniform provision and a single employer — offering a 'single neck to sever', as it were.

Indeed, some economics-of-bureaucracy theorists, such as Niskanen believe that when it comes to public bureaucracies, allocative and X-efficiency is inversely related to scale of operations, dismissing entirely the conventional Adam Smith argument for efficiency gains from increasing scale of operations. If monopoly provision of public services is unavoidable, a preference thus develops for small-scale rather than large-scale monopolies, on the grounds that X-efficiency and loss of information about consumer preferences becomes more serious the wider the jurisdiction of the monopoly concerned.

In general, economics-based theories of administration see performance contracting as more conducive to X-efficiency than direct employment in a master-servant mode, especially in monopoly situations. It is, of course, recognized that transactions costs will militate against performance contracting over direct employment in circumstances where there is a combination of limited rationality, high uncertainty (such that all possible contingencies cannot be easily specified in the terms of the contract), high opportunism and small numbers of transacting parties. Williamson (1975) provides a classic analysis of the limits of performance contracting in terms of the inherent difficulties of writing a workable contract in such circumstances.

However, while recognizing that performance contracting is highly problematic in circumstances of high uncertainty/limited rationality/high opportunism/small-numbers, the economics-of-bureaucracy school worry even more about the potential X-inefficiency problems of direct employment, particularly in the context of large, hierarchical (and often monopolistic) enterprises (Liebenstein, 1976). In such circumstances, problems of 'information-impactedness' (Williamson,

1975) are likely to be endemic. There will be ample scope for accidental or deliberate distortion of information as it travels up or down the hierarchy, and incentives to minimize organizational slack will in general be weak.

Worries about X-inefficiency from direct employment go back at least to Adam Smith, who thought that such problems were inherent in large-scale employment enterprise (Rosenberg, 1960: 563). Nowadays much writing has been devoted to the X-inefficiency problem, the distortion problem in employment hierarchies, and what is usually termed the 'principal/agent' problem more generally, to denote all circumstances in which one person acts for another. The argument goes that performance contracting, unlike the open-ended employment contract, forces attention to be directed towards performance standards and unavoidably builds in time limits for review and renewal of the contract.

A normative implication, flowing from much writing on the economics of public bureaucracy, is a general preference for multiple-provider structures of public service provision over single-provider structures. Orthodox public administration theory looks unfavourably on duplication and rivalry in the provision of public services, on the standard Chadwickian argument that competition is wasteful and centralized administration efficient (Crain and Ekelund, 1976: 149–62). But many modern economics-of-bureaucracy writers are distrustful of the Chadwickian argument, although they accept the Chadwickian case for 'competition for the field' for unavoidably non-contestable markets such as piped water supply and local telephone service.

Apart from that, the preference is for simultaneous rival supply rather than periodic competition for the field, and for overlapping jurisdictions rather than for tidy, mutually exclusive areas of responsibility. The argument goes that rivalry will serve to limit organizational slack, as in the classic economic analysis of competitive supply. Even where competition to supply is impossible, the argument goes that overlapping jurisdictions may serve to reduce distortion of information in hierarchies and subject policy initiatives to more rigorous tests of broad acceptability and of robustness of cause-effect assumptions built in to those initiatives.

Public choice theorists in general prefer public services to be financed by per-unit charges on users rather than from periodic allocations from general tax funds. Again, this preference is based on arguments about allocative efficiency, and to some degree X-efficiency too. The argument goes that per-unit user charges are less distorting of information about user preferences than applies in the case of services provided from block budgets, allocated periodically from general tax funds. (For a brief account of the general fund financing problem, see Mueller, 1979: 90–6.)

It is held that the latter introduces a strong degree of moral hazard into consumer behaviour, leading to dishonest preference revelation, inflated demand or over-consumption, since individuals pay for service from general taxes rather than paying for units of service as they use them, which would oblige them to balance off the benefits obtained from the extra unit of service against the benefits which could be obtained from using the money which that unit would cost for other things. To Niskanen (1971: 143), the effect of general-fund financing of public services is like that of averaging the bill for a group of diners at a restaurant. Each diner has an incentive to order a more expensive meal than he would do if he had to pay for what he individually consumed. Moral hazard combined with opportunism serves to push up collective costs.

Apart from the effect of general-fund financing on the behaviour of opportunistic consumers, writers on the economics of bureaucracy commonly hold that such financing also encourages opportunism on the part of producers. Since such an arrangement forces service producers to bargain periodically for block budget allocations out of general tax funds, they have an incentive to distort information about demand and to conceal information about the production function for the service (that is, the costs associated with alternative ways of providing the service). This line of argument goes that the budgetary process will turn into a political poker game, marked by concealment of information, histrionics, melodrama, contrived crises, and frequent deadlocks. Budgetary allocations will reflect the political bargaining skills of service producers, not necessarily what consumers want.

All public choice theorists recognize, of course, that for some services — namely, pure public goods — per-unit user charges are by definition not feasible. In such circumstances, a favourite prescriptive formula is the Wicksellian case for earmarked taxes attached to each public good. This, it can be held, may make the costs of particular services more visible to the community at large than would apply in a general-fund-financing regime and may thus be more likely to match the sums allocated to each service to demand for those services by consumers exposed to information about their costs rather than operating in conditions of moral hazard.

More controversially, some economics-of-bureaucracy writing may serve as intellectual underpinning for the 'New Right' preferences for providing public services through private or independent enterprises, rather than through public bureaucracies. That is, arguments about allocative efficiency can be brought to bear on this area of administrative design. The standard economics-of-bureaucracy argument notes as of fundamental importance the fact that ownership of public bureaucracies is, by definition, not transferable through sale of assets, stock exchanges and liquidation through bankruptcy. That means that any surpluses or losses from the operation of public bureaucracies are compulsorily diffused among the population at large. Which in turn means, so the argument goes, that incentives for limiting organizational slack will be relatively weak in public bureaucracies as against transferable-ownership enterprises. In order to limit X-inefficiency, a heavy apparatus of audit and evaluation will be needed. To be effective, this itself will be very costly and the elaborate record-keeping and statistical returns that it requires from bureaucracies will further increase their operating costs.

By contrast, an enterprise with transferable ownership will be subject to pressure to limit organizational slack without very elaborate procedures for external checking, oversight, reporting and record-keeping, providing (and this is, of course, a crucial assumption) that it operates within the context of a well-informed, sophisticated and competitive capital market. That is, even in the absence of product-market competition, a transferable-ownership enterprise which fails to operate at the least-cost combination of inputs will make it profitable for speculators to take over the ownership of the enterprise at a depreciated price, in the expectation of making capital gains consequent on operating the enterprise with lower-cost inputs. In the extreme case, of course, transferability of ownership will cause the assets of the enterprise to be broken up altogether through the process of bankruptcy and put to more productive uses in other hands. This cannot occur even in theory for public bureaucracies (Wagner, 1973).

Moreover, where ownership of enterprises is transferable, it is possible to reward those who direct them by stock options. Where such options form a substantial part of the remuneration package of a senior official, he or she has a personal stake in making profitable long-term investment decisions. Where ownership is not transferable, and high officials are paid only from fixed salaries, the incentive for the self-regarding opportunist is to favour investments which bring maximum present benefits to producers — which may mean favouring investments which are far from profitable or appropriate in the long term.

It may also be held that direct political oversight (another defining feature of public bureaucracies) will make evaluation of enterprise performance problematic. Part of the case for direct political direction is that 'wider issues' can be introduced into the performance of a public service at any time. That means that any service provided through public bureaucracy is likely to become overlaid with purposes extraneous to that service, rather than a simple matter of carrying out a specific service at least cost — for instance, sanctions against disfavoured foreign regimes, support for ailing enterprises, 'close support' enforcement of other political measures, and so on.

A case can obviously be made for flexible, multiple-purpose, politically-directed enterprises. There are many advantages in such organization in an area such as law enforcement. But it inevitably means that the output or cost-effectiveness of any such enterprise will be very hard to evaluate against any clear-cut yardstick. Non-politically sensitive issues will be hard to disentangle from politically sensitive ones, offering considerable scope for strategic behaviour by opportunistic bureaucrats. For this reason, the normative implication of much economics-of-bureacracy writing is to avoid the classic public bureaucracy form, especially when it comes to routine or specific tasks like emptying septic tanks or operating bus services.

UK service delivery trends in practice

This section explores the hypothesis that the five normative preferences discussed above have in fact underlain UK administrative trends over the recent past — looking mainly at the period since the mid-1960s, but not sticking rigidly to that period.

It is not, of course, suggested that UK governments and public service providers over this period might consciously have fashioned their designs on theoretical works in the economics of bureaucracy or public choice more generally. Indeed, they could scarcely have done so, given that such approaches only re-emerged in the modern literature on bureaucracy in the 1960s and the public choice approach only developed to a 'text book' stage in the 1970s. Rather, what is of interest is whether a change in the general social climate might have led to a modification of traditional design principles for public services in the world of practice at the same time (and perhaps under the same social pressures) as the economics-of-bureaucracy approach developed in the academic world.

There is little sign of actual administrative trends in the UK reflecting a preference for smaller rather than larger scale of service provision over the past two decades. Indeed, since the return of fire services from national to local government operation after World War Two, there has been no really big transfer of service responsibilities from central to local government control. The process, currently in operation, of winding up (central government-appointed) New Town Corporations in England and Wales and transferring responsibility to local, elected authorities, might count as such a shift, although it is really a transfer from local appointed authorities to local elected ones and in that sense it does not really reduce the scale of service provision.

Over a very long period in Britain, public service responsibilities have been taken away from local authority level provision to national level provision, e.g. prisons in the 1870s, gas, electric, power and health care in the 1940s, driver and vehicle licensing in the 1970s. The 1970s in particular saw a major shift to larger scale of provision. A single public gas corporation replaced 12 area gas boards and a central Gas Council: 10 water authorities in England and Wales replaced 187 water-supply undertakings, 1393 local sewerage authorities and twenty-one river authorities (Greenwood and Wilson, 1984: 200). As in many other countries, local authorities themselves were concentrated into larger and fewer units, though the process was taken further in Britain than in comparable European countries. In the 1970s, the first two tiers of local government in Great Britain were cut down from 1822 separate authorities to only 452. Such changes, of course, go directly against the normative preferences usually associated with the public choice and economics-of-bureaucracy school.

Have the 1980s witnessed a turn of the tide — a swing towards a 'small is beautiful' mood and against the 1970s fashion for large-scale provision? There is not much sign of it. Firstly, no major services organized at national government level have been returned to local authority control. Indeed a national public prosecution system is proposed in England and Wales (similar to the Scottish system), replacing the traditional system whereby local police conducted prosecutions on their own account, such that there was no formal central political control over police prosecution policy. The possibility that UK local authorities might use their planning powers as a lever for licensing local cable TV stations (as in the USA) was hastily removed by legislation in 1983, so that a central Cable Authority had sole control over cable TV licensing.

Secondly, privatization of formerly government owned enterprises, to be considered below, has not in general been accompanied by a reduction in scale of provision. Where services have been privatized, for instance, telephones, and gas, they have been retained as national-scale enterprises rather than broken up into localized units (as in the case of telephone service in the USA). The same goes for the transfer of garbage collection services to private contractors in many local authorities, where a single contractor has been chosen for each area rather than a more decentralized or rival-provider structure.

Thirdly, some attempts have been made since 1980 to cut back numbers of middle-tier or top-tier authorities for some services, but in all cases 'reduction in scale' is decidedly ambiguous. The abolition of Area Health Authorities in England and Wales in 1982 (intermediate 'representative' bodies) and a later shift towards a business management style in the National Health Service is difficult to interpret readily on a centralization/decentralization scale. The same goes for the 1986 abolition of the Greater London Council and the six Metropolitan County Councils (large urban authorities for the big conurbations) in England, with their services being performed by a mixture of centrally-appointed local boards (London transport, for instance) and the existing lower-tier authorities (districts, or boroughs in the case of

London), operating through joint boards for police, fire and public transport.

This is certainly a step towards more multi-organizational provision, but less clearly towards reduction in operational scale, since many of the services formerly performed by the abolished authorities will continue to be carried out on the same scale by new joint boards or special-purpose authorities. Moreover, these changes are occurring in the context of sharply increasing financial control over local government by central government, creating stronger pressures for uniformity of service provision rather than the reverse.

Indeed, any signs of reducing scale of service provision over the past two decades are faint and ambiguous. Radio and TV broadcasting is perhaps the clearest long-term case, with the coming of regional level independent TV broadcasting stations to supplement the former BBC monopoly in the 1950s, a parallel development of independent local radio stations in the 1970s, and of city-level cable TV stations in the 1980s. Beyond this, evidence for widespread scale reduction is hard to find, and it is very difficult to make out a case that actual administrative trends in the UK over the past decade have in any way followed the economics-based preference for small-scale monopolies in public service provision rather than large-scale ones. At most, it might perhaps be argued that (1) some *new* services have recently emerged (as indeed such services have done in the past) on a small-scale, localized basis, as in the case of hospices for the terminally ill; and (2) that the 1960s and 1970s passion for increasing the scale of public service provision in the name of economies of scale and operating efficiency (as for instance, in driver and vehicle licensing) has passed.

Trends on scale of service provision have apparently not followed the normative principles of the economics of bureaucracy school. But trends in the contracting/employment dimension over the past two decades perhaps show some movement towards those principles, from such fragmentary evidence as can be mustered. For instance, an approximate yardstick of contract purchasing by central government can be obtained by deducting public service pay costs from the amount spent on current goods and services. That item rose from 43 to 52 percent of total budgetary estimates between 1963 and 1984, as can be seen in Table 6.1. In the field of research and development, work financed by government but performed by outside institutions rather than direct government employees, increased by about 10 percent as a proportion of all central government-financed R and D between 1964 and 1984, as can also be seen from Table 6.1.

Similarly, in the realm of more mechanical or 'dirty' work, there has been a steady trend in the UK since the 1950s to replace blue-collar civil servants by contracting arrangements with private firms, especially in defence. Table 6.1 gives some indication of the scale of this shift. The same goes for cleaning of government offices, where a shift to contract cleaning rather than direct-employment cleaning was well under way before Mrs Thatcher's government took office in 1979.

More generally, direct employment costs have been tending over a long period to fall as a proportion of central government spending. Figure 6.1 shows the proportion of total net UK estimates taken by direct public service pay and pensions, over the period 1961–62 to 1985–86 (a period over which a consistent run of figures can be obtained). The lower line shows the pay and pension costs of the civil service alone. The upper line shows pay and pension costs of the National Health Service and the armed forces as well as the civil service (it also includes a few other public bodies not financed by fees and charges, such as the UK Atomic Energy Authority). For both categories of service, it can be seen that pay costs have shown a considerable, if erratic, fall over the period as a whole. It can also be seen that the record of the two main political parties in office is not obviously different in this respect, in spite of the considerable institutional representation of public service labour unions in the structure of the Labour party.

All the evidence does seem to point to a trend towards performance contracting rather than direct employment, a trend which seems to have pre-dated Mrs Thatcher's government. Of course after 1979, contracting out became a matter of doctrine rather than a pragmatic response to pressures to cut costs. In 1980, the government announced that tasks then performed by 11,000 direct civil service employees (in areas such as building supplies, maintenance and cleaning) would be contracted out (Heald, 1983: 307). In fact, between 1980 and 1984, over 14,000 jobs in the civil service disappeared as a result of contracting-out and privatizing functions previously performed by direct employees (Dunsire, Huby and Hood, 1985: Table 7). In the armed forces, contracted-out tasks include medical services and foreign languages teaching (4000 military jobs were planned to be replaced by contract services in these areas in 1985–86).

Unfortunately, there are no centrally-collected figures for contracting-out in local authorities and health authorities. But there seems to have been some shift to contracting-out of laundry and cleaning services in National Health Service (NHS) (government) hospitals. These services were traditionally performed by direct employees (in 1981, *The Economist* (19 September 1981: 56) reported that only 2 percent of NHS hospital cleaning was contracted out), but in 1984 government ministers directed District Health Authorities to put some 2000 cleaning contracts out to tender over the next two years (*The Economist*, 26 May 1984: 60). By November 1985, 360 tendering exercises for catering, cleaning and laundry work had been carried out,

TABLE 6.1
Contracting versus direct employment: some indices

(1) UK central government spending on current goods and services[a] *less* public service pay costs, as percent of total supply estimates 1963/64 to 1984/85		(2) UK 'industrial' civil servants as percent of all UK civil service staff, 1960/61, 1985/86		(3) Extramural government-financed R and D as percent of total government-financed R and D, 1964–84	
		1960–61	40.9	–	–
		1961–62	39.8	–	–
		1962–63	39.1	–	–
1963–64	43.4	1963–64	38.1	1964	56.8
1964–65	42.8	1964–65	37.1	–	–
1965–66	42.7	1965–66	35.9	–	–
1966–67	40.9	1966–67	35.0	1967	55.1
1967–68	41.8	1967–68	33.7	–	–
1968–69	40.8	1968–69	32.0	–	–
1969–70	38.3	1969–70	31.3	1970	56.7
1970–71	35.4	1970–71	29.7	1971	60.1
1971–72	33.3	1971–72	28.9	1972	63.5
1972–73	34.6	1972–73	28.2	1973	63.4
1973–74	37.9	1973–74	27.3	1974	62.7
1974–75	36.8	1974–75	26.4	1975	62.5
1975–76	36.7	1975–76	25.5	1976	63.2
1976–77	38.2	1976–77	24.2	1977	63.8
1977–78	39.7	1977–78	24.5	1978	65.6
1978–79	40.5	1978–79	23.2	1979	66.7
1979–80	41.9	1979–80	22.8	1980	67.6
1980–81	43.8	1980–81	22.5	1981	65.0
1981–82	46.4	1981–82	21.9	1982	62.5
1982–83	48.5	1982–83	21.2	1983	65.0
1983–84	50.6	1983–84	20.2	1984*	66.8
1984–85	51.8	1984–85	19.6	–	–
–	–	1985–86	18.7	–	–

Sources: (1) Memorandum by the Chief Secretary to the Treasury on the Supply Estimates.
(2) *Civil Service Statistics*.
(3) *Economic Trends*.

Notes:
[a] (i.e. total spending less interest, subsidies, grants, loans, transfers)
[b] ('public service pay costs' means costs of pay and superannuation of civil service, armed forces, NHS and other miscellaneous public bodies)

* – provisional

FIGURE 6.1
Public service pay as percent of net total UK estimates, 1961–62 to 1985–86

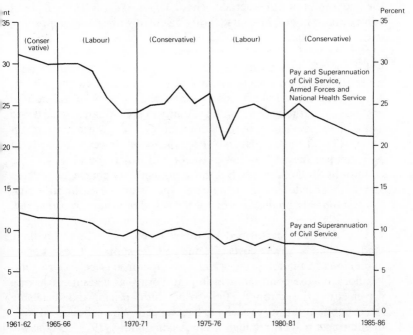

with 107 contracts going to private companies and 253 retained by Health Authority staffs (*Financial Times*, 2 November 1985). The government claimed that total savings from contracting-out in the NHS in 1983–84 amounted to £9.4m in a full year — just over 1 percent of the total laundry and domestic and catering budget (cf. HC 339, 1984–85, xix–xx). This is a distinctly undramatic outcome, in view of the benefits that were held to be gained from contracting-out such work.

In local authorities too, there has been a modest shift to contracting-out of services traditionally performed by direct employment, particularly street cleaning and garbage collection. Southend Borough Council was the first to change to private contractors for garbage collection and street cleaning in 1981, and eighteen other district and borough councils in England and Wales had followed suit by mid-1984 (*Which*? July, 1985: 328). In early 1985, central government announced that it would legislate to compel local authorities to introduce competitive tendering for garbage collection, catering, cleaning streets and buildings, and maintaining grounds and vehicles, but this plan was shelved in November 1985.

If there has been a shift towards performance contracting rather than direct employment in the provision of public services in the UK, has it brought about the beneficial results in terms of performance that the economics-of-bureaucracy school might expect? The effects of contracting-out are, of course, hotly disputed with strong opposition to contracting-out from public sector labour unions. Indeed, evaluation of the effects of a move to contracting-out is complicated by several well-known factors. Firstly, it is, in many cases, easier to quantify what a service costs than the standard of performance. In the UK, as elsewhere, some studies of contracting-out have revealed substantial cost savings in the short term. But quality of performance is harder to assess. The main thrust of the labour union case against contracting-out is that it saves costs at the expense of lower standards of performance (as well as lower wages and less favourable working conditions for employees). But the argument is, of course, conducted largely by anecdote, and in any case depends on the assumption that lower standards, on the basis of lower costs, should never be preferred.

Secondly, there are first-level and second-level effects of opening up services formerly performed by direct employment to competitive tender. That is, lower costs obtained in the short run may not be maintained in the long run, when a contractor may be able to get a headlock on the contract-awarding authority, as a result of having driven competitors from the field by predatory pricing and of causing direct public authority capacity to be scrapped. Where the capital costs of entering a market are high, as in Adam Smith's (1978: 534) classic case of tax farming in eighteenth-century France, this problem is not a trivial one. Adam Smith actually preferred a continuous public monopoly never subject to competition in such cases.

Thirdly, in the process of contracting-out, pressures for greater efficiency in direct-employment units may be set up, so that the law of anticipated reactions comes into effect. For instance, municipal employees in Birmingham won the bidding when municipal sanitation services, formerly operated on a direct employment basis, were put out to tender in 1983, as a result of drastically cutting costs in their own operations. Indeed, a process of tendering makes it necessary to specify performance standards, often for the first time, and this itself may make for more systematic performance evaluation of direct-employment services.

Fourthly, if contracting-out does not bring the benefits that the economics-of-bureaucracy theorists might expect, that might be interpreted as a consequence of defective tendering and allocative arrangements, not necessarily as a basic refutation of the ideas of the economics-of-bureaucracy school. For instance, competitive tendering in the National Health Service since 1984/85 has been limited by the use of narrow approved lists in many cases (Hartley and Huby, 1985: 24–5), and of restrictions placed on direct-employment units to submit tenders in competition with private firms. Also, as mentioned earlier, some contract arrangements convey monopolistic rights for which might be provided by simulataneously competing enterprises (for instance, all garbage collection contracts in UK local authorities to date have been on a basis of monopolistic service rather than allowing users to choose among competing garbage collection enterprises, as in some areas of the USA).

Careful studies of the effect of contracting-out are conspicuous by their absence. A study by the Audit Commission in mid-1984 claimed that the majority of local authorities in England and Wales which provided garbage-collection on a direct employment basis did less well on a value-for-money basis than private contractors, but many were doing as well or better. A survey of contracted-out services in health and local authorities by Hartley and Huby (1985, 23–6) suggested that yearly cost savings from competitive tendering rather than direct employment averaged 26 percent, but there was a very wide range of outcomes, making this average rather artificial. Also they did not offer evidence on service quality.

For the most part, in the UK as in other countries (Sharkansky 1979: 116–8), the tasks which have been put out to performance contracts have been relatively routine operations, often involving mainly low-paid labour. Examples include cleaning, maintenance, laundry services in hospitals, municipal garbage collection, security services. But contracting-out is not entirely confined to such fields. As shown above, it operates in areas such as R and D, and is increasingly being used for professional services such as architecture by local authorities, and even for management and quality control of programmes, as in the case of the Youth Training Scheme, a training programme for unemployed school-leavers introduced by government in 1983 (HC 221, 1981–82).

As was noted earlier the economics-of-bureaucracy approach tends to imply a normative preference for multiple rather than single suppliers of service, if all else is equal. This sharply contrasts with mainstream public administration doctrines. Which way have UK trends gone over the past two decades?

There were certainly some shifts in the direction of multiple-provider structures over the past decade. For instance, long-distance bus transport was to a large extent deregulated in 1980, by removing the former legal ability of British Rail (government-owned monopoly rail operator) to object to any new bus service which might damage its revenue, removing the formerly privileged position of the government-owned National Express Bus Company in running inter-city bus services, and allowing operators to operate any service they wanted for any main route over 30 miles long. Between 1980 and 1983, the number of coach passengers rose from under nine million to over fourteen million, and British Rail was forced to improve the quality of rail services and cut fares. Similar, though less dramatic, moves were made in air transport. In 1982, British Airways' monopoly on major domestic routes was broken when a rival airline (British Midland) was licensed to compete with BA on the London Heathrow–Edinburgh and London Heathrow–Belfast routes (Barrett et al., 1984).

Moreover, as has already been noted, the area of choice in broadcasting has been opened up by the creation of independent local radio stations in the 1970s, and of cable TV stations in the 1980s. In telecommunications, the radical step of combining local telephone service and cable TV into a single operation, and organizing it through regional franchises, was not taken. However, a new entrant (Mercury Communications) was allowed into the trunk telephone market in 1980, breaking British Telecom's former monopoly in this area. Similarly, the supply of telephone handsets was opened up to a degree of competition in the 1980s, and a 'Parents Charter' in 1980 allowed parents more choice in selecting among local authority schools for their children, although it fell considerably short of establishing a right for parents to place their children in schools of their choice.

As was noted above, economics-of-bureaucracy theorists commonly prefer user charges as the basis for financing public services to periodic allocations from a general tax fund. Has there been a major shift in the UK over the past two decades away from reliance on general tax funds as the basis of financing public services, and towards user charges or earmarked taxes?

There is not much sign of this at central government level. Budgetary estimates each year contain figures showing the extent of departmental spending which comes from sources other than general tax revenue. That category of funding is termed Appropriations in Aid, and consists mainly of funds raised in the form of fees to users, and other miscellaneous receipts. There is no very clear long-term trend in this category of spending, as Table 6.2 shows. In fact, it was running slightly lower in 1985/86 than it had been in 1965/66, but the difference is very small. A similar picture, but for a shorter time period, emerges from figures given in the *National Income and Expenditure Blue Book 1985* (Table 7.2, 57) for fees and charges in central government, which remained fairly steady at just over 2 percent of total current account spending between 1974 and 1984.

In short, no very clear sign here of a shift away from general-fund financing towards fees and charges as the financial basis of public services over the past decade or two. And indeed, even if there *had* been a big rise in Appropriations in Aid, this would go only part of the way towards a preference for user-charge finance of public services, because although Appropriations in Aid are drawn from sources other than general tax revenue, they form part of an overall block budget which is politically allocated every year, and hence are subject to the vagaries of the general-fund style of budgeting which economics-of-bureaucracy theorists commonly distrust as an allocation process.

The same applies to charges on patients as means of financing the NHS. As can be seen from Table 6.2, the proportion of NHS total spending financed by user charges (as opposed to general taxes) fell back slightly over the period 1963–64 to 1982–83, rather than the reverse. While user charges were raised periodically over this period, the elderly, the young and those on low incomes are exempted from charges, so the scope for increasing revenue by raising user charges has hitherto been fairly small (Heald, 1983: 299–306).

At the level of local authorities, income from rents halved as a proportion of all local authority income between 1965–66 and 1984–85, as is also shown in Table 6.2. Unfortunately, there is no long run of figures for income from other fees and charges. Some figures are given in the 1985 *National Income and Expenditure Blue Book* (Table 8.2, 63) for the years 1977 to 1983. For those years, the proportion of fees and charges to total current account spending remained fairly steady, at just over 6 percent. However, figures for UK local authority fees and charges as a proportion of total expenditure supplied to us from the Chartered Institute of Public Finance and Accounting (CIPFA) for the period 1974/75 to 1981/82 show a distinct increase, from under 5 percent in 1974 to nearly 7 percent in 1981.

On this evidence, the trend to user charges appears somewhat faint. Of course, these figures could be masking the 'true' picture in some way. The fairly static or downward trend in user charges, contribution to public services, as shown in Table 6.2 might perhaps be explained by continuous hiving-off of user-charge-financed services to off-budget, semi-autonomous agencies, so that they disappeared from Appropriations in Aid figures and from other fee and charge returns. Alternatively, or additionally a fairly steady proportion of total expenditure covered by user charges might be consistent with increased imposition of such charges, if their effect was to choke off demand drastically, for instance in the field of health care. Both of these factors are imponderables.

When it comes to earmarked (service-specific) taxes, it is even harder to see any sign of a trend towards Wicksellian preferences. Over the past century and more, earmarked taxes have not been in favour in Britain. No new earmarked taxes have been introduced over the past two decades, and some have been abandoned. For instance, radio licence fees were abolished in 1970, and the 'Eady levy' on cinema ticket sales (which went into a fund for British film production) was suspended in 1983 and is in the process of being abolished at the time of writing.

Have such earmarked taxes as exist increased in salience over recent years? Table 6.3 shows four cases. There is not much sign that TV

TABLE 6.2

Indicators of user charges as percentage of total spending on public services (various sources)

(a) Appropriations in Aid as percent of total UK estimates, 1955–56 to 1985–86 (1)		(b) Patients' payments as percent of total spending on National Health Service 1955–82 (2)		(c) Fees and charges as percent of UK local authority spending CIPFA figures 1974–75 to 1981–82 (3)		Blue Book figures 1977 to 1983 (4)		(d) Rents as percent of UK local authority spending, 1954–84 (5)		(e) Fees and charges as percent of UK central government spending, 1974–84 (6)		(f) Rents as percent of UK central government spending 1954–84 (7)	
1955–56	7.4	1955	4.7	1974–75	4.6	—	—	1954	15.2	1974	2.6	1954	8.9
1965–66	10.4	1958	4.8	1975–76	4.6	—	—	1957	16.0	1975	2.3	1957	9.1
1975–76	8.5	1961	5.7	1976–77	5.0	1977	6.2	1960	16.4	1976	2.5	1960	9.9
1985–86	9.1	1964	4.7	1977–78	5.5	1978	6.5	1963	16.2	1977	2.5	1963	11.7
—		1967	2.1	1978–79	6.2	1979	6.6	1966	16.6	1978	2.5	1966	8.7
—		1970	3.0	1979–80	6.6	1980	6.6	1969	18.3	1979	2.1	1969	6.4
—		1973	3.5	1980–81	6.6	1981	6.6	1972	16.4	1980	2.4	1970	5.2
—		1976	2.2	1981–82	6.9	1982	6.8	1975	14.5	1981	2.4	1975	3.8
—		1979	2.3	—	—	1983	6.7	1978	11.3	1982	2.4	1978	1.1
—		1982	3.0	—	—	—		1981	10.6	1983	2.5	1981	0.8
								1984	7.4	1984	2.1	1984	0.7

Sources: (a) Budget Estimates.
(b) *Annual Abstracts of Statistics.*
(c) CIPFA.
(d) *National Income and Expenditure.*
(e) *National Income and Expenditure.*
(f) *National Income and Expenditure.*

TABLE 6.3

Indicators of earmarked taxes as contributions to funding of public services

(a) Rates (property taxes) as per cent of UK local authority total receipts, 1960–84		(b) British Broadcasting Corporation: ratio of tax income to income from government grants, 1964–5 to 1983–4		(c) Light dues as per cent of operating income of General Lighthouse Fund, 1971–2 to 1982–3		(d) Employees and employers National Insurance Fund contributions as per cent of National Insurance Fund benefit payments plus other current government grants to the personal sector	
1960	39.3						
1961	39.5						
1962	39.1						
1963	39.2					1963	61.2
1964	38.4	1964–5	5.61			1964	64.2
1965	38.8	1965–6	6.07			1965	64.9
1966	38.5	1966–7	6.17			1966	63.8
1967	37.8	1967–8	7.05			1967	60.3
1968	35.8	1968–9	7.26			1968	58.7
1969	35.2	1969–70	8.16			1969	56.9
1970	34.0	1970–1	7.24			1970	61.3
1971	34.0	1971–2	n.a.	1971–2	95.7	1971	59.1
1972	34.6	1972–3	8.39	1972–3	96.5	1972	57.2
1973	32.4	1973–4	8.20	1973–4	97.7	1973	61.4
1974	31.5	1974–5	7.14	1974–5	97.9	1974	63.6
1975	28.3	1975–6	7.97	1975–6	97.2	1975	66.7
1976	26.9	1976–7	7.49	1976–7	98.0	1976	66.2
1977	29.0	1977–8	7.89	1977–8	97.6	1977	63.1
1978	29.5	1978–9	8.48	1978–9	98.0	1978	54.6
1979	30.0	1979–80	9.11	1979–80	97.8	1979	55.0
1980	31.2	1980–1	9.10	1980–1	96.9	1980	54.6
1981	33.6	1981–2	8.97	1981–2	96.0	1981	51.2
1982	35.4	1982–3	9.64	1982–3	96.3	1982	49.9
1983	34.5	1983–4	9.05			1983	52.5
1984	34.3					1984	52.6

Sources: (a) *National Income and Expenditure*

(b) *BBC Annual Report and Handbook*

(c) *Accounts of General Lighthouse Fund*

(d) *National Income and Expenditure*

licence fees have changed very much as a proportion of total expenditure by the BBC, as is shown in column (b) of Table 6.3. The high visibility of the BBC's licence fee to taxpayers undoubtedly creates political resistance to tax increases, but central government sets the tax level rather than the BBC itself, so the process of fixing the tax has some of the characteristics of budget negotiations under general-fund financing. 'Light dues', shown in column (c) of the table, are a surviving relic of the pre-general fund financing era. They are taxes on ships entering port, which pay for lighthouses in the UK and Irish Republic, and provide the main source of lighthouse expenditure.

Local authority rates (property taxes) are not earmarked taxes in a true Wicksellian sense, but they are clearly reserved to a particular class of public services. As Table 6.3 shows, rates as a proportion of total local authority spending actually fell by 5 percent overall between the early 1960s and 1984. In fact as Table 6.3 shows, it had dropped by over 12 percent by 1976. It rose in the subsequent years, but still stayed well short of its mid-1960s level.

The other earmarked tax shown on Table 6.3 is National Insurance Contributions (social security taxes levied on employers and employees and paid into a special fund). National Insurance contributions rose considerably as a proportion of total UK tax revenue over the period 1963–81, according to Rose and Karran (1983: 58–9). At the same time, however, they fell back over the period 1963–84 as a proportion of the total sums paid out by government in social security payments (the principal element in 'current grants to the personal sector') reflecting, no doubt, rising numbers registered as unemployed. Even on this item, it is thus debatable whether there was any move to the Wicksellian earmarked-tax-financing principle.

Certainly, in the UK over the past decade there has been a big trend towards 'privatization'. Privatization is not a completely new development. For example, government-owned road haulage and iron and steel enterprises were privatized in the 1950s, British Lion Film Studios in 1964 (an early use of a 'golden share' arrangement), government-owned public houses, breweries, wool disinfection factories, a travel agency and a multitude of government-owned stocks in the early 1970s. All of these privatizations occurred under Conservative governments, but it is interesting to note that the current trend towards privatization of government-owned enterprises was, ironically perhaps, begun by a Labour government in 1977, with a big sale of stock in the part government-owned BP company, in order to raise revenue.

Since then, with the advent of a 'privatizing' Conservative government in 1979, the floodgates have been opened, with a transfer of over £6 billion of assets and about 400,000 jobs to privately-owned company-law companies (*Financial Times*, 20 July 1985). Private ownership rights had been introduced into twelve major corporations, plus a number of smaller enterprises. There were also substantial real estate disposals. They included sales of municipally-owned houses and flats, with approximately 13 percent of municipal housing stock in England sold between 1979 and 1985 and approximately 7 percent of Scottish municipal housing stock (*The Sunday Times*, 20 October 1985). In late 1985 about 100 complete municipal housing estates were reported to be up for sale to private building companies for development (*The Times*, 22 November 1985). Asset sales also included disposal of commercial and industrial assets of New Town Corporations (which raised over £500m between 1979 and 1985); sale of smallholdings and estates formerly owned by the agriculture departments and of forestry estates formerly in the hands of the Forestry Commission (which raised over £63m between 1981 and 1984, out of a planned £82m disposal programme (HC 233, 1984–85)).

There are plans for much more of the same. In mid-1985, government reported plans to transfer another 200,000 jobs to the 'private sector' before the next General Election, to change the proportion of GDP in the hands of government-owned enterprises from 10.5 percent in 1979 to 6.5 percent (*The Times*, 18 July 1985). In late 1985, plans for privatization were still further extended, doubling the asset sales target to £4.75bn per year for 1986/87 to 1988/89, mainly by the addition of the monopoly public gas corporation to the list of disposals. Interestingly, too, there were signs in mid-1985 of a softening in Labour Party opposition to the privatization programme. The Party's 1983 General Election manifesto declared that a Labour government would take over all privatized enterprises at the original sale price, but an economic programme agreed between the party leadership and the Trade Union Congress in 1985 contained no pledge to take over all privatized enterprises and promised only to re-establish public enterprise in 'Key sectors' (*The Sunday Times*, 11 August 1985).

Most of the privatization programme, however, has been geared more towards the raising of revenue other than by the politically painful process of extra taxes in a sluggish economy with high unemployment, rather than directed towards the favoured public choice goal of enhancing allocative or X-efficiency. In some cases, the potential allocative efficiency-enhancing effects of takeover through ownership transfer have been deliberately blocked, for national-security or other reasons, by institutional expedients such as 'golden shares' held by government (giving it powers to block takeover bids) or the retention of a controlling stockholding by government. In other cases, potential for improving X-efficiency by subjecting the enterprises in question to competition (as in the case of airlines, airport services, telephones) has been rejected in favour of making the enterprises in question a more attractive proposition to investors, thus commanding a higher price.

The theoretical effects of ownership transfer are therefore likely to be most marked for the smaller, non-strategic, competitive-market enterprises included in the privatization programme, since only for them is liquidation or transfer of ownership a real possibility (an example is a government-owned ship repair yard, Redheads of South Shields, which was bought by employees in a buyout move in 1983 and went into liquidation in 1985 (*Financial Times*, 20 July 1985)). In short, the privatization programme has been carried out in a manner which to some degree flies in the face of the theoretical X-efficiency arguments which might otherwise be led to support a case for privatization of ownership rights, even in monopoly enterprises.

Trends that do not fit?

Institutional design principles normally associated with economic approaches to administrative theory seem to have been followed in some, but by no means all, of the trends in British public service organization over the past two decades. Such principles cannot clearly be shown to be an academic echo of developments occurring in real life, nor as a blueprint which has been followed to the letter. Moreover, some trends have been occurring for which economists of bureaucracy and public choice theorists have not yet developed theory or clear normative preferences. Two in particular deserve a brief mention. Namely, the growth of do-it-yourself in public services and the development of 'hybrid' enterprises which are not the classic public bureaux of public choice theory, but are not really private or independent enterprises either.

Firstly, do-it-yourself versus specialization. One of the 'megatrends' identified by Naisbitt (1982) in his content analysis survey of US local newspapers is a trend towards self-help rather than institutional help. In this category come such developments as the hospice movement (already mentioned); 'homesteading' in run-down former public housing areas (one of the first large-scale schemes in the UK was produced by a Labour-controlled local authority, Glasgow District Council, in 1981); neighbourhood crimewatch groups; a shift towards personal responsibility for health care (for instance, in purchase of kits for personal monitoring of pregnancy, blood pressure, bowel cancer); and a general explosion of 'self-help' networks to pool information and resources and organized by the affected persons themselves — be it families with handicapped children, homosexuals combating AIDS, even parents of sleepless children. Such trends are also clearly at work in the UK, some of them perhaps to a lesser extent than in the USA.

This sort of development chimes in more clearly with 'new left' biases against specialization and 'disabling professions' (in the vein of Illich, 1972) rather than with any clear economics-of-bureaucracy or public choice preference. In so much as they mean less tax-financed expenditure, they may increase consumer choice. In so far as they are 'privatizing' trends (often involving non-profit voluntary collective action rather than services provided for profit), they perhaps offer increased opportunities for trade and exchange. But neoclassical arguments for economic efficiency in specialization might lead economics-based theories of administration to draw the line at ever more do-it-yourselfing in public service provision. After all, Adam Smith, the classical advocate of competition and private enterprise, actually favoured local monopolies over free competition if greater specialization could be developed thereby (Smith, 1978: 85–6).

Secondly, much of what has been happening in the organization of public services in the UK, as in other countries, has not been so much a shift from pure public bureaucracy to pure private enterprise, as a shift from pure or classic public bureaucracy towards more hybrid forms of organization, having some of the features of public bureaucracy and some of the features of private enterprise (see, for instance, Sharkansky, 1979). This applies, for instance, to the transfer of service responsibilities from local authorities to special-purpose boards (as with the abolition of the Greater London Council and the English Metropolitan County Councils) or of the creation of privately-owned enterprises either with substantial 'public power' privileges (as with telecommunications, gas, and possibly water and electricity in the future) or in which government can exert influence either through special shareholding arrangements or through monopsonistic power (for instance, in purchase of warships and weapons). The rhetoric (coming from both advocates and critics of these changes) of a clean shift from the public to the private sector does not quite match the messier reality.

Now economics-based approaches to administrative theory have not yet developed theory of para-government organization in a way which relates to any clear normative principle. Theories of capture of independent regulatory agencies by regulatees or of the interaction between bureaucratic producers and interest-group producers do not lend themselves to prescriptive application in quite the same way as the five neoclassical principles discussed previously. Indeed, there are clearly opposed factors to be weighed, from an economics-of-bureaucracy viewpoint, in a development of para-government organization. On the one hand, a shift from service operation by classic public bureaucracies to operation by hybrid enterprises may move towards some of the features of 'privatization' — but not, by definition, all of them. On the other hand, by setting public services in a context where they are *neither* overseen by day to day political direction and full-blooded public audit and accountability *nor* exposed to the potential for ownership transfer in the event of operating other than at least cost, there is a risk, in the worst case, of creating conditions for even greater X-inefficiency than economists of bureaucracy typically expect from the 'classic' public bureau. So far, neither economics-based approaches nor the mainstream approach to public administration offer any clear prescriptive principles for this growing area of public organization.

Summary and conclusion

Does this admittedly patchy and impressionistic evidence from the UK support the hypothesis that administrative trends in the past two decades have moved towards the normative principles commonly associated with economics-based approaches to administrative theory, rather than the orthodox principles of mainstream public administration theory?

In some dimensions, it would seem that this *is* the case. Privatization and contracting-out are clear trends, though the former is less clearly a long term trend than the latter. But this cannot be said of the other prescriptive principles of the economics-based approach. There is very little evidence of real reduction in scale in public service provision, and only some of rivalry and multi-organizational structures as a developing trend in public service provision. There is not much evidence of increased reliance on user charges in general as a way of financing public services, as a trend of the past two decades.

Moreover, even in those areas where trends have broadly gone in line with the five principles outlined, they have often developed in such a way that the efficiency enhancing effects expected by economics-based theory of bureaucracy are certain to be damped down, if not wiped out, for reasons that can easily be drawn from that theory itself. Examples are the handing out of work to franchisees on a monopoly basis, or the linking of privatization to monopoly and/or substantial barriers to ownership transfer. Clearly this opens up considerable scope for future argument about whether principles drawn from economics-based theory of administration 'failed' in the UK over this period, or whether they were not really tried.

Thirdly, some trends which seem to have been taking place are not easy to evaluate against the more obvious normative principles derivable from the economics-based approach to administrative theory. This applies particularly to the specialization versus 'do-it-yourself' dimension of public service provision, and to the shift to 'hybrid' enterprises providing public services, the latter being especially difficult to evaluate by the principles either of orthodox public administration theory or of the rival economics-based theories.

As was stressed earlier, the extent to which observable administrative trends follow or run counter to any given set of design principles tells us nothing about the value of those principles themselves. It does not necessarily tell us anything about the real influence of academic theorists, since the same principles might emerge spontaneously in the world of practice, in complete ignorance of their academic provenance. But it can give us some indication of which principles have been on the crest of the wave in practice, serving as a (perhaps unconscious) blueprint for, or at least a reflection of, what is actually happening. From this evidence, it would seem that in the world of practice as well as in the halls of academe, neither the mainstream Woodrow Wilson–Max Weber principles, nor the challenging economics-based principles, can quite claim the status of a dominant paradigm.

Note

This paper arises in part from research work supported by the UK Economic and Social Research Council (grant No, E 00232018). We are grateful for helpful comments from Keith Hartley of the University of York.

References

Audit Commission (1984) 'Securing Improvements in Refuse Collection'. Bristol, Audit Commission.

Albrow, N. (1970) *Bureaucracy*. London: Pall Mall Press.

Barrett, F. et al. (1984) 'The Crafty Traveller in Britain', *The Sunday Times Magazine*, 15 July 1984, pp. 31–3.

Crain, W.M. and R.B. Ekelund (1976) 'Chadwick and Demsetz on Competition and Regulation', *Journal of Law and Economics*, 19, pp. 149–62.

Dunleavy, P. (1985) 'Bureaucrats, Budgets and the Growth of the State: Reconstructing an Instrumental Model', *British Journal of Political Science*, 15, pp. 299–328.

Dunsire, A., M. Huby and C.C. Hood (1985) 'Whitehall in Retrenchment II: Plans and Out-turns', University of York, mimeo.

Greenwood, J. and D. Wilson (1984) *Public Administration in Britain*. London: Allen and Unwin.

Hartley, K. and M. Huby (1985) 'Contracting-Out in Health and Local Authorities: Prospects, Progress and Pitfalls', *Public Money*, September 1985, 23–6.

Heald, D.A. (1983) *Public Expenditure*. Oxford: Martin Robertson.

Illich, I. (1972) *Deschooling Society*. London: Calder and Boyars.

Kellas, J.G. (1984) *The Scottish Political System* (3rd edn.) Cambridge: Cambridge University Press.

Liebenstein H. (1976) *Beyond Economic Man: A New Foundation for Microeconomics*. Cambridge, Mass.: Cambridge University Press.

Mueller, D.C. (1979) *Public Choice*. Cambridge: Cambridge University Press.

Naisbitt, J. (1982) *Megatrends: Ten New Directions Transforming Our Lives*. New York: Warner Books.

Niskanen, W.A. (1971) *Bureaucracy and Representative Government*. Chicago: Aldine Atherton.

Niskanen, W.A. (1975) 'Bureaucrats and Politicians', *Journal of Law and Economics*, 18, pp. 617–43.

Niskanen W.A. (1980) 'Competition Among Government Bureaus' in C.H. Weiss and A.H. Barton (eds) *Making Bureaucracies Work*. Beverly Hills: Sage, pp. 167–74.

Ostrom, V. and E. Ostrom (1971) 'Public Choice: A Different Approach to the Study of Public Administration', *Public Administration Review*, 31, 302–16.

Ostrom, V. (1974) *The Intellectual Crisis in American Public Administration*, rev. edn. Alabama: University of Alabama Press.

Rose, R. and T. Karran (1983) 'Increasing Taxes? Stable Taxes or Both? The Dynamics of United Kingdom Tax Revenues since 1948'. Studies in Public Policy No. 116, Centre for the Study of Public Policy, University of Strathclyde.

Rosenberg, N. (1960) 'Some Institutional Aspects of the Wealth of Nations', *Journal of Political Economy*, 68, pp. 557–70.

Sharkansky, I. (1979) *Wither The State*? Chatham: Chatham House.

Smith, A. (1978) *Lectures on Jurisprudence*. R.L. Meek, D.D. Raphael, P.G. Stein (eds) Oxford: Clarendon Press.

Wagner, R.E. (1973) *The Public Economy*. Chicago: Markham.

Williamson, O.E. (1975) *Markets and Hierarchies*. London: Collier-Macmillan.

UK Government Publications

Cmnd 9576 1985, 127th Report of the Commissioner of HM Inland Revenue for the Year Ended 31 December 1984.

HC 221 1981–2, Report of the Employment Committee 1981–2: Youth Employment and Training: New Training Initiative.

HC 233 1984–5, 13th Report from the Committee of Public Accounts 1984–5: Disposal of Forestry Land.

HC 339 1984–5, 6th Report from the Social Services Committee 1984–5: Public Expenditure on the Social Services.

7
Productivity measurement in bureaucratic organizations

Richard Murray

This article deals with the theory of and the practical solutions to measuring productivity in bureacratic organizations. It ends by summing up the results from a broad programme to measure productivity in the public sector in Sweden for the years 1960–1980.

There are many good reasons for measuring productivity in the public sector — and many objections. The first good reason is to raise the quality of the national accounts. The general practice today is to assume zero productivity change. This is unsatisfactory when the public sector comprises 30 percent of the total work force. The second good reason is to fuel the budgetary process with some solid facts. Today most government agencies are governed by ministries that don't know what they are getting for their money. By supplying information on output and resources consumed on an overall level it becomes possible for the agency to present what it is producing and at what cost and consequently the ministry can refrain from detailed regulation of the means of production. The third good reason is to furnish managers of public agencies with relevant information for them to govern.

Objections have over time become quite numerous. Efficiency is what is relevant and it is asked whether productivity is at all related to efficiency. It is asserted that productivity cannot be measured in a meaningful way when there is more than one output. Some other objections are that: quality cannot be incorporated in a productivity measure and measures of productivity are of no practical use are some other objections. These and other objections are dealt with both theoretically and in order to point out practical methods to circumvent them.

Since 1982 a broad program of productivity measurements in the public sector has been carried out in Sweden. Measurements cover 70 percent of the public sector. Results, interpretations and experiences are presented.

Introduction

This chapter deals with productivity measurement in the public sector. It discusses the problems that immediately arise when measurement is attempted, asking whether is it possible and if so, is it meaningful? These are practical issues and nothing is so practical as a good theory. A solid theoretical foundation is essential in overcoming practical obstacles and recognizing what is and what is not a real obstacle.

The public sector has grown rapidly, but unlike the private sector its productivity has rarely been measured. One exception is the measurement of productivity in the US Federal Government undertaken by the

Bureau of Labour Statistics from 1967 and onwards. This chapter will examine the potential for and the purposes of productivity measurement, by discussing misconceptions about what productivity is, how it is measured and why it is measured.

The many purposes of productivity measurement

A prime purpose of public sector productivity measurement is to improve national accounts. The government sector constitutes between 20 and 30 percent of the labour force in most capitalist countries, and slightly less of Gross National Product (GNP). The contribution of the government sector to GNP is measured in the national accounts by the value of its inputs. Since outputs are assumed to equal inputs there cannot be any productivity change either positive or negative. By definition, it is zero.

A programme to develop output statistics for the service sector must include the private as well as the government parts of the sector. Problems are very much the same in each, as will be shown. The growth of the service sector is very rapid today and this is likely to continue. Whether we are getting more out of it than we have put into it over the years is a major question to answer, since it will have a tremendous impact on the well-being of nations in the future.

A second reason for making productivity measurements is to furnish the budgeting dialogue with solid facts. In programme budgeting the idea is that the budget office, which presumably acts on behalf of its political principals, should buy specified amounts of services from an agency and be able to appraise both what it is paying for and what it is getting. Counting and weighing the delivered goods then becomes essential. In the budget process the agency asks for more money on the grounds that inputs have become more expensive, the work has become more complicated, the number of cases handled has increased and the quality of work has risen, etc. The budget office tries to see through these veils and sort out the different factors, judging both their merits and importance in terms of appropriations. However, it will be at a loss to do so if it has no solid measures of output and productivity to call on.

There is a double purpose in this budgeting process which in practice the PPB approach never sorted out. Firstly, there is evaluation. What do we get for the money? Is it more or less than last year, and how does it compare with what we get in other areas? Secondly, there is a budgetary purpose involved. How much money does the agency need to produce what it is being asked to do?

A third purpose of productivity measurement is management, and this purpose has many subdivisions. The first one is assessment. How are we doing, are we doing better than last year, etc? For a government agency lacking the relentless judgement of the market, it is of prime importance to have some sort of feedback signal that continually informs it about peformance. Profits cannot be calculated but productivity can. Calculating productivity growth and rating itself against other firms is also of importance to the market firm, even though it has its profits as a yardstick of success. Profits are influenced both by productivity and prices, but prices are subject to the fluctuations of the market. Therefore, in order to assess the strength of the firm under less favourable market conditions, productivity has to be calculated.

The second subdivision is that of analysis. From the aggregate productivity figures some conclusions can be drawn. What is the cause of productivity slow down? Is it connected with shrinking production and fixed costs which have to be covered by fewer units, or is it due to rising resource use per unit produced? It also becomes possible to distinguish between rising costs due to a rise in input prices and those due to an increase in resource use per unit. Which inputs have increased the most are easily discernable. Last year can be compared with the year before and with other years or months and conclusions drawn about favourable and unfavourable conditions. Does productivity increase with increased production or not? In what way does the resource mix influence productivity? Have investments in computers over the last five years shown up in increased labour or total productivity?

The third way of using productivity measurement is for management to set goals for the organization as a whole, or as separate units, in productivity terms. For example, next year we are going to improve productivity by 2 percent. Success or failure can be discovered if productivity is measured.

Finally productivity measurement can be used in conjunction with incentives. Part of a productivity increase, which can be recalculated in savings, can be handed out to personnel in the form of a bonus. Closely connected with this use is that of delegation. Clear goals have to be set of which output and cost efficiency are the most important.

Objections concerning the relevance of productivity measures

Let us take as the starting point the statement that productivity measures something that, by definition, is irrelevant to efficiency. It measures the relationship between outputs of various sorts and resources used, but it says nothing whatsoever about the value of those outputs. This reasoning can be interpreted in different ways. One interpretation is that productivity is not efficiency and therefore productivity is of no interest, since efficiency holds the key. Another is that productivity is in principle related to efficiency, but that it is only under rare circumstances that measures of productivity change tell us anything about efficiency, because of the way in which productivity is measured. Let us start out by defining the concepts of productivity and efficiency.

Productivity is the relationship, or quotient, between output and input.

$$1.\ \text{Productivity} = \frac{\text{Output}}{\text{Input}}$$

Efficiency is the relationship between the effects of output, or the goal achievement, and input.

$$2.\ \text{Efficiency} = \frac{\text{Effects of output}}{\text{Input}}$$

If we study a private business firm, the relationship between productivity and efficiency can be described easily. For the firm the relevant effects of output can be defined as revenues. Revenues are the product of output (in physical terms) and prices earned on the market.

$$3.\ \text{Efficiency of a private firm} = \frac{\text{Output} \times \text{prices}}{\text{prices}}$$
$$= \text{Productivity} \times \text{Input}$$

From this, we learn that there is an immediate relationship between productivity and efficiency. Efficiency is proportional to productivity and changes in exactly the same way. A 2 percent rise in productivity is accompanied by a 2 percent rise in efficiency, assuming prices are unchanged.

The efficiency of a private firm should be measured in terms of profits. This is easily accomplished by extending formula 3. So efficiency is revenues related to costs. But what are costs? Costs are physical input quantities multiplied by their purchase prices.

Efficiency, measured as the relationship between revenues and costs, is the equivalent of productivity times the relationship between output and input prices.

$$3a.\ \text{Efficiency of a private firm} = \frac{\text{Revenues}}{\text{Costs}}$$

$$= \frac{\text{Output}}{\text{Input}} \times \frac{\text{Prices of output}}{\text{Prices of input}}$$

$$= \text{Productivity} \times \frac{\text{Prices of output}}{\text{Prices of input}}$$

The efficiency of the private firm is proportional to productivity and changes in the same way. In this version, the factor of proportion is the relationship of the prices of output to the prices of input.

If the measure of efficiency is equal to one, we would say that the firm breaks even. If it is larger than one then it is efficient and makes a profit, and if it is less than one then it is inefficient and makes a loss. However, this is something that productivity can tell us nothing about. Productivity is an output measure related to an input measure. It is, however, relative and what is high and what is low is a matter of comparison. Therefore we cannot know whether a single measure of productivity indicates that the business is efficient or inefficient.

Let us assume that the activity is not worthwhile, i.e. that it is inefficient. Every dollar spent produces one unit of output worth only 50 cents. If productivity increases by 75 percent so that the dollar produces 1.75 units of output worth 87.5 cents it is still a waste of resources. However, the waste is reduced from 50 cents to 12.5 cents per dollar of resources. So inefficiency has been reduced by 75 percent.

Measuring and thinking about productivity offers no panacea. It does not deprive the organization or its principals of their duty to consider whether output is worth the resources spent. An analysis of productivity does not make an analysis of efficiency superfluous. However, a rational and practical division of labour can be visualized. The efficiency of government bureaucracy is usually far more difficult to quantify than productivity. It often has to be estimated on an intuitive basis. Both the agency and its supervisors can concern themselves solely with productivity, once a programme of outputs and efficiency has been agreed on, i.e. once it has been decided that the value of a unit of output is greater than its cost and that it is the best design of outputs in relation to the goals set.

Another argument against the relevance of productivity admits its relationship to efficiency but denies its applicability. This argument can be summed up in the following way, 'the agency might be very productive but is doing the wrong things'. Only in those circumstances, where the agency is on the right track from the point of view of political priorities, does productivity have any relevance to efficiency. This argument applies to situations where the agency is producing at least two products. It can then happen that the agency favours production of the cheap, but politically less preferred product, and thereby increases 'productivity'. Efficiency does not, in that case, increase proportionately and might even decrease. Far from discrediting productivity measurements, this example lends itself beautifully to the demonstration of how such measures should be constructed.

Any measure of output including more than one product has to be an aggregate. The aggregation should be performed in accordance with the relative contribution of the different kinds of output to the goals of the organization. Their absolute contributions do not concern us. It is quite sufficient to weigh the products by their *relative* contributions, e.g. 'twice as much' or 'one third as much'. This assures us that a change in aggregate output corresponds to an equivalent change in goal achievement and that as a consequence a change in productivity corresponds to an equivalent change in efficiency.

It could well be that an agency has lower costs for one product in comparison to another, but that the products provide equal contributions to the over-riding goals of the agency. A change from the more expensive to the cheaper product will increase productivity, since the products have equal weights in the aggregate output. This is quite logical if we want the productivity measure to signal changes in efficiency. Setting weights proportional to the contributions made to the achievement of organizational goals will guarantee that the agency reaches the highest level of efficiency, when maximizing its output according to those weights.

In some respects, it is easier for the private firm to measure productivity than for the bureaucratic organization. A firm has the prices it gets for selling its products as natural candidates for weights. An agency, financed by appropriations, has no such prices. Its weights must be drawn from other sources. However, the differences must not be exaggerated. For the firm it is a matter of judging what the weights should be when maximizing long term profits. In this case, short term prices as weights may be misleading.

When there is more that one product, the following formula is used for calculating productivity.

$$4. \text{ Productivity} = \frac{\text{Output}(1) \times \text{Weight}(1) + \text{Output}(2) \times \text{Weight}(2) + \text{etc}}{\text{Input}}$$

Productivity is then the weighted sum of outputs divided by inputs.

This immediately raises the question, what if there is more than one input? Interestingly enough, the procedure by which inputs are aggregated is seldom questioned, although it poses the same basic problems. It is conventionally accepted that inputs should be aggregated by using their prices to give a total cost. For the profit maximizing firm, this is quite logical since the reduction in profits from using one unit of input equals the price of that input. However, many questions arise. Is the price of an input its normal price? How should the use of capital and machinery be evaluated? How should the use of other resources owned by the firm be evaluated? Do the price differences reflect differences in the quality of resources? Let us, however, accept the use of input prices as weights, and at the same time use the prices of outputs as the weights in the numerator.

$$5. \text{ Productivity} = \frac{\text{Output}(1) \times \text{Price}(1) + \text{Output}(2) \times \text{Price}(2) + \text{etc.}}{\text{Input}(1) \times \text{Price of Input}(1) + \text{Input}(2) \times \text{Price of Input}(2) \text{ etc.}}$$

$$= \text{Efficiency}$$

By referring back to equation 3a we see that productivity, thus measured, is just the same as efficiency. What distinguishes productivity from efficiency is that the weights of outputs and inputs need not be the absolute contributions to, and reductions from the goal, which in this case equals profits, but only the relative ones. Weights need only to be proportional to the absolute contributions and reductions in goal fulfilment. Proportionality is essential if changes in productivity are to reflect changes in efficiency. This attribute is quite useful when it comes to estimating weights.

Productivity does not take account of quality
Closely related to the objections concerning relevance is the assertion that productivity leaves out changes in quality. The presumption is that quality has increased and that this is not reflected in the quantification of output. Consequently, productivity change does not give a fair evaluation of organizational efficiency.

Why is it so often presumed in the public sector that quality has increased? Very often the story goes as follows. Nowadays production of the product requires more personnel, more sophisticated routines, new, expensive machinery, and so on, and therefore quality has improved. That is, quality is defined by the inputs used in production, or by the process by which production is carried out. Quality should, however, be defined in terms of an improved contribution to the goals of the organization, or its principals. If the principals are consumers, it is their evaluation of quality that should set the standard. If the design of a product is new and fancy but consumers do not value this more highly than they did the previous design, then there has been no quality increase. Similarly, if hospitals introduce single rooms for their patients, but the patients would prefer to have company, there has not been a quality increase but instead, a quality decrease. Bearing this in mind, it is obvious that quality changes should be treated in the same way as different products are aggregated into a comprehensive measure of output. The weighting of the product should reflect its relative contribution to the goals of the organization, or its principals. Therefore a quality increase will be reflected in a slightly larger weighting and a quality decrease in a slightly smaller weighting.

In principal, we have solved the problem of how to take account of changes in quality, but the need to work out a practical solution still remains. We will return to this issue later. At this stage it is well to remember that even when there are market prices by which to judge the relative merits of different qualities, it is sometimes difficult to set the appropriate weights. A reasonably good approximation can be made if the same basic product exists in varying qualities on the market. The relative prices can then be used as weights. If, however, the quality of the product changes over time, it is difficult to sort out how much of, for example a price increase, reflects quality improvement. Part of the price change, or even the whole of it, might be attributed to inflated input prices or lower productivity. A thorough investigation is needed to sort out the different components in the price change. This is everyday practice in determining changes in the consumer price index.

No conclusions can be drawn from productivity measurements

A common argument is that even if productivity is calculated accurately, no conclusions can be drawn about the causes of change and what should be done to remedy a productivity decrease or further a productivity increase.

Productivity can be measured in different ways. Far from being a weakness of productivity measurement this guarantees its relevance. Measurements of productivity can be designed differently, according to the purpose in mind and the answers that are sought. So what a productivity measurement tells us depends upon how it has been designed and the question it is intended to answer. To illustrate this we will look at what kind of productivity measurement is appropriate for which purpose, and what types of important information can be gained from each.

Suppose that we wish to evaluate an agency from the point of view of its principals. This is the perspective used in the national accounts, where the principals, as far as possible, are identified with the consumers. The question then is, how much more or less does the principal receive in output in return for the resources expended on production? Weights for the different kinds of output should reflect the principal's evaluation of their relative importance. However, since we intend to compare productivity say, over a twenty year period, we are faced with the question, what generation of principals should set the weights? From the point of view of the present generation, it is its preferences that should determine the weights of outputs. However, if the question we wish to answer is how much better off would our grandparents have been today judged from their point of view of twenty years ago, then their judgements twenty years ago on the relative importance of different outputs, should determine the weights. On the other hand, should we wish to evaluate the organization as such, a different approach might be relevant. Instead of counting just the output which has been both produced and consumed, it might be more to the point to count the potential output, or the capacity. In the case of a hospital, a distinction should be drawn between the number of beds used and the number of beds available.

From the point of view of organizational efficiency, it would be more relevant to choose weights for the outputs from the beginning of the period over which productivity is compared, rather than from the end, because that is the starting point for the organization's efforts.

This is especially relevant if weights are chosen to reflect productive capacity, rather than consumer preferences. Weights are then set proportional to the marginal costs of each product. Using these weights will produce a comprehensive measure of total output, which shows how much of the various combinations of outputs the organizations could produce. If we want to measure how organizational efficiency has developed, we should take marginal costs from the beginning of the period as the weights for outputs. Marginal costs at the end of the period are themselves the result of a successful, or unsuccessful, effort to improve productivity.

In an organization that, to any large extent, uses inputs bought from outside, its own efforts to increase efficiency will not be so visible if total cost productivity is calculated. In order to reveal organizational efficiency, productivity on a value-added basis should be calculated. This relates the 'value-added' by the organization to either the input of labour, or the combined input of labour and capital employed by the organization. Value-added is the difference between the value of the output when it is sold and the value of the purchased inputs, raw materials, rents, services, etc. It is what the organization adds in value by utilizing the purchased inputs. In order to calculate value-added, the value of output has to be determined, requiring prices for the outputs. However, the change in value added productivity can, with reasonable accuracy, be estimated even if output prices do not exist, as will be explained later.

At this point let us give the formulae for three different concepts of productivity, total or cost productivity, labour productivity and value-added productivity.

6. Total (Cost) Productivity $= \dfrac{\text{Output}}{\text{Costs}}$

7. Labour productivity $= \dfrac{\text{Output}}{\text{Labour Input}}$

8. Value-Added Productivity $= \dfrac{\text{Output} \times \text{Prices of Purchases}}{\text{Labour Input}}$

$$= \dfrac{\text{Value Added}}{\text{Labour Input}}$$

One final point about the choice of productivity measure concerns the choice of price indices. Since what interests us is productivity change, we have to compare both output and costs at different times. To eliminate the effect of inflation, inputs have to be evaluated at the same prices. The technique is that of deflating costs in current prices by an input price index.

Let us now look at how the change in productivity is calculated. Productivity has to be measured for two different time periods, or for two or more organizational units, if the aim is a productivity comparison. This has to be done in a way that makes the comparisons meaningful. That means we have to choose one set of weights and use them for aggregation of outputs for both periods, just as we have to choose one set of input prices to aggregate inputs for both periods. In order to simplify the notation let us call a sum of several terms SUM, e.g. Sum Outputs × Weights means the sum of a series of terms consisting of the product of one output and its weight. Output for the first period is termed *Outputs 1* and the weight for period (1) is likewise called *Weights 1*. Using this definition, productivity during period (1), with weights from period (2) is

$$9a. \text{ Productivity (1)} = \frac{\text{Sum Outputs (1)} \times \text{Weights (2)}}{\text{Sum Inputs (1)} \times \text{Prices (2)}}$$

and productivity for period (2), also with weights for period (2) is

$$9b. \text{ Productivity (2)} = \frac{\text{Sum Outputs (2)} \times \text{Weights (2)}}{\text{Sum Inputs (2)} \times \text{Prices (2)}}$$

Productivity change is the ratio of productivity in the latter period divided by productivity in the former period.

$$10. \text{ Productivity Change} = \frac{\text{Productivity (2)}}{\text{Productivity (1)}}$$

If productivity has increased, this ratio is larger than one. If it has decreased, it is smaller than one. Often it is calculated as a percentage change which turns the formula into the following.

$$11. \text{ Percentage Productivity Change} = \left\{ \frac{\text{Productivity (2)}}{\text{Productivity (1)}} - 1 \right\} \times 100$$

If the productivity change takes place over a number of years, we might want to have the annual productivity change calculated as a compound rate of interest. The annual productivity change is calculated by the formula

$$12. (1 + \text{Annual Productivity Change})^{\text{Number of Years}}$$

$$= \frac{\text{Productivity (2)}}{\text{Productivity (1)}}$$

To get the annual productivity change in percent terms it has to be multiplied by 100.

Formula 10 can therefore be written as

10a. Productivity Change =

$$\frac{\text{Sum Outputs (2)} \times \text{Weights(2)}}{\text{Sum Outputs (1)} \times \text{Weights (2)}} \times \frac{\text{Sum Inputs (1)} \times \text{Prices (2)}}{\text{Sum Inputs(2)} \times \text{Prices(2)}}$$

This highlights the fact that outputs from both occasions are weighted by the same weights — in this case from period (2) — and that inputs are, in the same manner, weighted by prices from period (2).

As far as inputs are concerned, the aim is to remove the disturbing influence of inflation. When comparing the consumption of resources they have to be evaluated at the same prices. One way to do this is to add together a series of terms consisting of the product of an input quantity, e.g. hours of work, square-metres of floor space, number of pencils, light-bulbs, and its price. This can be very tedious, if it is at all possible. Alternatively, the cost in current prices can be deflated by a price index for those inputs. Such a price index is a weighted sum of prices. The weights in this case are the amounts of input. The relevance of the particular price index has to be seriously examined by asking questions such as 'Is the mix of inputs used by the agency similar to that of the price index?' However, given that we have a relevant price index 10a. can be rewritten:

10b. Productivity Change =

$$\frac{\text{Sum Outputs (2)} \times \text{Weights (2)}}{\text{Sum Outputs(1)} \times \text{Weights(2)}} \times \frac{\dfrac{\text{Costs(1)}}{\text{Price Index (1)}}}{\dfrac{\text{Costs(2)}}{\text{Price Index(2)}}}$$

From 10b it is quite obvious that price indices play an important role. More often than not, several indices must be used, one price index for each category of inputs, e.g. a wage index for labour, a rent index for floor space, a price index for materials. Costs are deflated category by category, and then added together to make up costs in fixed prices.

Now let us return to the choice of price indices. Prices for the agency may have developed differently from prices in general. The question is then, whether this difference should be allowed to affect the measured change of productivity. It can be argued that a gain in relative prices should be attributed to the organization. If, for example, an agency by hiring more low-paid workers succeeds in lowering its wage bill, deflating costs in current prices, using the general price index will result in a smaller increase of resource costs than using the agency's own price index. In this case, real costs are measured by the value of the resources in alternative uses. So from the point of view of society at large the change in productivity is more favourable than internal efficiency would suggest.

Deflating the value-added in production poses even more tricky questions. Value-added in current prices could be deflated by a general consumer price index. The resulting value-added in fixed prices reflects how much the value-added of a firm or a sector of the economy is worth, in terms of consumer goods. Fixed price value-added productivity, calculated in this way, will show how much labour, in different firms or sectors of the economy, produces in terms of consumer goods. This is, of course, of interest when it comes to allocating labour throughout the economy. Value-added calculations such as these will reflect relative price changes, so that productivity in a sector will increase merely because prices of its products have gone up more than consumer prices in general.

By comparing productivity over periods of time and between similar organizations, opportunities for finding the causes behind performance increase tremendously and the means by which to improve the output/input ratio. It is possible to go further and deepen the analysis in a consistent way by breaking down productivity change into its various components. In short, productivity measurement is a very fruitful starting point. It does not, even in its most refined applications, furnish concrete suggestions about what to do to remedy the situation, but what instrument of analysis does?

Productivity is influenced by so many external factors

The results from productivity measurements in Swedish national government agencies has often been seen as unfair (when they are negative) and not to reflect the stress and speed with which work is done. In fact, it is often felt at the agencies that efficiency today is much higher than it was ten or twenty years ago. Another reaction is that the measures are unfair because they are influenced by many factors that are external to the agency. This is true, at least in principle, while at the same time it provides a bridge between the agency's experience of the increasing intensity of work and the measured negative productivity development. If there are external factors causing productivity to decline, they could very well outweigh an increasing internal efficiency. Discussing who bears the responsibility for the development of productivity at an agency becomes a deep philosophical issue.

'Demand' as a concept does not fit in well into the setting of bureaucratic production. Nevertheless, we will use it to describe the externally generated workload. It may be generated by 'customers' or by parliament, and it reflects a demand, usually at zero price, for the services of the agency. Demand can fluctuate, which necessitates the adjustment of the supply of these services. If fewer criminals are sentenced to jail, the supply of cells should be reduced in order to avoid excess capacity. Productivity is, of course, dependent on technology and technology develops outside the agency. Therefore, it is up to the agency to utilize new technology, and even to refrain from investing in it when it does not pay to do so.

It is often thought that the productivity of services cannot be improved, or if it can be done, then it can only be achieved by lowering the standard of the service. The prospects for productivity improvement cannot be visualized unless changes, sometimes radical, in the end-product are accepted. The one-man bus is an example of a productivity improvement. Of course a ride on a one-man bus is not the same as a ride in a bus that has both a driver and a conductor, but is the difference so great as to justify regarding the two kinds of rides as wholly separate products? Or is this an example of an improvement in productivity being won by an equivalent reduction in quality? Neither seem to be reasonable objections.

There are all kinds of social change that affect productivity. Clients and witnesses at courts may plead their cause at greater length, which makes trials much more time consuming. There are legislative changes that affect productivity. New rules for income tax may require new routines for checking tax assessments.

It is worth noting that none of the above mentioned causes of productivity change has anything to do with 'slack' in the organization. There may be no slack at all, or it may be unchanged, nonetheless, productivity changes due to these factors.

An incomplete understanding of the many factors that influence productivity, besides slack, explains some of the controversy surrounding productivity studies. People may perceive that life in the agency is more hectic than ever. Productivity may still be reported to have declined. In the light of their own experience this may seem to be unbelievable.

In a broad programme of productivity measurement, it is just as important to enquire into the causes of productivity change, as it is to measure those changes. Therefore, any efforts on a broad scale to have agencies report productivity should include measures to examine the whole range of factors reviewed here.

Productivity measurements will be misinterpreted, misused and create the wrong incentives

One of the criticisms against productivity measurements claims that all facts and figures are misinterpreted and misused, at least to some degree and that, therefore, it is better to refrain from collecting such data. It should be noted that this risk exists in all empirical investigations. Therefore, all facts and figures have to be treated with caution. If possible the degree of uncertainty should be stated. Although measurements of probability for productivity calculations, such as confidence intervals, are not feasible, it is possible with sensitivity analysis to work out the effect on the productivity calculation of changing crucial assumptions.

We turn now to the criticism that, no matter how educational the reports on productivity are, there is still a risk that they will be misunderstood. To accept this point of view and refrain from collecting any data, is the standpoint of the agnostic. The dilemma of the agnostic is what then to base actions upon. It is not possible to plan and carry out a sensible programme unless one has some understanding of the facts. If empirical data is discarded as a source of such understanding, what is the alternative?

Measurements of productivity and output will most likely affect behaviourial patterns. This is so even if no material rewards are tied to them. Attention is focused on these measures and thereby call forth behaviour that is consistent with promoting goals expressed by these measures. But are there dangers in this?

In most bureaucratic organizations it is very worthwhile focusing attention on one over-riding goal. Many of the problems of bureaucratic organizations derive from the lack of clear goals, from the multitude of conflicting goals, and the lack of priorities. Even if it turns out not to be possible to measure productivity reliably, it will prove to be a very healthy exercise for any bureaucratic organization to go through the steps in constructing a productivity measure.

Once a routine for handling productivity reports is set up, incentives will consciously or unconsciously be created. Incentives might be subtle and consist of money for development projects, easier recruitment, promotion of executives, renovation of office buildings, etc. The point is that they will develop in any case and that it is as well to be aware of this and use the incentives consciously in ways that are thought to be suitable for the development of the whole organization.

It is an advantage if incentives can be tied to productivity, rather than to other more or less one-sided success indicators. This is because productivity captures comprehensively so many of the relevant aspects of the agency's performance at the same time. If instead, incentives are tied only to output, results can be disastrous unless there is a definite limit on resources.

The potential for productivity measurement and practical solutions to measurement problems

The potential for productivity measurement is far greater than is usually imagined. It depends on the one hand on the ability to solve practical measurement problems in a theoretically satisfactory way, and on the other, on the degree of regularity and uniformity in production.

Guidelines for the services produced, guaranteeing equal treatment, have often been laid down in law. When there are no such guidelines, professional standards have developed. Over the years these change very slowly.

Production of public services often takes place on a large scale. This ensures regularity. The composition of items does not change a lot and the changes that do occur are smooth. All of this facilitates measurement. A third factor could be added that increases the potential for productivity measurement, that of accepting a 'reasonable degree of accuracy' in the measurements. It is impossible to achieve such accuracy in the measurement of productivity, as was the case in old-fashioned auditing where it was expected that the accounts were correct down to the last penny. It is only by accepting a reasonable degree of accuracy that it becomes possible at all to carry out productivity measurements. The general emancipation from old-fashioned auditing has paved the way for productivity measurement.

The problem that looms the largest is that of setting the weights for different outputs. It happens only sometimes that priorities are expressed clearly. On occasion priorities can be derived from the relationship between outputs and an over-riding goal. If, for example, the handling of a private individual's assessment of income brings in, on average, one quarter of the tax receipts that the average private enterprise assessment brings in, then the commonsense priority would reflect this difference. The relative importance of various outputs can also be inferred, from the costs of those outputs. The reasoning here is that it is logical to infer that an output that costs twice as much as another is also valued twice as highly. An example of this is that parliament must place a value on saving lives that is at least as high as the costs that go into life-saving. Finally, by the same reasoning, it is possible to infer weights from the costs of production at the agency itself.

A further approximation is to take the average costs as weights instead of marginal costs, on the assumption that they are proportional to each other. Going one step further, labour input is often used for weighting, on the same assumption. There is an obvious danger in this practice, that in changing from production of an output with costs relatively higher than its value to an output with costs relatively lower, than its value will not show up as a productivity increase. A change in the opposite direction should decrease productivity, but aggregating outputs by weights that reflect relative costs will not reveal that either.

The definition of two sets of weights, 'outer' and 'inner' weights, is called for. Outer weights reflect the preferences of the agency's principal. Inner weights reflect the production capability within the agency. Inner weights are marginal costs or approximations of these. Using one or other set of weights has different implications. Using outer weights will make the productivity measurement reflect the ability of the agency to choose the right mix of outputs, i.e. 'to do the right things'. However, a productivity increase in that case may have nothing whatsoever to do with producing anything more efficiently, that is, with less resources. On the other hand, using inner weights will reflect changes in inner efficiency, producing outputs with more or less resources. However, it will not register improvements due to reallocating production capacity from lesser to more highly valued outputs. It is a matter of preference what kind of weights are used. In non-market organizations, productivity is usually measured with a bias in favour of reflecting inner efficiency, whereas productivity in market organizations is usually measured with a bias in favour of reflecting outer weights. It is as well to bear this in mind when comparing productivity in the government sector with that of free enterprise, since it is probable that the government sector will show a somewhat less favourable productivity increase.

Productivity, measurement and quality change
We now turn to the fundamental problem of quantifying quality changes. There are several basic methods to deal with. What in principle seems an easy method is to consider outputs of differing qualities as quite separate outputs. In practice it is sometimes difficult to do this. If outputs with different qualities exist side by side, for the year for which the weights are calculated (the base year) estimating separate weights for outputs of differing qualities is just the same as for different outputs. However, if quality has changed, so that outputs of lower quality have been succeeded by outputs of higher quality, estimating weights is more difficult. In principle, knowledge is required of the weight that the lower quality output would have had if it had existed in the base year. We then have to calculate how much less the lower quality output would have cost to produce, using the cost and technology of the base year. This is liable to give too high a weight to the old quality, otherwise it is difficult to see why it is no longer produced. On the other hand, calculating the difference in costs, assuming the use of the technology that existed when the old quality output was produced, will overestimate the weight of the new quality output in relation to the old. Otherwise it is inexplicable why the new quality product was not produced at that time. New quality outputs often occur in connection with the introduction of new technology that has substantially lowered prices. In this instance, overestimation would be considerable. For example, it is often thought that the value of the new services introduced in connection with computers is tremendous, since it was almost impossible to produce the same services with old technology. It is more logical to value the new services by the cost difference using new technology, since it is in this situation that the choice is being made.

On occasions it is possible to quantify quality directly. Upon closer inspection it sometimes appears that quality differences really are differences in quantity. For example, different courses have different numbers of lessons. If outputs are identified according to the number of learning occasions, the quality problem transforms into a quantity problem that can be solved by counting the number of lessons.

There are two lines of retreat if quality cannot be judged in either of these ways. The first one is to remove all costs associated with changes in quality. The productivity measure will be partial as it will include neither the quality change, nor its accompanying costs. The second is to investigate all kinds of quality or goal achievement indicators. Of course goal achievement may be influenced by outside factors as well, and if that seems probable it has to be taken into account too. If there are no signs of a change in goal achievement, aside from what has taken place as a result of outside factors, then it is quite logical to assume that no qualitative change has taken place.

Productivity measurement is very much faciliated by the fact that productivity is a measure of comparison. It is sufficient to have relative weights, since that is the only thing that affects the change in productivity. In a similar manner, what we need is only an estimate of the change in output. If we know that various types of outputs have all changed in exactly the same way, it is sufficient to know the change in just one of these outputs. It is also possible to use outside factors as estimates for output.

Since it is only relative weights and relative change in outputs that count, quite robust results can be produced in many instances. Another way of explaining this is to say that if all outputs change in the same way, weights do not matter at all. Or, if outputs change in only slightly different ways, weights have to differ by a lot in order for results to be affected.

The relativity of productivity measures allows us to cope with heterogenous outputs. It is a frequently voiced objection that no services are ever identical and therefore can not be added together. Heterogeneity may exist but summation nevertheless be possible, as long as the heterogeneity is constant. By that we mean that the more valuable (or costly) types of outputs have a constant share of the total mass of outputs.

Which price indices should be used to deflate costs in current prices? We do not need a price index that is constructed from the prices of those inputs that are, in fact, used by the agency in production. What we do need is an index that moves in the same way.

Finally, a few words about costs. Cost elements that are difficult to assess can be left out of the calculation, if it is reasonable to assume that those costs make up a constant proportion of total costs (in fixed prices).

Productivity change in the Swedish Government 1960–1980

In Sweden a programme for measuring productivity change was started in 1982. It has been led by a committee under the Department of Finance (Expertgruppen för studier i offentlig ekonomi, abbreviated to ESO). The experiences and theoretical developments related above stem from that work. The studies cover 70 percent of the governmental sector in Sweden. They cover 75 percent of the municipal sector and 55 percent of the national government sector.

These studies show that the opportunities for measuring productivity are great. Still they do not give the full picture of what is possible. In the first place, there are several other national government agencies that could very well have their productivity measured. In the second place what is possible today is limited by the statistics that exist, and statistics could be developed in the future to permit productivity measurements not possible today.

Measurements have been guided by the principles and theoretical foundations already explained. The point of departure has been the national accounts. This has had a number of consequences. As far as possible, definitions and evaluations of output and quality are made from consumer perspective, with the consumer at times being represented by political bodies. Costs are calculated in the same way as in the national accounts which, among other things, means that interest rate expenses do not count as costs but are seen as transfers. Value-added taxes are not included in costs. The base year used is 1980, i.e. weights for outputs are taken from that year, as well as prices for inputs.

Wherever possible, outputs are measured in conformity with how government consumption is recorded according to purpose in the national accounts. This means that large sections of the government sector are measured across several agencies. Two examples of this are day care centres for children and homes for the elderly, whose production in the whole country was measured and related to costs according to what is registered as government consumption under these headings. Within the national government administration the approach has been to investigate agency by agency, or sometimes individual systems of agencies. For example, the national tax organization includes several whole agencies and also parts of some other agencies. All of these have been lumped together and their combined resources have been related to a final output from the whole system. That means that we have not dealt with intermediary products within the system. Final output from one agency can in this aggregation appear as an intermediary output, since it is an input into another agency.

This is in sharp contrast to the approach of the US Bureau of Labor

Statistics. In that approach labour productivity is calculated for a large number of intermediary outputs. These productivity measures are then aggregated simply by weighting them according to the labour share. This method poses some tricky aggregation problems. If the purpose of the measurements is to evaluate productivity change for an agency as a whole, the result with this approach can be strikingly different from that of the final output approach. In principle, the two approaches will yield the same result if partial productivity measures are aggregated on the basis of value-added, but this is a difficult concept to apply within an organization.

All of the studies deal extensively with the question of defining final output. A list of some of the major outputs from the various parts of the government sector that are included are found in Appendix 1.

This is just a sample of outputs that have been measured. For some agencies twenty-five to forty separate outputs have been aggregated. The study of the health care sector in effect contains over three hundred outputs with separate weights. There are also studies with very few outputs, like that of housing and community planning. Its output is not measured directly, but considered to vary consistently with the amount of building construction, as measured by the volume of investments at fixed prices.

An interesting comparison can be made to see the effect of disaggregation into more outputs. The results for the health care sector, in a study using 312 different outputs, can be compared with a study that only has 40 outputs. The health study with 312 outputs reported a productivity change of –2.0 percent per year over the period 1970–80. The study with only 40 outputs reported a change of –2.4 percent per year. This suggests that it makes relatively little difference if outputs are highly disaggregated, or if they are treated in fairly large aggregates. Although it is not possible to generalize from one example, we need not reject out of hand even fairly composite output measures.

All of the results shown in Table 7.1 are of total (cost) productivity. The overall picture is one of negative productivity change. Outputs from the government sector in 1980 cost in real terms 20–80 percent more than they did twenty years before. It is true that there has been an expansion in output. In many sectors it has doubled. However costs have increased even more.

Can this apparent deterioration in productivity be vindicated by an improvement in the quality of the services? Substantial efforts to measure quality change have been made in all of the studies. The most serious problems in estimating quality change are met within the health care sector. However, not all quality improvements are left out of the output measures. Shorter hospital stays show up in the number of patients admitted, and more expensive (higher quality?) treatment shows up in an increasing share in total output of high-cost (high

TABLE 7.1
Productivity change in the Swedish government sector
1970–80, percent per year

Sector	1960–65	1965–70	1970–75	1975–80	1970–80
General administration	+0.1	–3.7	–5.5	+4.5	–0.6
Police, justice	–7.5	–2.7	–6.3	+3.1	–1.6
Defence	—	—	–0.1	–1.0	–0.6
Education	+3.9	–4.6	+0.3	–3.2	–1.5
Health	–3.6	–3.7	–1.4	–2.2	–1.8
Social Security	–0.4	–2.6	–4.8	–0.2	–2.5
Child, old-age care	—	—	–2.8	–0.4	–1.6
Planning	—	—	+0.2	–8.9	–4.5
Libraries	–5.4	+6.4	+0.7	–5.5	–2.4
Roads etc	+1.5	+2.2	+0.1	+0.4	+0.2
Total			–1.4	–1.6	–1.5

weight) treatments. Adjusting for the added costs of single-rooms for hospital patients, has a small impact on the results. The major quality change still not accounted for is the condition in which patients leave the hospital and that, by all accounts, has improved a lot.

In the study of national government administration, several adjustments for quality were included in the output measures. For example, allowances were made for over-crowded prisons, greater exactness in the disbursement of social insurance, change in the types of crimes solved. In several other studies important goal-achievement indicators were investigated in the search for quality change. In most cases little change could be observed. The Meteorological Institute, however, reported a substantial increase in the probability of correct prognoses. In this case it was not possible to quantify the quality increase, so that a true measurement of productivity could not be calculated. Several tests were performed to check the sensitivity of the results to changes in the assumptions.

In the studies of national government administration different sets of weights were tested. Even large variations in the weights up to ± 50 percent produced only moderate effects on the results. Deficiences, such as the lack of complete cost data, the use of investment expenditures instead of depreciation expenses, missing outputs, and different price indices were tested in sensitivity analyses. From this study it is safe to conclude that the deficiencies — more often than not working in different directions — taken together don't influence the annual productivity change, over the 20 year period, by more than ± ½ percentage points. This overall negative picture conceals more positive elements. A positive result was attained in the case of roads. This was due to an increased use of the roads supplied by the government. Within the social welfare sector, children's day care has had positive productivity change during the 1970s by 0.9 percent per year. Within the national government administration, the National Housing Organization, the Customs Authority, the Labour Market Training Board and the Meteorological Institute all show positive productivity change over the period 1960–80.

The results vary between the different time periods. Perhaps the most striking result is that all of the agencies in the national government administration which were studied had a positive productivity change 1975–80, in contrast with previous periods which, on the whole, were negative.

Productivity change in the national government administration is shown in Table 7.2

TABLE 7.2
National government administration, productivity change
percent per year 1960–80

	1960–65	1965–70	1970–75	1975–80	1960–80
National labour market board	−1.9	−7.4	−3.5	+1.9	−2.8
National Housing Board	+5.0	−0.6	+6.6	+2.0	+3.2
Courts	−5.4	−0.9	+1.3	+2.8	−0.6
Prisons	−5.6	−6.0	−11.0	+0.3	−5.6
Enforcement service	—	−4.1	−4.9	+3.1	−2.0[1]
National Board of Agriculture	−5.0	−1.6	+0.6	+1.1	−1.3
Central Office of the National land survey	−4.0	+0.3	−2.9	+2.5	−1.1
Police	—	−1.8	−6.2	+3.6	−1.5[1]
National social security organization	−1.0	−2.6	−4.8	−0.2	−2.4
National tax administration	−2.9	−7.1	−6.4	+5.1	−2.9
Board of customs	+5.0	+5.2	−4.3	+4.1	+2.4
Meteorological institute	−3.1	+4.2	−3.7	+4.7	+0.5
Patent and registration office			−4.3	−3.2	−3.7[2]
Weighted average	−2.0	−3.3	−5.2	+2.5	−2.0

[1] 1965–80
[2] 1970–80

It is also interesting to compare the performance of the government sector with that of the private service sector. Based on the statistics of the national accounts, the change in total (cost) productivity of the private service sector is calculated in the Table 7.3.

TABLE 7.3
Private service sector, productivity change 1965–80,
percent per year

1965–70	1970–75	1975–80	1965–80
0.9	1.8	1.2	1.1

The private sector performs better than the national government administration over the period, taken as a whole, but in the period 1975–80 this is reversed, as the productivity of the national government administration improved and private service sector productivity growth fell. The national government administration even had a productivity growth larger than the private sector taken as a whole!

As mentioned earlier, the output measures for the private service sector are rather shaky and this fact should be borne in mind. It is fair to say that the output measures that have been calculated for the government sector as a whole are far better, on average, than the ouput measures for the private service sector. It is, therefore, up to critics of public inefficiency to demonstrate with improved measurements that the private sector is really doing better.

To compare the private and public sector a more relevant measure to use would be valued-added productivity. As already discussed, it is possible to calculate the change in value-added productivity for the government, non-market sector. Briefly, the calculation is based on the assumption that output in the government sector is worth what it costs in one year, the base year. In that way it becomes possible to calculate the value of the output in fixed prices for the whole period studied. Purchases, also in fixed prices, are deducted from this value. What remains is value added, in fixed prices. Its increase or decrease, in relation to the input of hours worked, is the change in value-added productivity.

The value of output in fixed prices might be incorrect, either too high or too low, but the inaccuracy has to be very large in order for it to affect significantly the change in value-added productivity. If the value of output is wrong by 20 percent, under the circumstances of production of services in the government sector, this affects the calculated annual rate of change of productivity by, at most, 0.34 percent over the period of twenty years. The stability of the results is due to the fairly low share of purchases in total costs.

Table 7.4 shows valued-added productivity in the private service sector and the national government administration.

Now that we have seen a number of studies on productivity change within the government sector, it becomes possible to start inquiring

TABLE 7.4
Private service sector and national government administration change
in value-added productivity, per year, 1960–80

	1960–65	1965–70	1970–75	1975–80	1960–80
Private service sector	+2.3	+2.3	+3.8	+2.4	+2.9
National government administration	–1.4	–1.9	–4.6	+1.3	–1.7

into the causes of the observed development. Some general conclusions can be drawn from the study of the national government administration:

– A slower rate of increase of resources improves the productivity performance of the agency, a faster rate of increase worsens it.

– In periods of fast increase of output — mostly exogenously determined, from the point of view of the agency — productivity increases (or falls less).

– Overall productivity performance seems to be the result of chance, since it appears that no one, neither the budget office nor the agency itself, has had the faintest idea of how output and real resource costs have developed.

– Labour productivity deteriorated less than total (cost) productivity, which indicates the substitution of other costs for labour.

– Heavy investment in electronic data processing is not reflected in increased productivity, nor in a slower deterioration, at least in the period shortly after the investments.

– It is possible that the increased productivity 1975–80 is the result of investments in computers in the 1960s.

– Those agencies that have shown a positive productivity change do not use more electronic data processing than others.

– The same would seem to be true for organizational change. It might be so that organizational change leads to improvement in productivity but not until several years afterwards.

One final remark about these studies is that it proved useful to perform them with a task group which had the responsibility both for initiating the separate studies and for quality control. If productivity measurement is going to be used in the political assessment of priorities, or in the budgeting process, and if they are to be produced with a wide coverage and at the same time, the work should be carried out in this way. However, that leaves unfinished the important task of introducing productivity measurements as management tools at the agencies themselves.

Appendix I

Sector	*Output*
Health care	Patients admitted
	Out patient visits
	Bed-days for in-patients
Education	Hours of attendance at school by pupils
Social welfare	Children admitted to day-care centres
	Hours of care
	Number of recipients
	Bed-days
Defence	Hours of attendance at flight training
	Days of training of conscripts

Sector	Output
Roads	Ton-miles
	Person-miles
Public libraries	Book loans
Housing and community planning	Volume of building construction
National government administration	
National Labour Market Board	Job applicants
	Hours of attendance at training
National Housing Board	Housing loans processed and
	administered
Courts	Sentencing of offenders
Prisons	Internment places used
Central Office of the National Land	Number of proceedings
Survey	Number of maps
	Revenue in fixed prices
National Tax Administration	Number of income tax returns processed
Enforcement service	Number of proceedings
National Board of Agriculture	Number of consultations with farmers
	Inspections carried out
Board of Customs	Customs declarations
National Social Insurance organization	People insured
	Number of disbursements
Police	Solving of crimes
	Patrol hours
Meteorological Institute	Prognoses made

References

Den offentliga Secktorn — Produktivitet och Effektivitet, Bilaga 21 till Lååangtidsutred-
  nungen, 1987

Offentliga tjänster - sökarljus mot produktivitet och användare, rapport till Expertgruppen
  för studier i offentlig ekonomi, Ds Fi 1986: 13

Public Services — A Searchlight on Productivity and Users, Report to the Expert Groups
  on Public Finance, the Swedish Ministry of Finance

Statlig tjänsteproduktion, Produktivitetsutvecklingen 1960–80, Statskontoret, rapport
  1985: 15

US Office of Personnel Management, *Federal Productivity Measurement, A Report and
  Analysis of FY 1979 Data*. Washington DC February 1981

8
Functional and dysfunctional bureaucracies

Krister Ståhlberg

Introduction

Bureaucracy is a dominant feature of the Finnish political system. There have been several studies documenting growth trends, with regard to the number of bureaux, the number of bureaucrats and the amount of money consumed by bureaucracy during recent years (Lundquist and Ståhlberg, 1983). At the same time studies concentrating on the internal side of bureaucracies or on bureaucratic evaluation have not been all that many. From the point of governability the work of bureaucracies has received too little attention. In the aftermath of the economic difficulties faced by many countries during the 1970s a renewed interest in the internal workings of bureaucracies has ensued originating in the attempts to curb the growth of bureaucracy and make it more effective.

In this chapter we discuss the findings from two case studies, open-ended evaluations of two bureaucracies in Finland at the country level (län). Using different sources of data we followed the work of the county educational bureaux during the 1970s; these bureaux were created at this time to assist in the implementation of a large primary education reform. They are located within the county administration, placed hierarchically beneath the Ministry of Education and the Board of Education (Skolstyrelsen). They have a supervisory and advisory position in relation to the local level where responsibility for primary education is located.

One focus of these case studies is the discussion of dysfunctions in bureaucracies according to the Robert Merton's theory concerning the bureaucratic personality. The first study seems to fit Merton's notions perfectly, whereas the second study gives scant support to the idea of dysfunctional bureaucratic learning. Faced with contradictory evidence with regard to the Merton model, the logical task is to ask whether there are modifications or additions that should be made to it in order to account for the findings in both the case studies. What follows is not a strict attempt to evaluate the model, but rather an attempt to point at some interesting questions concerning bureaucracies, especially whether bureaucracies in different settings are, to a varying degree, prone to display dysfunctional patterns of behaviour.

Bureaucratic dysfunctions

Weber's model of bureaucracy has been contested, but here we follow the standard text book presentation of Weber's position. (Weber, 1947; Blau, 1955; Albrow, 1970). Weber has, perhaps unjustly, been interpreted as enumerating characteristics of an organization that functions effectively. At least he chose features in his model which link up with each other in a way that makes for rational calculation within the organization. This more pleasant picture of bureaucracy has been challenged over and over — Weber has not duly considered informal organizations that tend to develop within formal organizations. As Blau points out, such informal organizations are not merely idiosyncratic deviations from the formal rules, but form consistent patterns that are new elements of the organization.

The informal side of the organization may or may not contribute to the organizational attainment of goals. In the positive case, Blau speaks about functions and in the negative case, about dysfunctions, building upon the concepts introduced earlier by Merton. Merton recognized that the bureaucratic structure modelled by Weber may not have only apparent positive consequences. There may be negative and unforeseen consequences (Merton, 1957), especially dysfunctional organizational learning. Organization members generalize a response from situations where the response is appropriate to situations which result in unanticipated and undesired consequences by the organization. Simon and March outline the Merton argument in a simple model (Figure 8.1)

FIGURE 8.1
The Merton model

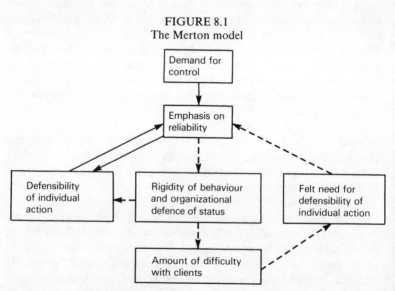

Source: Simon and March, 1958: 41.

According to the model, there is a need on the part on the top hierarchy within the organization to control what is going on at lower levels as part of the quest for reliable performance within the organization. Merton speaks about discipline and conformity. We may also talk about accountability and predictability. Standard procedures are established and control is directed by means of these procedures.

The stress on reliability implies that there is a reduction of personalized relationships within the organization. An organization is a set of relationships between roles. It follows that the internalization of the rules of the organization is increased, resulting in a displacement of goals, and thus means or rules become goals. Categorizing is used as a decision-making technique and the search for alternatives is decreased. These features all combine to make the organization rigid in its behaviour, which results in dysfunctional learning and increased difficulties with clients.

Merton mentions other structural factors that are conducive to rigidity. Career considerations make for adherence to rules and there may also develop an *esprit de corps*. This in turn makes for a sanctification of the organization in the eyes of the bureaucrats, which may be strengthened by an ideology portraying the bureaucrats as public servants. Difficulties with clients increase the need of bureaucrats to justify and defend their behaviour, which leads to emphasis on reliability and conformity with bureaucratic rules.

The sequence described is indicated in the model by the broken lines, a dysfunctional circle related to the need of the organization to maintain good client relations, and to serve its clients according to its tasks. The model suggests why an organization faced with client difficulties may react in a way which takes the organization from bad to worse. Merton notes that clients often look for personal relationships with the organization, while it favours depersonalized relations in the same way as it prefers depersonalized relations internally. For Merton, the bureaucratic personality stands for a permanent behavioural disposition on the part of the officials, partly determined by the very structure of the bureaucracy. At the same time as the Weberian bureaucratic structure makes for accountability and predictability, it has dysfunctional consequences as well.

Merton deduces the dysfunctional consequences from the general structure or formal structure of the bureaucracy, thus, leading us to expect that in similar bureaucracies similar dysfunctional patterns will occur. In the present context this means that within both of the educational bureaux studied, dysfunctional patterns of a similar kind would prevail. If this is in fact not the case, the theory about bureaucratic dysfunctions must be made conditional on additional factors.

Two cases studies of county educational bureaux

The county educational bureau were created by governmental ordinance issued in 1970 as part of a general educational reform. At the county level — there are twelve regional county authorities in Finland which are part of the state administration — there had earlier existed educational supervisory officers. These supervisors did not function within the general county administration and they did not have any real bureau at their disposal. In order to carry out the major primary education reform it was widely felt that the existing network of supervisors would not suffice.

A closer examination of the decision-making process leading up to the educational bureaux, revealed some interesting aspects of administrative reform. The process should be seen as an incrementalist process rather than as a rational one. Over the years the final administrative solution became less and less challenging to different types of interests. The setting of goals for the reform points in the same direction, and goal-statements have been classified during the process according to a distinction between real goals (i.e. goals expressed independently of the means chosen making some kind of evaluation of consequences possible) and mere adminstrative principles (i.e. situations in which the means is in fact the goal). It may be shown that there are practically no real goals set for the administrative reform, apart from the task to further the implementation of primary education reform. Statements of administrative principles abounded; co-ordination, efficiency, comprehensiveness, democracy, etc. What is typical of the formulation of these goals is that the administrative solution chosen is seen to satisfy the 'goals'; no indication of an independent future state of affairs to tied to the principles can be found. Neither can comparisons be found between different possible administrative solutions with regard to these principles.

The political parties were generally uninterested in the administrative reform and concentrated on the primary education reform itself. This may be one of the reasons for the widely differing interpretations given to many of the administrative principles, as well as the neglect of the position taken by Parliament on the administrative question. As Parliament approved a bill on the Board of Education, it added a unanimous statement maintaining that all forms of schools ought to be administered by the new bureaux. In total disregard of this statement, the President issued the ordinance creating county educational bureau with supervisory functions only over primary and secondary schools, but not vocational schools.

In many respects the county educational bureaux are 'ideal' bureaucracies. These bureaux are part of the general county administration headed by a county governor. The head of the bureau is responsible to the county governor, but has a fairly wide decision-making power himself. Only questions of general importance for the county have to be submitted to the governor. Assistant heads may be found within the bureaux of three counties having a sizable Swedish speaking minority population. In these three counties the assistant head of bureau has the same position as the head of bureau with regard to questions concerning the educational system of the minority; there are parallel Swedish schools in all local governmental units with a Swedish minority of sufficient size. The educational supervisors are hierachically subordinated to the heads of the bureaux. The bureaux have planners and research personnel, and backup staff such as typists, clerks, etc. and the number of personnel has grown continually during the 1970s. We can look at two educational bureaux in Table 8.1.

TABLE 8.1
The increase in personnel within two county educational bureaux

Type of personnel	Åbo County		Vasa County	
	1973	1981	1973	1981
Higher (heads and supervisors, planners, etc.)	16	21	13	15
Lower (clerkcs, etc.)	8	21	5	12
Total	24	42	18	27
of which: Finnish	20	34	13	18
Swedish	4	8	5	9

Source: Annual reports of Åbo County and Vasa County.

The county educational bureaux are administrative bureaucracies, as they do not take part in the production and delivery of educational services. As an administrative agency the bureau is subordinated to the Board of Education. The bureau must submit a decision for final approval to the central board, or it may only attach its opinion to the proposal coming from the local level on its way to the central level. For minor matters concerning decisions made at local level, the county bureau has the power to make the final decision. During the 1970s powers at regional level were strengthened, but they are still not considerable.

Generally speaking the educational bureau has three kinds of duties

1. *Supervisory duties:* matters in which the county has to approve lower level decisions on their way for final approval at the central level. The provisions in laws and ordinances regulating these supervisory tasks were almost innumerable and very detailed. It is hardly an exaggeration to maintain that the educational sector is the most regulated of all public administration sectors. From a judicial point of view these provisions are of a comparatively high level; that is, they are found in laws and ordinances and not within circulars and directives

issued by the central boards. Consequently, these legal documents have to be changed fairly often, which makes for time consuming decision-making processes, at least in comparison with the easily formulated and issued directives. Old administrative traditions have not been overcome within this traditional public sector.

2. *Planning duties:* functions were linked to the efficient implementation of the primary education reform and during their first years of existence work was intensive. The regional officers took part in the preparation of local educational plans. During the second half of the 1970s, having successfully participated in the implementation of the reform, the bureaux were given an additional planning duty to assist in implementing a new and important educational reform at the intermediate level — vocational education and high schools. The unregulated activities within this second group of duties may take a considerable time, but they leave little official marks, whereas the first group of duties, as a rule, resulted in formal documents of decisions.

3. *Service production:* the bureau participates in and organizes courses for teachers and personnel within its district covering administrative questions within the educational sector or professional questions for the teachers relating to substantive matters or questions of a pedagogical nature. Compared to the administrative and planning duties, this category is of lesser importance although it has been growing.

TABLE 8.2
Number of registered decisions leaving the educational bureau

Year	Åbo County	Vasa County
1970	4224	4475
1972	6524	6742
1974	6496	6922
1976	5631	5230
1978	4402	4301
1980	4549	4254

Source: Annual reports of Åbo County and Vasa County.

It is difficult to estimate just how much time the bureaucrats spent in performing these duties, but statistics may be obtained on the number of formal decisions registered each year within the two boards (see Table 8.2). The figures shown in this table lend themselves to two different observations. Firstly, we may conclude that since the variation in time over the number of decisions made is so similar, the number of decisions should be seen as a direct indication of the hierarchically subordinated position of these bureaux vis a vis the central Board of Education. Secondly, interestingly enough, the number of formally made decisions has clearly decreased during the 1970s, whereas, as noted earlier, the number of personnel has continued to increase. There are no signs of the personnel growth coming to an end, although the growth slowed down due to the state's fiscal difficulties. There is no indication of an increase in the number of formally made decisions. On the contrary, Parliament has adopted new acts decentralizing decision-making powers to the local level, thus eliminating some of the burdens at regional level. The transfer of matters from central to regional level will not compensate for those matters transferred still lower.

This looks like a growing bureaucracy with less and less to do. What seems to occur is an instance of a succession of goals. The bureaux increasingly turn their attention to matters of planning and guidance vis a vis the local level, a both interesting and comfortable shift of focus for the bureaux. The work becomes more stimulating as planning is more interesting than approving petty decisions made by others; planning and guiding are more difficult to evaluate than administrative work resulting in formally registered decisions. This succession of goals may be described as bureaucratic evasion of goals.

Case I: Åbo County
Within the case studies the intensive data being gathered was only about bureau questions on the Swedish minority population. Within Åbo County the Swedish population is not very large. The county itself has ninety-four local governments and a total population of more than 700,000, making it one of the largest counties. The number of local governments incorporating the Swedish part of the county educational bureau is only about ten.

The position of the minority could be shown by looking at the work load of the Finnish and the Swedish parts of the educational bureau. On the Finnish side we find eight educational supervisors, each covering 87 schools, 12,500 students and 662 teachers working full time. On the Swedish side we find only one supervisor for forty-one schools, 3600 students and 250 teachers. This uneven distribution of work has, as could be expected, resulted in tensions between the majority and minority. We found a number of such cases in interviews with higher personnel within the bureau, both in the Finnish and Swedish sections.

The interviews with the Swedish personnel indicated that two kinds of attitudes prevailed concerning the appropriate role of the bureau. It was generally admitted that the bureau assisted the local governments in their educational administration, but some officials stressed the role of a state supervisor in local governments more than others. Others spoke more about the advisory role, especially in educational and pedagogical matters, emphasizing what has come to be called the qualitative improvement of education. Among these was also found an attitude of 'one-up-manship', being a spokesman for the local governments vis a vis the state.

This difference in attitudes can be accounted for to some extent by the respective duties of the officers. However, the difference is not one between equal partners. Thus, it is fair to say that the traditionalistic and legalistic 'spokesman of the state' attitude was the one which characterized the bureau for an outside observer. The powers of the bureau were clearly vested among the traditionally oriented officials. In fact some client interviews suggested that clients did not really find it worth their while to turn to the officials with a 'modern' attitude for advice. The reason for this was simply that the word of these officials did not matter. Power was perceived to reside with the assistant ahead of bureau and his assistant, not with the supervisors.

The local governments are clients of the bureaux in matters in which they have to seek advice or approval of decision at the local level. The bureaucratic hierarchy showed itself also in the attitude that one could not bypass the regional officers and turn directly to the state central officers. Such local behaviour was also looked upon with much suspicion among the regional officers. The interaction between local and regional bureaucrats is fairly frequent. Local educational officials turn to the regional officials for advice at least once a week and during other periods, twice a week. Often local officials ask for advice on how local decisions ought to be made in order to avoid regional complaints or disapprovals of local decisions at a later date. This interaction forms the exclusive local, informal contact with the regional level. Local elected educational councillors very rarely meet with regional officials or even speak with them on the phone. The client interaction on the part of the county bureau is, therefore, mainly one of bureaucrats interacting with each other.

Educational officers of the local governments were interviewed in order to map the client attitude to the bureau. It turned out that the local governments within the county were divided regarding this attitude. The officials representing a larger population base were more favourably disposed toward the county bureau than were their counterparts in small local governments. These critical officers also happened to work within local governments on the periphery. They represented small local governments located within the archipelago. Within this area the population is very small and is scattered over many islands. These small local governments are in many respects deviant cases within the total educational system.

During the time the primary education reform was implemented, a parallel reform attempt was made in amalgamating local government units. An important argument in this reform attempt was that the new educational system needed a population base of at least 8000 people in order to allow for efficient educational solutions, meaning a certain number of students at every age level. The small island local governments have a population base ranging between 200 and 1500 as compared to the Swedish population in the two cities included in our ten communes, that is Åbo with approximately 8500 and Pargas with 7000.

The critical officials often perceived the regional bureau as state police looking after them. Since they often had special problems they did not like the way the regional bureaucrats categorized them and, in their opinion, treated them unfairly because they did not fulfil all the average requirements. They perceived the county bureaucrats as 'petty' bureaucrats occupied by interpreting impossible rules, instead of helping the small local governments to change the rules or to get exception from the rules.

One major issue did much to inflame relations between these local governments and the regional bureau. The regional bureau at the Swedish side refused to support the islanders[1] petition about a secondary school. The Finnish side at the regional level did support a comparative petition for a Finnish school, although the number of Finnish speaking population on the islands is only a fraction of the Swedish speaking population. The Swedish county officials were, of course, perceived to be totally addicted to the rules, with no understanding of the islanders' special situation, who earlier had to send their children away for secondary education. In the political game that ensued the islanders came out as winners. It turned out that the regional governor understood their predicament and the central level bureaucrats, as well as the politicians, were favourably disposed. This loss of face on the part of the regional officials hit them hard and many school-examples were cited by these officials in bureaucratic defence as part of a local newspapers debate during the conflict.

From the client interviews the impression given was that this client difficulty has continued and that the bureau has, in many instances, been rule ridden in its handling of decisions submitted to it by the local islands' governments. In some cases they have been overruled by the Board of Education. This seems to be an instance of client difficulties that ought not to be there and that have elicited a bureaucratic defence mechanism much in the way described by Merton.

It should be noted that interviews with local educational councillors supported the results obtained in the interviews with local officials. In fact, the councillors were more critical on average towards the county bureau than the officials. This is easy to understand since they do not have first-hand knowledge of the county, but heard about the county position from their officials and probably associated the county with the whole legal system surrounding education. Their comments on 'the impossible jungle of paragraphs' can be understood in this context.

Still the instances in which the county stands against the local units are not that frequent. Most of the decisions made at the county level are a matter of routine and the local units have learned to prepare correct proposals. Throughout 1970s the relative amount of refusals of approval decreased and today they account for less than one-tenth of the yearly decisions made by the Swedish officials. The main reason for this is because major decisions on how to organize and carry out local education were made at the beginning of the 1970s in connection with the implementation of the education reform. This mandated the local government to prepare educational plans and teaching programmes, as well as general regulations for the local school system which were to be approved either at county or central level. When these plans and programmes were prepared the relative amount of supervisory refusals was larger and they concern just these types of submission from the local governments.

Case II: Vasa County

Although Vasa County is smaller than Åbo County, 430,000 people in fifty-eight local governments, the Swedish speaking minority is considerably larger. Swedish speaking people totalled less than 30,000 in Åbo County, but in the Vasa County they number almost 100,000.

In Vasa County they have five Finnish educational supervisors on which fall on an average 95.2 schools, almost 11,000 students and 610 teachers. On the two Swedish supervisors fall 72.5 schools, 7516 students and 450 teachers each. The burden on the Swedish supervisors is clearly larger than the burden on the supervisor in Åbo County, but again smaller than on their Finnish counterparts within Vasa County. We have found many indications of language group tension between the bureaucrats. Although there is a variation among the local governments within the Swedish section, it is not of the same kind as in Åbo County. The Swedish population within the local governments is much more homogeneous than in Åbo County. Although the smallest local governments have a population of only 1000 and the largest a Swedish population of 15,000, most of the local governments still fall within a reasonable range of 3000 to 8000 inhabitants.

The bureaucrats within the Swedish section of the educational bureau have a high degree of solidarity and similar attitudes. They do point out that they are a state agency at regional level, but they perceive themselves to be spokesmen for the local governments. Even if they sometimes have to use regulations against the local governments they feel that the section and the local government are part of the same system and it is the system that should be blamed and not the section. It seems that the language group has much to do with this attitude. The officials often stress the difficulties with the Finnish section and point to the need for alertness in order to get their share of the common resources of the bureau. They even indicate the need to be in touch with the central level in order to get first hand information of what is going on in good time to defend their position within the bureau. Instances were found where common resources have to some extent been withheld by the majority group.

Whereas the bureaucrats within the section in bo County were of a relatively different educational background and of highly varying age, the Vasa County section is characterized by homogeneity. Most of the bureaucrats are of middleage with a long, common work experience. The relationship measured by the interaction between local governments as clients and the bureau is very much of the same type as within Åbo County. Once or twice, every second week, local officers are in touch with the regional bureaucrats in order to consult on some question on their agenda. Local councillors almost never meet with the regional officials.

Local officials within Vasa County generally have a different attitude toward the regional bureau than their Åbo County counterparts. They share almost all the sentiments expressed by the regional bureaucrats, and they perceive the regional officials as helpful and willing to champion their cause. Local officials believe that their regional colleagues try to stretch the interpretation of rules as far as possible in the direction of the local governments. They also have adopted the language group view held by the regional bureaucrats. Obviously, they are part of a minority group crossing the administrative levels, and in this respect they are not alone. Even if the local councillors may be slightly more critical than their bureaucrat servants, they still must be classified as very positive toward the regional bureau.

In many respects the homogeneity characterizing the bureaucrats within the bureau holds for the local officials as well. A large majority of them have held their positions since the educational reform was planned and they have a similar teachers' education as background. This also makes them different from their Åbo County counterparts, where many were not formally competent for their job and had varying educational background; nor had they stayed as long in their jobs on an average.

The background of regional and local bureaucrats within the Vasa County may well account for the development toward a marked *esprit de corps*. In the beginning when the educational reform was implemented and some local units were amalgamated — officially voluntarily but, in fact, under pressure — conflicts did occur between the local and regional level but there are few traces left. Now the common 'enemy', the language majority group, seems to be the one to unite against. This concurs nicely with the general impression that the Swedish speaking population within Vasa County has much in common with the general ethnic mobilization that has swept over Europe.

In this case we have an instance of a bureaucracy, working well at least with regard to its client relations. Although the bureau implements the same regulations as the earlier one, the clients perceive this differently. They readily blame the legalistic chaos of the educational system, although they put very little of the blame on the regional bureau. On the contrary, they perceive the bureau to be working for their interests. This may only be an attitude, because asked to name some concrete instances in which the regional officials had successfully championed their cause, few examples could be found. This bureau cannot do much more than the other bureau, but it has succeeded in doing what it does in a co-optive way, with a common frame of reference between the local and regional officials evolving from the interaction. This second case does not bear out the argument made by Merton about the bureaucratic personality. On the contrary, the dysfunctional sequence of his model does not seem to be activated.

How to make the Merton model more inclusive

Speaking in the general terms, it seems that Merton develops his argument with a preoccupation for internal structural features of the bureaucracy, perhaps because of a simple view of the Weberian concept of bureaucracy. Merton thus tries to deduce negative aspects from the bureaucratic features which Weber had singled out as conducive to rational calculations.

We should, of course, keep in mind that our first case seemed to fit the Merton argument. The second case did not, however. We do not have good reasons for expecting bureaucracies everywhere, with the same internal features, to display bureaucratic dysfunctions. Bureaucracies are part of a larger structure which may contribute toward a favourable or unfavourable adaption of the bureaucracy to its environment. The two cases suggest some interesting relationships of bureaucracies to their surroundings which may account for their different degrees of success.

A first factor to be singled out is the *degree of variation* found *among the clients*. Bureaucrats in Åbo County are faced with a more difficult administrative situation regardless of how benevolent they feel towards their clients. Among their client local governments only few seem to fit the ideal underlying the primary education reform. Typically, difficulties with clients are not found regarding these local governments. Problems seem to be connected to the majority of the local governments in the periphery. These local governments are characterized both by very small populations (Iniö 250; Houtskär 700; Korpo 1000; Nagu 1400; Västanfjärd 900; and Finby 1000) and scattered geographical conditions. Most of them are located on a large number of small islands. This factor may be operationalized in terms of the degree of deviation from explicit or implicit average norms used within the policy sector. A bureaucrat may be tempted to defend unpopular but necessary decisions by referring to the rules and regulations, thus creating a disposition in that direction. Such a disposition can, of course, be expected to result in a rule-fixation, even in cases where these rules do, in fact, allow for varying interpretations. This disposition may well mean that the rules are sanctified, in the way Merton has pointed to. Many of our respondents in these small local governments expressed disappointment on this point. They could not understand why the regional bureaucrats did not actively try to find exceptions to the rules that create difficulties for the small local governments. At the central level they found much more understanding of their specific circumstances.

The relative homogeneity of the client local governments in Vasa County made a different attitude possible. The county bureaucrats made many references to the dullness of their routine work. They took little interest in reviewing local decisions, probably because these generally fitted the rules. They did not point out that the local officials had adapted well to the regulations after some initial problems when the educational reform was implemented. What challenged these regional bureaucrats was to get different educational experiments going. Their interest clearly focused on championing new solutions. Educational experiments give new resources and they give the experimenters a sense of uniqueness. This probably contributed to good client relations.

A second factor could be called the *extent to which bureaucrats and clients form a policy community*. There are, in the light of our case studies, three aspects of this factor. The first aspect concerns a common *socialization* of bureaucrats and clients. Within Vasa County homogeneity could be found in this respect. All of the eleven local officials interviewed were men. Seven of these had been in their job for at least ten years. Only one of the officials was under forty years of age. All eleven had some kind of teacher's education as a background and seven of them had completed academic degrees. This background fits very well with the background of the regional bureaucrats too. It is not surprising that many respondents pointed to the closeness of relations within the Swedish part of the educational administration; comparing this to the larger Finnish side where personal acquaintance is less frequent.

In contrast bureaucrats at regional and local levels in Åbo County form a heterogeneous group. Many officials lack formal competence of their job and have shorter experience of them. Typically again, the bureaucrats within the positive local governments did, in fact, form a much more homogeneous group.

A second aspect of the policy community is the extent to which the *decision-making cultures* of bureaucracy and clients are similar. Inˆbo County the island local governments have a tradition of layman administration which is different from the tradition of the regional bureaucracy where the educational supervisors have a long and 'classic' bureaucratic tradition to lean on. The islanders perceive rules as something that have to change in order to fit what they feel is necessary, whereas the regional bureaucracy has much of the opposite view. It is perhaps needless to point to the communication difficulties that arise in such a situation.

The policy culture of the clients within Vasa County was much closer to that of the regional bureaucracy, characterized by the trust in their local officials expressed by many of the local councillors. They looked upon the educational administration as an area for bureaucrats. This contrasted with many of the views in Åbo County, where they had experienced a fight for their secondary school which was clearly political, aimed at overcoming the bureaucratic resistance.

A third aspect of the policy community seems to be the role played by the *belongingness to a language minority group*. We must first note that the internal bureaucratic relations in the bureaux were similar in this respect. In both cases the minority perceived the majority as unduly privileged. This reaction is understandable against the background that all bureaucrats work within the same bureau, but they have a different burden to carry. In Vasa County one of the biggest problems, according to the minority representatives, was to get rid of this close connection with the majority. According to the minority they ought to have a bureau of their own, in order to avoid the tensions that go with the distribution of resources allocated to the present bureau as a whole. In Åbo County the situation was looked upon in much the same way, although the tensions were perhaps not perceived to be as great.

There seems to exist some kind of threshold above which the minority gets activated in a way that contributes toward a policy community between clients and bureaucrats. Although in Vasa County the number of Swedish speaking people within the local governments is not very large, it is true that in all local governments their share of the population is considerable. In thirteen of the sixteen local governments the Swedish speaking people are in fact in the majority. In the three remaining local governments their minority position is strong (Vasa 28 percent, Karleby 22 percent and Kaskö 28 percent). This contrasts with the situation in Åbo County. In local governments where the Swedish speaking population is in a minority, this minority position is marked (bo 5 percent and Finby 16 percent). The rest of the local governments except Kimito and Pargas (69 percent and 62 percent respectively) are strongly dominated by the language minority. We could perhaps argue that in Vasa County both the number of minority speaking people and their share of their respective local government contribute toward an optimistic attitude, whereas the size of the Swedish speaking population in Åbo County and the very small share of the population in the county administration city, Åbo, are conducive to a pessimistic view. This, in turn, would make for conflict between the purely Swedish local governments in the periphery and the bureaucrats resident in the city.

Conclusion

In the Merton model the bureaucratic personality is an intervening variable between dysfunctional patterns of behaviour and the internal structure of the bureaucracy. The personality or behavioural disposition that follows from the internal structure of the bureaucracy makes a correct adaption to client difficulties less likely. There seem, however, to be other factors operating too. We have pointed to the importance of external structural variables regarding the relationship between the bureaucracy and its environment, especially its clients. These external structural conditions could either make dysfunctional patterns of behaviour more likely, thus aggravating the dysfunctional sequences in the Merton model, or make them less likely, thus eliminating the negative influences of the internal bureaucratic structure upon personality.

References

Albrow, M. (1970) *Bureaucracy*. London: Pall Mall.

Blau, P. (1955) *The Dynamics of Bureaucracy*. Chicago: University of Chicago Press.

Lundquist, L. and K. Ståhlberg (eds) (1983) *Byråkrater i Norden*, Åbo: Stiftelsens för Åbo Akademi forskningsinstitut.

Merton, R. (1957) 'Bureaucractic structure and personality' in Merton, *Social Theory and Social Structure* originally published in 1940. New York: The Free Press.

Simon, H. and J. March (1958) *Organizations*. New York: John Wiley.

Ståhlberg, K. (1983) Länsskolavdelningen vid länsstyrelsen i Åbo och Björneborgs län: En fallstudie i utvärderingsproblem kring en förvaltningsreform. Åbo: Statens utbildningscentral (mimeo).

Weber, M. (1947) *The Theory of Economic and Social Organization*. Glencoe: Free Press.

III
NORMATIVE CONSIDERATIONS

9
Giving direction to permanent officials: signals from the electorate, the market, laws and expertise

Richard Rose

Quis custodiet ipsos custodes

Public policy is purposeful. Without a sense of direction provided by formal or informal signals, civil servants would be completely directionless, lacking a sense of what they were supposed to do. The problem that this chapter addresses is: what gives direction to civil servants?

In the classic Weberian conception, civil servants are defined as bureaucrats applying the law (Weber, 1948: 196ff). Bureaucrats follow impersonal rules rather than the directives of a party or a personal patron. But the law can only provide limited guidance about how officials ought to behave since the law is full of 'interstices' that someone must fill in. Since no set of laws can anticipate every situation, an element of discretion is inevitable. Furthermore, many laws emphasize procedure rather than substance. Therefore, the law can only be one source of signals directing civil servants, it cannot be the only source.

The source of the signals directing public officials is an empirical question as well as a normative concern. To consider only what civil servants ought to do may tell us little about the important empirical question: among a multiplicity of signals — from the law, expertise and the market as well as the electorate — which are most important in giving direction to civil servants?

Civil servants are often subject to pressures from many different elements in the political system. Elected office holders are one important source of direction. But the will of politicians cannot override the law and unless laws are changed they must be obeyed. Moreover, while the wants of politicians are important, if the money raised by taxing the market is insufficient to finance them, this too must be heeded. Many public employees are professional experts in such fields as health care, education, and highway engineering, and they respond to direction from professional expertise too.

To enquire about the multiplicity of signals directing civil servants is to pose a question of applied cybernetics. It raises issues about fundamentals of political power as well as about communication (Deutsch, 1966). For example, the problem of party government can be defined as that of finding ways in which elected politicians can ensure that the signals from the electorate are stronger than the signals that civil servants derive from their own expertise (Rose, 1986).

The first task of this chapter is to define and compare the variety of signals that give direction to civil servants. The second task is for each signal to be identified as being particularly important for some types of programmes, and laws and expertise are shown to influence the largest proportion of public money and public employees. The concluding section considers whether the current mix of signals tends to be consistent or inconsistent with the values on which representative government is based in a mixed economy welfare state.

Multiple signals in the policy process

Most discussions of the role of public officials in government start from the assumption that all officials conform (or should conform) to a single type, the bureaucrat. The term is used even when the context makes it very clear that it is inappropriate. For example, important studies of atypical public officials, the higher civil servants working closely with politicians to make policies, have titles such as *Bureaucrats and Politicians in Western Democracies* (Aberbach et al. 1981), and *Bureaucrats and Policymaking* (Suleiman, 1984). Being a civil servant is not proof of being a bureaucrat. The books in question describe public officials who are as much involved in the policy process as are elected officials.

A multiplicity of signals implies variety among civil servants. Ideal-type categories of officials may be differentiated according to the priority given to a particular type of signal, law-bound bureaucrats; servants of elected policymakers; professionals possessing expertise in a substantive programme; and employees of public enterprises that sell their output in the market. As subsequent discussion will demonstrate, the clarity of these ideal types is purchased at the price of a substantial distortion of reality. One important feature of public officials is that they are not usually subject to a single type of directive, but to a mixture of signals.

Signals from laws

By definition, bureaucrats carry out the law. In a trivial sense all officials (whether elected politicians or civil servants) must abide by the law and no government official can systematically engage in illegal activity. However, the scope for discretion within the law is substantial. The question then arises, under what circumstances can officials be expected to act as rule-bound bureaucrats?

A lowly position in the organizational hierarchy of a public section organization is an indicator that an official is subject to a high degree of regulation. In ideal-type models of representative government, these regulations have two sources, laws, and also directives from elected politicans. The two sources are meant to be complementary.

Laws confer statutory powers and duties upon public sector organizations. In an organization, laws set parameters within which both elected officials and civil servants can act (Rose, 1986a; Page, 1985). Inasmuch as laws and written regulations cannot prescribe action in every contingency, then directives may be provided by top elected officials to fill in the gaps in laws. The minister's directives are not meant to contradict but to complete the law by providing a valid interpretation of the interstices of legislation (Bell, 1982: 17ff).

In the classic model of a hierarchical public sector organization, the minister is responsible for giving direction to high-ranking civil servants, who in turn send signals down the line to low-status officials at the base of the organizational pyramid. Since officials at the base of an organizational pyramid are far more numerous than those on top, this implies that most civil servants work primarily according to laws and directives derived from statutes, and their interpretation by elected politicians.

The extent to which low-level officials can have their actions determined by rules is problematic, not certain. The extent to which official discretion can be minimized is influenced by inherent characteristics of programmes and their delivery. It is far easier to specify and enforce rules and regulations upon postal workers than social workers, or upon a social security official using a computer to process pension claims than upon an official trying to market holiday travel on a state-owned railway. In a book entitled *Street-Level Bureaucracy*, Lipsky (1980: xi) argues that the lowest-level offices in 'schools, police, and welfare departments, lower courts, legal service offices and other agencies' are staffed by people who 'have wide discretion over the dispensation of benefits or the allocation of public sanctions'. A lowly status and salary is not a guarantee that an official is rulebound without discretion.

The signals constituting informal, and therefore 'unofficial', rules of conduct are maintained by a process of role socialization into a particular job. This transmits many values and beliefs about what is and is not done in the job. While occupation-specific, all informal norms have one thing in common: they provide alternative signals from those of the statute book.

Signals from expertise

Expertise signals how to define problems within a programme area; how to deal with the substantive problem presented (e.g. treat a hospital patient, teach a child to read, or build a public road); and how to evaluate the performance of a public organization.

Expertise is codified knowledge, the directives it gives are much clearer than the vague preferences of the electorate, or the procedurally significant but substantively vague injunctions of many laws. It can be acquired through formal training prior to entering public employment, or as a necessary condition for entry. For example, a teacher must have a teacher-training certificate, and a public health officer a medical qualification. Expertise is in part acquired through on-the-job experience.

Expertise is defined by experts rather than by statutes or elected officials (Dahl, 1970). It is often codified by professional associations, which publish standards defining what is required of a person wanting to work in their field. There is often a symbiotic relationship between professional associations and government. In the case of teachers, the state normally defines by law the educational qualifications required for teaching. But these laws are greatly influenced by the recommendations of teachers' associations and unions. Where government is not the dominant employer, as in legal practice, the professional association may be granted the authority to codify qualifications which gain the force of law. Even when expertise is sanctioned by statutes, it usually reflects the standards and interests of professionals more than elected legislators.

When expertise is learned on the job, it will not be formally codified; it will be expressed in standard operating procedures learned as part of informal role-socialization. These routines are derived by experience in dealing with problems in a practical way; they are not laid down in statutes. While Lipsky (1980: xii) rejects the idea that laws can control 'street level bureaucrats', he does emphasize that these officials develop norms of behaviour, 'modes of mass processing that more or less permit them to deal with the public'. This is a functional imperative for dealing with clients on a mass basis.

Expertise may be endorsed by elected officials and by the law, but it is not defined by these sources. In one sense, it is defined by results: it should prescribe, for example, how to build bridges safely, or treat patients in ways that lead them to recover rather than die. Institutionally, expertise is defined by professionals, who often collaborate in professional associations that bring together public employees with their fellows working in the private sector.

Signals from professional expertise are first and foremost important to experts. A medical doctor remunerated by the state does not regard himself as an official in an administrative hierarchy (*angestellte*) but as a free professional (*frei beruf*). The signals to which the doctor pays most attention are those provided by medical colleagues, and not by the electorate, the market or laws. While no set of experts can be completely isolated, least of all when providing a public service, people whose job qualification is a reflection of expertise will give it high priority.

In dealing with experts, elected officials are trebly handicapped. First of all, they are handicapped by ignorance; a legislator simply does not know how surgery is conducted, or how a water authority provides healthy water. Secondly, elected officials usually have low status when confronted with a consensus of expert opinion. Upon recognizing their ignorance, elected politicians may decide to let the experts decide. Only when experts disagree do politicians make decisions *faute de mieux*. Thirdly, experts are often not employed in a ministry. The specialist attributes that make them experts often lead them to work 'off line' in para-state organizations, or in the extreme case of a 'fee-for-service' national health system, as self-employed doctors.

Market signals

A defining attribute of a market is the exchange of goods between buyers and sellers. Most public goods and services are not sold but given to recipients free of charge; hence, market signals cannot operate. The absence of a market for most public goods and services severely inhibits the practical application of economizing techniques in government (cf. Self, 1975; Rhoads, 1985). Public employees are not paid on commission like salesmen in private sector firms, for normally they do not sell their services. Nor can higher civil servants be awarded stock options as an inducement to succeed, for ministries, courts and local authorities are not for sale. American attempts to pay performance-related bonuses to some senior civil servants have illustrated the difficulties of trying to apply market rewards to non-market activities (Ingraham and Ban, 1984).

There is one substantial, albeit neglected field of public policy where market signals do exist, however, and that is public enterprises. By definition, public enterprises are organizations that produce goods and services sold to consumers, such as electricity, coal, rail transport, postal services, steel, and motor cars. Selling their output makes public enterprises similar to private enterprises. But inasmuch as they are subject to state ownership and can draw upon tax revenue as well as market revenue, public enterprises differ from private enterprises (Vernon and Aharoni, 1981).

Like their private sector counterparts, public enterprises receive signals from the market about the demand for their products at a given price; this information is collected daily as part of routine operations.

Electricity or rail revenues provide evidence of how much people have paid to consume these public services. Moreover, public enterprises routinely collect information about the utilization of capacity. They know what percentage of electricity generating capacity is in use, and what percentage of seats are occupied on rail journeys.

The information generated by market signals can be used by public enterprises to evaluate the efficiency of their operations: the higher the utilization of their productive capacity, the more efficient an enterprise is. It can also be used to assess future demand, when decisions are required about investing in expansion or cutting back services. Notwithstanding difficulties in evaluation that have some private sector parallels (cf. Millward and Parker, 1983), public enterprises can make use of market signals, and the signals the market sends are continuous and public knowledge.

Employees of public enterprises are usually distinctive because they tend to identify with their industry rather than with the public sector per se. This is particularly the case in organizations that originated as private enterprises prior to being nationalized, for example, steel, or compete with private sector firms, as do motor-car manufacturers. The senior officials heading these enterprises are likely to be recruited on technocratic grounds. Many will have had an industry-specific training in a relevant engineering or scientific field of expertise; others may have training in commercial fields, such as accountancy, marketing or business administration. Workers in public enterprises usually organize by their industry (e.g. railways, postal workers) rather than joining general civil service unions.

Public enterprises must respond to more than the market; otherwise the rationale for public ownership is merely historical and accidental. The fact that enterprises are owned by the state makes elected officials to some extent answerable to the electorate for the enterprises. If an enterprise makes a loss, extra-market considerations become even more significant, for tax revenues can subsidize it. In the absence of a conventional profit constraint, public officials in charge of a public enterprise may maximize prescriptions of their expertise, and unions may bargain for higher wages or the retention of employees surplus to market needs, on the grounds that this provides a 'social' return.

Signals from the electorate

Civil servants are peculiarly ill-suited to identify and interpret signals from the electorate; their choice of career debars them from the experience of an elected politician. Those officials in European countries who do stand for office must go on leave from the service, and often do not return to civil service posts; they are a very small percentage of total public officials.

The electorate does not send clear and precise signals to policymakers. Voters do not 'choose' policies; even in the atypical circumstances of a referendum, voters do not choose the question that they vote upon (Butler and Ranney, 1981). Any popularly elected government can assert that it is doing 'what the people want', for otherwise it would not have been elected. However, the statement is true only insofar as it is tautological. Every study of the actual working of government emphasizes imperfections in the communication process between electors and elected officials (Key, 1961).

Public opinion surveys, whether by academics or by party organizations, show that the electorate has few opinions about issues, and these often concern generalized goals, e.g. peace and prosperity, or doing something unspecified about inflation and unemployment, rather than choices about specific programmes that are the day to day stuff of government activity. Nor is this surprising, for the ordinary voter lacks the expertise and involvement in public affairs of a politician, or a civil servant.

Politicians are specially sensitive to the electorate for reasons that have little to do with giving direction to civil servants, and a great deal to do with their own political careers. Since an election result can terminate a minister's career, that is sufficient motivation to pay attention to signals from the electorate. When elected politicians look to the electorate, they are first of all concerned with signals about their electoral standing and their personal popularity, rather than with popular assessments of policy alternatives. Within the governing party, politicians are not only concerned with mobilizing support for their actions but also with mobilizing support for their career ambitions.

The priority that elected politicians give to public relations rather than public programmes is a very clear signal to higher ranking civil servants who advise them in the ministries. These officials — the French *hautes fonctionnaires*, the British administrative class, or the American senior executive service — are directed toward what the French call *la politique politicienne*. A civil servant drafting a speech for a minister or answers to awkward questions from Parliament is not engaged in administration, but is acting as a 'closet politician'. The minister's involvement with his personal career and lack of strong attachment to a department or expertise (Rose, 1987; Headey, 1974) further attenuates the signals that civil servants may receive from elected officials.

Insofar as an elected official does want to send a directive to those delivering the services for which he is nominally answerable, it must often be an 'indirect' directive. Whereas the ideal-type model of political authority assumes that a low-status official works in the same organization as a minister, this is normally *not* the case. Three-quarters of all public employees work outside the ministries that are meant to provide central direction to government. They are employees of local or regional councils, public enterprises, health services, or other specialist bodies (Rose, 1985, Tables 1.10, 1.12). A Cabinet minister who thinks that the law empowers him to give direction to everyone working on 'his' programmes can have directives challenged by the heads of other public agencies who employ the persons who actually deliver the services for which the minister is nominally responsible (Hanf and Scharpf, 1978; Page, 1985a: Chapter 3).

The good news about public officials is that they live in an environment that is rich in signals; the bad news is that the signals are not always in harmony. A directive to obey the law can lead to complaints about excessive concern with procedures, and inflexibility in the face of substantive problems. A directive to respond to the electorate can lead to complaints about partisan bias. A directive to respond to market signals can lead to complaints about crass commercialism. Experts can be criticized for being more concerned with expert standards than with the persons whom they are meant to serve.

Relating signals to public policies
In government, there is no shortage of signals for public officials: the political problem, and thus the analytic problem, is to determine under what circumstances and to what extent each signal is appropriate to guide public action. The activities of civil servants are means to policy ends; they are not ends in themselves. Students of public administration or specialists in bureaucracy may, for purposes of their particular concern, treat the behaviour of civil servants as their dependent variable. But from a public policy perspective, these actions are intervening variables in the production of programme outputs.

The signals that officials receive are about substantive programmes of government; the programmes, like the signals, are diverse. The signals sent to public employees tend to be specific to a programmatic task, for a public employee is assigned particular duties and responsibilities within a specific institution, e.g. a health service, a public enterprise, or a ministry. Given the differences between the offices that public officials can hold, the question follows: which signal is dominant for a particular public policy? Are all signals equally important, or do signals differ in their significance from programme to programme?

In order to address these questions, we need to identify the attributes of public programmes that cause signals to vary. By definition, we would not expect market signals to be important in the non-market provision of education. Nor would we expect signals from laws to be particularly important in military defence, for major national security issues rarely turn on matters of international law. When examining public programmes, we can expect to find generic programme attributes relevant across national boundaries, and differences between programmes within a national political system (Rose, 1985a, 1985b).

Two distinctions are of fundamental importance in understanding the signals that public officials receive. The first is the distinction between collective goods as against private goods. (Olson, 1965). *Collective goods* affect all citizens, and cannot be sold in the market place because no one can be excluded from receiving these outputs of government. Defence against foreign invasion and the maintenance of public order are classic collective goods programmes. Conventional market signals cannot operate because of the non-excludable characteristic of collective goods, but this does not mean that citizens are 'voiceless' (cf. Hirschman, 1970).

In economic terms, many of the programme outputs of the public sector are private goods and services. *Private goods* are provided to identifiable individuals and organizations who can be excluded from their receipt. Education, health care, and social security payments are no less private benefits than restaurant meals or clothes, simply because they are produced by public employees. Receipt of private goods may depend upon legal, not pecuniary considerations. In the extreme case of education, the law not only offers a free education to every child but also compels children to be educated. Education remains a private good whether it is provided free of charge by a public institution, or is paid for in the private sector.

A second distinctive feature of public programmes is that private goods may either be sold or provided without charge and financed by taxes. Most of the major services of the contemporary welfare state are given away rather than sold, e.g. education, health and pensions. These goods are described as *merit goods*, which are socially so desirable that public laws authorize their provision to citizens without payment (Musgrave and Musgrave, 1980: 84f).

The decision about whether or not a particular private good is classified as a merit good is a political decision. Some public employees produce goods and services that are sold to consumers, e.g. electricity, coal, postal services, rail, bus and air fares. This remains the case even though heat, light and travel can be considered just as much necessities as education and health care (cf. Rose, 1986b). When the outputs of public employees are sold, then market signals are available; market signals are not available when these services are given away without charge.

These distinctions produce a fourfold typology of public programmes, contrasting pure and deviant collective goods, and private merit benefits with the benefits sold by public enterprises (Table 9.1). Here, the relevant task is to consider the signals that each type of programme is likely to send to civil servants.

TABLE 9.1
Alternative modes of providing public programmes

Programme type	Means of Provision	
	Non-market	Marketed
Collective	(i) Pure collective goods (defence)	(ii) Deviant goods (debt interest)
Private	(iii) Merit goods (education, health)	(iv) Public enterprise products (gas, post)

Expertise and electorate (pure collective goods)
By definition, the market cannot provide signals for the provision of goods for which no charges can be levied. Equally important, the law cannot direct how the nation should be defended in an insecure world, nor can it determine the conditions in which public order can be upheld in a world in which authority rests upon consent.

The pervasive significance of collective goods issues invariably makes them of concern to elected politicians and the electorate. When matters of war and peace are at stake, elected politicians are bound to give direction, for they are the legitimate authorities to decide whether or not a nation should go to war. Significant diplomatic matters are the province of a few top politicians, and contemporary governments pay heed to public opinion, for a military confrontation is difficult to sustain without popular backing.

Politicians turn to military experts for an assessment of the forces required in a given situation, and an estimate of the risk of failure. In the face of domestic disorder, elected politicians will be under popular pressure to 'do something' about rising crime or riots, and they depend upon the advice of police and intelligence experts about what can or should be done.

Laws and markets (deviant collective goods)
Logically, this category appears an impossibility because of the problem of marketing goods from which recipients cannot be excluded. However, debt interest payments can be considered a deviant example, for no citizen can be excluded from paying a share of interest on debts that government has accumulated, and the payment of debt interest is an increasingly important element in the national budget.

The law and the market provide the dominant signals determining what public officials do about debt interest. Laws obligate the government to pay interest on past debts, the market determines what the interest rate is. Experts forecast but do not control interest rates in today's open international economy. Politicians cannot choose the interest rate that the electorate would like, nor does debt interest reflect the public choice of the government of the day; it is the unintended cumulative result of choices taken by politicians in the past (Rose and Karran, 1984).

Laws and expertise (merit goods)

By definition, the market can provide little direction for the provision of benefits given to citizens without charge as acts of public policy. At any given point in time, the strongest signals come from public laws, for laws determine the content of benefits, and who is entitled to receive them.

Social security benefits are distinctive merit goods for laws can send signals sufficient without the intervention of expert judgements. The output of social security programmes consists of cash payments to the elderly and others entitled to such benefits. Public money is transferred directly to the recipients, who can claim a pension without expert intervention. The great bulk of social security benefits are routinely administered by low-status public officials applying the law.

In the case of education and health, public funds are paid to teachers, doctors and nurses expert in the production of these services. The law can lay down conditions of entitlement to these services. But expert standards give strong signals to professionals, determining formally and informally exactly what services are provided within the law. The expert content of the services inhibits elected politicians from giving directions. Since citizens receive merit goods without charge, they cannot send signals through the market to professional providers.

Market and elected officials (public enterprise products)

The dominant signal for public enterprises comes from the market. If people buy more electricity or take more airplane rides, this is a signal to the appropriate state enterprise to produce more of the product. Reciprocally, if people buy less coal or take fewer train rides, this is a signal to reduce production or services. Elected officials provide a secondary source of signals, indicating the amount of money available from the fisc to subsidize, on social or political grounds, provision of some services at sub-market prices. In theory, elected officials could provide an unlimited subsidy to a public enterprise to keep prices of a particular service low, or to maintain in employment workers in a politically sensitive constituency. In practice, elected officials expect public enterprises to raise nearly all their revenue from the market, and offer only supplementary grants from the fisc.

Neither the law nor expertise provides much direction to public enterprises. Laws do not signal how public enterprises must be operated; they only lay down conditions under which they conduct their business. Experts within an industry may have definite views about production and investment in the development of new products.

But expert influence will be limited to what is deemed financially feasible in the market, as modified by limited subsidies from the fisc.

Altogether, the four different types of programmes show that it is inadequate to describe public officials as bureaucrats single-mindedly applying the law. The law does send important signals directing the handful of public officials concerned with debt interest payments. In the provision of merit benefits, the law determines eligibility. But only in social security is legal eligibility sufficient to determine a programme. Often, the signals that laws give are procedural rather than substantive. Nor can we say that public officials do what the electorate wants, for the guidance the electorate gives elected officials is relatively weak in many programme areas. Signals from the electorate lay down broad guidelines, positive and negative, in defence, and in the maintenance of public order. The support of the electorate, or at least its tolerance, is important in determining the level of subsidy provided to a public enterprise with revenue from the market insufficient to meet market costs.

Signals from expertise are important for pure collective goods, and for many merit benefits. In national security, diplomats and military officials continuously advise elected officials and expertise not only shapes their advice but also how elected officials perceive the world. In health, the care that the patient gets is what the medical profession prescribes. In education the instruction that a child receives in a classroom is determined by the teacher's professional standards.

Market signals are not so much absent in government as they are overlooked. Public enterprises are rarely discussed, yet public ownership prima facie makes them part of government. The same is true of debt interest. The significance of market signals for public enterprises cannot be dismissed in an era in which these public sector organizations account for about one-quarter of all public employees (Rose, 1985). Nor can debt interest be dismissed when it accounts for a higher proportion of public expenditure than does defence, and is approaching education's claim on the fisc (OECD, 1984; Rose, 1985c: Table 4).

Given that examples can be cited for the significance of each type of signal, the question arises, which signals are most important in giving direction to public programmes? To answer this question, two complementary types of data can be utilized, public employment figures for six major Western nations, and OECD data about public expenditure in nineteen advanced industrial nations. Public employment data indicate the number of officials directed by each type of signal. Public expenditure data indicate how much money is affected by each type of signal. The two answers are not identical, for two big-spending programmes, social security and debt interest, are not labour intensive and one labour-intensive programme, public enterprises, is not tax revenue intensive, because of the availability of market revenues.

To produce quantitative indicators of the importance of different signals, public employment and expenditure data were categorized on a programme by programme basis according to the principles discussed above. Defence was assigned to expertise and the electorate, as was a general administrative factor; health, education, social security and other social programmes to the law and expertise; public enterprises to the electorate and markets; and debt interest to the law and the markets. Double-counting recognizes that two types of signals can affect a particular programme. The results are intended to indicate the relative importance of different types of signals rather than precise measures, for inevitably the categorization does not take into account signals of lesser importance, or which may be important only in part of a programme area.

TABLE 9.2
Relative importance of signals for public programmes

| Signals | Relevance to: | |
	Public employment %* (1)	Public expenditure %* (2)
Expertise	77	56
Law	52	74
Electorate	48	26
Market	23	23

Sources: (1) Public employment data averaged from detailed programme data for Britain, France, Germany, Italy, Sweden and USA; see Rose, 1985, Tables 1.10, 1.12. (2) Public expenditure data averaged from OECD data for seven major programmes (total, 41.8 percent of GDP), reported for up to nineteen countries; see Rose, 1985c: especially Table 4.

*Columns total to more than 100 percent, since more than one signal can affect public employees or public expenditure.

Signals from expertise and from laws tend to dominate public resources; this is true whether public employment or expenditure is the measure (Table 9.2). Moreoever, the difference is so substantial in the weight assigned to the two most important and the two least important signals that it should be valid, notwithstanding the rough-and-ready nature of the indicators employed. More than three-quarters of public employees have an expertise that is likely to affect programmes; public enterprises are the exception in being less dominated by experts. Expertise is important but less dominant for public expenditure, since it does not direct the routine payment of social security benefits or debt interest.

Laws give substantial direction to public employment and public expenditure. More than half of public employees are in programmes for which laws are important in specifying conditions of entitlement, i.e. education, health and social security. Typically, the laws define groups that are eligible to receive services of public employees, and indicate what their entitlements are. Laws are important in determining three-quarters of public expenditure. The so called 'uncontrollable' programmes of the budget are in fact controlled by statutes that persist with the force of inertia (Rose, 1986).

Politics and markets are often exaggerated as forces in government (cf. Lindblom, 1977) for while substantial in the absolute sense, each is relatively less important than signals from the law and expertise. Signals from the electorate can be important in classic defining concerns of defence and public order, and also in providing 'more than the market' signals for public enterprises. But in each case they operate in conjunction with signals from other sources.

Markets are very important in signalling demand for public enterprises: market signals explain why some public enterprises grow while others contract, and this pattern is true across Western nations (Rose, 1985: Table 1.8). Market signals also determine how much government must spend in interest payments on its debt. But most public programmes cannot be directly subject to market signals, for they are merit benefits provided free of charge, or collective goods for which no market exists.

While laws are primary sources of signals to civil servants, in no sense does this make officials bureaucrats. Most of the programmes for which laws produce signals are also subject to signals from other sources as well. Normally, these signals come from expertise, which may be formally codified and propagated through professional education and certification, or which may be the standard operating procedures of Lipsky's street-level bureaucrats.

Attempts to 'economize' politics, however elegant in the abstract, cannot provide positive direction to public officials as long as two conditions prevail. Most programmes are non-market, and economists have no agreed and precise empirical means for measuring the outputs and utilities of non-market goods. Until that occurs, public choice must be *political* choice and not a codeword for economic analysis in another mode. But political choice need not be choice by the electorate. In default of signals from the electorate, signals more often come from the inertia of laws enacted in the past and from the expertise of non-elected civil servants.

Implications for popular choice

The theory of democracy is simple, but the operation of democratic government is complex. The simple ideal — 'give the people what they want' — is far too simple. In an era of big government, popular preferences are inadequate to provide clear signals directing millions of public employees spending tens of billions of national currency. Just as government involves more than the market, so too it involves more than elections.

In the analysis of representative systems of government, it is appropriate to start from the ideal of popular choice: the actions of government should be consistent with the values and interests of citizens. The avoidance of the label of public choice is intentional, for public policy is not made in a simplified, idealized world in which public officials have wide scope for choice. In an era of big government, most of the big decisions about taxing and spending have already been taken, and are institutionalized in the bureaucracy and on the statute book (Rose, 1984; Rose, 1986c). The word popular is used to avoid confusing the role of public officials with the public qua electorate.

Consistency with popular choice

Given the primary importance of signals from the law and from expertise, the crucial question is, to what extent are they consistent with popular choice? The role of *laws* in public policy is often confused, or misunderstood (cf. Rose, 1986a). The laws that sustain the growth of government are not those that are the subject of judicial opinions, or cause controversy in Parliament. They are the old, widely understood and widely accepted laws that confer entitlements to education, health care, and social security benefits. The statute book is not so much a catalogue of prohibitions to citizens as it is a catalogue of benefits that public officials *must* provide.

The laws sustaining the major, and widely popular, programmes of the welfare state are measures that have been enacted by Parliament, and expanded to their present significance through representative political institutions. Signals from laws cannot be regarded as a denial of popular choice (cf. Lowi, 1969). The strongest criticism that can be made of laws is that they give great weight to the choices of past Parliaments and politicians, because they maintain their programmes in place through the inertia of the statute book. However, the fact that a law is not repealed can be reckoned as evidence of tacit acceptance of old laws, even if they are not what the government of the day would have chosen.

The capacity of laws to regulate and alter market conditions, marshalling political power against economic power, is recognized even when denounced as an 'imperfection' by free market economists (cf. Etzioni, 1985; Elkin, 1986). Today, neither experts nor party patronage machines decide who shall receive merit benefits since the law gives citizens a right to benefits. *Expertise* is specially important in determining how benefits are provided. The closer one approaches the point of delivery — the street level in Lipsky's sense — the more public service providers are likely to be sensitive to direction by expertise.

The expertise of professional public employees is not anti-social nor is it subversive of popular choice, just because it is so different from decisions by voting. Expertise results from processes that are necessarily social, involving the development of codes of conduct that can be widely transmitted. Professional associations often depend upon government for licensing authority, as well as for employment. Failure of professionals to deliver the goods — doctors to succeed in treating patients, or of teachers to educate most of their pupils — can produce a political counter-mobilization against experts for popular ends.

The use of *markets* to direct some public programmes is not inconsistent with popular choice. Every citizen spends more time participating in the market than in politics. A consumer makes far more choices in a week as an individual than a citizen as a voter is allowed to make in a year. Subject to income constraints, the market can do more to promote individual choices than can centralized decisions taken by experts, bureaucrats or politicians.

Whereas an election is a blunt instrument, aggregating millions of preferences, a market permits fine tuning. A party system may offer less than half a dozen choices to the voter, but a supermarket will offer thousands of different choices, and even a relatively restricted market, such as motor-cars, will offer dozens of alternatives. In mixed economy welfare states, the market remains the primary institution for allocating goods and services. In the average European country, 82 percent of final consumption is determined by non-governmental actors, as against 18 percent by the public sector (OECD, 1985: Table R6).

Given that all markets are imperfect, due to demand problems (e.g. income inequalities) as well as supply problems (e.g. oligopolistic or otherwise constrained competition), signals from the *electorate* are not the fundamental source of frustrating the realization of an ideal free market. Collective goods are technically incapable of market provision. To privatize military defence and the maintenance of public order would be to deny government the attributes of a modern state, a monopoly of the use of coercion. It would put up for auction decisions about such 'priceless' political values as national independence, and the security of the populace in an orderly and free society.

The limited involvement of the electorate in sending consumer-type signals is complemented by the limits upon elected officials acting like the managing director or owner of a firm. One reason for this is rarely faced up to: elected representatives today are more expert in being elected than in governing. Taking positions in Congress or securing an improved position within a parliamentary or extra-parliamentary party can be more important than the consequences of laws for which a Congressman votes, or of the actions that civil servants take under the nominal direction of a minister (Mayhew, 1974; Rose, in 1987).

Signals at the margin

In an era of big government, the established programme commitments of government must be taken as given. A newly elected government, whatever the ideological orientation of its President or Prime Minister, has limited room for manoeuvre. Signals from laws and experts, not to mention the beneficiaries of the 'good' goods and services of the welfare state, have a great momentum. It is unrealistic for an elected politician to expect to overturn this structure, for there are many things stronger than parties (Rose, 1984a; Chapter 8). Once these inertia commitments are recognized as 'sunk' costs, the important consideration is change at the margin. What is the relative strength of different types of signals for year-to-year changes in public programmes?

The Manpower and Social Affairs Divison of OECD (1985a) undertakes analyses of the principal causes of change in social programmes accounting for much of the expenditure and employment in the contemporary welfare state. The influences identified, inflation, demographic entitlements, the relative price effect (i.e., disproportional increases in public sector wage costs), and increases in programme coverage or in the level of real benefit, can be aligned with the four types of signals analysed herein. Since social security is not a large public employer, it has no relative price effect. Therefore, health and education programmes, the other two very big programmes of big government, are most appropriate for examining the signals that alter public spending most at the margin.

Of all the signals determining expenditure change from 1975 to 1981, the strongest was a market signal, inflation (Table 9.3). Two-thirds to three-quarters of the extra tax revenue went to meet the general effects of inflation. While hardly surprising, the political importance should not be discounted. Elected politicians can be blamed for raising taxes to generate more revenue needed to deal with the consequences of inflation for public expenditure. They can be blamed again for failing to provide a greater volume of services, notwithstanding the increase in taxation.

For both health and education, the most important influence, after inflation, is that described by OECD as an increase in real benefits. Since these benefits are meant to be received by citizens, they can be regarded as evidence of programmes being directed by the goal (if not identifiable signal) of electoral wants. Raising benefit levels may be initiated by elected politicians, or by expert pressures on behalf of the clients of the programmes that they administer.

TABLE 9.3
Signals for marginal expenditure growth, health and education 1975–81

| | Percentage growth[a] | | | |
	Health		Education	
Market (inflation)	68	(9.5)	78	(9.5)
Electorate (coverage, real benefits	20	(2.8)	11	(1.4)
Expertise (relative price effect)	7	(1.0)	11	(1.3)
Law (demographic entitlement)	4	(0.6)	0[b]	(0)
Total	99	(13.9)	100	(12.2)

[a] Proportion of growth accounted for by each signal given first. Contribution of each signal to the annual percentage rate of growth is given in parenthesis.
[b] Demographic impact negative (–0.4).

Source: OECD (1985a: Table 5) 'The Decomposition of the Growth Rate of Social Expenditure'; for seven major OECD countries, America, Britain, Canada, France, Italy, Japan, and the United States.

Experts have interests too: these are signalled in wage demands. The extra 'rent' that experts gain, the relative price effect resulting from wage costs rising faster than productivity, is a familiar phenomenon in labour-intensive service industries.

At the margin, the entitlements embedded in laws now account for very little change. For example, demographic pressures pushed up health spending by 0.5 percent, and depressed education spending by 0.4 percent. The importance of laws is in sustaining the *base* of demand for these programmes. The base is six to eight times the size of the cumulative marginal increase examined here.

The OECD (1985a) analyses are indicative, not conclusive. Yet the pattern found is consistent, when data is examined for a variety of programmes, a variety of countries, and for two time periods, the relatively affluent era from 1960–75 as well as a time of fiscal stress since 1975. The effects of laws, expertise, the market and the electorate differ as between programmes or from time to time, but all must be taken into account in a multivairiate analysis of giving direction to public officials.

Neither iron cage nor anomie
The perspective of public officials could theoretically reflect one of several extreme conditions. A government that was totally directed by laws would be a government living in an 'iron cage' of bureaucracy. An official would have no flexibility, and the resulting rigidity would be unpopular with both elected officials and citizens. Alternatively, a modern state could not be run without some laws to give direction to civil servants; otherwise, they would work in a state of anomie.

To subject civil servants solely to signals from the electorate would be to deny the significance of their expertise, and ultimately to invite blame for failing to warn against the disjunction between short term popular wants and long term satisfaction. While the exclusive dominance of expertise might be possible in non-democratic systems, it cannot be all-important in any system of democratic government.

The market is even less suited to be the sole source of signals for government. The importance of money in public finance is as a means to an end, not as an end in itself. Most public expenditure is for the provision of non-market goods and services. Contemporary advanced industrial nations have explicitly *rejected* the market as the ultimate arbiter of all things, by the provision of social welfare services as merit goods. In theory, it is possible to conceive of a regime in which most outputs currently provided without charge by government are sold. But empirical analysis must start with what is; the authority of law is used to give away valued social goods, thus dispensing with conventional market signals.

From the perspective of ordinary citizens, multiple signals can be regarded as a surety of better public policies. This proposition rests not only upon a recognition of the advantages of redundancy, but also takes into account the fact that citizens are accustomed to live in a 'mixed' society, that is, a society in which their welfare is the product of the market, the household, and also the state (Rose, 1986b). A plurality of signals offers the potential to produce a more appropriate mix of public goods and services than placing total reliance upon only one signal, whether from laws, expertise, markets, or elected officials.

Laws provide a base line of continuity in public programmes, guaranteeing entitlements to citizens, and procedural protection against unfair or inequitable treatment by civil servants or elected officials. The ballot box provides a very rough and ready mechanism by which citizens can express preferences, not only about private benefits but also about such important collective goods as national security and public order. Expertise provides a form of 'trusteeship' or 'guardianship', insofar as ordinary individuals cannot and do not expect to be competent to give direction for every problem about which government acts (Dahl, 1970). The market provides a fourth and familiar way in which citizens can vote with their pocketbook for or against some public sector goods and services.

The signals to public officials are not so numerous as to create confusion. Their multiplicity may be a source of conflict, but there is no a priori assumption of cognitive dissonance, i.e. mutually incompatible and peremptory directives. It would also be unjustified to assume that the sum of signals was guided by a 'hidden hand' that assured a perfect equilibrium. It is more appropriate to say that multiple signals require civil servants to be able to balance more than one directive. The higher one rises in the civil service and the closer a public official is to elected policymakers, the more likely this is to be the case. To paraphrase Harry Truman's injunction that politicians who cannot stand the heat should stay out of the kitchen, one might add: *Civil servants who can't stand the clamour should avoid high-ranking positions.* Work at the non-bureaucratic level of the civil service is inevitably accompanied by signals as diverse and noisy as those of a lively kitchen.

Note

The work reported here is part of a research programme on the Growth of Government of the Centre for the Study of Public Policy, supported by British Economic and Social Research Council grant HR 7849/1.

References

Aberbach, J., R.D. Putnam and Bert Rockman (1981) *Bureaucrats and Politicians in Western Democracies.* Cambridge, Mass.: Harvard University Press.

Bell, John (1982) *Policy Arguments in Judicial Decisions.* Oxford: Clarendon Press.

Butler, D.E. and A. Ranney (1981) *Referendums.* Washington DC: American Enterprise Institute.

Dahl, Robert A. (1970) *After the Revolution.* New Haven: Yale University Press.

Deutsch, K.W. (1986) *The Nerves of Government.* New York: Free Press.

Elkin, Stephen (1986) 'Regulation and Regime', *Journal of Public Policy* 6, 1, pp. 49–71.

Etzioni, Amitai (1985) 'The Political Economy of Imperfect Competition', *Journal of Public Policy*, 5, 2, pp. 169–86.

Hanf, Kenneth and F.W. Scharpf (eds) (1978) *Interorganizational Policy Making.* London and Beverly Hills: Sage.

Headey, Bruce (1974) *British Cabinet Ministers: The Roles of Politicians in Executive Offices.* London: Allen and Unwin.

Hirschman, Albert O. (1970) *Exit, Voice and Loyalty.* Cambridge, Mass.: Harvard University Press.

Ingraham, Patricia W., and Carolyn Ban (eds) (1984) *Legislating Bureaucratic Change: the Civil Service Reform Act of 1978.* Albany: State University of New York Press.

Key, V.O. (1961) *Public Opinion and American Democracy.* New York: Alfred A. Knopf.

Lindblom, C.E. (1977) *Politics and Markets.* New York: Basic Books.

Lipsky, Michael (1980) *Street-Level Bureaucracy: Dilemmas of the Individual in Public Services.* New York: Russell Sage Foundation.

Lowi, T.J. (1969) *The End of Liberalism.* New York: W.W. Norton.

Mayhew, David (1974) *Congress: the Electoral Connection.* New Haven: Yale University Press.

Millward, R. and D. Parker (1983) 'The Incentive Effects of Taxation' in R. Millward et al., *Public Sector Economics.* London: Longman, pp. 199–274.

Musgrave, R.A. and P. Musgrave (1980) *Public Finance in Theory and Practice.* New York; McGraw–Hill.

OECD (1984) 'Domestic and International Developments', *Economic Outlook*, No. 36.

OECD (1985) *Economic Outlook* No. 37.

OECD (1985a) *Social Expenditure 1960–1990.* Paris: OECD.

Olson, Mancur (1965) *The Logic of Collective Action.* Cambridge, Mass.: Harvard University Press.

Page, Edward C. (1985) 'Laws as an Instrument of Policy', *Journal of Public Policy*, 5, 2, pp. 241–66.

Page, Edward C. (1985a) *Political Authority and Bureaucratic Power*. Brighton: Wheatsheaf.

Rhoads, Steven E. (1985) *The Economist's View of the World*. New York: Cambridge University Press.

Rose, Richard (1984) *Understanding Big Government*. London and Beverly Hills: Sage.

Rose, Richard (1984a) *Do Parties Make a Difference?*. London: Macmillan, 2nd edn.

Rose, Richard (1985) *Public Employment in Western Nations*. Cambridge: Cambridge University Press.

Rose, Richard (1985a) 'The Programme Approach to the Growth of Government', *British Journal of Political Science*, 15, 1, pp. 1–28.

Rose, Richard (1985b) *Comparative Policy Analysis: the Programme Approach*. Glasgow: University of Strathclyde Studies in Public Policy, No. 138.

Rose, Richard (1985c) *How Exceptional is American Government?*. Glasgow: University of Strathclyde Studies in Public Policy, No. 150.

Rose, Richard (1986) 'Steering the Ship of State: One Tiller but Two Pairs of Hands', in Treasury and Civil Service Committee, *Civil Servants and Ministers: Duties and Responsibilities*. London: HMSO, HC 92–II, pp. 301–14.

Rose, Richard (1986a) 'Law as a Resource of Public Policy', *Parliamentary Affairs*, Summer, pp. 297–314.

Rose, Richard (1986b) 'Common Goals but Different Roles: the State's Contribution to the Welfare Mix', in R. Rose and R. Shiratori (eds) *The Welfare State East and West*. New York: Oxford University Press.

Rose, Richard (1986c) 'Choice and Inertia as Alternatives for Revenue Change'. Athens: Paper to 42nd Congress of International Institute of Public Finance, August.

Rose, Richard (1987) *Ministers and Ministries: a Functional Analysis*. Oxford: Clarendon Press.

Rose, Richard and T. Karran (1984) 'Inertia or Incrementalism? A Long-Term View of the Growth of Government', in A. Groth and L.L. Wade (eds) *Comparative Resource Allocation*. Beverly Hills and London: Sage.

Self, Peter (1975) *Econocrats and the Policy Process*. London: Macmillan.

Suleiman, Ezra (ed.) (1984) *Bureaucrats and Policy Making*. New York: Holmes and Meier.

Vernon, Raymond and Y. Aharoni (eds) (1981) *State-Owned Enterprises in the Western Economies*. London: Croom-Helm.

Weber, Max (1948) in H.H. Gerth and C.W. Mills, *From Max Weber*. London: Routledge and Kegan Paul.

10
Comparing bureaucracies
Edward C. Page

Introduction

There does not appear to be much that distinguishes one nation from another if one examines recent writings on bureaucracy in Europe. Such differences that exist are matters of *style* or 'standard operating procedures' rather than substance (Richardson, 1982). There is a dominant accepted theme in much of this writing that executive decision-making is sectorized: it takes place in distinctive subgroups within the executive, each involved in a complex process of consultations or negotiations with interested parties. Government is fragmented. The importance of decisions taken at the top (e.g. by cabinets or ministers) has, according to this view, been overrated in the past. Moreover, the impact of decisions taken at the top diminishes as one considers the ubiquitous problems of implementation.

The impression of homogeneity given by such literature is, however, counter-intuitive. Based as it is upon American experience and the rich and imaginative studies of the US federal bureaucracy, it is difficult to imagine that political systems with different historical experiences, different 'state traditions', different institutional structures and different patterns of civil service careers among other things should be so closely identical to each other and the USA (Dyson, 1980). This intuitive reaction is confirmed by a close reading of the classic chronicles of everyday life of officials in Germany, France, USA and UK (Hockerts, 1980; Grémion, 1979; Heclo, 1977; Kaufman, 1981; Heclo and Wildavsky, 1981). These people inhabit very different worlds.

There are no general theoretical frameworks which allow one to distinguish between salient and marginal differences of bureaucracies. This could possibly account for the paucity of truly comparative studies of bureaucracy as opposed to collections which describe the civil service and related institutions in different countries (Ridley, 1979). This paper seeks to help fill this gap in the study of comparative politics through setting out a comparative approach to bureaucracy derived from the work of Max Weber and applied to the contemporary systems in Germany, France, USA and UK (Page, 1985).

Weber's perspective has two main uses. The first use provides a common set of questions and concepts which can be applied cross-nationally as it facilitates the comparison of bureaucratic systems. It sets out the salient features of bureaucratic systems and points to the dimensions along which they may vary in such a way as to avoid the problems of making divergent systems appear homogeneous or producing results that are so configurative that it is impossible to characterize broad systemic similarities and differences. Weber's perspective derives its concepts and measures from a central set of normative concerns: the exercise of political leadership in bureaucratic systems. This constitutes the second reason for the usefulness of the Weberian perspective; it allows us to consider the normative implications of the development of bureaucracy and its environment for the nature of democracy and public influence in political systems.

Weber's approach

The focal point of Weber's analysis of bureaucracy was political leadership. On the basis of the ideal typical characteristics of bureaucratic rule he identifies a danger that government may become dominated by bureaucrats and a bureaucratic ethos. While he is not as fatalistic about this as is often alleged, the nature of the ideal type of bureaucracy contains this tendency. Without potent political leadership, publicly articulated political preferences cannot shape state action and officials can, indeed must, govern virtually alone.

Weber's approach offers a framework that concentrates directly upon one of the oldest and most important questions of political science — the scope and nature of political activity. The framework is set out in the four remaining sections. The following section explores the degree to which the conditions inherent to bureaucratic systems of government are found in each of the four countries cited, and the implications this has for the nature of political authority. 'The constraints on bureaucratic power' examines the degree to which existing institutions, parliaments, pressure groups, law courts, advisers and collegial decision-making institutions may limit the influence of bureaucracy. The third examines the constraints on political authority and characterizes the basic differences between the four countries on the basis of the Weberian perspective. Lastly, the conclusion offers an evaluation of the usefulness of the Weberian perspective.

Bureaucracy and the limitations on political leadership

The reliance upon bureaucracy imposes constraints on those who occupy the senior positions of political legitimacy (whether party politicians, monarchs or dictators) because of factors related to the *permanence* of the career-based administrative staff. One of the main features of 'ideal-type' bureaucracy is that the administrative staff is permanent and full time. Officials in the ideal-type possess specialized skills that are in part the result of specialized training. For this reason, Weber defines bureaucratic rule as that which is based upon knowledge. The officials in this system have a greater stock of knowledge than those whose will they are opposed to be faithfully executing. Consequently, the power of officials is 'constantly a very strong one and under normal circumstances one which towers above that of any others' (Weber, 1972: 572).

The career basis of administrative officials varies. In each of the four countries discussed in this chapter, there is a degree of political appointment which runs counter to the principle of a permanent civil service (Dyson, 1977; Suleiman, 1974; Heclo, 1977; Fry, 1985). However, only in the US does this amount to a strong dichotomization of officials into permanent and political groups. While such political appointments can be made in France and Germany, these are usually drawn from the ranks of permanent civil servants, while the choice of top officials has traditionally been far more restricted. Only Britain conforms relatively closely to the ideal type of permanent career civil service insofar as the most senior positions are concerned.

Does the training for a career service, however, bring the type of skills which are likely to strengthen the role of the official? The degree to which training or educational background is technical depends, of course, upon how one interprets the term 'technical.'. If one regards technical training to involve the social or natural sciences then only the USA conforms reasonably closely to the ideal type. However, if one regards legal training as the appropriate skill for public administration then Germany would fit with the ideal type. The French system of training could similarly be called technical since those who reach the top levels of the civil service have been recruited through a system which specializes in the training of public officials in special schools, most notably the Grandes Écoles and the École Nationale d'Administration (ENA). Only in Britain, with its preponderance of those who have a humanities background, is it difficult to find a criterion which would allow the training of civil servants to be called technical.

It may be doubted in all four countries that the type of educational background of officials, however technical, is particularly specialist in the sense of providing a training directly relevant for the nature of a top official's job. The argument that technical training is particularly specialist in this sense is a dubious one. As Suleiman suggests (1978), the education provided in the Grandes Écoles and the ENA is frequently assumed to be highly specialist. Yet the training that civil servants receive at the ENA has little to do with the type of work that they subsequently do, neither is it particularly specialized. Similar questions could be raised about the specialist nature of technical training in Germany and the USA — the work of top officials is far from technical. As Rose (1981) argues, familiarity with solid state physics might be of less use in interdepartmental bargaining than intimacy with the Peloponnesian War.

Although Weber did stress the importance of technical training he also argued that it was not the sole source of expertise upon which the power of the official is based (Weber, 1972: 855). Skills and expertise are also built up during the official's career. The fact that civil servants develop in the civil service means that they have been in the service a long time before they come to occupy senior positions. Aberbach, Putnam and Rockman (1981: 68) found that the senior officials covered in their study in Britain had been in the civil service for twenty-eight years on average, while in France the period was normally twenty-two years, in Germany twenty-one years and in the USA twenty-three years. If specialist knowledge is based on service experience, permanent civil servants have over twenty years apprenticeship in this field. As Rosen (1981: 204) writes, 'career executives are usually experts in a particular subject, they know the territory, the laws, the interested power centres, and what has worked or failed and why.'

It must not, however, be assumed that Weber is suggesting that a bureaucratic elite, single and cohesive, is likely to take over from the elected representatives of government. Government organization is diffuse (see, for example, Kaufman, 1981; Darbel and Schnapper, 1969; Mayntz and Scharpf, 1975; Hood and Dunsire, 1981). Moreover, as the literature on 'bureaucratic politics' suggests, your position or organizational affiliation also helps to shape your goals and values. Hence, one would expect that with this differentiation comes the potential for conflict among discrete government organizations and even within them.

However, in Weber's analysis, official dominance does not only emerge where a cohesive civil service elite exists. Differentiation and sectorization may prevent the dominance of a single elite, but they also make it far more difficult to exercise control. Weber's discussion of Imperial Germany and Imperial Russia shows that bureaucracy can limit political leadership through its differentiation. The administrative staff of these systems was characterized by Weber as displaying 'satrapic conflicts', referring to the territorial potentates of Persia (Weber, 1958: 326).

To use more recent terminology, it is precisely the pluralist nature of the administrative staff that limited the ability to exert political leadership in Imperial Russia and Germany, and if there is bureaucratic dominance in the modern period in each of our four countries, it is more likely to result from the satrapic internal conflicts than from the cohesiveness of a dominant bureaucratic elite. Given that the administrative staff is potentially in a powerful position in all four countries, what constraints exist to limit their power?

The constraints on bureaucratic power
There are a variety of institutional limitations upon the development of bureaucratic power, in particular, Parliament, interest groups, collective cabinet authority, ministerial advisers, and courts of law. How effective are these in asserting publicly established priorities upon the private world of bureaucratic politics?

The role of Parliament
For Weber the contribution that Parliament could make in limiting bureaucratic dominance was twofold. First, Parliaments can influence directly through mechanisms such as the initiation and amendment of legislation, the budgetary process and scrutiny committees. Second, and probably more importantly, he argued that Parliament provided a crucial training ground for political leaders: those who have skills to mobilize public support for their preferences and can sustain these within a bureaucratic system. This second role of legislatures will be discussed on pages 243–4.

Only the US legislature can be regarded as an important constraint on official dominance in the first sense. Mezey (1979) argues that the legislatures of the UK, West Germany and France can be termed as 'reactive' while the US legislature is 'active'. The term reactive refers to the domination by the executive of the policy-making process with the legislature reacting to, possibly modifying, decisions taken elsewhere. Such a view of the European legislatures would be supported by the preponderance of successful legislative initiatives originating within the executive, the relatively weak powers of amendment or at least passive use of these powers, the executive-dominated budgetary process and the reluctance shown by legislative scrutiny committees to inflict serious embarrassment upon a government which a majority of members of the legislature support (Page, 1985). Of course, the precise powers of legislatures and the willingness of their executives to use them varies from country to country, time period to time period, and issue to issue. However, in most cases, the constitutional limitations upon legislatures plus the importance of party cohesion for the conduct of government means that legislatures cannot be seen as controllers of the executive, and by extension the administrative staff, in France, Britain and West Germany.

In the USA, however, the reverse applies. Much of the legislation reaching the statute books originates within the legislature. Presidential initiatives have relatively low chances of success without substantial amendment, therefore Congress plays a crucial role in the budgetary process. In the post 1974 period, there has been a massive expansion in the scrutiny role of Congress; a role enhanced by the huge staffs employed by Congress as well as the importance of Congressional support for government agencies in the budgetary process. Moreover, the low level of party cohesion in Washington DC means there are fewer limitations on Congress availing itself of its substantial powers than are found in European legislatures.

Interest groups

While it is conventionally argued that interest groups serve to limit the degree to which officials may dominate, Weber is rather more ambivalent about the role of interest groups in bureaucracy. On the one hand, he suggests that groups have the potential for cultivating the form of political leadership which was so necessary in preventing a bureaucratic system from degenerating into rule by officials, along with other areas such as journalism and party organization. On the other hand, Weber points to the way in which such developments could strengthen the role of officials; not only does the influence of interests detract from the authority of the political leader, but interest groups also represent a source of expertise which can be utilized by officials to enhance their own position (Weber, 1972: 576). This corresponds with a number of diagnoses of the role of interest groups in the USA. For example, Beer argues that functionally defined 'professional-bureaucratic complexes' limit the scope for decisions reflecting 'concerted action toward national priorities and problems' (Beer, 1977: 9–10).

The activity of pressure group politics, as opposed to pressure groups as a potential recruiting ground for political leadership, serves above all to weaken the scope for political leadership, possibly also strengthening the power of officials. It means that state action might be contingent upon the consent that can be mobilized within the process of negotiation with groups, which centres upon the executive agencies in each of these four countries, rather than the political authority of government. This suggests that political authority can best be exercised in bureaucratic systems where there is a relatively wide scope for making government decisions *non-negotiable* with groups; where the government has control over which of the ubiquitous interest group demands action and how it acts upon these demands. The degree to which an interest group interacts with the administrative staff and constrains political leadership varies, *ceteris paribus*, cross-nationally with the variability of the scope for non-negotiable policy-making.

The USA offers the clearest example of a political system with narrow scope for non-negotiable policy-making. While the imagery used to describe the importance of interest groups differs among different authors, using terms such as 'issue networks' and 'iron triangles', studies of policy-making in Washington DC have tended to emphasize the importance of interest groups in a more or less fluid triadic relationship with executive bureaux and Congressional committees and subcommittees (Heclo, 1978). Moreover, the number of interest groups and their importance appears to have grown rapidly in the past twenty years. These groups have tended to develop specifically to influence the political system in Washington, with many groups having no national organization of any significance outside of their Washington DC lobby (Walker, 1983). The importance of the groups can be seen in their significance as 'inside players' in the policy process along with the judiciary, the President, Congress and the executive agencies. In the USA, groups constitute a strong constraint upon executive policy-making which, along with other features of the American system of government, such as the diffuse structure of the executive itself as well as the structure and influence of Congress, serve to fragment executive authority and limit their scope for non-negotiable policy-making.

This limited scope for non-negotiable policy-making in America contrasts sharply with the broader scope that exists in France. Of course, interest groups influence government in France too. However, the relationship between groups and government officials is one in which government officials dominate to such an extent that Hayward refers to pressure*d* groups in France. There are two sorts of evidence that one can point to in order to substantiate this. First, Suleiman's (1974) study shows that top officials made a distinction between legitimate 'professional' and non-legitimate 'pressure' groups, which in their minds appeared to come close to notions of corruption, and discriminated between those groups they wanted to pay attention to and those they sought to ignore. Second, there are numerous cases of major policy changes followed by government over the protests of major interests. In the case of the modernization of French agriculture — frequently cited as one of the only major policy areas in which group pressures are powerful — the government's proposals were opposed by the group with which it usually dealt, the Fédération Nationale des Syndicats d'Exploitants Agricoles, so the government simply sought the collaboration of its youth wing, the Centre National des Jeunes Agriculteurs (Keeler, 1981). In contrast to the USA, there exists in France greater scope for the government to derive policies and priorities without significant group involvement and sell these policies to groups afterwards if needs be.

While it is quite clear that the United States and France represent two extremes among our four countries with respect to the negotiability or non-negotiability of policy-making, the nature of policy-making in Germany and Britain is more hazardous to characterize. Traditionally, studies of interest groups in Germany since 1945 have emphasized the importance of interest groups. In 1955 Theodor Eschenburg's *Herrschaft der Verbände?* (*Dominance by Groups?*) argued that the underassertive state (*Unterstaat*) towards which West Germany appeared to be developing was the initial reaction to the overassertive state (*Überstaat*) of the National Socialist era; the Germans had developed an underrespect for the principle of state authority, a *Staatsunlust*, and an overrespect for pluralism and, in particular, interest groups. In Eschenburg's formulation, groups looked set to predominate the German policy-making process; ministries were staffed with interest group representatives, as were the specialist Bundestag committees, and groups influenced the choice of government officials (Eschenburg, 1962). Despite the subsequent criticisms (for a discussion of the criticisms see Rausch, 1976), Eschenburg's thesis appears to be upheld by subsequent studies (Braunthal, 1965: 231). Ellwein's (1974: 486) survey of interest group activity in West Germany concludes that the group system has a 'conservative effect and creates limits on the room for manoeuvre in policy-making which can make the social system incapable of innovation'; for example, the opposition of industrial groups managed to obstruct the development of environmental protection policies in the 1960s. Dyson (1982) points out the importance of group interests in German policy-making; delays and shifts in nuclear policy reflected the emergence of environmental groups, reforms of health policy were 'characterized by a stalemate of opposed interests and consequent immobility of policy' and on economic policy the state relied heavily on 'the social partners [i.e. capital and labour groups] to work out acceptable economic solutions'. The resulting 'collaborative style' of policy-making 'emphasises the need to accommodate group pressures in order to maintain social peace' and suggests a far more limited role for non-negotiable sphere of state activity than Britain and certainly France.

The evidence suggests that in Britain government is conducted routinely by the executive on the basis of group consultation is extremely well documented in Richardson and Jordan's *Governing Under Pressure* (1979). Yet it would be a mistake to equate the routine of consultation with a narrow scope for non-negotiable policy. Undoubtedly, the evidence strongly suggests that the British style of policy-making, like the German one, lays stress on group participation and the avoidance of 'electoral politics and public conflict in order to reach consensus or "accommodation" in the labyrinth of consultative machinery which has developed' (Jordan and Richardson, 1982: 81). However, as Jordan and Richardson stress, a policy style refers to 'standard operating procedures' and '*preferred* operating procedures'. This suggests the possibility that preferred procedures are those which, under certain circumstances, can be abandoned when the desire to achieve the outcome of a policy is stronger than the preference for the standard procedures. This has become increasingly apparent under the Conservative government of the early 1980s. The rhetoric of the Conservative party, with its 'anti-corporatist' strategy has emphasized its ability to ignore powerful interests. Moreover, the rhetoric does refer to changes of substance. Groups, such as doctors or even local government associations were, in the 1970s, conventionally assumed to have privileged access to policy negotiation within the executive. Yet the Conservative government has shown its preparedness to ignore the most persistent pleas of these groups. The government has also displayed a similar preparedness to ignore the expressed interests of other groups such as Trade Union Congress (TUC) the Confederation of British Industry and the Police Federation in key areas of government policy. Of course, one must not exaggerate the extent of the rejection of interest group consultation and negotiation. Yet British government appears to have greater discretion in defining not only which groups are included and excluded, but in defining issues which exclude any substantial group involvement or negotiation at all. Certainly this conclusion is supported by the contrast with West Germany — Dyson (1982: 45) argues that 'the idea of a sphere of non-negotiable policy has, therefore, been less apparent [in West Germany] than in Britain'.

Certainly, a distinction can be drawn between USA and West Germany on the one hand and France and Britain on the other. The distinction is of the degree of group involvement and the scope for non-negotiable policy-making, with non-negotiable policy more likely to be found within Britain and France than in Germany and the United States. The implications of these findings are that in Germany and the US executive leadership, whether by officials or politicians, is substantially constrained by the constellation of outside pressures. Here the systems are unlikely to be a system of *Beamtenherrschaft* because the administrative system is relatively open to interest group pressures. While this may serve to limit the development of *Beamtenherrschaft* (rule by officials), it also limits the scope for exercising political authority.

Cabinets, advisers and courts

Weber discusses two further limitations to dominance by officials. The first, collegiality, refers to the sharing in decision-making by those formally outside the direct hierarchy of an administrative organization. As Albrow (1970: 47) explains, 'bureaucracy [for Weber] meant that, at each stage in the official hierarchy, one person, and one person only, had the responsibility for taking a decision. As soon as others were involved in taking that decision *as of right*, then the collegial system was being employed'. This can be taken to refer to two sorts of limitation on the power of officials; that emanating from the principle of Cabinet government and that which results from the use by ministers of advisers to formulate policy and run their departments. The second of these further limitations stems from the nature of bureaucratic systems as forms of ideal typical rational-legal rule; governments can be 'bound by legal norms and acquired subjective rights' (Weber, 1972: 158) with courts as the main channels for observing these norms and rights.

The principle of Cabinet government is, of course, one of the main targets of the literature describing the sectorization of government policy making. This underlines the fact that in each of the four countries the role of Cabinet as an initiator of decisions, or even as a body to which many decisions of substance taken within government departments are referred, is limited. Perhaps its collegial role is most limited in the USA; Fenno's (1959) classic study indicates the 'essential powerlessness' of the American 'Cabinet'. This 'Cabinet' is weak in giving policy advice; communication between agencies usually only occurs 'on the lucky chance that something might pop up during casual Cabinet conversations', it does not settle inter-agency conflicts and even its decisions can be ignored or misinterpreted. Yet even in Europe, with an apparently stronger tradition of Cabinet government, Cabinet involvement in decision-making rarely conforms to the model ascribed to it in Britain by the 1918 Haldane Committee as the 'mainspring of policy' (Mackie and Hogwood, 1983). Most important, items tend to be decided on before, if at all, they ever reach Cabinet. In Britain, this leads Richardson and Jordan (1979) to conclude that 'very much in British politics can be understood without reference to the Cabinet'. In France, the presidential Council of Ministers has tended to adopt a minor role in policy-making, mainly because of the way in which the council worked 'afforded scant opportunity for the working deliberations that resolve disagreements and settle problems' (Andrews, 1981: 35). In Germany, the constitutional *Ressortprinzip* that gives formal autonomy to individual ministers further limits the powers of the Chancellor and the Cabinet. As Mayntz (1980: 155) suggests, in Germany Cabinet decisions mostly approve those decisions taken elsewhere, either within the ministries or by interdepartmental committee.

Advice and intelligence can strengthen the role of heads of executive departments, and in each of the four countries ministers, bureau chiefs and cabinet secretaries can expect advice from a wide variety of sources. Perhaps the only strongly institutionalized source of policy advice is to be found in France, where the ministerial *cabinets*, which are supposed to function as the eyes, ears and mouth of the minister within his department, are an integral part of the ministerial structure with the Directeur of the *cabinet* endowed with the authority of the minister. Although the members of the *cabinets* are generally top officials, raising the argument that it constitutes yet another area of political influence dominated by civil servants, it certainly has the potential for strengthening the minister's role rather than for actually controlling the administration. Similar institutionalization of advice specifically for the minister is not found in the other three countries.

Although almost all ministers have advisers, the role of stable sets of ministerial advisers appears relatively weak. In Britain, Young and Sloman (1981: 91) comment that advisers are 'at best . . . a minor cosmetic on the granite face of the body politic: good for appearances, even for a politician's self-regard, but not likely to change very much.' Dyson (1977) discusses the failure in Germany of 'policy planning' units within ministries, although he does suggest that 'invisible planners' in the form of special personal groups outside the formal structures operate in a 'quiet but occasionally influential manner'. In the USA, studies of the executive have shown that advice flows very freely and that much of top political executives' time is taken up with receiving it (Kaufman, 1981). Yet the ability to use information is curtailed by the highly limited nature of executive leadership; that of 'nudging agendas, priorities and decisions' (Kaufman, 1981: 149). With the possible exception of France, advisers do not appear to be a particularly powerful counterweight in the balance of power between the minister or political executive and his permanent staff, however beneficial an effect they may have on the quality of policy-making.

Almost by definition in rational–legal systems, courts have some role in scrutinizing the actions of government. In Britain this role is limited through the absence of a written constitution. This means that judicial review, as understood in the other three countries as a means of evaluating the consistency of the laws and actions of the government of the day with a higher constitutional law, does not exist. In Britain, judicial review has a more limited meaning — examining the legality of administrative actions according to existing statutes and precedent. Moreover, even in his limited conception of the term, courts in Britain rarely use their discretion to challenge the executive, making judicial opposition to the government an 'aberration which occurs most infrequently and in very special circumstances' (Griffith, 1981: 227). This application of judicial review contrasts with the USA where through interpreting the constitutionality of government actions the courts (above all, the US Supreme Court) have influenced not only individual rights but a whole range of public policy issues including education and pollution (see US ACIR, 1981a; 1981b). Johnson (1982) argues that the German *Bundeverfassungsgericht*, or Federal Constitutional Court, matches the US Supreme Court in its influence in policy-making. Such a contention is difficult to establish, however, it does point to the importance of the courts decisions in domestic as well as foreign policy. Certainly, the US and German court systems have constraints upon the executive and this contrasts with the British system. Their powers are also greater, or at least have been more consistently used, than those of the French *Conseil Constitutionnel*, originally set up as an executive device to maintain the subordination of the legislature. The Conseil has, however, developed a more activist role, frequently critical of the government, especially after 1974 when the rules governing access to the Conseil were changed to allow matters to be referred to it through petitions of sixty deputies. Its decisions include declaring that the budget in 1979 was unconstitutional, and the re-evaluation of the level of compensation offered to industries taken into state ownership in 1981. Yet, as Hayward (1983: 141) suggests, the Conseil has generally been reserved in the use of its powers, preferring 'to steer a middle way . . . between a quietist acknowledgement that the will of the people's representatives should prevail and activist temptation of government by judges who lay down the law to politicians prone to put short-term expediency before the protection of basic rights'.

Constraints on Political Authority

Political leadership
Weber identifies the institutions that might be expected to prevent official dominance — the legislature, interest groups, courts of law, advisers and collegial bodies. In the three European countries, the impact of these institutions upon official dominance is only limited: the executive dominates the legislature; where court activism can claim a number of important successes, as in Germany, judicial review is still not invoked as a matter of routine; collegial bodies as well as political advisers and appointees may strengthen the hand of the minister but do not guarantee that the voice of public officials is weak. Only in Germany and the USA do interest groups serve to limit the scope for non-negotiable policy-making. Yet even here, the bureaux are central to the network of negotiation. The forces which are present to limit official dominance are generally weak. However, the influence that emerges from institutions is not the only or even the most important means of limiting 'Beamtenherrschaft'. For Weber, Beamtenherrschaft could only be avoided effectively through the assertion of political leadership.

Weber's conception of political leadership can best be understood as a contrast to his more pessimistic writing on the subject of bureaucracy. A system of Beamtenherrschaft is a 'lifeless machine'. Free will is suppressed in the 'cage of bondage' resulting from the development of bureaucracy as a rational form of social organization. However, it is possible for individuals to rise above the constraints of the lifeless machine. Political leaders, those with political skills and public democratic legitimacy, offer the only real alternative in a bureaucratic system of government to the 'pacifism of social impotence under the wing of the only totally certain inescapable power — that of the bureaucracy in the state and the economy' (Weber, 1972: 836). Political leadership involves using the skills of persuasion and compromise, the ability to sacrifice the 'less for the more important', acquired in the competition for votes and a career in politics, to assert the values and choices of the politician. A bureaucratic system without political leadership will, of course, carry on the process of government. However, the decisions taken within it will be subject to logic internal to administrative organizations rather than to any publicly expressed values and preferences. Peters' (1981) counter-factual discussion on the 'problem of bureaucratic government' as well as Diamant's (1968) factual analysis of the French Fourth Republic show this. Weber's framework does allow an examination of the different sources of limitations on political leadership in each of the four countries.

The constraints of supply and authority
While interest group and legislative influence can be found in all countries, some countries are more centripetal than others. The weak role of pressure groups in France contrasts with the importance of the changing array of 'issue networks' that act as 'inside players' in the policy process in Washington, and makes France far more centripetal than the USA. Britain and Germany are not as centripetal as the USA; the British Parliament has a far more limited role in policy-making than the German Bundestag (King, 1975), yet in neither does the legislature have the degree of influence found in the US Congress. On the basis of the centrifugality introduced by interest group pressures, the evidence suggests that the British executive has far greater scope for ignoring group pressure (and has done so to an increasing extent since 1979) than its German counterpart. In Germany, a number of studies of policy formation and implementation have suggested that interest groups have severely constrained government action across a number of issues: such as urban policy, energy policy and regulative policy (Scharpf et al., 1976; Mayntz, 1978; Dyson, 1982). Thus we would expect Germany to be relatively closer to the USA than Britain in terms of the centrifugality of the system. This characterization of three out of the four countries is supported by the survey evidence presented by Aberbach et al. (1981: 230) who argue, on the basis of the frequency of contacts between top officials on the one hand and interest groups and members of legislatures on the other, that Britain 'fits our expectation about centripetal systems quite well', the USA is the prime example of a centrifugal system and Germany 'appears to be evolving in directions similar to (but not coincident with) American institutional patterns'.

There are thus two forms of systemic constraint on political leadership in our four countries. First, a constraint of supply which exists when the structure of political careers appear less likely to generate the form of political leadership discussed by Weber: a politician with the ability and experience to mobilize public support and skill to achieve important objectives through the sacrifice (i.e. compromise) of less important ones. Second, a constraint of authority which exists when pluralistic constraints, characteristic of centrifugal political systems, make the exercise of political leadership exceptionally difficult even on a highly limited scale.

France: a problem of supply?

It is quite simple to challenge some of the more naive beliefs about the nature of the French administrative system that were held until around ten years ago. The French administrative system was supposed to produce a cohesive elite, drawn from a narrow social stratum, acquiring common values and lasting friendships in the *Grandes Ecoles*. This specialist training underpinned the power of top officials; they constitute a technocratic elite within the French political system. Suleiman (1974; 1978) has shown the error of such a simplistic view. Neither a *Grandes Ecoles* training nor common social background can be expected to create homogeneous political values. Moreover, the specialism of the training at the *Grandes Ecoles*, and especially at the *Ecole Nationale d'Administration*, the most important source of recruits for the highest positions in the administration, is largely mythical, with few undergoing training relevant to their future tasks.

Suleiman concludes that top officials in France constitute an élite only insofar as they cohere to protect their corporate interests, especially when the status of the civil service or a particular corps within it is under threat. Their specialist training serves to underpin their extreme eligibility for top posts in the public, semi public and even private sector. Yet Suleiman distinguishes between this 'corporate identity', which is concerned with attitudes and behaviour connected with the civil service (primarily over matters of status and power within the politico-administrative system) and specific functional policy preferences. He argues (1978: 247), for example, that it would be 'difficult to pinpoint a coherent set of policies that the Inspection des Finances or the Corps des Mines are committed to within the areas of the economy or energy.'

Nevertheless, most studies of the French politico-administrative system tend to stress the importance of the civil service in the process of the policy-making: in both the initiation and the processing of policies. The influence that it exerts is not that of a cohesive elite with a clear set of policies, instead it reflects the interests, frequently conflicting, of different corps within it. That is to say, as with the satrapic conflicts observed by Weber in Imperial Germany, the development of policy takes place on the basis of criteria, divisions and conflicts reflecting the social relations within the bureaucracy rather than the imposed priorities of political leadership.

This is especially apparent in the work of Catherine Grémion (1979;

1982). Grémion documents a substantially different picture of the role of civil servants in policy-making to the more traditional one which sees the civil servants as relatively constrained by their corps allegiances Crozier, 1964; 1970; 1974). The principle of *détachement*, which allows civil servants to work for a period outside their usual posts without loss of any privileges that go with their usual posts, has created a more mobile and more broad minded (in the sense of being less bound to think and act on the basis of corps loyalties) group of top officials which Grémion terms the civil servants *hors machine*. Such officials are 'relatively open to outside pressures and are prepared to overlook the rationality of the corps' (Grémion, 1979: 394). The experience of mobility creates '*reseaux* of solidarity' which cross corps divisions and are capable of exercising a dominant influence on executive action. This contrasts with the position of the more traditional civil servants who work *dans la machine* in the sense that they follow the career paths usually associated with their corps and consequently are likely to reflect in their thoughts and actions the interests of that corps.

Grémion does not suggest that the groups of *hors machine* civil servants interested in particular policy problems, which she terms *familles d'esprit*, are the sole source of policy initiatives. Indeed, in one of her case studies, regional reform, the development of the policy within the administration tended to reflect the more traditional corps system. Yet in others, such as Grémion's case of housing finance reform in the 1970s, the *hors machine* officials were extremely important.

The distinction between the processing of policy *dans la machine* on the one hand and *hors machine* on the other in Grémion's work reflects a duality within the French politico-administrative system that has been noted elsewhere (Hayward, 1982). It has been considered to be an innovatory style of policy-making in which a mobile and relatively open administrative elite innovates and accommodates divergent interests both within and to a degree outside the civil service, and a more ponderous style in which initiatives are blocked or altered by the obstruction of different corps. Both models are more or less consistent with the characterization of the constraints on political leadership resulting primarily from constraints of supply. Whether policy is made *dans la machine* or *hors machine*, neither political leadership, nor indeed many other forms of open political control, have a strong capacity to intervene in the policy process in view of the importance of the constellation of interests within the civil service. Even where the *familles d'esprit* initiate policy, ministers frequently have the role of 'providing the necessary backing for the initiative' (Hayward, 1982: 122).

Leaderless democracy in the United States

Leaderless democracy is a term used by Weber (1972: 850) to describe systems in which political leadership fails to emerge and policy is formulated on the basis of relatively unstructured (through the party system) interactions between a variety of democratic forces, above all interest groups and groups within the legislature. As such, it reflects constraints upon political leadership both of supply and authority. The absence of a pool of political leadership in the USA and the powerful pressures upon the executive emanating from outside the department — from groups and the legislature — have already been discussed. The consequences that this has for political leadership have been pointed out by a number of American commentators. Seidman (1980: 322), for example, points out that political appointees:

> . . . rarely bring to their jobs the unique combination of political insight, administrative skill, leadership, intelligence and creativity required for the management of heterogeneous institutions with multiple and sometimes conflicting purposes. Most are content to be a 'mediator-initiator' or a reactor to initiatives coming from the White House, the Congress, the bureaucracy and the several constituencies represented by the department.

Kaufman's (1981) study offers a similar picture. Reflecting on the nature of leadership he argues that most studies of the policy process in the USA, whether they assume that the executive consists of interrelated networks of policy activists or isolated organizations with no contact or co-operation between them, come to the same conclusion: 'the administrative system is not fully under control'.

Without political direction the system cannot become (as in the case of France) dominated by officials since the officials themselves are part of a highly complex web of relationships, involving Congress, the President and his office, interest groups and other executive agencies with no one able to sustain any exclusive claim to authority. Thus officials are better regarded as participants in this process than in control of it. As Heclo (1978: 105) suggests,

> . . . a somewhat new and political dynamic is being played out in the world of political administration. It is not what has been feared for so long: that technocrats and other people in white coats will appropriate the policy process. If there is to be any expropriation, it is likely to be by the policy activists, those who care deeply about a set of issues and are determined to shape the fabric of public policy accordingly.

In the USA the wide distribution of authority and the atomization of influence means that neither political executives nor top civil servants are at the apex of an organization which is hierarchically structured and over which they have a monopoly of control. Political executives preside over organizations that make claims on public authority for legal authorizations and financial support, yet are not themselves subject to the public authority of political leadership. In consequence, the outcome of policy processes, as in France, tends to reflect the relationships that exist within a particular set of national policy communities rather than any publicly expressed political preferences. Yet here the policy communities appear more complex, unstable and involve a broader range of interests than in France.

Wolin shows how such a pluralistic system contrasts with more traditional views of political authority by arguing that since legitimacy is something that has become associated with groups, 'public authority has no source of power peculiarly its own'. Instead, public authorities become the representatives of 'residual constituencies that . . . have not been wholly absorbed into the dominant groups' such as the ethnic and racial minorities, farm workers, unorganized industrial workers and those who are almost totally dependent upon the welfare state; 'In other words, public authority has the constituency of the powerless.' This is similar to Heclo's conclusion.

> . . . the first and foremost problem is the old one of democratic legitimacy . . . political executives get their popular mandate to do anything in the bureaucracy secondhand, from either an elected chief or Congress. The emerging system of political technocrats makes this democratic weakness much more severe. The more closely political administrators become identified with the various specialised policy networks, the farther they become separated from the ordinary citizen. Political executives can maneuver among the already mobilised issue networks and may occasionally do a little mobilising of their own. But this is not the same thing as creating a broad base of public understanding and support for national policies. (Heclo, 1978: 118)

Such creation of public understanding and support is the essence of the form of demagogic leadership of Weber's definition; it is largely absent in the USA in which the scope for non-negotiable policies which exclude interest group bargaining and bargaining with the legislature is limited.

West Germany: the reaction to the strong state

The German political system does not appear to have particularly strong constraints on political leadership which result from the supply of political leaders: there is a pool of politicians who have pursued a political career within the Bundestag, a political party, an interest group, or state and local government. In addition, German politicians are likely to gain insights into the operation of executive organizations through activity on the Bundestag committees, and the post of *parlamentarischer Staatssekretär* offers further such opportunities. Unlike the USA and the UK, few analyses have emphasized the problem of the supply of leaders in Germany. Johnson (1982a: 156), does the reverse when he suggests that political leadership in Germany has been 'pragmatic, flexible in its response to demands voiced within the political system and, at its best, decisive and public spirited', although he also notes an increasing degree of introspection within the parties which leads them to 'show signs of becoming less concerned to a broad band of public opinion . . . than with their own programmes and internal arguments.' Nevertheless, this is referred to as a potential rather than an actual danger. Consequently, if there are major constraints upon political leadership in Germany, we may expect them to be constraints of authority.

In Germany, as elsewhere, group consultation takes place. Often it does so on a statutory basis. Group influence is reinforced through the relative power of the Bundestag committees (at least in European terms) which provide an additional target for interest group activity as does (to a decreasing extent) the process of appointing *politische Beamte*. The centrifugality of the German system is further reinforced by the federal structure. The federal government has relatively few functions which it carries out without state and local collaboration, and the second chamber, the Bundesrat, further increases the influence of state government in federal policy-making.

Dyson (1982) shows the importance of group pressures as a limitation on the exercise of political leadership. Health policy groups, representing medical professionals and health insurance organizations, played an important role in blocking reform of the health service. Of course, medical professionals exert extensive influence over the shape of health policy in most western nations, yet in Germany group influence appears to be a characteristic found in a large number of policy areas. In nuclear energy policy, the contentiousness of the issue, which caused conflict within the different sectors or *Ressorts* involved as well as from outside groups, resulted in an attempt to 'design procedural policies of agenda management and consensus' and avoid raising issues that provoked group conflict. Similarly, in economic policy-making, 'concerted action', a form of 'corporatist' voluntary regulation of economic policy by the state, labour and capital, was essentially a 'convenient device for issue management and consensus formation in the face of politically sensitive industrial problems like coal and steel' (Dyson, 1982: 39).

Similarly, Fritz Scharpf and his colleagues (1976) pointed to a model of 'policy interpenetration' which emerges from the centrifugal nature of the German bureaucratic system, although the Scharpf et al. work stresses the role of divisions within the state organization, the *Ressortpartikularismus*, of the different sectors of different federal ministries as well as the horizontal division between federal, state and local government. Policy making, because of the importance of these divisions, tends to produce the quest for conflict avoidance strategies in which contentious issues are isolated and set aside. The results of this process are an inability to produce policy instruments likely to have much resemblance to those which are desired. For example, the rationale of regional policy is that it seeks to *target* money for industrial developments towards particular regions. However, in the German case, the 'norm' (so conflicts can be avoided) produces a regional policy based more closely on a 'fair shares all round' basis.

Britain: a particular problem of supply

The British system has already been described as more centripetal than the German one (for elaboration on this see Page, 1985). Consequently, we may expect the limitations on political leadership in Britain to be constraints of supply. This might at first appear counter-intuitive since the British system has a clear pool of politicians, Members of Parliament who can be recruited to ministerial offices. Indeed, the German *parlamentarischer Staatssekretär* system was borrowed from British experience. The problem of supply results is apparent from the fact that despite the sort of political career that is absent within the USA, relatively few ministers would conform to a model of political leadership of the type found within Weber's discussion. Headey's (1974) study offers persuasive evidence that ministers only infrequently have the sort of skills and priorities that might be expected of a political leader. Headey distinguishes between five different types of ministers; policy initiators (who promote their own policy initiatives); policy selectors (who accept the objectives of the department and see their role as choosing between alternatives presented to them by officials); executive ministers (who are concerned with particular aspects of the management of their ministry and in maintaining morale); ambassadors (who see themselves as responsible for maintaining good relations with interest groups and Parliament), and minimalists (who simply conceive themselves to be the person who signs official documents, who bats for the department in Cabinet and makes sure that he does not make any blunders in Parliament). Headey found that twenty-three out of his sample of fifty ministers interviewed regarded themselves as 'policy initiators'. However, many of these

> appeared to be doing no more than paying lip service to a constitutional norm that said that a Minister should 'decide his policy objectives' or 'dominate his department' or 'make an impact on policy — so that everyone knows he has been there [in the Department]' (Headey, 1974: 71)

A more accurate description of policy initiation, that of courting opposition within the department through overlooking 'the existing objectives and policies of their departments' and succeeding in 'exacting policy programmes based upon objectives defined by themselves or their party' (Headey, 1974: 191), covered fewer of the sample of fifty ministers. Headey states that on such a definition 'at least nine' of the sample could be termed 'initiators'. Generally, he (1974: 271) concludes that British politicians are 'not qualified . . . to act as policy initiators'.

Headey gives two major reasons for this. The first one is that British ministers are in office for a relatively short time, between two and three years, while in Germany the duration is longer, for around four years (Paterson, 1982: 106) In addition, German ministers are more likely to have developed a specialist knowledge of the affairs of their ministries than their British counterparts (von Beyme, 1983). It takes, Headey estimates, approximately three years to see a complex policy initiative through to completion, and ministers without particularly well-defined policy objectives before their appointment in a ministry (a clear majority, see Headey, 1974: 174) require time to evolve them. The average of three years is therefore not only a problem for the minister who is appointed at the outset of the formation of the government, it is also a problem for the minister taking over for the remaining period, a maximum of two years before the election. In a similar vein, *The Economist* (22 October 1983) commented on the alteration of government posts under Mrs Thatcher's leadership; 'frequent reshuffles were the easiest way of ensuring that civil servants rule the country'.

The second reason results from the nature of party government in Britain (Rose, 1974). One main condition of party government is that parties in opposition generate 'do-able' and detailed statements of policy intentions. Yet in Britain the specification of detailed programme objectives in controversial areas has proved to be extremely divisive. Moreover, the distance of the party in opposition from the centres of political power means that it has little status in consultation with interest groups and is open to the charge by the government that such policy proposals are based on incomplete knowledge of the relevant facts and issues at stake.

To argue that a characteristic limitation of political leadership in the bureaucratic system of government in Britain is the supply of political leadership by no means suggests that ministers are invariably or even frequently 'weak' — at the mercy of the suggestions coming from their departments. There is too much evidence pointing to the existence of strong ministers and, above all, the importance within any government department for it to have a 'strong' minister. Heclo and Wildavsky (1981: 132) argue that 'civil servants invariably prefer a strong to a weak minister . . . Given a choice between someone who passively accepts their advice and interests and someone who can effectively protect and advance the departmental interests, the Treasury and the spending departments would unanimously choose the stronger character.' Similarly, Headey's (1974: 142) questioning of top civil servants shows that 'almost to a man civil servants claim to prefer a minister who puts them on their mettle, annotates their papers, poses shrewd questions in office meetings, disputes received departmental assumptions and throws out ideas for further consideration.'

However, such a conception of strength and the ability to assert an individual judgement is significantly different from the model of political leadership set out in Weber's writings. Indeed, this conception of strength is something that would be expected of a good official as well as a good minister (Weber, 1958: 322–23). The strength of the strong assertive minister in Heclo and Wildavsky's study, as well as the preferred strong minister of civil servants, is that of the 'policy selector' in Headey's study rather than the 'policy initiator'. The difference between the two is not purely in the cliché that advice offered by civil servants to the 'policy selector' minister is limited and therefore subject to his available options being under the control of the officials. There is strong evidence to support this argument in studies of the civil service (Kellner and Crowther Hunt, 1980). Indeed, the nature of advice probably means this is invariably true, whether such options are consciously or unconsciously limited. The more important difference between even the aggressive policy selector and the policy initiators is that the selector is responding to cues for political initiative either emanating from within the department or filtered through it rather than mobilizing political support for his own initiative. As Headey (1974: 160) writes,

> probably the ideal situation for a policy selector is one in which there is a large number of proposals in the departmental pipeline. These proposals may be evaluated both in terms of their intrinsic usefulness and the extent to which sponsoring them is likely to enhance the Minister's and the Government's standing.

This distinction between policy selectors and policy initiators is also important in distinguishing between the more preferred from the less preferred type of minister from the officials' perspective. Since to exercise leadership means to exert one's preferences over and above existing departmental inclinations, it appears almost axiomatic that to exercise political leadership is to court some opposition from within the department (Headey, 1974: 211). This is supported by the preference found by Headey (1974: 153) among civil servants for policy selectors over policy initiators. While he argues that there is 'no suggestion that civil servants tend to reject non-conforming ministers like the body tends to reject transplanted organs' because of the strong and pervasive sense of loyalty in the British civil service 'in the highly competitive worlds of Westminster and Whitehall a minister needs all the support that he can get, and it seems reasonable to conclude that policy selectors are at an advantage over policy initiators'.

Conclusions

There are at least three major benefits to be derived from applying Weber's ideas. First, the approach allows the identification of salient differences between the bureaucratic systems of different countries. The differences that exist are not solely to be found in the internal structure of the administration itself, but also within the conditions prevailing in the proximate environment with which the permanent administrative staff interact. Complexity and bargaining may indeed be universal, but the differences in institutional structures and relationships are so great that it is impossible to equate the constraints upon, say, top officials in the United States that result from legislative and interest group activism with those that face top officials in France. In each of the four countries the position of the administrative staff displays broad structural features which Weber's analysis helps to pinpoint.

The second advantage of the Weberian perspective is that it focuses attention once again, in the European context, upon a central question in the study of bureaucracy — how political choices can be made in bureaucratic systems. Many studies of bureaucracy seek to establish the degree to which civil servants or ministers have power. Such studies are more or less doomed to be inconclusive. Not only do we lack any common definition of power, we also lack agreed means of detecting it, let alone comparing it cross-nationally. Moreover, such studies that exist rely heavily on case study material, frequently so sparse that broader theoretical generalizations are impossible. Weber's analysis, however, focuses attention upon the degree to which a particular activity, the exercise of political authority, can be found within a particular governmental system. The American literature, from which a significant portion of modern European studies borrow, has for a long time had this as a central practical, if not theoretical, concern (compare Long, 1981 with Richardson, 1982). In this respect, Weber's concerns are with a *political science* of bureaucracy rather than the form of analysis of power within administrative systems more characteristic of *organizational sociology* which originated with an entirely different set of concerns from those displayed by Weber (Mayntz, 1965).

The third benefit is that Weber's analysis raises important normative concerns which are often lost in more recently published European studies researching public administration. Complexity in policy formulation, the policy-making process and policy implementation are the dominant message that comes across from studies which examine the executive in action. The conceptual terminology used to deal with this complexity — policy styles, sectorization, bottom-up policy-making among many others — has been impressive. What such studies do, however, is set out what Wolin would term the actions of the 'new organizational statesmen'; the institutions to which they belong, the values that they have, the routines and processes through which they seek to influence policy and so on. It matters little who they are, whether ministers, civil servants, legislators or lobbyists; they are of interest if they seek to influence, or actually have influence on, the shape of public policies. Weber's perspective makes it clear that it does matter who they are, and, more importantly, whether they have skills of political leadership. Without such skills and the capacity to exercise them, the public world of politics would be reduced to the private world of the organizational statesman.

References

Aberbach, J.D., R.D. Putnam and B.A. Rockman (1981) *Bureaucrats and Politicians in Western Democracies*. Cambridge, Mass.: Harvard University Press.

Albrow, M. (1970) *Bureaucracy*. London: Macmillan.

Andrews, W.G. (1981) 'The Collective Political Executive under the Gaullists', in W.G. Andrews and S. Hoffman (eds) *The Fifth Republic at Twenty*. Albany: State University of New York Press.

Beer, S.H. (1977) 'Political Overload and Federalism', *Polity*, 10, 1: pp. 5–17.

Braunthal, G. (1965) *The Federation of German Industry in Politics*. Ithaca: Cornell University Press.

Brittan, S. (1975) 'The Economic Consequences of Democracy', *British Journal of Political Science*, 5, 2, pp. 129–59.

Crozier, M. (1964) *The Bureaucratic Phenomenon*. London: Tavistock.

Crozier, M. (1970) *La societée bloquée*. Paris: Le Seuil.

Crozier, M. et al. (1974) *Où va l'administration française?* Paris: Les Editions d'Organisation.

Darbel, A. and D. Schnapper (1969) *Le système administratif*. Paris: Mouton.

Diamant, A. (1968) 'Tradition and Innovation in French Administration', *Comparative Political Studies*, 1, 2, pp. 251–74.

Dyson, K. (1977) 'The West German party book administration: an evaluation', *Public Administration Bulletin*, 25, pp. 3–23.

Dyson, K. (1980) *The State Tradition in Western Europe*. Oxford: Martin Robertson.

Dyson, K. (1982) 'West Germany: The Search for a Rationalist Consensus' in J. Richardson (ed.) *Policy Styles in Western Europe*. London: George Allen and Unwin.

Ellwein, T. (1974) 'Die gossen Interessenverbände und ihr Einfluß' in R. Loewenthal and H.-P. Scharz (eds) *Die Zweite Republik*. Stuttgart: Seewald.

Eschenburg, T. (1963) *Herrschaft der Verbände?* (2nd edn.) Stuttgart: Deutsche Verlagsanstalt.

Fry, G.K. (1985) *The Changing Civil Service*. London: George Allen and Unwin.

Grémion, C. (1979) *Profession: Décideur*. Paris: Gauthier Villars.

Grémion, C. (1982) 'Le milieu décisionnel central', in F. de Baecque and J-L. Quermonne (eds) *Administration et politique sous la Cinquième Republique*. Paris: Presses de la Fondation Nationale des Sciences Politiques.

Griffith, J.A.G. (1981) *The Politics of the Judiciary* (2nd edn). Glasgow: Fontana.

Hayward J.E.S. (1982) 'Mobilizing Private Interests in the Service of Public Ambitions: the salient elements in the dual French policy style' in J. Richardson (ed.) *Policy Styles in Western Europe*. London: George Allen and Unwin.

Hayward, J.E.S. (1983) *The One and Indivisible French Republic* (2nd edn.)

Headey, B. (1974) *British Cabinet Ministers*. London: Allen and Unwin.

Heclo, H. (1977) *A Government of Strangers*. Washington DC: Brookings.

Heclo, H. (1978) 'Issue Networks and the Executive Establishment' in A. King (ed.) *The New American Political System*. Washington DC: American Enterprise Institute.

Heclo, H. and A. Wildavsky (1981) *The Private Government of Public Money*. London: Macmillan.

Herzog, D. (1982) *Politische Führungsgruppen*. Darmstadt: Wissenschaftliche Buchgesellschaft.

Hockerts, H.G. (1980) *Sozialpolitische Entscheidungen im Nachkriegsdeutschland*. Stuttgart: Clett Cotta.

Hood, C.C. and A. Dunsire (1981) *Bureaumetrics*. Farnborough: Gower.

Johnson, N. (1982a) 'Parties and the Conditions of Political Leadership' in H. Doering and G. Smith (eds) *Party Government and Political Culture in Western Germany*. London: Macmillan.

Johnson, N. (1982b) 'The Interdependence of Law and Politics: Judges and the Constitution in West Germany', *West European Politics*, 5, 3, pp. 236–52.

Jordan, A.G. (1981) 'Iron Triangles, Woolly Corporatism or Elastic Nets: Images of the Policy Process', *Journal of Public Policy*, 1, 1, pp. 95–123.

Jordan, A.G. and J. Richardson (1982) 'The British Policy Style or the Logic of Negotiation?' in J. Richardson (ed.) *Policy Styles in Western Europe*. London: George Allen and Unwin.

Kaufman, H. (1981) *The Administrative Behaviour of Federal Bureau Chiefs*. Washington DC: Brookings.

Keeler, J. (1981) 'The Corporatist Dynamic of Agricultural Modernisation in the Fifth Republic' in W.G. Andrews and S. Hoffman (eds) *The Fifth Republic at Twenty*. Albany: State University of New York Press.

Kellner, P. and Lord Crowther Hunt (1980) *The Civil Servants* London: Futura.

King, A. (1975) 'Overload: Problems of Governing in the 1970s', *Political Studies*, 23, 2/3, pp. 284–96.

Long, N.E. (1981) 'The SES and the Public Interest', *Public Administration Review*, 41, 3, pp. 305–12.

Mackie, T.T. and B.W. Hogwood (1983) 'Cabinet Committees in Executive Decision Making'. *Studies in Public Policy*, No. 111. Glasgow: University of Strathclyde.

Mayntz, R. (1965) 'Max Webers Idealtypus der Bürokratie und die Organisationssoziologie', *Kölner Zeitschrift für Soziologie und Sozialpsychologie*, 17, pp. 493–502.

Mayntz, R. (1978) *Soziologie der Öffentlichen Verwaltung*. Heidelberg: Mueller.

Mayntz, R. (1980) 'Executive Leadership in Germany. Dispersal of Power or "Kanzlerdemokratie"?' in R. Rose and L.N. Suleiman (eds) *Presidents and Prime Ministers*. Washington DC: American Enterprise Institute.

Mayntz, R. and F.W. Scharpf (1975) *Policy Making in the German Federal Bureaucracy*. Amsterdam: Elsevier.

Mezey, M.L. (1979) *Comparative Legislatures*. Durham, NC: Duke University Press.

Page, E. (1985) *Political Authority and Bureaucratic Power: A Comparative Analysis*. Brighton: Harvester Press.

Paterson, W.E. (1982) 'Problems of Party Government in West Germany' in H. Doering and G. Smith (eds) *Party Government and Political Culture in Western Germany*. London: Macmillan.

Peters, B.G. (1981) 'The Problem of Bureaucratic Government', *Journal of Politics*, 43, 1, pp. 56–82.

Rausch, H. (1976) *Bundestag und Bundesregierung*. Munich: Beck.

Richardson, J.J. (ed.) (1982) *Policy Styles in Western Europe*. London: George Allen and Unwin.

Richardson, J.J. and A.G. Jordan (1979) *Governing Under Pressure*. Oxford: Martin Robertson.

Ridley, F.F. (ed.) (1979) *Government and Administration in Western Europe*. Oxford: Martin Robertson.

Rose, R. (1974) *The Problem of Party Government*. Harmondsworth: Penguin.

Rose, R. (1981) 'The Political Status of Higher Civil Servants in Britain', in Public Policy No. 92. Glasgow: University of Strathclyde Studies.

Rose, R. (1984) *Understanding Big Government*. London and Beverly Hills: Sage.

Rose, R. and E.N. Suleiman (eds) (1980) *Presidents and Prime Ministers*. Washington DC: American Enterprise Institute.

Rosen, B. (1981) 'Uncertainty in the Senior Executive Service', *Public Administration Review*, 41, 2, pp. 203–7.

Scharpf, F.W., B. Reissert and F. Schnabel (1976) *Politikverflechtung: Theorie und Empirie des Kooperativen Föderalismus in der Bundesrepublik*. Kronberg: Scriptor.

Seidman, H. (1980) *Politics, Position and Power* (3rd edn). New York and Oxford: Oxford University Press.

Suleiman, E.N. (1974) *Politics, Power and Bureaucracy in France*. Princeton: Princeton University Press.

Suleiman, E.N. (1978) *Elites in French Society*. Princeton: Princeton University Press.

Sundquist, J. (1981) *The Decline and Resurgence of Congress*. Washington DC: Brookings Institution.

Thoenig, J–C (1973) *L'ère des technocrates*. Paris: Editions d'Organisation.

Thoenig, J–C. and E. Friedberg (1976) 'The Power of the Field Staff. The Case of the Ministry of Public Works, Urban Affairs and Housing in France' in A.F. Leemans and A. Dunsire (eds) *The Management of Change in Government*. The Hague: Martinus Nijhoff.

US Advisory Commission on Intergovernmental Relations (1981a) *The Conditions of Contemporary Federalism: Conflicting Theories and Collapsing Constraints. A–78.* Washington DC: ACIR.

US Advisory Commission on Intergovernmental Relations (1981b) *An Agenda for American Federalism: Restoring Confidence and Competence. A–80* Washington DC: ACIR.

von Beyme, K. (1983) *The Political System of the German Federal Republic*. Farnborough: Gower.

Walker, J.L. (1983) 'The Origins and Maintenance of Interest Groups in America', *American Political Science Review*, 77, 2, pp. 390–406.

Weber, M. (1958) *Gesammelte Politische Schriften*. 2e Auflage, Tübingen: J.C.B. Mohr.

Weber, M. (1972) *Wirtschaft und Gesellschaft*. 5e Auflage, Tübingen: J.C.B. Mohr.

Wolin, S.H. (1961) *Politics and Vision*. London: George Allen and Unwin.

Wolin, S.H. (1981) 'The American Pluralist Conception of Politics; in A.L. Kaplan and D. Callahan (eds) *Ethics in Hard Times*. New York: Plenum Press.

Wolinsky, O.H. (1973) *The French Deputy*. Lexington: Lexington Books.

Young, H. and A. Sloman (1981) *No Minister*. London: BBC Publications.

11
Politicians and bureaucrats in the politics of policy-making

B. Guy Peters

Introduction

One of the most crucial areas of institutional politics in contemporary industrialized democracies is in the interaction between political executives and career civil servants. These interactons are crucial for the capacity of government to perform its routine tasks, and to make and implement the decisions required of a modern political system. Also they are important for the functioning of an effective political democracy. Political executives, either elected directly by the people or appointed by those who have been elected, are presumed to hold a mandate to enact and implement the policies they advocated during their electoral campaigns. But those political executives are constantly reporting that they believe themselves to be thwarted in their policy-making efforts by the power of an entrenched public bureaucracy.[1] The road blocks actually presented by the bureaucracy are not placed there because of a desire to sabotage one set of political leaders or another for partisan reasons. Rather these blocks arise as large organizations tend to proceed from inertia and to persist in their routine unless stopped. In addition, bureaucrats and their organizations tend to believe that they understand the policy area in question better than the political executive, who may be in office only a short time.[2] For whatever reasons, many ministers or cabinet secretaries believe themselves to be inhibited in producing the policies they desire.

If the perceptions of these political executives are accurate, there is a need for two types of effort. One is an analytic effort to develop a better conceptual understanding of the politics that occur across and within the real and perceptual gulf separating these groups. The second is the problem of designing institutional arrangements which will allow the energizing of bureaucracies by political leaders while still preserving the permanence, expertise and partisan (if not policy) impartiality of the public bureaucracy.[3]

Two fundamental points should be made before embarking upon the more substantive portions of this chapter. First, the previous paragraphs appear to resurrect and to enshrine the relics of the (hopefully) long-dead dichotomy between politics and administration.[4] To some extent, this appearance is quite correct, but in others it is not.

On the one hand, we are recognizing quite explicitly that administration is not merely the execution of policies decided upon by political officials; that point is quite central to the entire concern of the paper. Indeed, administrative officials are deeply involved in policy-making and fight for their own positions and for their own conceptions of 'good' policies. But, on the other hand, although they are both engaged in policy-making, political and administrative leaders play very different roles in the policy process. Their permanence, longer time perspective and functional expertise all provide the career civil servant with a different view of policy and policy-making than that held by the political executive. The political executive is only in 'town' for a short period of time and has to accomplish something in that time — if only so he or she can come back at some time in the future — and cannot afford to advocate policies which, although they may be technically superior, take a long time to come to fruition.[5] Also, the identification of a career civil servant with a single department or agency (especially in the USA, although this is true in most other systems after some point in an individual's career) may make the civil servant's perceptions of desirable policies quite different from those held by the politician. Finally, the politics of the career civil servant are organizationally based rather than partisan. The civil servant is engaged in politics to protect or to promote an organization and the values that it embodies rather than to promote a political party or political career.

A second preliminary point to be made is that there has been relatively little theoretical development concerning the relationship of political executives and career civil servants. This is true for individual nations, and is especially true of comparative studies of their interactions. There is certainly no shortage of studies of higher civil servants and a large number of political executives; however, it is fair to say that much less has been done to analyse patterns of interactions between these two sets of actors in the policy-making process.[6] There are, of course, some notable exceptions, such as the work of Robert Putnam and his collaborators, and Hugh Heclo's work on the United States, but the majority of evidence regarding ministers and their civil servants is anecdotal.[7] And much of this material has come from the writings of retired ministers, e.g. Richard Crossman, Barbara Castle, Lord Crowther Hunt, Michael Blumenthal.[8] This is the principal type of evidence available for some of the points made in this chapter. However, there is a need to mesh that evidence within a broader analytic and comparative framework. This chapter will be a preliminary attempt at such organization and analysis. It will focus to some extent on what is known about civil servants and political executives in the United States, then will fit that pattern into comparative frameworks to aid an understanding of the generic phenomenon with which we are concerned.

Five models of interaction

Our statement that there has been a relative absence of theoretical developments concerning the relationships between senior civil servants and political executives may be thought to be excessively harsh and ill-informed. There have been, in fact, five very basic and, each in its own way, extreme models of the relationship between civil servants and their nominal political masters. These models have only occasionally been consciously articulated as such, consequently we have been forced to extract and synthesize in order to present these models in a more explicit form. Moreover, these models are to some degree extreme, and in several instances approach being 'Ideal Type' constructions, which illuminate the real world by abstracting from it and providing a standard against which to compare reality. Few if any systems of executive politics in the real world will fit these models exactly. Moreover, almost any national or subnational system will at times display at least one aspect of all the models. However, it is hoped that by developing these models and explicitly exploring some apparent relationships with other characteristics of executive politics that our understanding of politics within the executive branch can be enhanced.

The formal model

The first of the models of interaction is the 'Formal–Legal' model in which the policy-making role of the civil servant is reduced to saying 'Yes, Minister'.[9] This model has been developed less in a formal sense in the USA than in other countries (perhaps especially the UK), but it has certainly been clearly articulated. The Wilsonian approach to public administration stressed this conception of the civil servant's role.[10] In addition, numerous statements appearing in the popular media, regarding the inappropriate powers being granted to bureaucrats in making policy and the related loss of democratic control, are indicative of the existence of this model in the popular mind. Many of the numerous attempts at reforming the executive branch of government have been oriented toward improving the control of the President and his appointees over permanent civil servants within the executive branch.[11]

The Formal–Legal model is obviously a caricature of the role of bureaucrats and ministers in making policy; this was probably the case even as Wilson and Weber wrote their conceptions of the respective roles.[12] It is important, however, as a normative standard against which to compare real patterns of interaction and policy-making. Putnam's conception of the 'classical bureaucrat', for example, has been shown to be a useful standard against which to compare the attitudes of real world bureaucrats in a number of countries.[13] And this model also serves as useful fiction, allowing civil servants a great deal of functional responsibility while retaining political responsibility in the hands of elected executive officials.[14] Finally, it is, despite being a caricature to more detached analysts in academe, a model that many real-world executives (especially political executives) carry with them into their work. This can, of course, present a great deal of difficulty for those political executives, and may be the source of much of their reported frustration in exercising the powers of their office.

Village life

A second model of the relationship between civil servants and political executives might be termed the 'Village Life' model. Although Heclo and Wildavsky applied this term specifically to the values of British civil servants working within the Treasury, rather than the relationship of those civil servants with their political 'masters', the idea of an intergration of values through socialization and recruitment appears quite applicable to the analysis of political and bureaucratic elites.[15] In this second model, senior civil servants and political executives are conceptualized as having relatively similar values and goals, with the most important perhaps being the maintenance of the government and the smooth functioning of the executive branch.[16] In this conception of executive branch politics, the political and bureaucratic elite coalesce against outside interference in their own tightly constrained little world. One scholar has gone so far as to advocate the development of a field of 'executive-bureaucratic policies'.[17] His argument is that the views and interests of the two sets of actors at the top of organizational pyramids are sufficiently similar to make their interactions, and pattern of policies which emerge, more readily explicable by examining them as one group rather than two. Such a conceptualization would, of course, conform rather closely to the arguments of various elite theories and Marxist critiques of contemporary capitalist societies as being dominated by a single class which seeks to maintain its own interests rather than following the tenets of democratic theory and mass opinion.[18]

A second point of similarity between the two sets of elites is their common interest in the management of the state.[19] Both sets of executives find it advantageous to advance their careers through effective management and appropriate decision-making. However, this point of similarity may be extremely variable across political systems and across individuals and structural positions within political systems. An American political executive is more likely to regard management as an important demand of his or her job, everything else being equal, than would a British or Canadian counterpart.[20] This might be especially true of assistant secretaries who are close to the day-to-day management of their organizations, and who must demonstrate managerial abilities in order to further their careers.[21] Within the upper echelon of bureaucracy in the USA, Heclo reports the presence of a number of institutionalists whose primary goals appears to be the effective management of their organization and of government in general.[22] Szablowski regards these managerial values and concern to be more broadly distributed throughout the public services and political executives of the four countries he has studied so that almost all of those occupying these types of positions would have very strong managerial and elitist positions.[23]

Finally it should be pointed out that in many political systems the administrative and political career structures are not as isolated and distinct as is sometimes assumed. In fact, the separation that is assumed to exist is often an extrapolation of the British experience, or an extrapolation from normative writing on the politics–administration dichotomy. For example, in the United States, the absence of a higher civil service, in the sense of the European context, means that there is substantial overlap of administrative and political officials, and at times their functional responsibilities may be similar.[24] In France, although the *grand corps* are career civil servants, they move freely from administrative to political positions and function as an all-purpose elite for French society.[25] Similarly, a large number of West German politicians are civil servants on leave from the civil service but able to return. As civil service rank and status in most European countries go with the individual, not with the particular position held, it is quite possible for these individuals to move freely from politics to administration and back again. Therefore, to some degree, the sharp distinction sometimes drawn between the two career structures may be overly sharp, and the same individuals may simply wear different hats at various stages of their own careers as the leaders of their country.

However, it is important to bear in mind that, in general, politicians and administrators do have different careers and different occupational perspectives.[26] The differences are very often in terms of time. The politician has a short time within which to reach his goals while the career bureaucrat may have a lifetime.

The functional model

The third model is, to some extent, a subset of the 'Village Life' model, but with one important difference. While the Village Life model assumes an integration of political and administrative elites throughout the upper echelons of government, the 'Functional Village Life' model will rather posit an integration of elites along functional lines. There would be close ties among civil servants and political executives within the same functional area, e.g. health, and links to other people in that area such as legislative committees and interest groups. There would be less linkage to other civil servants or other political elites. Thus, this third model would bear some resemblance to numerous descriptions of corporatism or neocorporatism in a number of European countries, and to the literature on 'iron triangles', 'cozy little triangles', or 'issue networks' in American politics.[27] The model of relationships in which we are interested need not carry along with it all the intellectual baggage associated with those other terms, but there are points of similarity which are interesting and important.

The implications for politics of the Functional Village Life, or simply Functional model, are rather different from the Village Life model. In the Village Life model, the elite integration presented was centred around the values of an upper echelon of public executives, where an attempt was made to differentiate 'us' from 'them' solely on the basis of position within government; it was a horizontally connected elite whose principal interest appeared to be the smooth functioning of the system. This implies a certain absence of content; 'whatever is best administered is best governed.'[28] Such an arrangement need not be totally devoid of content, but there is a tendency to stress form over substance. One may hear in this at least a faint echo of many of critiques which have been levelled at the Whitehall system of government in the United Kingdom.[29]

The Functional model, on the other hand, is oriented toward vertical integration and more extensive contacts with the society as a whole — or at least with specified segments of that society. In such a model of executive interactions, political and administrative elites within a specific policy sector will be allied against political and bureaucratic elites from other policy sectors. The conflicts that are expected to arise would be over money, personnel, legislative time and all the other factors which give one agency or policy precedence over another.[30] In these political encounters, policy and organization are more central than elite status or conflict reduction.

The Village Life and the Functional models need not, of course, be mutually exclusive, and in the real world are closely intertwined. Although the types of conflict over policy and money described may occur within the executive elites, there is a common tendency to attempt to contain it and to present a united front to outsiders. This is especially true in political systems within a parliamentary form of government where, despite sharp internal battles — both within Cabinet and between Cabinet and civil servants — once a decision has been taken a relatively united front must be presented to those on the outside of government.[31] It may be hypothesized that only the type of elite integration described as the Village Life model would permit sharp disagreements over policy to be fought out without severe threats to stability, not to mention individual careers. Disagreements may be permitted so long as they are kept in house and confined to those who are all a part of the small, tight governing group.

The adversarial model

The fourth model is, to a great extent, the converse of the Village Life model, and it is perhaps the most commonly articulated model of the interactions between these two sets of policy makers. This is the 'Adversarial' model, in which the political executive and the senior civil servant are assumed to be competitors for power and control over policy. In this model the civil servant frequently is cast in the position of saying 'No, Minister', or more commonly saying nothing at all then proceeding to do whatever he thinks best.[32] This model can be taken seriously even if the reader does not take the politics–administration dichotomy seriously. Even if those two activities are inextricably intertwined, the individuals who occupy positions within either career structures, may still regard themselves as competing for power with the incumbents of the other career structure. Most commonly, this model has been articulated as the political executive attempting to recapture the organization from the civil servants, although civil servants might argue that their departments are captured by outsiders who do not understand either the policies being administered or the procedures through which they are administered.

The conflict described through the Adversial model may arise in one of several ways. The first is simply passive or unintended conflict. The bureaucracy is there, and thereby is a challenge to an incoming political executive. Even if the bureaucracy — or more exactly a particular organization — or an individual civil servant does not oppose the policy ideas of the political executive, inertia and the persistence of old habits may make change difficult. Policies may be labelled 'infeasible' simply because they have not been done that way before. Any political executive coming to office with an idea of changing policy quickly will be rapidly disappointed.[33]

The adversarial relationship between the bureaucracy and the political executive may be more active and intentional. This more purposeful conflict may arise from several sources. The most frequent difference is over the content of specific public policies. As we have discussed in other writings, organizations do have ideologies about the manner in which policies should be designed and implemented, and these ideas may well differ from those of the political executives.[34] In such situations, there will be conflict over the shape of policy, frequently followed by a period in which the bureaucracy will delay and attempt to outlast the politician. It will require especially skilful and persistent political executives to overcome a civil service staff which has decided to dig in and outwait their nominal political masters.

A second source of conflict is the survival of the organization. The one task which civil servants tend to regard as most crucial in their political masters is the ability to win battles for their organization over budgets and personnel, and over policy issues considered important by members of the organization. Consequently, civil servants will tend not to support a political executive they regard as weak or ineffective in dealing with other politicians, and may actively work to have that person removed.[35] And perhaps the greatest faux pas a political executive can make is, like Terrel Bell at the US Department of Education, to argue for the abolition of the organization.[36] This would certainly engender conflict with the organization's civil service staff.

A partisan conflict over policy between civil servants and political executives. Given that we have been stressing the differing career structures within the organization, with the civil servant being characterized by political neutrality, this may now be a doubtful proposition. But, as we have also pointed out, it is easy for civil servants to become politicized. This politicization may be inadvertant, as in the case of a single political party being in office for a long period of time. When there is a change in ruling parties, the new political executives frequently find that the civil service is populated largely by individuals who agree with the policies of the previous government. This need not be the result of an attempt to pack the civil service with opponents to any alternative government. Rather, it may be simply the selective attraction of individuals to the civil service who believe in the current government's programme. So, the bourgeois coalition coming to power in Sweden after over three decades of Social Democratic government might have had cause to question the willingness of the bureaucracy to co-operate with any policy changes.[37] The Nixon administration in the USA expressed a belief that the social services departments of government were loaded with Democrats attracted to government office during the Kennedy and Johnson administrations.[38] The Reagan administration has made similar claims about a number of agencies, perhaps most notably the Environmental Protection Agency.

Civil servants may also accept political tasks. There are provisions in the West German administrative structure for civil servants to take on political tasks, although they accept the possibility of retirement when there is a change in government, or even a change of minister.[39] Heclo points out the number of civil servants in the USA who are in political posts, at least on temporary assignments.[40] The provisions of the Civil Service Reform Act of 1978 make that even more likely. And literature abounds with examples of civil servants who were attracted by the glamour of politics, flew too close to the fire, and eventually were burned by their political attachments. Sir William Armstrong's involvement with the Heath government in the UK is an important example.[41]

Finally, the civil service may become politicized and partisan because of actions taken by a government concerning the civil service itself. One such example is the attacks on civil service pay and perquisites by the Reagan administration and the reactions by the federal civil service.[42] A more extreme example is the Thatcher government in the UK. These issues of pay have been combined with conflicts with workers over the right to belong to a union at the Government Communications Headquarters (GCHQ): this action produced very strong civil service reactions against the government.[43] The reactions against those personnel policies may be translated into opposition to all government policies.

When conflicts based upon partisan allegiances and identifications arise, these might be dismissed simply as partisan, rather than as part of the patterns of institutional politics we have been discussing. However, given the civil service status of at least one set of the actors involved, this cannot be done so easily except perhaps when civil servants adopt manifestly political stances. Civil servants are still civil servants and can wrap themselves in the legal cloak of civil service protections, as well as in the moral cloak of being above politics. The civil service status and the intermingling of institutional and partisan conflict makes the task of the political executive faced with recalcitrant individuals and organizations all the more difficult.

The administrative state model

A fifth model of the interactions between administrative and political executives is termed the 'Administrative State' model. This model reflects an increasingly common perception that the decision-making of government is dominated by bureaucracy.[44] We have explored some of the implications of the model rather fully elsewhere, and will not belabour the points made in this paper.[45] However, the fundamental conception contained in the model (that of the increasing workload being placed upon government — even to deregulate requires a great deal of effort — and because of the complexity and technical content of that workload bureaucracy has come to dominate decision-making), is an important perspective on institutional politics in contemporary political systems. Legislative bodies or essentially amateur political executives do not have the numbers or capabilities to handle the work-load required of modern government, and consequently the important work on policy is left to the permanent civil service.[46] Certainly legislatures still pass laws, and their appointees still are nominally in charge of government, but all of those political actors may ultimately be in the control of the bureaucracy, which has greater access to the information upon which decisions are based. The bureaucracy also controls much of the government's procedural machinery and can structure or accelerate or delay decisions through their mastery of procedures. This model does not depend upon a conscious plot by the career civil service, nor is it necessarily a condemnation of bureaucracy.

Most of the abdication of authority by political leaders can be seen as being done voluntarily and perhaps even as being in the public interest through the production of technically superior decisions. However, this model of modern governments' decision-making is quite different from that found in most textbooks on democratic government, and is the exact opposite of the Formal–Legal model previously discussed.

The differences between the Adversarial model and the Administrative State model may appear rather slight; however, they are important. In the Adversarial model, it is assumed that the political executive is the prime mover in the decisions which are taken, and the moral imprimateur, coming from the electoral process, will supply that individual with great powers. The bureaucrat is seen as a contender for power and this concept is based primarily upon technical information, mastery of procedures and simple longevity in office. And in the Adversarial model it is assumed that one side or the other will 'win' at different times, depending upon the nature of the conflict and the mobilization of their respective resources at that particular time. In the Administrative State model, on the other hand, the bureaucracy is visualized as victorious, with the political executives and the legislature reduced to, as Grosser put it, 'participants in a process of registration'.[47] It is important to remember, however, that both of these intellectual models are of a more complex reality, so that they will exist primarily in the minds and the words of detached analysts.

Summary
The five models of interactions among bureaucrats and political executives are something akin to Ideal Type models: no system of government will display all of the patterns of behaviour outlined. Page's chapter in this book details the extent to which the Formal–Legal model describes empirical reality. Both national systems and the relationships of individual ministers and civil servants may contain some elements of all the models, and may also change rapidly depending upon the issues or the individuals involved. However, by using these models, we are attempting to illuminate and understand the complexity of the real world.

Characteristics of the five models
On the basis of the brief presentations of each of the models presented in this chapter, as well as the other writings concerning these patterns of interaction, several dimensions can be isolated which should further illuminate the differences among these intellectual models. Table 11.1 presents a simplified description of the five models of interaction in terms of five dimensions. These dimensions should capture the major differences among the five models and serve as a guide if empirical observations of such systems of interaction were to be performed. We

TABLE 11.1
Characteristics of the models

	Tone	Winners	Conflict resolution	Style	Impacts
Formal–Legal	Integrative	Politicians	Command	Authority	Variability
Village Life	Integrative	Both	Bargaining	Mutuality	Management
Functional Village Life	Integrative	Both	Bargaining	Expertise	Interest dominance
Adversarial	Adversarial	Variable	Power	Conflict	Variability
Administrative State	Integrative	Civil Service	Abdication	Expertise	Stability

do not, however, presume to present any clearly coded rules for what are essentially nominal and descriptive categories.

The first dimension is labelled 'tone', to describe something of the general tenor of the interactions among the participants. Four out of the five models are described as having a rather smooth or integrated pattern of interaction. As should have been anticipated, the 'tone' of the Adversarial model is much sharper and combative. The participants in this system can be expected to display some suspicion and difficulties in working relationships. Such working relationships are important for humane reasons: they are also important for the successful management of the organization. In addition, conflicting systems tend to build in excessive redundancies, checks and counter-checks, slowing down the execution of policies and even preventing the implementation of a policy in anything approaching the form intended.[48]

The second dimension of variation concerns who wins in the political process within the executive branch. Clearly, if the Formal–Legal model is seen as the most appropriate, the political executives will be masters over policy. In that model it is the task of the political leaders to shape decisions, and the task of the bureaucrats to implement those decisions. At the other end of the spectrum, the Administrative State model would have the bureaucrats as the real makers and implementers of policy, while politicians would be useful primarily in the legitimation of their actions rather than acting as decision makers. In both of the models outlined, political and bureaucratic elites are equal victors in the process, but are victors against possible intruders rather than against each other. In both the Village Life and the Functional models the two elites coalesce at the expense of other elites. In the Village Life model, the political and bureaucratic elites coalesce against legislators and other groups in the society in order to maintain their privileged position in government.

The Functional model would allow for more openness to societal influences than would the Village Life model, but there is still an attempt to partition one portion of government off from another. Finally, the Adversarial model would not predict any particular winner in all cases. Instead, winners and losers would be determined by the specific set of issues and conditions existing at the time.

The third dimension to be considered in the description of these models of interaction is the style of conflict resolution practised by the participants of the networks of institutional politics. Again the Formal model is the easiest to describe, with conflicts being resolved almost automatically through law and hierarchical command — 'Yes, Minister' is the accepted form of conflict resolution. Again, at the other end of the spectrum, in the Administrative State model, conflict is resolved or avoided through the virtual abdication of policy-making responsibilities by elected or appointed political executives in favour of public bureaucracy. This abdication may not be a conscious one, but it is nonetheless real. In the Village Life and Functional models conflict resolution is conducted through bargaining. Given that these two models assume a high degree of integration and common interest in maintaining the elite's interests against real or imagined threats from outsiders, the best means of dealing with conflict is to bargain. Such bargaining might occur within the elite as a whole or within a particular sub-set of the elite, depending upon the perspective adopted. And the integration of values of the elite members — be it system wide or functional — will facilitate the bargaining and also limit the scope of the conflict that emerges to more narrow and technical issues.

The fourth dimension of importance in describing the patterns of interaction between political and bureaucratic executives is the *style* of interaction, and thereby essentially the style in which politics is conducted. Within both the Functional and the Administrative State models, this interaction occurs on the basis of expertise. In both of these systems of interaction, the important attribute is the possession of expert knowledge of the policy area.[49] Participants in the functional model use expert knowledge to exclude potential interlopers into their policy area, while those in the Administrative State model can use expertise to counteract the formal, legal powers of their political masters. That formal power would, of course, be expected to manifest itself in the Formal–Legal model, in which the legitimate ruling status of the political executive is accepted by the bureaucrat. In the Village Life model, the acceptance of their mutual elite status, and the ability to use that status and the associated personal and professional contacts, gives the residents of the village great power over any potential competitors. Lastly, power and the ability to muster whatever weapons are available — including such things as formal position and policy expertise — is the medium of exchange in the

Adversarial model. On any particular issue, either sets of actors may be able to muster differing amounts of their own resources in order to 'win' that policy conflict.

Finally, there is the dimension of the *impacts* of these differing systems of interaction on the policies adopted by government. For two of the systems, we would hypothesize that the effects on policy would be quite variable.[50] If the Formal model was to operate as it is alleged to, and there was a change in office in a democratic political system, then changes in governing political parties should produce changes in policy. There is, of course, strong evidence to indicate that policy is *not* that changeable.[51] Likewise, if the Adversarial model allows one of the two sets of contending elites to win on different issues at different times, variability in policies could be expected. This would, of course, be compounded by the variability in political party control that would determine the policies stressed by the political executives office, as in the Formal model. In contrast, the policies emerging from the Administrative State model should be more stable. The permanent civil service would be in charge and would tend to preserve much of the status quo despite the attempts of political executives to produce change. But, of course, bureaucrats are not totally devoid of ideas for change and improvement themselves. Some have argued that these ideas arise totally out of self-interest (for larger budgets), while others have argued that the ideas arise from professional training and from a sincere interest in improving society.[52] But for whatever reasons, bureaucrats can serve as sources of policy change. Changes proposed by civil servants tend to occur within the context of an existing policy paradigm and typically constitute only incremental departures from the status quo, but they are changes nonetheless. The Village Life model can also be expected to be associated with policy stability, although much of the concern of the participants in such an arrangement would be for systematic management rather than on altering the details of operating policies.[53] And lastly, although the policies adopted through a Functional model may be quite similar to those found in the Administrative State model, there should be greater impact of the connections to groups in the society than might be true of the Administrative State model.

Explaining types of executive systems

We should again emphasize that in the real world it may be difficult to distinguish neatly and clearly any one of these patterns of interaction from another, especially without empirical research directly related to the topic. However, these dimensions should provide some ideas as to the types of factors that must be considered when attempting to distinguish between the several models, and can be considered hypotheses with regard to the effects of a particular pattern of elite interaction on the policies adopted by government. However, this leaves yet another question; what factors might predict the development of one pattern versus another in different political systems, or within parts of a single government? Obviously, there are a huge number of such factors — some of which will be personal and idiosyncratic — and to isolate the effects of any single factor in such a diffuse and complex pattern of interaction is a difficult logical problem. However, we can generate a set of hypotheses and muster some corroborating evidence that may assist in clarifying how this one crucial area of policy-making fits within the overall pattern of policy-making in Western, industrialized societies.

Issues

Perhaps the simplest factor that could explain the presence of one pattern of interaction would be the specific issues being considered. This type of explanation might be useful for only a limited range of issues. The clearest type of issue affecting patterns of interaction between civil servants and political executives would be an issue which clearly affects the civil service as an institution, e.g. pay, perquisites, or unionization.[54] In these cases one should expect either the Adversarial model or the Administrative State model to develop. Whichever one did develop would depend, of course, upon the strength of the political executives and a number of other factors. The important point here is that an issue of this type will clearly pit the bureaucracy and those who might wish to control it against one another. Also, as some issues of this type can become highly politicized, e.g. unionization and pay comparability, the boundaries of the conflict may be extended to the broader social and political arena, generally giving political executives additional resources in their struggles to control the bureaucracy.[55] Attempts by public employees to use their organization's power tends to provoke public resentment and provide support for political executives.

Another aspect of an issue which may be hypothesized to be related to the pattern of interaction between civil servants and political executives would be its technical content. The more technical the issue, the more power the permanent bureaucracy would tend to have, and consequently the more the interaction pattern would tend to approximate the Administrative State model. The control of information will, except perhaps when political executives counterattack through the use of personal advisors, appointed commissions and the like, have the determining influence on many decisions in government.[56] It should be pointed out that many decisions over which the bureaucracy has a controlling influence will provide little direct benefit to the civil servants; they may gain nothing except the beneficial feeling of a job well done.[57] But they will control decisions nonetheless, and a feeling of technical mastery may be all that they sought from the outset.

Finally, the degree of public, and especially organized public, concern over a particular issue will influence patterns of interaction. If the issue is considered important by an organized group in the society, and there are means of group access to government, then something approaching the Functional model of interactions is likely to develop. This is especially true if there has been a stable pattern of interaction among concerned groups — civil servants, political executives, legislative actors, and the interest groups — which has developed and would facilitate early consultation and a policy proposal that all concerned can accept. In the dynamics of the Functional model, most likely the political executive would be the outsider, especially if there has been a recent turnover in the party controlling government. And it is quite possible in such a case that the Functional model of interaction would evolve into the Adversarial one, with the civil service and its pressure group allies confronting the novice political executive. This outcome would be especially likely if the party coming into power had made campaign commitments to alter the practice in specific policy, or which had ideological predispositions that would be hostile to the interest groups in the areas.[58]

The political executives

Another factor, which would be hypothesized to affect the pattern of interaction between civil servants and the political world in which they live, is the nature of both the political executives and the bureaucrats. Both sets of actors in these interchanges have characteristics that will affect their interaction with the other, and arguably political executives will be less variable than the bureaucratic executives and the bureaucratic systems with which they interact. The patterns of recruitment for political executives and their involvement in the policy process appear to be less varied than the greater variability of bureaucratic systems. But there are still important variations in the nature of political executives which will influence their effectiveness and their mode of interaction with civil servants. One such factor is simply the number of political executives. The comparison between the number of American and British political appointees has been made many times.[59] When a change in the governing party occurs in the UK only several hundred people lose their jobs, whereas in the USA several thousand lose their jobs. With more political executives active in government, it is only natural that there would be a greater attempt on the part of those executives to attempt to control the direction of government policy; otherwise, why are they there? But it is not only the number of readily identifiable political executives occupying formal governmental positions which should be counted.

Frequently an apparently small number of political leaders will surround themselves with a number of independent advisors and associates who may not occupy any formal position, who may be paid out of either public or private funds, and who may increase substantially the capability of the political executive to exercise his control, or at least compete for control. Thus, ministers who have the assistance of bodies such as *cabinets* and personal secretaries would be more likely to engage in adversarial relationships with the permanent civil service than would those such as the average minister in British government, who has little personal assistance other than that provided by civil servants.[60] Even British government, however, is now populated with more independent advisors than in earlier years, with Mrs Thatcher in particular seeking advice from outside the civil service.[61]

A second characteristic of political executives influencing their patterns of interaction with the civil service is the type of training they have received, and their career patterns. Here we can easily contrast the generalist orientation of British political executives with the more specialized selection of executives in the United States, West Germany or Sweden.[62] Generalists will have less capability of contesting issues on substantive grounds than would political executives with more specialized training, or a career pattern which forces them to specialize early on in their careers. Thus, generalist political executives may be expected to be associated with the Administrative State, or the Village Life models of interaction, depending upon several other factors. They may also be found associated with the functional patterns of interaction although very much as junior partners to the more specialized civil servants and interest group leaders in these sub-systems.

A third characteristic of political executives, which may be hypothesized to affect their interactions with civil servants, is the fundamental forms of government of their country. The demands of Cabinet government and collective responsibility may require a more adversarial stance of the political elites vis-a-vis civil servants that would be true in other forms of government. Moreover, Cabinet government may, because of the apparently closer connection between electoral choice and those occupying office, push towards the Formal–Legal pattern of interaction. This may be especially true when there is a pervasive theory of very extensive responsibilities of the minister for the activities of the department, whether or not that extreme position is actually carried out in practice.[63]

Another factor affecting executive interactions, not unrelated to the impact of parliamentary government, is the role conception of political executives. Principally, this is a question of whether they regard themselves first as politicians, or first as policy makers and departmental managers. It may be difficult to unravel these two strands of the political executive's role, although there have been several interesting studies on this subject. Headey, for example, has discussed a variety of roles which ministers in Britain's government have adopted for themselves, and Putnam and his associates have provided some information concerning the attitudes and role perceptions of politicians who are in frequent contact with civil servants.[64] We would hypothesize that an executive who conceived of his role as that of the politician might adopt relatively simplistic conceptions of the relationship with a bureaucrat, adopting either a Formal–Legal conception of their relationship, or gratefully accepting the Administrative State and leaving all the nasty work of running the Ministry to the permanent staff. Those who regarded their tasks as policy entrepreneurs or as managers would be more likely to engage in some form of conflict with the civil service, or if through their external job experiences they were members of larger issue networks, they might well adopt a functional conception of the role of political executives. Such role distinctions have a great deal to do with career patterns in political and social life, just as the earlier distinction between generalist and specialist patterns of training affected the relationship between ministers and civil servants. If the criteria for recruitment of political executives is the ability to pacify one wing of the party or another, or the ability to win a certain type of constituency, the behaviour of the executives in office would be very different to those who are selected for their knowledge of a particular type of policy. Clearly, those who regard themselves as policy entrepreneurs would be more interested in engaging in conflicts over policy than would those who thought of their role primarily as political and electoral. Of course, policy and electoral success may be closely related, but individual political elites may stress one over the other, and that emphasis can affect their interactions with their bureaucratic staff members.

The openness of the government and its ministries to the organized groups in society will influence the manner of interaction between the political elites and their civil servants. This is, of course, in some ways almost a definition of the Functional model, but the influences may extend beyond this one model. If there is a general openness towards interest group influence, and if their political executives tend to be recruited from different career structures and lack that close connection with societal interests, then rather than a functional pattern of interaction developing, an adversarial relationship could be expected. On the other hand, if the political system is not generally open and accepting of interest group influences, the possibility for developing the elitist, Village Life pattern of interactions is that much greater.

The training, careers and role conceptions that political executives bring with them to office will tend to influence the manner in which they interact with the permanent civil service staff they find when elected to office. More importantly, it may influence the effectiveness of those executives in performing the tasks they were elected or appointed to perform. The political executive who comes to office ignorant of the responsibilities to be performed and of issues in the policy area is not likely to further the cause of democracy. And the effectiveness of the political executives in implementing policies will, to some degree, be dependent upon the characteristics of the civil servants with whom they must interact.

The civil service

This naturally brings us to a discussion of some of the characteristics of civil servants and bureaucratic systems which influence their inter-actions with their political 'masters'. Perhaps because of our own training and interests there does appear to be more variability in bureaucratic systems than among political executives. These differences can, however, be broken down into several sub-categories of characteristics.

Training

One of the principal factors affecting the relationships between civil servants and their political executives is the type of training received by civil servants. Different countries have developed a variety of patterns in the training of their civil servants and these may be hypothesized to affect relationships with political executives. One pattern of training might be termed the Oxbridge pattern, after the two major British universities that have traditionally provided (and continue to provide) the majority of upper civil servants — as well as political executives — for the British government. The training that these future executives receive generally has little to do with the roles they will occupy later in their careers as it has been oriented toward the humanities.[65] This training pattern has tended to create a tightly integrated elite with relatively little substantive training in any particular policy area. It also makes the upper civil service and political executives more alike. In short, such a pattern of training should be conducive to the develop-ment of the Village Life model, which to some degree is itself abstracted from British government.

A second pattern of training, which is characteristic of much of Western Europe, is the use of the study of law as a grounding for the civil service. The model German, Austrian, Dutch or Scandinavian civil servant will have taken a degree in law before entering the upper civil service. This legal training tends to be carried over into job performance, as a result there is perhaps a greater tendency towards adopting the Formal–Legal model than would otherwise be the case.[66] The legal statement of the relationship between civil servants and politicians in almost all political systems is that political leaders are to make policy decisions and the civil servants are to implement them.

Legal training may make the civil servant more willing to accept this formalistic conception of the role. This certainly does not mean that civil servants in West Germany or Scandinavia are robots blindly following the dictates of politicians: indeed, there are numerous examples of conflicts over policy between the two groups. But it does mean that it is easier for a civil servant trained in a legal tradition to accept a more narrowly circumscribed conception of the proper functions of the civil service.

A third pattern of training for civil servants is typified by the ENA in France, in which prospective civil servants receive a distinctive training above and beyond that received in any post secondary educational institutions. This training tends to create a class out of the upper civil service, separating the 'Enacrats' both from political executives and from other members of the civil service.[67] Everything else being equal, we would hypothesize that such a pattern of training would tend to create a differentiation between the higher ranked civil servants and the political executives, and thus create the conditions for an adversarial relationship between the two groups. We would be quick to point out, however, that in the French case the elite for the entire social system comes from the public bureaucracy and tends to infiltrate not only from the political executive but from the private sector as well.[68]

Finally, there is a functional pattern of training for the higher civil service. Such training is rarely intentional, but is more simply the education in specialities given to students who then later elect to join the civil service. This pattern of training is perhaps best typified by the civil service in the USA which tends to employ people on the basis of some functional expertise.[69] And this will, in turn, produce a civil service that tends to be very well versed in the policies they administer and who may well be able to defeat any political elites coming to office who are not so well acquainted with those issues in question. And given that the agencies for which these civil servants will also work tend to have close connections with the interest groups in the respective policy area, they may frequently be part of functional patterns of interaction, with the political executives being perhaps the least important constituent. This pattern has been moving towards a more adversarial model as the development of 'issue networks' has produced more knowledgeable political executives.[70]

Careers

The career pattern of civil servants is related to the patterns of training previously described, and may also have an independent influence upon the patterns of interaction between civil servants and political executives. The standard differentiation made in civil service career patterns is between generalists and specialists. The career patterns fostered by individual administrative systems may either reinforce or counteract the pattern of training received by the civil servant before entering the service. For example, the training received by British civil servants is quite general, and relatively frequent movement of younger civil servants between jobs reinforces that generalist perspective. On the other hand, although law is an all-purpose, general training for the civil service, once selected the typical Swedish or Danish civil servant will remain within a single organization for a good part, or all, of his career.

Just as with generalist patterns of training, generalist career patterns would tend to create something of a Village Life relationship between civil servants and political executives. This career pattern reinforces a variety of contacts among the civil service and with political executives, while at the same time it reduces any commitment to a particular policy area. The generalist career pattern tends to give the individual civil servant some sense of the generic problems of government, consequently this may limit his willingness to press the claims of one department or agency against the overall demands of centralized control and management.[71]

Rather obviously, the specialist career patterns would be hypothesized to produce rather different patterns of behaviour. This pattern might be best exemplified by the civil service system in the Scandinavian countries which, although they have central standards for civil servants, leave the majority of personnel decisions to the individual ministries and boards. Although individuals may at some time in their career apply for other positions and in turn be appointed to them, the model civil servant will spend a career within a single organization. It would be hypothesized that career patterns, or the somewhat more centralized pattern in the United States, might be related either to an adversarial relationship with political executives or to the Functional model of interaction. In either instance, there would not be the integration across agencies predicted with a generalist career pattern.

Specialized bureaucratic organizations

Several specialized career structures within public bureaucracies also may have an influence on patterns of interaction. Most notably, the corps structures that exist in France, Italy and Spain may produce highly integrated subsets of individuals within the bureaucracy, which have a pronounced organizational identity of their own. Particularly in France, these civil servants are not confined to their nominal functional designations (e.g. Inspection des Finances), but constitute an all-purpose elite for government and society. The personal contacts, prestige and knowledge that members of these corps obtain enables them to manage their own village very well, and the entire society not too badly.[72]

Another specialized structure, atlhough not nearly so clearly defined as the grand corps, are the 'Superbureaucrats'.[73] These are the civil servants who work for the co-ordinating organizations within government. These organizations, such as the Office of Management and Budget in the USA, the Treasury in the UK, the Privy Council Office, Treasury Board Secretariat etc. in Canada, and a host of other organizations, attempt to co-ordinate fiscal, personnel and legal actions across a wide variety of organizations in government. Although there are a number of career civil servants who are employed by these organizations, they have a special relationship to politics, and are charged with implementing the wishes of a government to perhaps a greater extent than civil servants in operating departments. If the civil servant is willing to accept a position in one of these organizations, this implies a willingness to accept the wishes of his political executives. Furthermore, these civil servants do not have the organizational turf and clientele to protect as do their counterparts in line agencies; one major part of their functions is to subsume those interests into a broader national interest (as defined by the party in power). Rather obviously then, civil servants in these central organizations might be expected to engage in the Village Life relationship with their political masters, and to take the part of their organizations against the interest of line agencies.

And the same reasoning applied to the macro-level of government organization might also be applicable to lower levels of organization. There are generally staff civil servants in most public organizations, and it could be expected that they would be more likely to accept the viewpoints of political appointees than would members of the line components of these organizations. It is also quite possible that as these staff civil servants become identified with the personal viewpoints of one or more political executives, their careers in that particular position will be more brief than would be true of the line civil servants.

Role conceptions
As with the political executives, there is an important psychological element in the roles adopted by civil servants in their relationships with political executives. To some extent, these role conceptions will be developed and reinforced by some of the structural factors already mentioned, but they are also the products of cultural patterns in the society.[74] Societies and their members regard hierarchical relationships, such as would be found in the Formal–Legal model, quite differently. They also regard conflict among individuals very differently and further develop different mechanisms for coping with potential conflict.[75] Interpersonal relationships within organizations will be influenced by such cultural patterns, perhaps in particular the willingness of civil servants to accept the hierarchical authority of

someone nominally above them in an organizational chart. There are also differing concepts of the meaning of government and the public sector and this will also have important consequences for the manner in which the government can be managed. In short, the relationships between civil servants and their nominal superiors will be greatly influenced by the images that civil servants (and perhaps the society as a whole) carry in their heads of what those relationships should be.

Conclusion
It is now perhaps obvious to even the casual reader that this is more of a research agenda than a formal statement of findings. However, the understanding of the relationship between members of the executive branch, who just happen to have arrived in their positions through different routes is quite important for the management of contemporary political systems and for the functioning of political democracy. If electoral politics and the politics within elective offices in selecting a government are to mean anything, then those who emerge from the selection process must be able to govern. In the majority of cases, however, those who come to office deplore their difficulties in governing. On the other hand, there is an argument to be made in favour of experience and longevity in office, and for the continuation of policies which have shown themselves to be at least marginally effective. It is this conflict between popular choice and stability and between democracy and technocracy that motivated some of the concern expressed in this paper.

How can we devise an arrangement which preserves both the values of popular control through the electoral process and permanence, expertise and non-partisan nature of the civil service? The first possible answer is that this is impossible and that those who design the institutions of government should forget about it. A second and only marginally more satisfying answer is that this is simply a trade-off. We should perhaps be content with certain institutions being dominated by the will of the elected executives, while the majority of line institutions are dominated by expert and permanent civil servants. This dichotomy between expert civil servants and amateur but earnest political executives may be excessively simplistic, as many political executives may come to office with a substantial knowledge or interest in what they are administering, but they may still find themselves considered outsiders simply because they are not members of the organizations on a permanent basis. In general, there may be a trade-off between the two sets of values which will provide some guidance in designing institutions and allocating responsibilities among them.

A third proposal has been made to try to redress any imbalances in power between political and bureaucratic executives by improving the quality of the executives being recruited. This plea has been made several times in the United States, and has also been made in other countries.[76] The problem is always to obtain political executives who can manage large organizations, who have political skills, and who have some substantive knowledge about a policy area. And if such talented people can be found, they are generally so well paid in the private sector that they cannot be attracted into the public sector. This assumes that the career structures of government would be sufficiently open to allow them to participate.

On the other hand, a plea has been made to tame the civil service, and to place people in charge of organizations who will be subservient to political authority. Here we have almost the reverse problem as the one with the political executives. The individuals who rise to the top of the bureaucratic ladder are apparently too talented. This is to some extent as it should be, and we as citizens should not want agencies managed by less than competent individuals, neither by individuals who do not have ideas nor the determination to implement them. This then implies a rather basic trade-off in the role of public bureaucracy. On the one hand we want it to be docile and subservient to political authority while on the other hand we want it to be dynamic and highly skilled.

It may be that the roles assigned to the members of the executives of industrialized democracies are contradictory and confusing. We want our political executives to be the best available with leadership and managerial talent but only want to pay them a pittance compared to their worth in the market. And we want to make them responsible for a number of other political forces too. We want dynamic and aggressive civil servants who will in turn cower when a politician speaks. Until these contradictions can be corrected the problems of executive leadership in government will not be resolved.

Notes

1. As noted below, much of this sense of justification may be the result of unreasonable expectations.

2. For the latter point see Charles T. Goodell (1983) *The Case for Bureaucracy*. Chatham: Chatham House.

3. This is, therefore, similar to the now classical concept of 'neutral efficiency'. See James W. Doig (1983) 'If I See a Murderous Fellow Sharpening a Knife Cleverly . . .', *Public Administration Review*, 43, pp. 292–304.

4. James W. Doig (1983) 'If I See a Murderous Fellow Sharpening a Knife Cleverly . . .', *Public Administration Review*, 43, pp. 292–304.

5. See Thomas P. Murphy, Donald E. Neuchterlein, and Ronald J. Stupak (1978) *Inside the Bureaucracy: The View from the Assistant Secretary's Desk*. Boulder: Westview.

6. There appears to be the need for more careful qualitative analyses. See for example Colin Campbell (1983) *Governments Under Stress*. Toronto: University of Toronto Press; Herbert Kaufman (1981) *The Administrative Behavior of Federal Bureau Chiefs*. Washington DC: The Brookings Institution.

7. Robert Putnam (1973) 'The Political Attitudes of Senior Civil Servants in Britain,

Germany and Italy', *British Journal of Political Science*, 3, pp. 257–90; Samuel Eldersveld, Sonia Hubee-Boonzaijer and Jan Kooiman (1975) 'Elite Perceptions of the Political Process in the Netherlands', in Mattei Dogan *The Mandarins of Western Europe*. New York: John Wiley; Thomas J. Anton (1980) *Administered Politics: Elite Political Culture in Sweden*. Boston: Martinus Nijhoff; Robert Putnam, Joel Aberbach and Bert A. Rockman (1981) *Politicians and Bureaucrats*. Cambridge, Mass.: Harvard University Press.

8. Richard Crossman (1975) (1977) *The Diaries of a Cabinet Minister*, Vols. 1–3. London: Hamish Hamilton and Jonathan Cape; Barbara Castle 'Mandarin Power', *The Sunday Times*, 10 June 1983; Peter Kellner and Lord Crowther-Hunt (1980) *The Civil Service*. London: Macdonald; Hugo Young and Anne Sloman (1982) *No, Minister: An Inquiry into the Civil Service*. London: BBC TV; Hugo Young and Anne Sloman (1984) *But Chancellor: An Inquiry into the Treasury*. London: BBC.

9. *No, Minister*, as both a book and a BBC TV series, demonstrated a much more complex relationship, at least at the very top level of ministers and permanent secretaries.

10. Woodrow Wilson (1887) 'The Study of Administration', *Political Science Quarterly*, 2. pp. 209–13.

11. This has been one of the consistent recommendations of the several commissions on executive leadership in the United States.

12. See Edward C. Page (1985) *Political Authority and Bureaucratic Power*. Knoxville: University of Tennessee Press.

13. Robert Putnam (1973) 'The Political Attitudes of Senior Civil Servants in Britain, Germany and Italy', *British Journal of Political Science*, 3, pp. 260–63.

14. See B. Guy Peters (1978) *The Politics of Bureaucracy*. New York: Longmans, pp. 31–6.

15. Hugh Heclo and Aaron Wildavsky (1974) *The Private Government of Public Money*. Berkeley: University of California Press, pp. 76–119.

16. Such common values are made more likely by the increasing use of administrative personnel in political posts, as well as attempts to place more political appointees in nominally administrative positions. See the articles by Renate Mayntz and Bernard Gournay (1984) in Bruce L. R. Smith (ed.) *The Higher Civil Service in Europe and Canada: Lessons for the United States*. Washington DC: The Brookings Institution.

17. See George Szablowski, 'Executive-Bureaucratic Policies'. Paper presented to the 1981 Convention of the Midwest Political Science Association.

18. Ian Gough (1979) *The Political Economy of the Welfare State*. London: Macmillan.

19. See Richard E. Neustadt (1973) 'Politicians and Bureaucrats', in American Assembly, *Congress and America's Future*. Englewood Cliffs: Prentice-Hall, pp. 118–40.

20. Thomas P. Murphy, Donald E. Neuchterlein and Ronald J. Stupak (1978) *Inside the Bureaucracy: The View from the Assistant Secretary's Desk*. Boulder: Westview.

21. Thomas P. Murphy, Donald E. Neuchterlein and Ronald J. Stupak (1978) *Inside the Bureaucracy: The View from the Assistant Secretary's Desk*. Boulder: Westview.

22. Hugh Heclo (1977) *A Government of Strangers*. Washington DC: The Brookings Institution, pp. 151–2.

23. George Szablowski, 'Executive-Bureaucratic Policies'. Paper presented to 1981 Convention of the Midwest Political Science Association.

24. Hugh Heclo (1984) 'In Search of a Role: America's Higher Civil Service' in Ezra N. Suleiman (ed.) *Bureaucrats and Policymaking*. New York: Holmes and Meier.

25. Ezra N. Suleiman (1974) *Politics, Power and Bureaucracy in France: The Administrative Elite*. Princeton: Princeton University Press, pp. 271–7; Ezra N. Suleiman (ed.) (1984) 'Bureaucracy and Politics in France', *Bureaucrats and Policymaking*. New York: Holmes and Meier.

26. See footnote 5.

27. Richard Rose (1980) 'Government Against Sub-Governments: A European Perspective on Washington', in Richard Rose and Ezra N. Suleiman (eds) *Presidents and Prime Ministers*. Washington DC: American Enterprise Institute, pp. 284–347.

28. Of course, in the Village Life model the difference between administration and government is minimal.

29. Peter Kellner and Lord Crowther-Hunt (1980) *The Civil Service*. London: Macdonald; Richard Chapman (1978) *Your Disobedient Servant*. London: Chatto and Windus.

30. This is the feudal conception of government described by Natchez and Bupp (1973) 'Policy and Priority in the Budgetary Process', *American Political Science Review*, 67, pp. 951–63.

31. While many of the conventions of cabinet government have been strained in Britain, e.g. Mrs Thatcher and her semi-public conflict with the 'wets', they retain a surprising amount of power.

32. Hugh Young and Anne Sloman (1982) *No, Minister* (London: BBC).

33. See Dom Bonafede (1979) 'A Day in the Life of a Cabinet Secretary', *National Journal*, 11, pp. 792–3; Hobart Rowan 'Kreps' Introspective Farewell', *Washington Post* (3 November 1979).

34. B. Guy Peters (1978) *The Politics of Bureaucracy*. New York: Longmans, 65–9.

35. Hugh Heclo and Aaron Wildavsky (1974) *The Private Government of Public Money*. Berkeley: University of California Press, pp. 134–8.

36. *The Washington Post* (14 August 1981).

37. Unfortunately, Anton's book on Swedish bureaucracy, while excellent, ends its narrative before this change occurred.

38. Joel D. Aberbach and Bert A. Rockman (1976) 'Clashing Beliefs within the Executive Branch: The Nixon Administration Bureaucracy', *American Political Science Review*, 70, pp. 456–68.

39. Renate Mayntz (1984) 'German Federal Bureaucrats: A Functional Elite Between Politics and Administration', in Ezra N. Suleiman (ed.) *Bureaucrats and Policymaking*. New York: Holmes and Meier.

40. Hugh Heclo (1977) *A Government of Strangers*. Washington DC: The Brookings Institution, pp. 36–41.

41. Peter Kellner and Lord Crowther-Hunt (1980) *The Civil Service*. London: Macdonald, pp. 184–5.

42. B. Guy Peters (1986) 'Administrative Change: Are the Cuts Worth It?' in Charles Levine (ed.) *The Unfinished Agenda of Civil Service Reform*. Washington DC: The Brookings Institution.

43. B. Guy Peters, 'Administrative Change: Are the Cuts Worth It?' in Charles Levine (ed.) *The Unfinished Agenda of Civil Service Reform*. Washington DC: The Brookings Institution.

44. This perception is shared by the political left, which also appear to believe they would win in a more 'democratic' government.

45. B. Guy Peters, (1981) 'The Problem of Bureaucratic Government', *Journal of Politics*, 43, pp. 56–82.

46. Richard Rose (1974) *The Problem of Party Government*. New York: The Free Press, pp. 379–426.

47. Alfred Grosser (1975) quoted in M. Dogan *The Mandarins of Western Europe*. New York: John Wiley, p. 7.

48. For one more extreme view see Orion F. White (1969) 'The Dialectical Organisation: An Alternative to Bureaucracy', *Public Administration Review*, 39. pp. 32–42.

49. This is true even in countries, for example the United Kingdom, where civil servants are not recruited on the basis of expert knowledge.

50. This is more than just an easy way out of a problem. There are real reasons to expect variability.

51. This assumes parties do make a difference. See Richard Rose (1980) *Do Parties Make a Difference*. Chatham, NJ: Chatham House.

52. See William Niskanen (1971) *Bureaucracy and Representative Government*. Chicago: Aldine Atherton; Francis E. Rouke (1979) 'Bureaucratic Autonomy and the Public Interest, *American Behavioral Scientist*, 22, pp. 537–46.

53. Hugh Heclo and Aaron Wildavsky (1974) *The Private Government of Public Money*. Berkeley: University of California Press.

54. The PATCO strike is an obvious example of this extension.

55. B. Guy Peters (1978) *The Politics of Bureaucracy*. New York: Longmans, pp. 189–96.

56. This is one of the fundamental premises upon which much of the literature on public bureaucracy takes an economic perspective. For example, see William Niskanen (1971) *Bureaucracy and Representative Government*. Chicago: Aldine Atherton.

57. This appears to be a fundamental weakness of the simple utility maximizing approach to bureaucracy, e.g. Niskanen. Most bureaucrats can gain very little for their efforts at expanding the budget. See Christopher Hood, Meg Huby and Andrew Dunsire (1984) 'Bureaucrats and Budgeting Benefits: How Do British Central Government Departments Measure Up?' *Journal of Public Policy*, 4, pp. 163–79.

58. The experience of the bureaucracy during the Reagan administration has been a useful test of this proposition.

59. Most notably Richard E. Neustadt (1969) 'White House and Whitehall', in Richard Rose (ed.) *Policy-Making in Britain*. London: Macmillan.

60. See Rudolf Klein and Janet Lewis (1977) 'Advice and Dissent in British Government: The Case of Special Advisers', *Policy and Politics*, 6, pp. 1–25.

61. Some have advocated bringing even more informal advisors into British government. For example, see Sir John Hoskyns (1982) 'Whitehall and Westminister: An Outsider's View', *Fiscal Studies*, 3, 162–72.

62. Renate Mayntz (1980) 'Executive Leadership in Germany: Dispension of Power or "Kanzler-demokratie" ', in Richard Rose and Ezra N. Suleiman (eds) *Presidents and Prime Ministers*. Washington DC: American Enterprise Institute.

63. Maurice Wright (1980) 'Ministers and Civil Servants: Relations and Responsibilities', *Parliamentary Affairs*, 33, pp. 293–313.

64. Bruce Headey (1974) *British Cabinet Ministers*. London: George Allen and Unwin; Thomas J. Anton (1980) *Administered Politics: Elite Political Culture in Sweden*. Boston: Martinus Nijhoff, pp. 85–94.

65. This remains the case even after the charges proposed by Fulton in 1964. See John Garrett (1980) *Managing the Civil Service*. London: Heinemann, pp. 11–27.

66. See Barbel Steinkemper (1974) *Klassiche und politische Burokraten in der Ministerial-verwaltung der Bundessrupublik Deutschland*. Köln: Carl Heymans.

67. This is indicated, in part, by the increasing level of professional employment in the civil service. See Frederick C. Mosher (1978) 'Professions in the Public Service', *Public Administration Review*, 38, pp. 144–50.

68. Ezra N. Suleiman (1968) *Elites in French Society*. pp. 226–35; C. Alphantéry et al. (1968) Princeton, NJ: Princeton University Press *Pour nationaliser l'Etat*. Paris: Editions de Seuil, pp. 193ff.

69. This is indicated, in part, by the increasing level of professional employment in the civil service. See Frederick C. Mosher (1978) 'Professions in the Public Service', *Public Administration Review*, 38, pp. 144–50.

70. Hugh Heclo (1970) 'Issue Networks and the Executive Establishment', in Anthony King (ed.) *The New American Political System*. Washington DC: American Enterprise Institute; A. Grant Jordan (1981) 'Iron Triangles, Woolly Corporatism, or Elastic Nets: Images of the Policy Process', *Journal of Public Policy*, 1, pp. 95–124.

71. Peter Kellner and Lord Crowther-Hunt (1980) *The Civil Servants*. London: Macdonald, pp. 22–45.

72. Ezra N. Suleiman (1984) 'Bureaucrats, Politics and Policy Making in France', in Ezra N. Suleiman (ed.) *Bureaucrats and Policymaking*. New York: Holmes and Meier.

73. Colin Campbell and George J. Szablowski (1979) *The Superbureaucrats*. Toronto: Macmillan of Canada.

74. David Nachamias and David H. Rosenbloom (1978) *Bureaucratic Culture: Citizens and Administrators in Israel*. New York: St Martins, pp. 10–20.

75. See for example, Henry Eckstein (1966) *Division and Cohesion in Democracy*. Princeton: Princeton University Press.

76. Frederick V. Malek (1978) *Washington's Hidden Tragedy*. New York: The Free Press: Lawrence E. Lynn, Jr. (1981) *Managing The Public's Business*. New York: Basic Books.

12
A cultural theory of responsibility

Aaron Wildavksy

The theatrical definition of 'responsible' from the compact edition of the *Oxford English Dictionary* — 'an actor who undertakes to play any part which may be temporarily required' — explains the difficulty we have all had in coming to terms with this concept. Responsibility is so integral a part of human relationships that in its various meanings it serves as a synonym for almost every important political word. As Webster's *Dictionary of Synonyms* so clearly states, '*responsible, answerable, accountable, amenable, liable* are comparable when they mean subject to an authority which may exact redress in case of default. *Responsible*, *answerable*, and *accountable* are etymologically very close, all meaning capable of being called upon to answer, or to make amends to someone for something. They are, therefore, often used interchangeably.' Other political terms, such as power, influence, control, also come into play. Returning to Webster's *Dictionary of Synonyms* '*accountable* is much more positive than *responsible* or *answerable* in its suggestion of retributive justice in case of default . . . *Amenable* and *liable* especially stress subjection and suggest the contingency rather than the probability or certainty of being called to account. One is *amenable* (to someone or something) whose acts are subject to the control or the censure of a higher authority, and who, therefore, is not self-governing or absolute in power; as, a despot is *amenable* to no will other than his own.' Fault or blame or subject to sanction or required to give an explanation also appear as synonyms.

Who is responsible to whom in regard to what matters? Such a question could serve as the leitmotif for the study of politics itself. The protean character of responsibility, however, does not mean it is useless for political enquiry — on the contrary, it is essential. What is missing from the definitions are the answers to the question. This paper shall try to show that answers to questions about the family of synonyms surrounding responsibility vary with people's visions of the good life. Since what matters most to people is how they wish to live with other people, responsibility is a function of culture — the shared value justifying social relations that differentiate ways of life.

The dimensions of cultural theory are based on answers to two questions: 'Who am I?' and 'How should I behave?' The question of identity may be answered by saying that individuals belong to a strong group, a collective, that makes decisions binding on all members or that their ties to others are weak in that their choices bind only themselves. The question of action is answered by responding that the individual is subject to many or few prescriptions, a free spirit or one that is tightly constrained. The strength or weakness of group boundaries and the numerous or few, varied or singular, prescriptions binding or freeing individuals are the components of their culture.[1]

Strong groups with numerous prescriptions that vary with social roles combine to form hierarchical collectivism. Strong groups whose members follow few prescriptions form an egalitarian culture, a shared life of voluntary consent, without coercion or inequality. Competitive individualism joins few prescriptions with weak group boundaries, thereby encouraging ever new combinations. When groups are weak and prescriptions strong, so that decisions are made for them by people on the outside, the controlled culture is fatalistic.

The social ideal of individualistic cultures is self-regulation. Its adherents favour bidding and bargaining in order to reduce the need for authority. They support equal opportunity to compete in order to make arrangements between consenting adults with a minimum of external interference. They seek opportunity to be different, not equality of condition to be the same, for diminishing social differences would require a central, redistributive authority.

Hierarchy is institutionalized authority. Its members justify inequality on grounds that specialization and division of labour enables people to live together with greater harmony and effectiveness than do alternative arrangements. Hence hierarchies are rationalized by a sacrificial ethic: the parts are supposed to sacrifice for the whole.

Committed to a life of purely voluntary association, egalitarians reject authority. They can live a life without coercion or authority only by greater equality of condition. Thus egalitarians may be expected to prefer reduction of differences — between races, or income levels, or men and women, parents and children, teachers and students, authorities and citizens.

FIGURE 12.1
Models of four cultures

Strength of group boundaries

		Weak	Strong
Number and variety of prescriptions	Numerous and varied	Apathy (Fatalism)	Hierarchy (Collectivism)
	Few and similar	Competition (Individualism)	Equality (Egalitarianism)

An apathetic culture arises when people cannot control what happens to them. Since their boundaries are porous and the prescriptions imposed on them are severe, its subjects develop fatalistic feelings — what will be, will be. There is no point in them having preferences on public policy because what they prefer would not, in any event, matter.

Responsibilities vary with cultures

Any broadly gauged moral theory is necessarily a theory of social-cum-cultural responsibility: who ought to be accountable to whom in regard to what? What culture attempts to do is internalize the rules of accountability. By understanding these rules specifying proper social relationships, cultural theory attempts to explain and predict how people try to hold each other responsible. If the central intuition of this paper is correct, in that responsibility is central to social life, it should be possible to restate cultural theory in terms of the family of synonyms surrounding responsibility. And so, I think, it is. The group dimension answers the question of *to whom* the individual is responsible, to a collective with strong boundaries or whether the person is a free spirit able to transact on his or her own behalf. The prescription dimension answers the question of *for what* the individual is responsible, rules made by others or by him-/herself. What advantage is there, if any, in passing the concept of responsibility through the lens of cultural theory, of refracting responsibility through a cultural prism?

A single dimension does not a culture (or a responsible individual) make. Knowing that one is dealing with a strong collective of people whose decisions are binding on its adherents is a valuable piece of information. By itself, however, it cannot tell us whether the individual adherent is subject to command from above or must personally agree with every decision he or she considers important. Nor does the extent of these boundaries indicate to people involved whether certain individuals should perform specific functions or whether they ought to be involved in (almost) everything. Only by adding in the element of prescription, which Mary Douglas calls the 'grid' of social life, do we get at the scope and direction of activity. How much is the individual responsible for his or her specialty or all large choices and should she support the existing authorities or condemn them? Whether one feels responsible for exerting authority over others or is duty bound to unmask and undermine that authority is not a function solely of collectivism, but it is also whether minimal versus maximal prescription is considered normal. Adherents of hierarchy support, adherents of equality undermine, and individualists seek to avoid established authorities.

Knowing that group boundaries are weak helps the observer. Without boundaries to safeguard, for instance, meaning that no one is responsible for maintaining what is not wanted, there is no pollution. Differences between the pure and the contaminated are unnecessary when there is no social body with distinct social practices to be protected. Adding a dimension makes a big difference. When weak group boundaries are combined with binding prescriptions, for instance, individuals lose all sense of responsibility. Controlled by others, unable to defend themselves, they become fatalists. Joining weak prescription to weak groups, by contrast, so that individuals are encouraged to transact with whoever they want, changes their sense of responsibility. Responsibility for their own achievements goes up but responsibility for others goes down.

Preferences come from cultures: envy, blame, inequality, fairness, growth, scarcity, leadership, uncertainty, participation

The dimensions of cultural theory, because they are crucial dimensions of social life, also comprise the matrix out of which different senses of responsibility, matching the different cultures, are associated. I will argue that each culture generates characteristic responsibilities. These characteristics should be viewed as part of an 'as, if, and when' theory; individuals who identify with each of the various cultures are predicted to adopt as their own those responsibilities that they believe, correctly or mistakenly, are likely to help strengthen their way of life.

A suggestion by Jon Elster, adjusted to say that it is political cultures into which people are socialized, sets out the structure of the cultural argument.

> Desires are shaped, predominantly, by socialization. This does not mean that one is socialized into desiring some particular good, regardless of costs. Rather the idea is that one learns from socialization how to trade off different goods against each other . . . One should not seek in socialization the direct spring of action, only the cause of certain preference schedules that, in a given environment, may lead an action to be preferred to the feasible alternatives . . . First a causal explanation of desires, then an intentional explanation of action in terms of the desires, and finally a causal explanation of macro-states in terms of the several individual actions.[2]

First, people adhere to cultures. Second, their desires or preferences come from internalizing the social relations these cultures embody, employing them as scanning devices to determine essentially which preferences are culturally supportive. Third, people decide whether to pursue their cultural preference in view of other considerations, the rewards and penalties, that may affect them. The macro- or large-scale institutional behaviours are made up of individuals acting out their cultural biases. It is individuals as social creatures, not only being moulded by but actively moulding their social context — running the maze and shaping it — that are the focus of cultural theory.

Cultures answer questions about life with people. How is order to be achieved and maintained? Is there to be leadership and, if so, by whom? How are the goods of this world to be secured and divided up? How is envy to be controlled, inequality to be justified or condemned, blame for misfortune to be apportioned? How is responsibility to be allocated?

Envy

Envy is not correlated with the size of social differences alone, rather with their acceptability. The crucial question for social science is not whether there are large differences in individual or group resources in most places — (surely there are) but whether these are rationalized as natural or unnatural, right or wrong, appropriate or illegitimate. Hence envy is an especially difficult problem for egalitarians. If all members are supposed to be equal (how else would you get voluntary agreement on political processes and public policies?) then this egalitarianism must show in the outer appurtenances of life — plain food, meals without main courses (as in vegetarianism), simple clothes, redistribution of income, bare furniture, unornamental 'worker' housing, the life of the humble style. Suspicion is on all members, especially leaders, to see that they do not elevate themselves above others. Conversely, each member is responsible for preventing other members from lording it over them.

The humble life, to say the least, would hardly be appropriate in market individualism, whose rationale depends on competitors' ability to appropriate the benefits of the risks they take. Conspicuous consumption, or making a fetish out of commodities, may be a rational effort to point to where the power is in order to gain adherents in a network for future ventures. Since some people display much more of the goods of this world than others, however, envy is bound to rear its ugly head. Individualists combat envy by attributing personal success to good luck and/or good performance while failure they attribute to bad luck or poor performance. Those who complain are told 'You have had your chance' (e.g. opportunity is equal) and will have it again if you are not irresponsible. Naturally, fatalists know no envy, because, for them, to use Mrs Gaskell's evocative term, life is like a lottery. Lacking control over their lives, they cannot be responsible for what happens to them.

Control of envy in hierarchy is more interesting because it is more necessary. After all, hierarchy is institutionalized inequality. Ostentation is reserved for the collectivity — grand palaces, public works, ornate buildings in which the complexity of design mimics the near-infinite gradations of social structure. Hierarchs may wear faded finery at home; however, the army and the marching bands and the tombs of founders are bedecked in all splendour. The individual is reponsible to and for the condition of the collective. As education inculcates the desirability of differences, envy is deflected by arguing the appropriateness of specialization and the division of labour. Experts do know best. Leaders are to be loved because they sacrifice themselves by going out first in battle; or by subsidizing medical care and pensions; or by donating museums and libraries; or by suffering for their followers. It is the belief that office provides not power over others but a burden to the holder that dampens envy.

Blame
When things go wrong, however, as they must in all cultures, who is to blame? Fatalists blame fate, hierarchs cannot blame the collective however. 'System blame', blaming the relationship between the parts and the whole on which they pride themselves, would amount to self-destruction. This quite clearly would not be acceptable to them. Hierarchies are famous for their blame-shedding techniques. Responsibility is hidden or diffused (the same thing) among numerous offices. Investigations are quashed or forbidden by official secret acts. Blame is shifted to deviants. They do not know their place. They must be subject to re-education or belong in asylums, working on the premise that a person would have to be mad to object to a collective way of life. To egalitarians, however, who reject authority, it is precisely the system (some combination of individualism and collectivism) that is insane — coercive and inegalitarian. If they had their way, suicides would be owed redress by the implacable institutions that drove them to their undeserved deaths. Were society differently organized, murderers would not want to kill their prey. Since good people are corrupted by evil institutions, the eglitarian task is to unmask authority by revealing the connection between apparently benign institutions and the cancers they actually cause. Cultural solidarity is maintained by portraying external forces as monstrous, and by accusing deviants of secretly importing evil ways ('hidden hierarchies') to corrupt the membership. Consequently, egalitarians search for insidious contamination from secret external sources, the turncoats, the political radishes, the witches, who have brought duplicity into their innocent garden.

However, individualists can hardly claim to be innocent; they are supposed to know what they are doing. The whole point is to outguess the future; if it were knowable, there would be no need for entrepreneurs. Hence, individualists can blame bad luck or personal incompetence or any combination thereof, providing that the system, in their case competitive individualism, is blameless. People may be dumb, as economic individualists say, but markets are always smart.

Anyone who thinks that attribution of responsibility is not diagnostic should consult Verba and Orren's table addressing that very question to a variety of elites. Who, they ask, is responsible for poverty in America, the poor or the system?

TABLE 12.1
Poverty in America[3]

Group	Fault of poor	Fault of system
	%	%
Business	57	9
Labour	15	56
Farm	52	19
Intellectuals	23	44
Media	21	50
Republicans	55	13
Democrats	5	68
Blacks	5	86
Feminists	9	76
Youth	16	61

Using cultural shorthand, individualists blame the poor (business-men, 57 percent), so do hierarchists (Republicans, 55 percent), while egalitarians (feminists, blacks, Democrats, 68 percent to 86 percent) fault the system.[4]

Inequality
Every regime has to confront inequality of condition. Egalitarians abhor inequality; it can never be justified. Cultures that embody it are guilty of perpetrating the silent death of institutional oppression. For fatalists, inequality is the norm; they are ruled by others. Hierarchists give more help because the 'unequals' are part of their own people for whom they feel responsible. Their justification of inequality is the same as for the system itself: different roles for different parts is healthy for the system as a whole. Essential order, hierarchical collectivists claim, can be achieved only by agreeing to accept inequality. In return, all members of society are supposed to get equality before the law in order that their claims may be adjudicated on a consistent and predictable basis. Assuming responsibility — adjudicating 'who has the right to do what' — is essential in maintaining distances and differences in hierarchies.

Economic growth
Abundance increases the temptation to differentiate, which interferes with equality. Thus egalitarians do not prefer economic growth. Far better for egalitarians to concentrate on equal distribution, which keeps their people together, than on unequal development, which pulls them apart.

Wealth creation belongs to the established cultures, although in different ways. The promise of hierarchies is that collective sacrifice will lead to group gain. Thus they plan to reduce consumption to create capital to invest for future benefits. Should its solidarity be threatened, however, the hierarchy may adopt a limited redistributive ethic, buying off discontent, limiting exchange so as to limit losers. Not so competitive individualists. They seek new combinations to create new wealth so that there will be more for all and they can keep more.

Uncertainty

Just as cultures are fundamentally concerned with moral order (the shared values and social practices that constitute them), they must also cope with uncertainty about which norms apply in a given circumstance. Answering the question of who is responsible for the good and bad things is the same as choosing the best and worst ways of life.

Adherents of hierarchical cultures try to negotiate their environments in order to reduce ambiguity in the structure of roles, which they regulate themselves. They will intervene to dampen economic fluctuations or to punish deviance, giving up efficiency in order to reduce variations in behaviour that threaten established relationships. Fatalists accept uncertainty as they do everything else — it being beyond their control. Individualists welcome the uncertainty that creates their opportunities. Individualism copes with extreme uncertainty by doing more of what it does best, i.e. by trial and error through competition. Egalitarians abjure competition. How, then, do they cope with uncertainty? Where the hierarchy stresses clarity in role definition, so that performance can be attached to position, the egalitarian culture embraces ambiguity, so that no one has authority.

Leadership

Hierarchies tie authority to positions.[5] Hence hierarchies are pro-leadership cultures, shoring it up at every opportunity, protecting it when under attack, shedding and diffusing blame, keeping information under close control. Market cultures treat leadership like any other commodity — they pay as little for it as they can. They seek to make it unnecessary by self-organization through bidding and bargaining. When conditions, such as external attack, make a modicum of leadership necessary, it is limited in time and authority; the hope being that the meteoric leader who flames bright and then burns out will retire when the task is completed. Egalitarians actively reject leadership as a form of inequality. When the existence of their organization is threatened, however, they will accept charismatic leadership as a substitute for authority.

Apathy

The very same failure to vote may be appropriate or inappropriate, legitimizing or destabilizing, depending on the social context. Adherents of each culture select meanings of apathy (as of activity) to support their preferred power relationships.

Egalitarians rationalize by rejecting established authority, arguing that there is no real participation. Power is 'unmasked' by showing that fatalism is the true location of the mass of citizens. Like the wonderful Steinberg cartoon in *The New Yorker*, where Manhattan grows so large the rest of the country recedes from view, egalitarians see fatalists as most of the people, a nation metaphorically populated by 4200 oligarchs, 2000 egalitarians and 200 million apathetics. Egalitarians constantly seek to recruit supporters from fatalists who, they claim, are apathetic because decisions are made for them by the establishment. The hierarchists' counterclaim that apathy is functional (inactivity implies consent) is derided as ideological window dressing. High rates of general participation across a broad scope of issues, by contrast, would undermine hierarchical rule. How could principles of hierarchy be maintained if each is responsible for all?

Individualists do not have to take the rate and scope of activity as a measure of their virility. They are responsible for results, for outputs, not for inputs. If it is worthwhile for people to participate, they will; if not, they will not. Should voting decline, for instance, this might indicate that the probability of an individual influencing events is so low that a rational person would not bother.

What is responsible for a low rate of voting? Egalitarians answer that either the 'system' excludes people or that voting is ineffectual; supporters of hierarchy reply that voters are so satisfied they are willing to leave things to those who are better qualified; members of markets respond that voting is not worth the effort it takes.

However, let us turn the tables. Suppose you wish to oppose prevailing policies that you believe confer undue advantage on people who are already well off. Who will assume responsibility for redressing your grievance? Individualists may like large differences or they may well ask whether it is worth their while to participate in view of the low probability of success. Hierarchists may support existing authority or they may believe it is not their place to act. Fatalists think there is no point in acting because they will not make a difference. Under such circumstances, you may be grateful for the existence of egalitarians who are prepared to throw body and soul into the fray, who never seem to tire, and who feel personally responsible for righting wrongs, provided only that yours is an inegalitarian wrong.

The cultural allocation of responsibility

Responsibility is the grand regulator of human life. It is not too much to say that the social relations that make life human revolve around the allocation of responsibility. Trying to hold other people accountable for their actions is a fair description of social life. Whether it is or is not desirable to be held responsible depends upon whether the act ought to be done by the actor within a given cultural context. Cultures determine the behaviour that is deemed good or bad. A strong leader who exercises full authority within his station would be praised in a hierarchy, while exactly the same behaviour would be condemned in an egalitarian culture because commanding others is wrong. To egalitarians, accumulating more than others is wrong, but is a positive requirement for individualists and a sign of favour for hierarchists.

For *what* are people responsible? Believers in hierarchy are supposed to maintain, egalitarians to diminish, and individualists to increase differences among people. To *whom* are people responsible? Individualists are responsible for themselves, including the agreements they make with others; hierarchists are responsible to those in authority; egalitarians are responsible to their collective, providing they have participated in its decisions.

Who escapes responsibility? Cultures with strong boundaries never blame the collective, but they seek to avoid blame in different ways. Hierarchies blame individuals for not following the rules. Since individuals are born bad but may be improved by good institutions, it is the institutions that must escape blame. Egalitarianism's only rule is diminishing differences. Thus egalitarians excoriate established authority, thereby shifting responsibility to external forces. Believing as they do in results, individualists have the most difficulty in escaping from responsibility. When pressed, they seek bankruptcy or claim bad luck and try to begin anew.

Each culture has a characteristic problem with responsibility. By seeking to shed blame, hierarchists make change difficult. They face stultification. By externalizing blame, egalitarians drive conflict underground. They face splits or persecution. By building ever greater networks, individualists reduce their chances of starting again. They face manipulation from the 'big men' (to use the language of New Guinea anthropology) who convert them into 'rubbish men'. What can be done?

Whatever their immediate rationale, whether hierarchies are traditional ('it has always been done that way'), ascriptive (the divine right of kings) or scientific (the merit principle), their motivation is the same: to solve the problem of social order by encouraging individuals to sacrifice for the collective. Individuals are both united through strong group boundaries and separated by them, so as not to conflict with each other, by innumerable prescriptions according to role. The advantage of hierarchies, assuming individuals give them their allegiance, is that they minimize internal conflict while maximizing external strength. The disadvantages of hierarchical structure are well known.[6] The top levels (the 'upperarchy') may exploit the bottom levels (the 'lowerarchy'). Officers may desert their men in battle. As each level aggrandizes its own expenses, with members unable to decrease them, hierarchies may cost more than the services they provide. 'Who has the right to do what' is essential for defining roles, so process often triumphs over purpose. However, this stock phrase is misleading, for in hierarchies the process is part of the cultural purpose. Since authority is attached to position, leadership outside of role expectations is rejected. Hierarchies are famous for rigidity, and this has its roots in rejection of information that does not come through the proper channels. Rigidity is also rooted in the reluctance to accept blame for fear of damaging the system. Signatures-cum-clearances are hostages against retribution. If this syndrome of difficulties constitutes the hierarchy problem, what constitutes the solution?

Context is all: no culture exists alone. Every organization of scope and complexity is a compound of cultures. The relative power of each culture in comparison to the others determines what it can do. The solution to the hierarchy problem, therefore, is to surround it with a sufficient force of other cultures to mitigate its excesses without depriving it of the ability to maintain order.

The tendency to shed blame may be mitigated by constant criticism from egalitarians. The system is to blame; this and that authority are guilty until proven innocent. What egalitarians call 'unmasking' may well expose faults. Throwing hierarchies into competition, moreover, as with political parties in elections or bureaux for budgets, gives each an incentive to expose the other. Rival sources of information (and informants) help to reduce rigidity. Individualism's emphasis on results, 'the bottom line', as capitalists call it, helps break down the hierarchical over-emphasis on process.

Cultural pluralism is the solution to the problem of responsibility. With hierarchy, there is sufficient structure to know who is supposed to act; with egalitarianism, there is sufficient criticism to know what was done; with individualism, there is sufficient competition to create a standard of comparison between what should have been and what is. Of course, with cultural pluralism, it becomes more difficult to know who or what is to be counted as responsible. There is no perfect way. Only fatalists are inherently irresponsible and no one wants to trade places with them.

Notes

1. Cultural theory comes from the work of Mary Douglas. See especially her *Natural Symbols* (1970) (Harmondsworth: Penguin); and 'Cultural Bias', in Douglas (1982) *In the Active Voice*. London: Routledge and Kegan Paul.

2. Elster, Jon (1983) *Explaining Technical Change: A Case Study in the Philosophy of Science* Cambridge: Cambridge University Press, p. 85.

3. Verba, Sidney, and Gary R. Orren (1985) *Equality in America: The View From the Top*. Cambridge, Mass.: Harvard University Press, p. 74.

4. See Author's 'A World of Difference: The Public Philosophies and Political Behaviors of Rival American Cultures', forthcoming in Anthony King (ed.) *The New American Political System* (2nd edn). Washington, DC: American Enterprise Institute.

5. A more substantial analysis of leadership from this cultural perspective may be found in the Author's paper 'Political Leaders are Part of Political Systems: A Cultural Theory of Leadership', prepared for the Bentley Chair conference at the Workshop in Political Theory and Policy Analysis, Indiana University, 17 and 18 May, 1985. Published in Bryan D. Jones, (ed.) (forthcoming 1987) *Political Leadership: Perspectives from Political Science*.

6. See Jan–Erik Jane (1984) *The Concept of Bureaucracy*. Florence.

Index

Notes on the Contributors

Gert P. de Bruin is lecturer in Methodology and Formal Theory at the Department of Political Science, University of Amsterdam. His more recent publications mainly relate to problems of decision-making on public goods.

Donald Chisholm is assistant professor of Political Science at The Ohio State University. He has also taught at the University of California, San Diego, Michigan State University, and the University of California, Berkeley, where he received his Ph.D. His doctoral dissertation received the 1985 Leonard D. White Award of the American Political Science Association for the best dissertation in the field of public administration. His research interests focus on the design and behaviour of public organizations and problems of decision-making and policy analysis.

Andrew Dunsire has taught Administrative Theory for over thirty years with a brief two-year spell as a civil servant in the late 1950s. Since 1978 he has been head of the Department of Politics at the University of York. His major books include *Administration: the word and the science (1973); Implementation in a Bureaucracy* and *Control in a Bureaucracy* (both 1978); and (with C.C. Hood) *Bureaumetrics* (1981).

Christopher Hood is professor of Government and Public Administration, University of Sydney. He is the author of *The Limits of Administration* (1976); *Bureaumetrics* (1981); (with Andrew Dunsire); *Big Government in Hard Times* (1981); (with M. Wright, ed.); *The Tools of Government*; and *Administrative Analysis* (1986).

Jan-Erik Lane is professor at Umeå University. He has published numerous books and articles in the fields of Public Policy and Administration as well as Political Economy. He has edited *State and Market* published by Sage and *Politics and Society in Western Europe* with Svante Ersson also published by Sage.

Richard Murray has a Ph.D. in Political Economy from a dissertation on Local Government Finance in 1981. Since then he has worked with the Swedish Agency for Administrative Development on a programme for productivity measurements and key indicators for public authorities. At the present he is doing research at the Industrial Institute for Economic and Social Research.

Edward C. Page is a lecturer in Politics at the University of Hull. He has written in the fields of Public Policy and Administration and Urban Politics in journals such as *Public Administration, Political Studies, European Journal of Political Research* and numerous edited works. His recent book, *Political Authority and Bureaucratic Power*, was published in 1985.

B. Guy Peters is currently Maurice Falk Professor of American Politics at the University of Pittsburgh, after having taught previously at Emory University, the University of Delaware, and Tulane University. He has also held a Fulbright Professorship at the University of Strathclyde, and was Hallsworth Fellow of Political Economy at the University of Manchester. He is author of *The Politics of Bureaucracy, American Public Policy, Can Government Go Bankrupt?* (with Richard Rose), *Policy Dynamics* (with Brian Hogwood) as well as a number of other books and articles.

Professor Richard Rose, Director of the Centre for the Study of Public Policy at the University of Strathclyde, is currently completing a five-year programme of research on the growth of government. Among his books are *Understanding Big Government, Public Employment in Western Nations, Taxation by Inertia, Ministers and Ministries*, and *Presidents and Prime Ministers*. He has been a visiting fellow at policy research institutes in America and Europe, and his works have been translated into ten languages.

Rune J. Sørensen works as associate professor at the Department of Political Science, University of Oslo. He has done research on Public Budgeting and Public Finances. Sørensen has had his works published in Norwegian books and journals, such as *European Journal of Political Research, Scandinavian Political Studies*. He has contributed to *The Politics of the Public and the Private* edited by Jan-Erik Lane and to *Territorial Politics in Western Europe* edited by Michael Goldsmith and Edward Page.

Krister Ståhlberg, professor of Public Administration, Åbo Academy, is the author of several books on Finnish Public Administration, local as well as Central Administration. His books include: *Teori och praxis i kommunal planering* (1975); *Politik och planering* (1978); *Närdemokrati* (1979); *Självstyrd eller dräng* (1983). Ståhlberg is also the editor and co-author of several books and articles.

Aaron Wildavsky is professor of Political Science and Public Policy at the University of California, Berkeley. He was Dean of the University's

Graduate School of Public Policy from 1969 to 1977. He is author of *The Nursing Father: Moses as a Political Leader* (1984), co-author with Mary Douglas, *Risk and Culture* (1982), *How to Limit Government Spending* (1980), *Speaking Truth to Power* (1979), co-author with Nelson Polsby, *Presidential Elections* (6th edn, 1983) and co-author with Hugh Heclo, *The Private Government of Public Money* (2nd edn, 1981).